TEST PREP

FOR

Olesya Sitkowski

THE WESTERN HERITAGE

SINCE 1300

TWELFTH EDITION

AP® Edition

Joanna Cone

Frisco ISD
Frisco, TX

Patti Harrold

Harding Fine Arts Academy
Oklahoma City, OK

ISBN-10:   0-13-521759-8
ISBN-13:   978-0-13-5217597

 Pearson

www.pearsonhighered.com

1 2019

CONTENTS

PART I

INTRODUCTION TO THE AP®️ EUROPEAN HISTORY EXAMINATION

This section overviews the advanced placement program, introduces the types of questions you will encounter on the exam, and provides helpful test-taking strategies. It also explains the grading procedure used by the College Board. Finally, a correlation chart is provided that shows where key information commonly tested on the examination is covered in *The Western Heritage.* Review this section carefully before trying the sample items in the following part

PART II

TOPICAL REVIEW WITH SAMPLE QUESTIONS AND ANSWERS AND EXPLANATIONS

This section is keyed to chapters 1 through 22 in *The Western Heritage*. Part II overviews important information correlated to the 2019–2020 AP European Curriculum Framework and provides sample questions for every question type using the new AP exam format. Use these practice questions and essays to arm yourself thoroughly for the kinds of test items you will encounter on the AP exam. Answers and explanations are provided for each question for your further review.

Material in Chapter 1 will not be tested in the Advanced Placement exam. It introduces key events in pre-1450 European history that teachers may wish to discuss and explore with their students. The questions that follow are designed to ensure student comprehension and provide opportunities to practice the skills they will apply in the actual exam. In lieu of AP framework information, the answer key for this chapter references page numbers in the student edition.

CHAPTER 1

The Late Middle Ages: Social and Political Breakdown (1300–1453)

The late Middle Ages were an era marked by major social, religious, and health crises. War, plague, social unrest, and religious schism characterized this era.

THE BLACK DEATH

The Black Death, also known as the bubonic plague, came about as a result of decades of overpopulation, economic depression, famine, and bad health and hygiene in some European regions.

- **The Black Death** was named for the discoloration of the body. The belief is that it was introduced by seaborne rats from the Black Sea area. By the early fifteenth century, Western Europe had lost as much as 40 percent of its population to the plague.
- Lack of sophisticated medicine led to superstitions about the reasons for the plague, including poisoning.

THE HUNDRED YEARS' WAR AND THE RISE OF NATIONAL SENTIMENT

During the late Middle Ages, tremendous violence and political unrest led to the breakdown of European governments. Toward the end of the period, monarchs in England and France began to reassert their power; the Hundred Years' War was the result of their struggle for control.

- The Hundred Years' War (1337–1453) began when the English king Edward III claimed his right to the French throne after the death of Charles IV. The territorial proximity of England and France and their quarrel over the rights to Flanders exacerbated the dispute.
- English success in the war was due to its military superiority and its use of weaponry like the longbow. French weakness was due to territorial infighting and a lack of leadership.
- Fighting consisted primarily of sieges and raids. The battles of Crécy (1346), Poitiers (1356) and Agincourt (1415) were significant victories for the British. The Peace of Brétigny (1360) recognized English holdings in France, in exchange for Edward III renouncing his claim to the French throne.

- Joan of Arc (1412–1431), a peasant from Domrémy, who claimed she heard the voices of God, led the French to victory in the Battle of Orléans. Joan served as an inspiration for the French, who eventually defeated the English and won the war. Joan was later burned at the stake at Rouen as a heretic for refusing to recant her beliefs.

ECCLESIASTICAL BREAKDOWN AND REVIVAL: THE LATE MEDIEVAL CHURCH

- Pope Innocent III (r. 1198–1216) transformed the church into a secular power, creating a papal monarchy with a political mission that included the granting of *benefices* (church positions that provided income to the recipients) and declaring saints. Pope Urban IV (r. 1261–1264) continued the secularization of the Church by establishing its own law court, the Rota Romana, and by broadening the distribution of *benefices*. The College of Cardinals became politicized.
- Pope Boniface VIII (r. 1294–1303) refused the English and French efforts to tax the clergy, and issued a bull, *Clericis laicos,* which forbade taxation of the clergy without papal approval. Boniface was forced to make a concession to Philip the Fair of France, but the dispute led the two into further debates. In 1302, Boniface issued the bull *Unam Sanctum,* which declared that temporal authority was subject to the power of the Church. Pope Clement V moved the papacy to Avignon, to avoid a strife-ridden Rome and further pressure from the French king. The Avignon papacy was in appearance, although not always in fact, under strong French influence and the time in Avignon was called the "Babylonian Captivity," an allusion to the biblical bondage of the Israelites.
- Pope John XXII (r. 1316–1334) unsuccessfully tried to restore the papacy to Rome. William of Ockham and Marsilius of Padua protested papal power. John Wycliffe and John Huss led the popular lay movements, the **Lollards** and the **Hussites** (respectively in England and Bohemia) that protested the rights of the papacy.
- **The Great Schism** (1378–1417) occurred when Pope Clement VII, a cousin of the French king, was elected by a council of cardinals just five months after they had elected an Italian archbishop, Pope Urban VI. Two papal courts now claimed the right to power.
- Cardinals deposed both popes and elected a new pope, Alexander V. For a time, there were three popes who claimed spiritual authority.
- The Conciliar Movement, an effort to regulate the actions of the pope by councils, grew during this time. In 1414, the council of Constance met. In a document known as the Sacrosancta, the council recognized the Roman pope Gregory XII, and one pope ruled.

MEDIEVAL RUSSIA

Prince Vladimir of Kiev (972–1015) chose Orthodox Christianity as the religion of what would later become the Russian Empire.
- Kiev was a cultural center that rivaled Constantinople. Three cultural groups—the Great Russians, the White Russians, and the Little Russians (Ukrainians)—developed. Russia's hierarchical social structure divided freemen (clergy, army officers, **boyars**, townspeople, and peasants) from slaves. Debtors made up an intermediate group.
- Mongols, led by Genghis Khan, conquered Russia during the thirteenth century and Russian cities became part of the Mongol Empire until their liberation by Grand Duke Dimitri and Ivan the Great during the fifteenth century.

Multiple-Choice Questions

Questions 1–3 refer to the map below.

The Spread of the Black Death

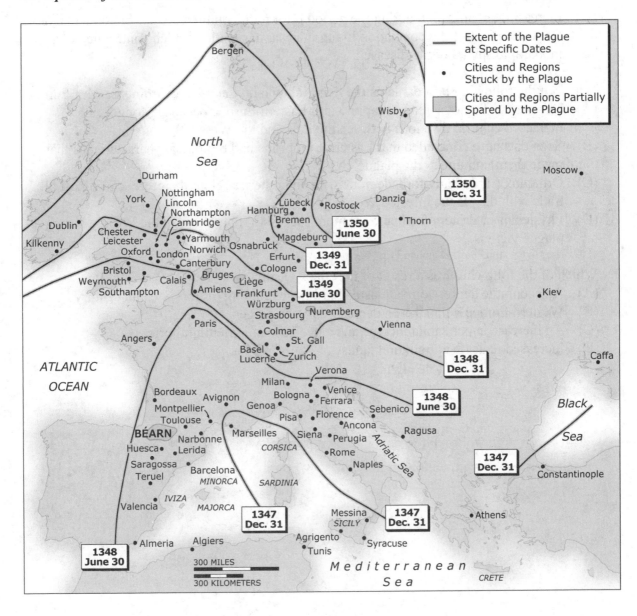

1. Which of the following was the most significant factor that contributed to the trends shown on the map?
   (A) The Hanseatic League's increased trade with the Ottoman Empire after their conquest of Constantinople helped to rapidly spread the bubonic plague throughout Europe.
   (B) The vibrant flagellant movement spread the bubonic plague rapidly from town to town as they travelled throughout the continent.
   (C) Increasing population combined with decreasing food supply prior to the outbreak of the bubonic plague weakened Europe's population, making it highly vulnerable to disease.
   (D) Increasing urbanization during the period prior to the outbreak of the bubonic plague led to over half of the population living in unsanitary cities, which contributed to a more rapid spread of the disease.

2. Which of the following best explains the trends shown on the map regarding Eastern Europe?
   (A) The plague did not spread as rapidly into Eastern Europe because Mongol rule increased cultural divisions between the East and the West.
   (B) Scientists have concluded that Eastern Europeans had biological characteristics that made them immune to the plague.
   (C) Orthodox Christianity forbade trade with any other religion; therefore, cutting off all trade with the plague infested West.
   (D) Physicians in Eastern Europe were more successful than those in the West in curing plague victims.

3. Which of the following was a result of the Black Death?
   (A) An economic depression that lasted until the beginning of the sixteenth century
   (B) Western Europe's population decreased by ten percent
   (C) An increase in per capita income and a decrease in agricultural prices
   (D) Increased rents on agricultural lands

Questions 4–6 refer to the passage below.

"In Florence, despite all that human wisdom… could devise to avert it, even as the cleansing of the city from many impurities by officials appointed… the refusal of entrance to all sick folk, and the adoption of many precautions for the preservation of health; despite also humble supplications addressed to God, and often repeated both in public procession and otherwise, by the devout; towards the beginning of the spring of the said year [1348] the doleful effects of the pestilence began to be horribly apparent by symptoms that [appeared] as if miraculous.

Not such were these symptoms as in the East, where an issue of blood from the nose was a manifest sign of inevitable death; but… it first betrayed itself by the emergence of certain tumours in the groin or the armpits, some of which grew as large as a common apple, others as an egg… which the common folk called gavoccioli. From the two said parts of the body this deadly gavoccioli soon began to propagate and spread itself in all directions indifferently; after which the form of the malady began to change, spots black or livid making their appearance in many cases on the arm or the thigh or elsewhere… and, being in ignorance of its source, failed to apply the proper remedies; in either case, not merely were those that recovered few, but almost all died within three days of the appearance of the said symptoms… and in most cases without any fever or other attendant malady."

Giovanni Boccaccio, Italian humanist, author, and poet, *The Decameron*, 1353

Source: From *The Decameron of Giovanni Boccaccio*, trans. J. M. Rigg (New York, 1930), p. 5.

4. Based on the first paragraph of the passage and the context in which it was created, it can be inferred that
   (A) city governments made no effort to slow down the spread of the plague
   (B) both peasants and nobles united against plague victims in order to halt the spread
   (C) everyone believed that the plague was sent by God to punish only sinners
   (D) religion remained important to most Europeans

5. The events described in the passage are reflective of which of the following continuities in medieval history?
   (A) There were frequent occurrences of bubonic plague occurring in Europe since the fall of the Roman Empire.
   (B) Europeans did not attempt to find a cure for any medical conditions in the centuries preceding the plague, instead relying upon God for miracle cures.
   (C) Death was a frequent companion to people during the high middle ages although the Black Death accelerated the death rate.
   (D) Science became more accepted by the Catholic Church as a possible solution to the Black Death.

6. Which of the following was an effort by landowners to avert the economic consequences of the events described in the passage?
   (A) Legislation that froze wages and restricted peasant movements
   (B) Legislation that enserfed the free peasantry
   (C) Enclosing all common lands in order to make additional profits
   (D) Experimentation with new forms of crop rotation to produce additional food

7

Questions 7–8 refer to the image below.

Edward III pays homage to his feudal lord Philip VI of France

Source: Snark/Art Resource, NY

7. Which of the following causes of the Hundred Years' War is best illustrated in this image?
   (A) Commercial conflict
   (B) English expansion
   (C) Nationalist animosity
   (D) Overlapping jurisdictions

8. Which of the following factors regarding the relationship between England and France prior to the Hundred Years' War is NOT reflective of the image?
   (A) France was militarily superior to England.
   (B) A series of weak English kings allowed French kings to dictate national policy.
   (C) The French abhorred English possession of lands in France because it hindered centralization.
   (D) The French Estates General had more control over French kings than the English Parliament had over English kings.

Questions 9–11 refer to the maps below.

The Hundred Years' War

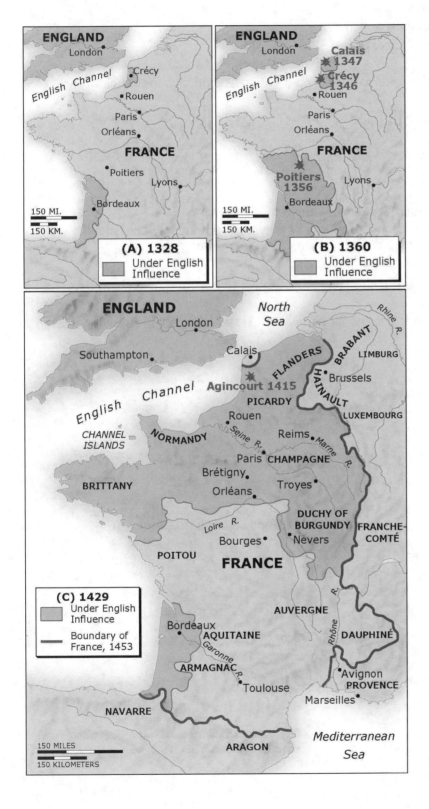

9. Which of the following was a significant factor that contributed to the changes to French territory shown on the maps?
   (A) Internal disunity in England
   (B) Internal disunity in France
   (C) France was fighting a defensive war
   (D) England was fighting a defensive war

10. An historian could best use the patterns shown on the map as evidence for which of the following?
    (A) French military superiority
    (B) English military superiority
    (C) The expansion of France
    (D) The weakness of Burgundy

11. Which of the following reversed the patterns shown on the map?
    (A) Joan of Arc's victory at Orleans inspired a new sense of French national identity.
    (B) Charles VII defeated the Duke of Burgundy and confiscated his territories and weapons to use against the English.
    (C) Eleanor of Aquitaine's marriage to Henry II of England occurred in exchange for English territories in France.
    (D) The French were the first to use the longbow in 1431, which enabled a quick defeat of their enemy.

Questions 12–13 refer to the passage below.

"Hugh of St. Victor… declares that the spiritual power has to institute the earthly power and to judge…. We can clearly prove from the order of the universe that the church is set above nations and kingdoms [Jeremias 1:10]…. It is the law of divinity that the lowest are led to the highest through intermediaries…. At Romans 13… the Apostle, having said that there is no power except from God… added: "And those that are, are ordained of God." If then there are two swords [governments], one spiritual, the other temporal, as can be gathered from the words of the Gospel, "Behold, here are two swords" (Luke 22:38), [to which] the Lord at once added, "It is enough" because these two swords suffice for the church, [then] it follows that these two swords, these two powers and authorities, are [both] from God, since there is no power except from God. But, therefore they must be rightly ordered since, what is from God must be ordered. [And] they would not be so ordered unless one sword was led by the other and one was under the other since, as Dionysius said, the law of divinity which God gave to all created things requires this…. Therefore the temporal sword, as being inferior, is led by the spiritual sword, as being superior, and the one is set below the other as an inferior below a superior."

Giles of Rome, philosopher and papal adviser, *On Ecclesiastical Power*, 1301

Source: *The Crisis of Church and State, 1050–1300* by Brian Tierney. Copyright © 1964 by Prentice-Hall, Inc. Copyright renewed © 1992 by Brian Tierney. All rights reserved. Also, https://cup.columbia.edu/book/giles-of-romes-on-ecclesiastical-power/9780231128032

12. The author of the passage would reject which of the following assertions?
    (A) The church is superior to secular authority.
    (B) Spiritual and secular authority can be equal.
    (C) Spiritual and ecclesiastical authority are the same.
    (D) The pope is the head of the Catholic Church.

13. The author of the passage would have supported which of the following?
    (A) Pope Boniface VIII's compromise with Philip the Fair in the late 1290s
    (B) Pope Innocent III's doctrine of *plenitude of power*
    (C) The *Pragmatic Sanction of Bourges*
    (D) The Conciliar Movement

Questions 14–15 refer to the passage below.

"That the material substance of bread and… wine remain in the Sacrament of the altar.

That Christ is not in the Sacrament essentially… in his own corporeal presence.

That if a bishop or priest be in mortal sin he does not ordain [effectively] ordain, consecrate, or baptise…

That it is contrary to Holy Scripture that ecclesiastics should have possessions.

That any deacon or priest may preach the word of God apart from the authority of the Apostolic See, or a Catholic bishop.

That no one is a civil lord, or a prelate, or a bishop when he is in mortal sin.

That temporal lords can at their will take away temporal goods from the church, when those who hold them are habitually sinful.

That the people can at their own will correct sinful lords.

That tithes are mere alms, and that parishioners can withdraw them at their will because of the misdeeds of their curates.

That friars are bound to gain their livelihood by the labor of their hands, and not by begging.

That… the ordination of clerics [and] the consecration of [holy] places are reserved for the Pope and bishops on account of their desire for temporal gain and honor.

That the excommunication of the Pope or any prelate is not to be feared, because it is the censure of antichrist.

It is fatuous to believe in the indulgences of the Pope and the bishops.

The Condemned Conclusions (London and Council of Constance) of John Wycliffe, 1382 and 1415

Source: *Documents of the Christian Church*, ed. Henry Bettenson (New York: Oxford University Press, 1947).

14. Which of the following could have influenced Wycliffe's ideas expressed in passage?
    (A) English kings support of the Avignon papacy
    (B) Anti-French policies of the English government
    (C) Anticlerical policies of the English government
    (D) The spread of Christian humanism to England

15. Wycliffe's ideas in the passage are most similar to those of
    (A) King Richard II
    (B) Philip the Fair
    (C) Wat Tyler
    (D) John Huss

12

Short-Answer Question

Answer a, b, and c:
1. a) Describe one significant <u>change</u> in the relationship between church leaders and secular rulers during the thirteenth and fourteenth centuries.
   b) Describe one significant <u>continuity</u> in the relationship between church leaders and secular rulers during the thirteenth and fourteenth centuries.
   c) Explain one significant effect of the changes in the relationship between church leaders and secular rulers during the thirteenth and fourteenth centuries.

Long-Essay Question

Evaluate the extent to which crop failures in the early fourteenth century contributed to the rapid spread of bubonic plague from 1348 to 1352.

ANSWERS AND EXPLANATIONS: AP® PRACTICE TEST

Multiple-Choice Questions

1. **C** (12th Edition p. 30) In addition to overcrowding in cities (although approximately 50% of the population did not live in cities), crop failures in the early-fourteenth century led to decreased food supplies. Prior to this period, population had increased dramatically, having doubled in the three previous centuries. All of this weakened the European population, making it particularly vulnerable to diseases such as the bubonic plague.

2. **A** (12th Edition p. 47) The Mongol conquest of Eastern Europe, including modern-day Russia and Ukraine, led to decreased contact between the people of this area with the people of Eastern Europe. As a result, the plague did not spread as rapidly into Eastern Europe.

3. **C** (12th Edition pp. 33–36) The depletion of the European population created opportunities for those who survived, resulting in a population with increased money to buy food, goods, and luxury items. Some historians believe that Europeans would not consume the amount of meat and fish that they did during the plague until the end of the nineteenth century.

4. **D** (12th Edition p. 31) The first paragraph infers both private and public appeals toward God. This is consistent with the importance of religion and the Church to most Europeans, even those who were uneducated.

5. **C** (12th Edition p. 33) Death rates were high during the middle ages. It is estimated that life expectancy was only half as long as in modern times and close to 50% of children would die before the age of 10.

6. **A** (12th Edition p. 30) Landowners often encouraged legislation that would restrict peasants from leaving their estates as well as freezing wages (in response to increased demand for labor in urban areas). For example, The English Parliament passed a Statute of Laborers in 1351 that limited wages and forbade peasants to relocate.

7. **D** (12th Edition p. 37) Edward III was sovereign in England, but he was also the subject of Philip IV and owned many lands in France.

8. **C** (12th Edition p. 37) French monarchs detested English control of lands in France because English kings, even though vassals to the French kings, did not often act that way. This hindered further centralization of France. After the Hundred Years' War, French King Louis XI, "the Spider," would further centralize power, creating Europe's first national army.

9. **B** (12th Edition p. 38) Although France was fighting a defensive war, internal problems in France, including a divided Estates-General and increased taxation of the peasantry, hampered French unity and led to several French losses. The French were unable to use their defensive (and nationalistic) advantage until the Battle of Orleans in 1429.

10. **B** (12th Edition p. 38) English infantry were more disciplined and used new weapons, including the longbow, successfully in the early stages of the war thus gaining additional territories in France as shown on the map.

11. **A** (12th Edition pp. 39–40) Joan of Arc's leadership during the siege and victory of Orleans as well as a quick succession of military victories against the English encouraged a new sense of French national identify. By 1453, the English were driven from most of the continent (although Calais remained in English hands).

12. B (12th Edition pp. 40–42) The author strenuously argues that one authority—the Catholic Church—must be over the other.

13. B (12th Edition p. 40) Giles of Rome, an ardent supporter of papal authority, would most likely have been supportive of Pope Innocent III's doctrine of *plenitude of power*. This doctrine essentially transformed the papacy into a political power with the spiritual sword (of the Church) more powerful than the temporal sword (of kings). Essentially, he believes that the pope is the highest spiritual authority and outranks kings.

14. C (12th Edition p. 44) These propositions are a harsh condemnation of the practices of the popes and other church authorities and were written in the context of an English government that was opposed to increased papal power.

15. D (12th Edition p. 45) Many Bohemians studied at Oxford during Wycliffe's lifetime and were most likely influenced by his beliefs. John Huss was the leader of the Hussite movement that advocated ideas similar to those of Wycliffe.

Short-Answer Question
(12th Edition pp. 40–46)

Possible responses to part a) include:
- Secular rulers became more powerful than church leaders during this period, for example, Philip the Fair of France sent an army to Boniface VIII's papal retreat and almost executed him.
- The papacy was moved to Avignon during this period and it appeared to be under French influence.
- Control of religion fell into the hands of monarchs.

Possible responses to part b) include:
- The Church continued to assert its authority against secular rulers, for example, Pope Boniface issued the *Unam Sanctum* in 1302.
- The Church continued (albeit with less success) to excommunicate secular rulers.

Possible responses to part c) include:
- Monarchies continued to centralize and grow in power, particularly France and England.
- The weaknesses of church leaders led to growing reform movements, particularly the Lollards in England and the Hussites in Bohemia.

Long-Essay Question
(12th Edition pp. 30–32)

Evaluate the extent to which crop failures in the early fourteenth century contributed to the rapid spread of bubonic plague from 1348 to 1352.

Reasons why crop failures played an extensive role in spreading disease rapidly might include:
- Crop failures during the early fourteenth century led to the greatest famine of the medieval period, especially in urban areas.
- The lack of nutrition weakened the European population and made it more vulnerable to the bubonic plague.

To a lesser extent, other reasons might include:
- Urban sanitary conditions were poor, which further hastened the spread of the disease.
- Many believed the plague was sent from God as punishment for the sinful ways of the world and recommended penance and repentance as the best way to stop the spread of the disease.
- The flagellants did nothing to stop the spread of the plague; indeed, their bloody bodies spread the disease.
- Many also believed in superstitious remedies that did nothing to prevent the spread of the plague.

CHAPTER 2

Renaissance and Discovery

The Renaissance era in European history is associated with Italy, whose city-states were venues for some of the most significant events of the period. Italy's strategic location at the crossroads of the East and the West enabled the country to achieve commercial prosperity during the late Middle Ages. Italian rulers and merchants served as patrons to the arts, government, and education, leading to an unprecedented cultural Renaissance, or rebirth.

THE RENAISSANCE IN ITALY (1375–1527)

The three major city-states in Italy during the Renaissance were Florence, Milan, and Venice.

- The Renaissance was shaped by its emergence in the context of Italian city-states. The merchants of these cities played an important role in Renaissance culture.
- The Treaty of Lodi (1454–1455) was a fragile alliance between the city-states of Naples, Milan, and Florence, and their rivals, Venice and the Papal States.
- Cosimo de' Medici (1389–1464) was a wealthy Florentine who manipulated elections and influenced the local council, the *Signoria*, in his uncontested control of the city. His grandson, Lorenzo the Magnificent (1449–1492) ruled Florence with a totalitarian regime from 1478–1492. The later Florentine ruler, Piero de' Medici, allied with Naples against Milan in 1494, and he was exiled after handing Pisa and other Florentine possessions over to Charles VIII of France.
- The Visconti family came to rule Milan in 1278, and the Sforza family took over in 1450. Both ruled without constitutional restraint or political competition. A Sforza, Ludovico il Moro, appealed to the French in 1494 for aid against Naples and its allies, an appeal that resulted in France's acquisition of Florence.
- In response to the takeover of Florence by Charles VIII of France, in 1495 Ferdinand of Aragon created the League of Venice, a counter alliance designed to protect Venice, Milan, the Papal States, and Emperor Maximilian I from France.
- Girolamo Savonarola (1452–1498), a radical Dominican monk, convinced a mob of Florentines to exile Piero de' Medici and claimed that France's victory was divine justice. Savonarola ruled Florence until his imprisonment and execution in 1498.
- Venice was an exception to the trend of despotic rule. It was ruled by a merchant oligarchy, a 300-member senate, and a judicial council.

AP® FRAMEWORK
TOPIC # 1.2, 2.6; LO: UNIT 1 A, B, C AND UNIT 2 E
KC:
1.1.I.A Italian Renaissance humanists, including Petrarch, promoted a revival in classical literature and created new philological approaches to ancient texts. Some Renaissance humanists furthered the values of secularism and individualism.

1.4.I.C Established hierarchies of class, religion, and gender continued to define social status and perceptions in rural and urban settings.

1.4.III.A Population recovered to its pre-Great Plague level in the 16th century, and continuing population pressures contributed to uneven price increases; agricultural commodities increased more sharply than wages, reducing living standards for some.

HUMANISM

The growth of humanism, the study and appropriation of the ideals expressed in Latin and Greek classics and other works of antiquity, played an important role in the Italian Renaissance. Humanists were innovative educators who believed in the importance of well-rounded education and in the noble ideals expressed by **Baldassare Castiglione (1478–1529)** in his ***Book of the Courtier.***

- Humanists espoused a program of study that included rhetoric, politics, moral philosophy, poetry, and history, which also embraced classical and biblical sources. In Florence, the Florentine Platonic Academy arose under the patronage of Cosimo de' Medici to enable humanists to devote their attention to Plato and the Neoplatonists.
- Scholars consider Francesco Petrarch (1304–1374) the "father of humanism." Other important works and authors of the era include *The Divine Comedy* by Dante Alighieri (1265–1321) and *The Decameron* by Giovanni Boccaccio (1313–1375).
- In art, new techniques like *chiaroscuro* and linear perspective were perfected and implemented by Renaissance artists of extraordinary talent, including Michelangelo Buonarroti (1475–1564), Leonardo da Vinci (1452–1519), and Raphael (1483–1520).

AP® FRAMEWORK
TOPIC # 1.2; LO: UNIT 1 B, C
KC:
1.1.I.B Humanist revival of Greek and Roman texts, spread by the printing press, challenged the institutional power of universities and the Catholic Church. This shifted education away from a primary focus on theological writings toward classical texts and new methods of scientific inquiry.

1.1.I.C Admiration for Greek and Roman political institutions supported a revival of civic humanist culture in the Italian city-states and produced secular models for individual and political behavior.

1.1.III.A In the Italian Renaissance, rulers and popes concerned with enhancing their prestige commissioned paintings and architectural works based on classical styles, the developing "naturalism" in the artistic world, and often the newly invented technique of geometric perspective.

THE NORTHERN RENAISSANCE

Northern humanism was stimulated by the learning imported by students returning to the Netherlands from Italy, and the movement was spread further by the effects of the French invasions of Italy.

- Northern humanism was supported by the Brothers of the Common Life, a lay religious movement based in the Netherlands. Northern humanists often had more diverse social backgrounds and were more interested in religious reform than were their Italian counterparts. They were able also to convey their educational ideals to more people as a result of Johann Gutenberg's invention of printing with movable type in 1450.
- Desiderius Erasmus (1466–1536), the most famous northern humanist, tried in his writings to unite the classical ideal of civic virtue with Christian ideals. His works embraced anticlerical views and satirized religious superstition. He produced a Greek edition of the New Testament (1516), and then a Latin translation of the Greek edition.
- The English humanist Thomas More (1478–1535) is best known for *Utopia,* a critique of society that envisioned an imaginary society based on tolerance and communal property.

AP® FRAMEWORK
TOPICS # 1.3, 1.4; LO: UNIT 1 D, E
KC:

1.1.III.B The Northern Renaissance retained a more religious focus, which resulted in more human-centered naturalism that considered individuals and everyday life appropriate objects of artistic representation.
1.2.I.A Christian humanism, embodied in the writings of Erasmus, employed Renaissance learning in the service of religious reform.

VOYAGES OF DISCOVERY AND THE NEW EMPIRE IN THE WEST AND EAST

Primarily economic motives led western European countries to the exploration of faraway lands. A quest for gold and spices led European explorers to Africa and India.

- Explorers such as Christopher Columbus (1451–1506), Amerigo Vespucci (1451–1512), Ferdinand Magellan (1480–1521), and Henry the Navigator (1394–1460) sought to conquer unknown worlds and bring riches and supplies back to Europe.
- The effects of discoveries on the culture and history of conquered peoples frequently involved exploitation and, in some cases, complete destruction.

AP® FRAMEWORK
TOPICS # 1.6, 1.7, 1.8, 1.9; LO: UNIT 1 G, H, I, J, K, L
KC:

1.3.I.A European states sought direct access to gold, spices, and luxury goods to enhance personal wealth and state power.
1.3.I.B The rise of mercantilism gave the state a new role in promoting commercial development and the acquisition of colonies overseas.
1.3.I.C Christianity was a stimulus for exploration as governments and religious authorities sought to spread the faith, and for some it served as a justification for the subjugation of indigenous civilizations.

1.3.II Advances in navigation, cartography, and military technology enabled Europeans to establish overseas colonies and empires.

1.3.III.A Advances in navigation, cartography, and military technology enabled Europeans to establish overseas colonies and empires.

1.3.III.B The Spanish established colonies across the Americas, the Caribbean, and the Pacific, which made Spain a dominant state in Europe in the 16th century.

1.3.III.C The Atlantic nations of France, England, and the Netherlands followed by establishing their own colonies and trading networks to compete with Portuguese and Spanish dominance in the 17th century.

1.3.III.D The competition for trade led to conflicts and rivalries among European powers in the 17th and 18th centuries.

1.3.IV.A The exchange of goods shifted the center of economic power in Europe from the Mediterranean to the Atlantic states and brought the latter into an expanding world economy.

1.3.IV.B The exchange of new plants, animals, and diseases—the Columbian Exchange—created economic opportunities for Europeans.

1.3.IV.C Europeans expanded the African slave trade in response to the establishment of a plantation economy in the Americas and demographic catastrophes among indigenous peoples.

Multiple-Choice Questions

Questions 1–2 refer to the following map.

Renaissance Italy

1. Which of the following best reflects the geo-political situation shown in the map?

(A) The political fragmentation of the Italian peninsula contributed to the development of new theories regarding the secular state.

(B) The political fragmentation of the Italian peninsula contributed to Italian nationalistic movements during the Renaissance.

(C) The Kingdom of Naples militarily dominated the Italian city-states throughout the fifteenth and sixteenth centuries.

(D) Rome and the Papal States had secular authority over all of the city-states due to the Donation of Constantine in the fourth century.

2. In which of the following ways did the geo-political situation shown in the map contribute to the Renaissance?

   (A) The central location of Rome ensured that Renaissance art and architecture were often commissioned by the Catholic Church.

   (B) Many of the rulers of the Italian city-states commissioned portraits and other works of art to enhance their prestige.

   (C) Italy's location on the Mediterranean ensured that the Renaissance would affect only the Italian states.

   (D) Italy's position in Europe as well as the urban nature of the Italian city-states guaranteed that only Italian universities could provide a humanist education.

Questions 3–5 refer to the passage below.

"All wives of artisans… should encourage their husbands… to get to work early in the morning and work until late…. [And] the wife herself should [also] be involved in the work to the extent that she knows all about it, so that she may know how to oversee his workers if her husband is absent, and to reprove them if they do not do well…. And when customers come to her husband and try to drive a hard bargain, she ought to warn him… to take care that he does not make a bad deal. She should advise him to be chary of giving too much credit if he does not know precisely where and to whom it is going, for in this way many come to poverty…

In addition, she ought to keep her husband's love as much as she can, to this end: that he will stay at home more willingly and that he may not have any reason to join the foolish crowds of other young men in taverns and indulge in unnecessary and extravagant expense… By treating him kindly she should protect him as well as she can from this. It is said that three things drive a man from his home: a quarrelsome wife, a smoking fireplace, and a leaking roof. She too ought to stay at home gladly and not go off every day traipsing hither and yon gossiping with the neighbours… That is done by slovenly housewives…"

Christine de Pisan, *The Treasure of the City of Ladies*

Source: The Treasure of the City of Ladies by Christine de Pisan, trans. by Sarah Lawson (New York: Penguin, 1985), pp. 167–168. Copyright © Sarah Lawson, 1985. Penguin Books Ltd.

3. The passage reflects which of the following continuities during the Renaissance period?
   (A) Improvements in literacy continued to be emphasized.
   (B) Women were expected to run the household in partnership with their husbands.
   (C) Unmarried women were expected to join religious orders.
   (D) Traditional gender hierarchies continued in both rural and urban settings.

4. The passage reflects which of the following developments of the Renaissance period?
   (A) Debates emerged regarding female education and women's roles within the family.
   (B) Population losses from the plague led to an increase in the number of females who worked.
   (C) Women should work, but their primary role in the family should be as caretakers.
   (D) Clerical positions were open to women.

5. Which of the following best explains why more people were influenced during the Renaissance period by ideas such as those expressed in the passage?
   (A) Compulsory schooling laws in the Italian city-states
   (B) The revival of classical schools of learning
   (C) An increase in the use of Latin
   (D) The invention of the printing press

Questions 6–8 refer to the passage below.

"The best of artisans [God] ordained that that creature (man) to whom He had been able to give nothing proper to himself should have joint possession of whatever had been peculiar to each of the different kinds of being. He therefore took man as a creature of indeterminate nature and, assigning him a place in the middle of the world, addressed him thus: "Neither a fixed abode nor a form that is thine alone nor any function peculiar to thyself have we given thee, Adam, to the end that according to thy longing and according to thy judgment thou mayest have and possess what abode, what form, and what functions thou thyself shalt desire. The nature of all other beings is limited and constrained within the bounds of laws prescribed by Us. Thou, constrained by no limits, in accordance with thine own free will, in whose hand We have placed thee, shall ordain for thyself the limits of thy nature. We have set thee at the world's center that thou mayest from thence more easily observe whatever is in the world…. Thou shalt have the power to degenerate into the lower forms of life, which are brutish. Thou shalt have the power, out of thy soul's judgment, to be reborn into the higher forms, which are divine."

Pico della Mirandola, Oration on the Dignity of Man (ca. 1486)

Source: Giovanni Pico della Mirandola, *Oration on the Dignity of Man*, in *The Renaissance Philosophy of Man*, ed. by E. Cassirer et al. Translated by Elisabeth Livermore Forbes (Chicago: Phoenix Books, 1961), pp. 224–225.

6. The passage is best understood in the context of which of the following developments during the Renaissance?
   (A) An increase in the study of scholasticism
   (B) A new emphasis on secularism
   (C) The increased importance of the individual
   (D) A revival of civic humanism

7. The passage most clearly shows the influence of which of the following trends in fifteenth-century Europe?
   (A) Christian humanism
   (B) Italian humanism
   (C) Boccaccio's *Decameron*
   (D) Castiglione's *The Book of the Courtier*

8. Which of the following was a result of the spread of ideas such as those expressed in the passage?
   (A) An increase in religious works such as Thomas à Kempis *The Imitation of Christ*
   (B) An increased emphasis by humanists on the study of the Book of Genesis (first book of the Bible)
   (C) A shift in education from theological to classical studies
   (D) A marked decrease in the number of Jesuit schools throughout the Italian states

Questions 9–10 refer to the passage below.

"In the Middle Ages both sides of human consciousness—that which was turned within as that which was turned without—lay dreaming or half-awake beneath a common veil. The veil was woven of faith, illusion, and childish prepossession, through which the world and history were seen clad in strange hues. Man was conscious of himself only as member of a race, people, party, family, or corporation—only through some general category. In Italy this veil first melted into air; an *objective* treatment and consideration of the state and of all the things of this world became possible. The *subjective* side at the same time asserted itself with corresponding emphasis; man became a spiritual *individual*, and recognised himself as such…

In far earlier times we can here and there detect a development of free personality which in Northern Europe either did not occur at all, or could not display itself in the same manner… But at the close of the thirteenth century Italy began to swarm with individuality… Dante's great poem [*The Divine Comedy*] would have been impossible in any other country of Europe… For Italy the august poet, through the wealth of individuality which he set forth, was the most national herald of his time…. This fact appears in the most decisive and unmistakeable form. The Italians of the fourteenth century knew little of false modesty or of hypocrisy in any shape; not one of them was afraid of singularity, of being and seeming unlike his neighbours."

Jacob Burckhardt, The Civilisation of the Renaissance in Italy, 1860

Source: Jacob Burckhardt, *The Civilization of the Renaissance in Italy*, translated by Samuel George Chetwynd Middlemore, 1890, p. 129

9. Which of the following characteristics of the Italian Renaissance would support Burckhardt's argument?
   (A) The Italian Renaissance humanist values regarding individualism were synthesized with the Catholic Church teachings regarding faith and reason.
   (B) The Italian Renaissance humanist values regarding individualism challenged the institutional power of the Catholic Church.
   (C) The Italian Renaissance focus on Greco-Roman works led to increased studies of Jesus's apostles' journey through the ancient Roman Empire.
   (D) The Italian Renaissance focus on humanism, secularism, and individualism was anti-Christian in nature.

10. Which of the following characteristics of Italian Renaissance art would support Burckhardt's argument?
    (A) Renaissance artists were the first to use vibrant colors in their works.
    (B) Renaissance artists' paintings and sculptures were primarily religious in nature.
    (C) Renaissance artists tried but failed to realistically paint individuals in their paintings.
    (D) Renaissance artists were influential to the development of the style of "naturalism."

Questions 11–13 refer to the image below.

Pedro de Alvarado Besieged by Aztec Warriors from the Codex Duran (sixteenth century)

Source: Codex Duran: Pedro de Alvarado (c. 1485–1541), companion-at-arms of Hernando Cortés (1845–1547) besieged by Aztec warriors (vellum) by Diego Duran (16th century), Codex Duran, Historia De Las Indias (16th century). Biblioteca Nacional, Madrid, Spain/Bridgeman Art Library

11. The image suggests which of the following as a reason for the European conquest of the Americas?
    (A) The English were the greatest military power in Europe during the sixteenth century.
    (B) Jesuit soldiers were more militarily advanced than the armies of the indigenous peoples of the Americas.
    (C) Europeans had technological advantages over the indigenous peoples of the Americas.
    (D) The indigenous groups in the Americas did not have a formal military structure.

12. Which of the following was LEAST important as a cause during the sixteenth century for events similar to those in the image?
    (A) The impulse to spread Christianity
    (B) Europeans' desire for more luxury goods
    (C) The search for gold and silver
    (D) Competition between Spain and England for territory in the Americas

13. Which of the following was a result of events similar to those in the image?
    (A) A slow and steady rise in prices (the Price Revolution) during the sixteenth century
    (B) The growth of Protestantism in the New World during the sixteenth century
    (C) The spread of Christian humanism in the sixteenth century
    (D) A shift in economic power to the Mediterranean states

27

Questions 14–15 refer to the passage below.

"You well know that in our dominion, there are certain bad Christians that… committed apostasy against our Holy Catholic faith… Therefore, in the year 1480, we ordered that the Jews be separated… hoping that by such separation the situation would be remedied. And we ordered… an Inquisition be established… Furthermore, we are informed by the Inquisition and others that the great harm done to the Christians persists… such Jews trying… to subvert our holy Catholic faith and trying to draw faithful Christians away from their beliefs…

Therefore… after much deliberation, it is agreed and resolved that all Jews and Jewesses be ordered to leave our kingdoms, and that they never be allowed to return."

The Alhambra Decrees, Ferdinand and Isabella, 1492

Source: Peters, Edward. "Jewish History and Gentile Memory: The Expulsion of 1492." Jewish History, Vol. 9, No. 1 (Spring, 1995).

14. An historian could use the excerpt as evidence for which of the following?
    (A) Jewish exiles from Spain primarily settled in Portugal.
    (B) The Spanish Inquisition only targeted Spanish Muslims.
    (C) Ferdinand and Isabella relied upon the papacy to settle religious issues in Spain during their reign.
    (D) New monarchies embraced religious uniformity as a way to further consolidate their rule.

15. In addition to the Alhambra Decrees, Ferdinand and Isabella also
    (A) ended the Inquisition after the successful creation of a Catholic kingdom
    (B) used marriage as a way to further consolidate their rule
    (C) fought wars against the English to respond to their intervention in the Dutch revolt
    (D) created the Court of the Star Chamber to enforce royal decrees

Short-Answer Question

Answer a, b, and c:
1. a) Explain one way in which the invention of the printing press transformed literature during the period 1450–1600.
   b) Explain one way in which the invention of the printing press contributed to the development of national culture during the period 1450–1600.
   c) Explain one way in which the invention of the printing press affected the Northern Renaissance during the period 1450–1600.

Long-Essay Question

1. Evaluate the extent to which the Renaissance fostered change in European politics and culture during the period 1450–1600.

ANSWERS AND EXPLANATIONS: AP® PRACTICE TEST

Multiple-Choice Questions

1. A   (KC: 1.1.I.C; LO: Unit 1 C) This map shows the political divisions of the Italian peninsula during the Renaissance era. This political fragmentation contributed to new secular political theories such as those espoused in Machiavelli's *The Prince.*

2. B   (KC: 1.1.III.A; LO: Unit 1 C) The politics of the Italian city-states led to increased competition among the Italian rulers. As a result, many Italian rulers often sponsored art works (including portraits) to enhance the prestige of the city-state and themselves.

3. D   (KC: 1.4.I.C; LO: Unit 2 E) Although the passage reflects enlightened views of women during the time period, there is also reference to women's subordinate role to their husbands in the second paragraph.

4. A   (KC: 1.4.IV.B; LO: Unit 2 E) Renaissance humanists often debated whether women should be educated and what should be their proper role in the household and society.

5. D   (KC: 1.1.II.A; LO: Unit 1 E) The invention of the printing press in the 1450s led to an increased number of both classical and vernacular works (such as de Pisan's) that were spread mostly through urban learning centers.

6. C   (KC: 1.1.I.A; LO: Unit 1 B) Della Mirandola considers humans to have unlimited potential, unlike other animals. This directly correlates with the Renaissance value of individualism. Renaissance humanists were not necessarily anti-church; however, they did value the individual more than did medieval scholars.

7. B   (KC: 1.1.I.A; LO: Unit 1 B) The idea of individualism, emphasized in the passage, was a direct result of the Italian humanist movement.

8. C   (KC: 1.1.I.B; LO: Unit 1 C) One of the effects of the growing emphasis on humanism, secularism, and individualism was that educational emphasis shifted away from the Church (scholasticism) and more towards the classics.

9. B   (KC: 1.1.I.A; LO: Unit 1 B) In the passage, Burckhardt discusses the Italian emphasis on individualism, a value of the Italian humanists. One important consequence of this were challenges to the Catholic Church's teachings. For example, a humanist, Lorenzo Valla, proved the Donation of Constantine to be false.

10. D   (KC: 1.1.III.A; LO: Unit 1 C) Burckhardt's discussion of individualism also contributed to new styles of art, primarily the use of naturalism. Renaissance artists successfully imitated nature in their works, further differentiating the movement from Burckhardt's references to the Middle Ages in the first few sentences.

11. C   (KC: 1.3.II; LO: Unit 1 G) This image depicts Spanish warriors armed with bows, rifles, and better defensive wear than their Aztec rivals. Advanced technology including guns, gunpowder, and horses allowed the Spanish to conquer the great Aztec and Inca empires.

12. D   (KC: 1.3.I, 1.3.II; LO: Unit 1 H) Although the English and Spanish were rivals during the sixteenth century, they were not yet competing for territory in the New World. The English would attempt to establish colonies toward the end of the sixteenth century but would not gain considerable territory until the seventeenth century.

13. A   (KC: 1.4.II.B; LO: Unit 1 M) One result of the European conquest of the Americas was the Price Revolution of the sixteenth century. This was a slow but steady inflation that occurred throughout the century partly as a result of the amount of bullion from the New World and also partly as a result of the population increase during this time period.

14. D   (KC: 1.5.I.A; LO: Unit 1 F) The new monarchies that developed at the end of the fifteenth century often relied upon religious uniformity to strengthen their rule. Ferdinand and Isabella, strongly Catholic, believed that one religion would help further unify their country.

15. B   (KC: 1.5.I.A; LO: Unit 1 F) Ferdinand and Isabella used marriage to consolidate their rule in Spain by uniting the Christian kingdoms of Aragon and Castile. Furthermore, they arranged their children's marriages (Joanna to Philip of Habsburg and Catherine to English heir Arthur) to build alliances and further strengthen Spain as a power, especially to counter the power of France.

Short-Answer Question
(KC: 1.1.II; LO: Unit 1 E)

Possible responses to part a) include:
- Dissemination of Italian Renaissance writers including Petrarch, Machiavelli, Castiglione, and Pico della Mirandola
- Dissemination of Northern Renaissance writers including Erasmus, More, and Rabelais
- The popularity of humanist writings throughout much of western and central Europe

Possible responses to part b) include:
- The increase in literary works written and printed in the vernacular
- The increase of political propaganda used by rulers to centralize their states

Possible responses to part c) include:
- The dissemination of works by Erasmus to reform the Church
- The dissemination of works by Martin Luther and others (e.g. Calvin) that led to the Reformation in various regions
- The printing of vernacular Bibles that enhanced popular access to Scripture

Long-Essay Question
(KC: 1.1.I, 1.4.IV, 1.5.1; LO: Unit 1 C, D, F)

Evaluate the extent to which the Renaissance fostered change in European politics and culture during the period 1450–1600.

Possible changes include:

- The Reformation (influenced by Christian humanism) that led to political divisions within the Holy Roman Empire
- The Reformation (influenced by Christian humanism) that led to civil war in France, the Spanish Armada, and the Dutch Revolt
- The emergence of New Monarchies in Spain, France, and England
- The development of Italian Renaissance art and Northern Renaissance Art
- The influence of Italian and Christian humanism
- The decline in the status of upper-class women
- Increased literacy in Protestant states (and later Catholic states led by the Jesuits)
- The dawn of a new age in learning that inspired the early Scientific Revolution
- The spread of cartography and its impact on navigation

Possible continuities include:

- Few changes in the lives of peasants
- Few changes in the lives of ordinary women
- The continued dominance of the Catholic Church in Italy, Spain, France, and southern Germany
- Little influence of Renaissance ideas in eastern Europe

CHAPTER 3

The Age of Reformation

The **Protestant Reformation** was a reaction against the traditions, policies, dogma, and abuses of the Catholic Church. Those who opposed the church were called Protestants for the various protests they waged. These protests altered the religious unity of Europe, brought about religious wars, and resulted in the fragmentation of the Christian faith into many different denominations.

THE PROTESTANT REFORMATION

Some of the issues that led to this religious shift away from the Catholic Church include:

- The Great Schism: Two different popes (Clement VII and Urban VI) claimed authority over the Catholic Church; this conflict was not resolved until the Council of Constance in 1414, and the overall result was the weakening of church unity, sales of indulgences, nepotism, and simony. These aspects of Catholic life angered many believers, who thought that they were not scripturally sound.
- Humanism: The rise of scholarship during the Renaissance, and humanists' interest in returning to classical texts made direct study of and access to the Bible of great importance.

AP® FRAMEWORK
TOPIC # 1.3; LO: UNIT 1 D
KC:
1.2.I.A Christian humanism, embodied in the writings of Erasmus, employed Renaissance learning in the service of religious reform.

PROTESTANT LEADERS

- Martin Luther (1483–1546), a German theologian,was discontented with the medieval Christian teachings that God required perfect righteousness for salvation. Luther argued on behalf of "justification by faith alone" whereby grace was given freely to those who believed in Jesus Christ. In 1517, Luther famously attacked the Catholic system of indulgences promoted by preachers like John Tetzel, when he posted his Ninety-five Theses on the door of Castle Church in Wittenberg. Condemned to heresy in 1520, Luther was protected by friends who hid him in a castle where he translated the New Testament into German, using Erasmus's Greek text and Latin translations.
- Ulrich Zwingli (1484–1531) carried the the Reformation to Switzerland. He was opposed to the sale of indulgences and to religious superstition. Zwingli successfully petitioned for the end to clerical celibacy and the clerical right to marry, which was adopted by all Protestant groups. Zwingli believed anything that lacked literal support in Scripture was not to be believed. He questioned traditional behaviors such as fasting, adoration of saints, pilgrimages, and other sacraments. His beliefs translated into a regime of harsh discipline in Zurich, and made Switzerland an example of puritanical Protestantism. Zwingli and Luther disagreed in the famous Marburg Colloquy (1529) over the presence of Christ's body in the Eucharist.

- John Calvin (1509–1564) was the leader of the Calvinists, who believed in divine predestination or the concept of "the elect" and the individual's duty to reform society according to God's plan. Calvin's *Institutes of Christian Religion* is a theological statement of the Protestant faith. Calvin believed in the unity of church and state, and he stressed the sovereignty of God over all creation. He instituted a theocracy in Geneva.

AP® FRAMEWORK
TOPIC # 2.2, 2.3; LO: UNIT 2 B, E
KC:
1.1.II.B Protestant reformers used the printing press to disseminate their ideas, which spurred religious reform and helped it to become widely established.
1.2.I.B Reformers Martin Luther and John Calvin criticized Catholic abuses and established new interpretations of Christian doctrine and practice. Responses to Luther and Calvin included religious radicals, including the Anabaptists, and other groups, such as German peasants.
1.2.II.B Some Protestants, including Calvin and the Anabaptists, refused to recognize the subordination of the church to the secular state.
1.2.I.C Some Protestant groups sanctioned the notion that wealth accumulation was a sign of God's favor and a reward for hard work.
1.4.III.C Social dislocation, coupled with the shifting authority of religious institutions during the Reformation, left city governments with the task of regulating public morals.
1.4.IV.B The Renaissance and Reformation raised debates about female education and women's roles in the family, church, and society.

THE ENGLISH REFORMATION

Protestant ideas did not take hold in England until the sixteenth century. Important figures are listed below.
- Martin Bucer, a Strasbourg reformer who influenced Calvin, was forced into exile during the Augsburg Interim and helped to draft the religious texts of the English Reformation.
- William Tyndale (1492–1536) translated the New Testament into English in 1524–1525, and it began to circulate in England in 1526.
- Cardinal Thomas Wolsey (1475–1540) and Sir Thomas More (1478–1535), chief ministers to King Henry VIII, guided the royal response to English Protestantism.
- Henry VIII (r. 1509–1547) was married to Catherine of Aragon, who did not produce a male heir; in order to divorce her and then to marry Anne Boleyn, he converted himself (and the rest of England) to Anglicanism.
- Thomas Cranmer (1489–1556) and Thomas Cromwell (1485–1540) were Lutheran sympathizers who helped Henry VIII declare himself supreme ruler over English affairs, which enabled him to take charge of the Church of England and put an end to Catholic interference with his policies.
- Edward VI (r. 1547–1553), Henry's son, presided over the flourishing of Protestantism in England. He oversaw the removal of most vestiges of Catholicism from churches and English life.

AP® FRAMEWORK
TOPIC #2.3; LO: UNIT 2 B
KC:
1.2.II.C Religious conflicts became a basis for challenging monarchs' control of religious institutions.

THE COUNTER-REFORMATION

The Catholic Counter-Reformation consisted both of reforms that sprang from within the church, and reforms that emerged in reaction to the Protestant Reformation.

- The Society of Jesus, also known as the Jesuits, was one of the most influential Counter-Reformation groups; it was founded by Ignatius of Loyola in the 1530s. Loyola's *Spiritual Exercises* embodied a program of spiritual disciplines that encouraged believers to transform their spiritual selves through discipline and practice.

- The Council of Trent, the result of an effort by Emperor Charles V to force Pope Paul to reassert church doctrine, met from 1545–1563, and was attended predominantly by Italians. The council made reforms in internal church affairs (including restricting the selling of church offices and religious relics), strengthened the authority of local bishops, and subjected them to new rules requiring them to reside in their dioceses and be visible and accessible to their congregations.

AP® FRAMEWORK
TOPIC # 2.5; LO: UNIT 2 D
KC:
1.2.I.D The Catholic Reformation, exemplified by the Jesuit Order and the Council of Trent, revived the church but cemented divisions within Christianity.

Multiple-Choice Questions

Questions 1–3 refer to the image below.

16th century Protestant woodcut.

Source: akg-images

1. The image is best understood in the context of which of the following characteristics of fifteenth and sixteenth century Europe?
   (A) The development of vernacular bibles
   (B) The spread of Italian humanism
   (C) Increasing church abuses
   (D) The Catholic Reformation

2. Which of the following movements influenced the ideas expressed in the image?
   (A) Italian humanism
   (B) Christian humanism
   (C) Renaissance art
   (D) Baroque art

3. Ideas such as those expressed in the image contributed to which of the following changes in sixteenth century Europe?
   (A) The development of new branches of Christianity in western Europe
   (B) The spread of Orthodox Christianity into central Europe
   (C) The southern German states' acceptance of Lutheranism
   (D) Limited religious toleration throughout western Europe

4. Images such as the Protestant woodcut above were used to justify which of the following?
   (A) German Peasant Wars of 1524–25
   (B) The Schmalkaldic War
   (C) The Peace of Augsburg
   (D) The Edict of Nantes

Questions 5–7 refer to the passage below.

"In conformity, therefore, to the clear doctrine of the Scripture, we assert, that by an eternal and immutable counsel, God has once for all determined, both whom he would admit to salvation, and whom he would condemn to destruction. We affirm that this counsel, as far as concerns the elect, is founded on his gratuitous mercy, totally irrespective of human merit; but that to those whom he devotes to condemnation, the gate of life is closed by a just and irreprehensible, but incomprehensible, judgment. In the elect, we consider calling as an evidence of election, and justification as another token of its manifestation, till they arrive in glory, which constitutes its completion. As God seals his elect by vocation and justification, so by excluding the reprobate from the knowledge of his name and the sanctification of his Spirit, he affords an indication of the judgement that awaits them."

John Calvin, "The Institutes of the Christian Religion"[on Predestination], 1541

Source: John Calvin, *The Institutes of Christian Religion*, translated by John Allen, 1844

5. Some historians may use the ideas of the passage to explain which of the following?
   (A) The only acceptable vocation for good Christians was to join the clergy.
   (B) Calvinist doctrine advocated a strict separation of church and state.
   (C) Calvinist doctrine advocated the idea that the bread and wine were only symbolic of the body and blood of Christ.
   (D) Some Protestant groups sanctioned the notion that wealth accumulation was a sign of God's favor and a reward for hard work.

6. People who accepted the ideas of the passage were more likely to believe which of the following ideas?
   (A) Women should be allowed to preach alongside men.
   (B) The "elect" should receive a formal education in monastic schools.
   (C) The church should not be subordinate to the state.
   (D) The concept of religious toleration should be afforded to all Christian sects.

7. Which of the following is true regarding Geneva under John Calvin?
   (A) Exiled Catholics from the German states settled there in great numbers to escape religious persecution.
   (B) The city government regulated public morals.
   (C) The city became the capital of the Swiss Confederation.
   (D) Authorities allowed for husbands to beat their wives, citing biblical examples for justification.

Questions 8–9 refer to the map below.

Religions in Europe c. 1560

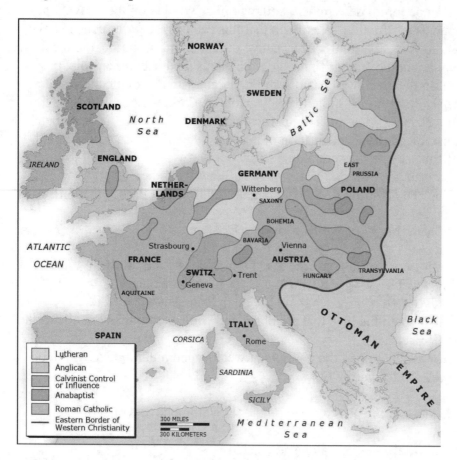

8. Which of the following led to the patterns shown on the map?
   (A) The dynastic wars between the Habsburgs and the Valois led to a religiously unified Europe.
   (B) The Ottoman conquest of eastern Europe led to a revival of Orthodox Christianity.
   (C) The defeat of the Holy Roman Emperor in the Thirty Years' War led to the unification of Germany.
   (D) Monarchs often initiated religious reform in the various states to help consolidate their rule.

9. Which of the following best explains the patterns shown on the map in Spain and Italy?
   (A) Both Spain and Italy had strong centralized monarchies that enforced Catholicism and severely punished "heretics."
   (B) Neither Spain nor Italy allowed church abuses prior to the Reformation; thus, there were very few opponents of Catholicism.
   (C) Both Spain and Italy were centers of the Catholic Reformation using the Inquisition and new religious orders such as the Jesuits to revive Catholicism.
   (D) Spain and Italy stayed out of European wars during the Reformation; thus, both were able to focus on combatting Protestants.

40

Questions 10–13 refer to the passages below.

Source 1

"I, N, with a firm faith believe and profess each and everything which is contained in the Creed which the Holy Roman Church maketh use of…

I most steadfastly admit and embrace Apostolical and ecclesiastical traditions, and all other observances and constitutions of the Church.

I also admit the Holy Scripture according to that sense which our holy mother the Church hath held, and doth hold, to…true sense and interpretations of the Scriptures. Neither will I ever take and interpret them otherwise than according to the unanimous consent of the Fathers.

I also profess that there are truly and properly Seven Sacraments of the New Law…

I embrace and receive all and every one of the things which have been defined and declared in the holy Council of Trent concerning original sin and justification."

The Tridentine Creed, 1564

Source*: The Tridentine Creed*, From TraditionalCatholic.net
http://www.traditionalcatholic.net/Tradition/Prayer/Tridentine_Creed.html

Source 2

…Let the following Rules be observed.

First Rule. The first: All judgment laid aside, we ought to have our mind ready and prompt to obey, in all, the true Spouse of Christ our Lord, which is our holy Mother the Church Hierarchical.

Second Rule. The second: To praise confession to a Priest, and the reception of the most Holy Sacrament of the Altar once in the year, and much more each month, and much better from week to week...

Third Rule. The third: To praise the hearing of Mass often, likewise hymns, psalms, and long prayers, in the church and out of it…

Fourth Rule. The fourth: To praise much Religious Orders, virginity and continence, and not so much marriage as any of these.

Ignatius Loyola, "Spiritual Exercises," 1522–24

Source: Ignatius Loyola, *The Spiritual Exercises of St. Ignatius of Loyola, Translated from the Autograph by Father Elder Mullen, S.J.* New York: P.J. Kennedy and Sons, 1914.

10. Which of the following was a result of the ideas expressed in both sources?
    (A) The Catholics and Protestants would be permanently divided because of irreconcilable doctrinal differences.
    (B) Religious wars raged throughout the Italian peninsula in response to increased persecution of Protestants.
    (C) The Catholic Church accepted the doctrine of justification by faith alone.
    (D) The Catholic Church sanctioned the legalization of vernacular Bibles in Catholic areas of Europe.

11. The ideas expressed in the first source reflect which of the following continuities regarding Catholicism in early modern Europe?
    (A) The continuation of the sale of indulgences
    (B) A reaffirmation of basic Catholic beliefs
    (C) The Catholic Church's refusal to address church abuses
    (D) A continuation of the idea of consubstantiation

12. The ideas expressed in the second source were different from Protestant beliefs in which of the following ways?
    (A) Loyola's *Exercises* were intended to teach adherents to meditate and interpret Christian doctrine individually.
    (B) Loyola's *Exercises* were intended to teach adherents to be prepared to die for their faith.
    (C) Loyola's *Exercises* were intended to teach adherents to be mindful of the Holy Trinity.
    (D) Loyola's *Exercises* were intended to teach adherents to submit without question to higher church authority.

13. In addition to the ideas expressed in Source 1, the Council of Trent resulted in which of the following changes regarding Catholicism in early modern Europe?
    (A) Religious orders were decreased in order to better control clerical behavior.
    (B) The Inquisition was moved from Spain to the Netherlands.
    (C) The Catholic Church formally recognized Protestant adherents as "separated brethren."
    (D) Steps were taken to eliminate the many church abuses that existed prior to the Reformation.

Questions 14–15 refer to the passage below.

Imagine what it would be like without women. The home, cities, economic life, and government would virtually disappear. Men cannot do without women. Even if it were possible for men to beget and bear children, they still could not do without women.

Martin Luther, Table Talk, c. 1531–1544

Source: *Luther's Works*, Vol. 54: *Table Talk*, ed. and trans. by Theodore G. Tappert (Philadelphia: Fortress Press, 1967), p. 161.

14. The passage is best understood in the context of which of the following?
    (A) The Catholic Church condemned both contraception and family planning.
    (B) Women were being accepted into the new "Scientific Academies."
    (C) The Renaissance and Reformation raised debates about women's roles in the family, church, and society.
    (D) The Protestant religious groups revered single women who chose to join a convent.

15. Ideas similar to those in the passage had which of the following effects in sixteenth century Europe?
    (A) Increased education for females
    (B) The liberalization of divorce laws in both Catholic and Protestant countries
    (C) A large increase in the number of female preachers
    (D) Earlier marriages

Short-Answer Question

Use the passage below to answer all parts of the question that follows:

"There is no question that printing played an important role in the spread of Protestant ideas. Historians have long noted the explosion of pamphlet literature that accompanied the Reformation, and pointed out that earlier, less-successful reform efforts lacked this powerful tool…After all the vast majority of Europeans were illiterate. We know that many ordinary people were deeply engaged in the religious upheavals of the sixteenth and seventeenth centuries. So how did the Reformation reach them?

We can start by recognizing that the print revolution went beyond the printed word. It also allowed for printed woodcuts and engravings…sometimes these images were meant to inspire and uplift."

Source: Robert Scribner, *Popular Culture and Popular Movements in Reformation Germany,* London: The Hambledon Press, 1987

Answer a, b, and c:

1. a) Explain how one piece of evidence <u>supports</u> Scribner's argument regarding the importance of the printing press.
   b) Explain how another piece of evidence <u>supports</u> Scribner's argument regarding the importance of the printing press.
   c) Explain how one piece of evidence undermines Scribner's argument regarding the importance of the printing press.

Long-Essay Question

Evaluate the extent to which political and economic concerns were the most significant factors that shaped religious reform as it spread across Europe in the fifteenth and sixteenth centuries.

ANSWERS AND EXPLANATIONS: AP® PRACTICE TEST

Multiple-Choice Questions

1. C (KC: 1.2.I.B; LO: Unit 2 B) The sale of indulgences, as shown in the Protestant woodcut, was one of many Catholic Church abuses that reformers highlighted to gain support. Woodcuts were used throughout Germany to gain backing from the large percentage of the population that was illiterate.

2. B (KC: 1.2.I.A; LO: Unit 1 D) The creator of the image as well as others unhappy with the Catholic Church in the early sixteenth century would most likely have been influenced by the ideas of Christian humanism. Christian humanists, such as Erasmus, were among those to call for reform and to eliminate church abuses in the period prior to the Reformation. Interestingly, Erasmus and many other Christian humanists did not support the formation of new Christian denominations.

3. A (KC: 1.2.I.B; LO: Unit 2 B) Church abuses (such as the sale of indulgences) and other major factors led to the permanent division of Christianity in western Europe. New Protestant churches included the Lutherans, Calvinists, Anabaptists, and Anglicans, among others.

4. A (KC: 1.2.I.B; LO: Unit 2 B) Much of the peasantry was illiterate and as a result, the woodcuts such as the one in the image had a good deal of influence. Inspired by Luther's revolt from the Church, German peasants revolted against the German nobles in 1524–25. Luther condemned these peasant revolts as he believed people were obligated to obey political authority.

5. D (KC: 1.2.I.C; LO: Unit 2 B) Calvin's emphasis on predestination, combined with the Protestant belief that all vocations were sacred, contributed to the belief that wealth accumulation could be indicative of God's good favor, leading to what is known as the "Protestant Work Ethic."

6. C (KC: 1.2.II.B; LO: Unit 2 B) Calvinists, along with Anabaptists, believed that the church should not be subordinate to the state. In fact, Calvin is thought to have called the city of Geneva the city of God because it was essentially a theocracy.

7. B (KC: 1.4.III.C; LO: Unit 2 E) Calvin's Geneva implemented religious laws that resulted from cooperation among civil and religious authorities. The Genevan Consistory enforced discipline throughout the city. For example, both adultery and Catholic leanings could lead to one being called before religious authorities.

8. D (KC: 1.2.II.A; LO: Unit 1 F) Not surprisingly, monarchs and princes often chose the religion of their subjects in order to consolidate power and control religious life. For example, the Tudor kings in England chose Anglicanism while the Peace of Augsburg allowed German princes to choose either Lutheranism or Catholicism.

9. C (KC: 1.2.I.D; LO: Unit 2 D) Both Spain and Italy were centers of the Catholic Reformation and used a number of techniques to combat Protestantism, including the Inquisition and the creation of the Index of Prohibited Books, as well as the creation of new religious orders.

10. A (KC: 1.2.I.D; LO: Unit 2 D) Both sources define the Catholic position and, as a result, the division in western Christianity would become permanent.

11. B (KC: 1.2.I.D; LO: Unit 2 D) One of the most important aspects of the Council of Trent was a reaffirmation of basic Catholic doctrine, further defining a difference with Protestant theology.

12. D (KC: 1.2.I.D; LO: Unit 2 D) Protestant faiths originated by standing up and disobeying the Catholic Church in order to reform. Loyola instead taught strict obedience.

13. D (KC: 1.2.I.D; LO: Unit 2 D) One of the most important changes that occurred during the Council of Trent was a purging of church abuses including the egregious sale of indulgences, simony, nepotism, absenteeism, and clerical immorality, among others.

14. C (KC: 1.4.IV.B; LO: Unit 2 E) Combined with the new ideas of the Renaissance, the spread of Lutheranism and other Protestant religions led to new debates about the roles of women regarding women's place in society, education, and family life.

15. A (KC: 1.4.IV.B; LO: Unit 2 E) As a result of Protestant ideas of "spiritual equality," women in Protestant countries were encouraged to be literate, with the expectation that they would model their lives in a Christian manner and teach their children to read the Bible.

Short-Answer Question
(KC: 1.1.II; LO: Unit 1 E)

Possible responses to parts a) and b) include:
- The printing press facilitated the spread of Italian humanism that later influenced Northern Renaissance writers such as Erasmus and Thomas More.
- The printing press enabled the publishing of materials in the vernacular.
- The printing press significantly reduced the cost of printed materials allowing such works as Erasmus's *In Praise of Folly* to influence Luther and other reformers.
- The printing press enabled Martin Luther's ideas to spread with stunning speed throughout the Holy Roman Empire.
- The printing press facilitated the spread of John Calvin's ideas and other Protestant reformers.
- Earlier reformers such as John Wycliffe and John Hus failed to achieve Luther's success largely due to lack of means to spread their messages.
- Visual material, such as woodcuts, could more easily be interpreted by illiterate people (such as many German peasants).

Possible responses to part c) include:
- Many peasants did, in fact, possess some literacy, although far fewer were able to write.
- The spread of ideas through word of mouth occurred before and during the Reformation era.

Long-Essay Question
(KC: 1.2.II, 1.2.III; LO: Unit 2 B, C)

Evaluate the extent to which political and economic concerns were the most significant factors that shaped religious reform as it spread across Europe in the fifteenth and sixteenth centuries.

Possible responses regarding political concerns include:
- Luther stressed the importance of obeying temporal authority, thus making Lutheranism appealing to German princes.
- German princes in the northern Holy Roman Empire often adopted Lutheranism and removed Catholic authority from their realms.
- Calvinist burghers in the Netherlands created a republic free of the authoritarian rule of the Habsburgs.
- French rulers, though Catholic, supported the Protestant Schmalkaldic League to weaken the Holy Roman Empire.
- Protestant reform movements grew in influence and threatened Catholic authority leading to religious wars.
- The Catholic Reformation was, in part, a political response to the spread of Protestantism.

Possible responses regarding economic concerns include:
- In Calvinist regions, the Protestant work ethic evolved into a mix of religious and economic concerns.
- Middle-class Calvinists became influential in Geneva, France, England, and Scotland.

Possible responses that regard other concerns (not political or economic) include:
- Social issues regarding the domestic role of women shaped Lutheran societies.
- Religious concerns (perhaps) played the primary role in the Catholic Reformation.

CHAPTER 4

The Age of Religious Wars

In this era, religious conflict among Protestants and Catholics and dynastic rivalries fueled wars.

THE FRENCH WARS OF RELIGION (1562–1598)

- French Protestants, or **Huguenots**, were under surveillance in France as early as 1520, when Lutheran ideas began to circulate in Paris. Huguenot persecution was essentially a policy under Henry II, and it continued until Henry IV (Henry of Navarre) took the throne in 1589.
- Catherine de Médicis, who served as regent for Charles IX, sought allies among the Protestant factions. In 1562, she issued the January Edict, which granted Protestants freedom to worship publicly outside towns and to hold synods.
- In March of 1562, a duke from the powerful Guise family led a massacre on the Huguenots, starting the French Wars of religion. In the series of wars that followed, Huguenots and their Protestant allies fought against the Guise faction. Catherine de Médicis aligned herself with the Guises, and plotted against Coligny, the leader of the Huguenots. Catherine supported the 1572 St. Bartholomew's Day Massacre, in which 3,000 Huguenots were killed. Within three days, 20,000 Huguenots had been executed.
- The Peace of Beaulieu, led by Henry III in May 1576, granted Huguenots almost complete religious and civil freedom, but within seven months, the Catholic League forced Henry to back down from these liberties. After Henry III's murder, the Protestant Henry IV (Henry of Navarre) rose to the throne, converted to Catholicism, and proclaimed a formal religious settlement with the Protestants. Called the Edict of Nantes and made on April 13, 1598, this proclamation recognized and sanctioned Huguenots' rights within France. It granted them freedom of worship, right of assembly, and a series of other liberties.

AP® FRAMEWORK
TOPIC # 2.4; LO: UNIT 2 B, C
KC:
1.2.II.B Religious conflicts became a basis for challenging the monarchs' control of religious institutions.
1.2.III.A Issues of religious reform exacerbated conflicts between the monarchy and the nobility, as in the French wars of religion.
1.2.III.D A few states, such as France with the Edict of Nantes, allowed religious pluralism in order to maintain domestic peace.

IMPERIAL SPAIN AND THE REIGN OF PHILIP II (R. 1556–1598)

Philip II of Spain was the extremely powerful Catholic ruler of Habsburg lands of Bohemia, Austria, and Hungary, as well as Castile, in Spain.

- Spain dominated the Mediterranean in the Battle of Lepanto, in which the Turkish fleet was brutally put down. Under Philip II, Spain annexed Portugal and gained access to their empires in Africa, India, and the Americas.
- Philip did not see similar success in his attempts to conquer the Netherlands. When Cardinal Granvelle attempted to institute ecclesiastical reform in the Netherlands, William of Orange and the Count of Egmont led the resistance. Egmont was executed, and the resistance was put down by the Duke of Alba, but the Dutch continued their campaign against Spanish governance.
- In 1576, Catholic and Protestant provinces came together in opposition to Spain in what is known as the Pacification of Ghent. True peace with Spain was not achieved until 1609, when the Twelve Years' Truce gave the northern provinces independence. Full recognition was finalized in the Peace of Westphalia in 1648.

AP® FRAMEWORK
TOPIC # 2.4; LO: UNIT 1 F, UNIT 2 B, C
KC:
1.2.II.B Religious conflicts became a basis for challenging the monarchs' control of religious institutions.
1.2.III.B Habsburg rulers confronted an expanded Ottoman Empire while attempting unsuccessfully to restore Catholic unity across Europe.
1.2.III.C States exploited religious conflicts to promote political and economic interests.
1.5.I.C New monarchies laid the foundation for the centralized modern state by establishing monopolies on tax collection, employing military force, dispensing justice, and gaining the right to determine the religion of their subjects.

ENGLAND AND SPAIN (1553–1603)

The Catholic Mary Tudor (Mary I) ascended the English throne after challenging the right of Protestant Lady Jane Grey. Mary brought sweeping change to England, restoring Catholicism and executing the Protestants Thomas Cranmer, Hugh Latimer, and John Hooper.

- Mary's half-sister, Elizabeth I, was her successor following a 1559 Act of Supremacy that undid much of the anti-Protestant legislation Mary had enacted. The act asserted Elizabeth's right as "supreme governor" over spiritual and secular affairs. Elizabeth strove to maintain a middle ground by not granting too much control to Catholics or Protestants.
- Facing a real threat from Spain, England allied with France in 1571. At this time, explorers Francis Drake and John Hawkins were preying on Spanish ships. Elizabeth's decision to execute Mary Stuart, Queen of Scots, an ardent Catholic and French royal with a legitimate heir to the Scottish throne, aroused Catholic anger.
- Philip II of Spain ordered his Armada to prepare for war with England. This battle resulted in a complete victory for England and encouraged European Protestants.

50

AP® FRAMEWORK
TOPIC # 2.4; LO: UNIT 1 F, UNIT 2 B, C
KC:
1.2.II.A Monarchs and princes, including the English rulers Henry VIII and Elizabeth I, initiated religious reform from the top down in an effort to exercise greater control over religious life and morality.
1.2.II.B Religious conflicts became a basis for challenging the monarchs' control of religious
1.2.III.C States exploited religious conflicts to promote political and economic interests.

THE THIRTY YEARS' WAR (1618–1648)

The Thirty Years' War was a complicated series of battles in four phases—Bohemian (1618–1625), Danish (1625–1629), Swedish (1630–1635), and the Swedish-French (1635–1648)—between countries with radically opposed political and religious agendas.

- In the Bohemian Period, Calvinists demanded more freedom from Catholic Habsburg ruler Ferdinand. Protestant nobility responded to Ferdinand's revocation of religious rights by throwing two of his regents out of a window in the "defenestration of Prague."
- In the Danish Period, King Christian IV of Denmark tried to bring Protestantism to Germany and was forced to retreat by Maximilian. In 1629, Ferdinand outlawed Calvinism by issuing the Edict of Restitution.
- In the Swedish Period, military tactics of King Gustavus Adolphus of Sweden helped Protestants win the battle at Breitenfeld. The Swedes refused to join the Peace of Prague Agreement—a compromise between German Protestant states and Ferdinand.
- The Swedish-French Period, the final phase of the Thirty Years' War, involved French, Swedish, and Spanish soldiers wreaking havoc in Germany. At the most destructive point in the war, religious issues became secondary to political ones.
- The Treaty of Westphalia of 1648 stopped Ferdinand's Edict of Restitution and recognized Calvinists. The independence of the Swiss Confederacy and provinces of Holland was proclaimed. German princes were acknowledged as the supreme rulers over their principalities. The treaty broadened the legal status of Protestantism in the realm, but it perpetuated Germany's internal division and political weakness.

AP® FRAMEWORK
TOPIC # 2.4, 3.6; LO: UNIT 2 C, UNIT 3 F
KC:
1.2.III.C States exploited religious conflicts to promote political and economic interests.
1.5.I.B The Peace of Westphalia (1648), which marked the effective end of the medieval ideal of universal Christendom, accelerated the decline of the Holy Roman Empire by granting princes, bishops, and other local leaders control over religion.
1.5.II.B Advances in military technology led to new forms of warfare, including greater reliance on infantry, firearms, mobile cannon, and more elaborate fortifications, all financed by heavier taxation and requiring a larger bureaucracy. New military techniques and institutions (i.e., the military revolution) tipped the balance of power toward states able to marshal sufficient resources for the new military environment.

Multiple-Choice Questions

Questions 1–5 refer to the passage below.

"It finally remains for me to solve a question of the greatest moment, namely, whether it is allowable…to offer resistance by armed force to tyranny assailing the true religion and even stamping it out as far as may be, and to contend against persecution…

What therefore will subjects have to do if on the other hand they are compelled by their ruler to worship idols?...But if the free exercise of the true religion has once been granted by means of decrees lawfully passed…then I declare that the ruler is so much the more bound to have them observed as a matter of religion is of greater moment compared with all others…If he acts otherwise I declare that he is practicing manifest tyranny; and with due allowance for the observations made above, [his subjects] will be all the more free to oppose him as we are bound to set greater store and value by the salvation of our souls and the freedom of our conscience than by any other matters however desirable. It should therefore now be no cause of surprise to anyone that our Lord Jesus Christ, the Prophets and the Apostles, too, or the other martyrs, since they were men in private station, confined themselves within the limits of their calling."

Theodore Beza, The Rights of Magistrates Over Their Subjects, 1574

Source: Translation by Henry-Louis Gonin, edited by Patrick S. Poole, Notes from the critical French Edition translated by Patrick S. Poole. http://pages.uoregon.edu/dluebke/Reformations441/BezaRightsofRulers.htm.

1. An historian could best use this source as evidence of which of the following?
   (A) French Catholics opposed the monarchy of Elizabeth I.
   (B) French Protestants opposed the monarchy of Henry of Navarre.
   (C) Most Protestant leaders advocated freedom of religion in their own lands.
   (D) Religious conflicts were used to justify revolts against monarchies.

2. Which of the following most likely inspired the ideas of the passage?
   (A) The Habsburg-Valois Wars
   (B) The Thirty Years' War
   (C) The French Wars of Religion
   (D) The Fronde

3. The conflict described in the passage ultimately led to which of the following?
   (A) The issuance of the Edict of Nantes, which allowed for the toleration of Huguenots in France
   (B) The issuance of the Peace of Augsburg, which allowed for the existence of Calvinism in the Holy Roman Empire
   (C) French military involvement in the Thirty Years' War
   (D) French military involvement in the Dutch revolt

4. Adherents to the ideas expressed in the passage would most likely have supported which of the following seventeenth-century events?
   (A) Mary, Queen of Scots' attempt to overthrow Elizabeth I of England prior to the English Civil War
   (B) The English Parliament's successful overthrow of Charles I during the English Civil War
   (C) Philip III's continued use of the Spanish Inquisition to maintain religious uniformity
   (D) Oliver Cromwell's appointment as "Lord Protector" of England

5. The ideas of the passage would have been supported by which of the following?
   (A) Supporters of Henry of Guise
   (B) Henry VIII of England
   (C) French Huguenots
   (D) Bishop Bossuet

Questions 6–8 refer to the image below.

The Milch Cow c. 1583

Not long time since I saw a cow
Did Flanders [Netherlands] represent
Upon whose back King Philip
[Habsburg] rode
As being Malcontent
The Queen of England giving hay
Whereon the cow did feed

As one that was her greatest help
In her distress and need.
The Prince of Orange milked the cow
And made his purse the pail.
The cow did sh** in monsieurs hand
While he did hold the tail.

Source: Universal Images Group/Getty Images

6. The activities depicted in this image represent which of the following events in sixteenth century Europe?
    (A) The defeat of the Spanish Armada
    (B) The wars between France and Spain
    (C) Religious wars in the Holy Roman Empire
    (D) The Dutch revolt against the Spanish

7. The image is best understood in the context of which of the following characteristics of sixteenth-century Europe?
   (A) The allure of gaining new territory was the most significant factor that led to European warfare during this time period.
   (B) Religious conflicts could often justify monarchical pursuit of political and economic interests.
   (C) European leaders often cooperated with each other in order to maintain a balance of power.
   (D) The stronger European powers exploited the nations that were not as militarily powerful.

8. Which of the following is true of Habsburg power during the time period in which this image was created?
   (A) The Habsburg defeat in the Schmalkaldic Wars led to the loss of Habsburg German territories.
   (B) Habsburg armies successfully led the Holy League to victory over the Ottoman Empire at the Battle of Lepanto, halting their advance into the Mediterranean world.
   (C) Philip II married Mary Tudor, adding England to Habsburg territories.
   (D) Philip II was able to successfully subdue the Dutch with the help of other European powers.

Questions 9–10 refer to the passage below.

"Where at the death of…King Edward VI there remained one uniform order of common service and prayer…in the Church of England…which was repealed and taken away…in the first year of the reign of…Queen Mary, to the great decay of the due honour of God, and discomfort to the professors of the truth of Christ's religion:

Be it therefore enacted…that the said statute of repeal, and everything therein contained…shall be void and of none effect…with the alterations and additions therein added and appointed by this statute, shall stand and be, from and after the said feast of the Nativity of St. John Baptist, in full force and effect…

And further be it enacted by the queen's highness…that all…ministers in any cathedral or parish church, or other place within this realm of England, Wales…or other the queen's dominions, shall…be bounden to say and use the…celebration of the Lord's Supper and administration of each of the sacraments, and all their common and open prayer, in such order and form as is mentioned in the said book…

And that if any manner of parson, vicar, or other whatsoever minister…shall wilfully or obstinately…use any other rite, ceremony, order, form, or manner of celebrating of the Lord's Supper, openly or privily…or shall preach, declare, or speak anything in the derogation or depraving of the said book… shall be thereof lawfully convicted, according to the laws of this realm…"

Queen Elizabeth I, The Act of Uniformity, 1559

Source: Gee, Henry, and William John Hardy, ed., *Documents Illustrative of English Church History* (New York: Macmillan, 1896), 458–67.

9. The passage can be used as evidence to support which of the following?
    (A) Religious reform during the sixteenth century was mostly initiated by monarchs and princes.
    (B) Elizabeth I rejected all of the Catholic practices in the Church of England.
    (C) Elizabeth I issued religious reform without the consent of Parliament.
    (D) England accepted the Calvinist doctrine of "predestination,"

10. Which of the following resulted from ideas such as those expressed in the passage?
    (A) Greater clerical control over countries that broke away from the Catholic Church
    (B) The elimination of religious dissenters due to the power of the state
    (C) The development of the first political parties to provide a forum for religious debate
    (D) Increased monarchical control over moral issues in the state

11. The Act of Uniformity was written in context with which of the following?
    (A) Elizabeth executed her cousin Mary, Queen of Scots for conspiring with Catholics to overthrow her.
    (B) Elizabeth's succession to the throne resulted in the overthrow of her sister, Mary I.
    (C) Elizabeth's succession to the throne occurred after a period of religious turmoil during the reigns of her siblings, Edward VI and Mary I.
    (D) Philip II also claimed the English throne when Elizabeth was crowned.

Questions 12–13 refer to the image below.

Bohemian protesters throwing three of Holy Roman Emperor Ferdinand II's Catholic agents out of windows at Hradschin Castle in Prague in 1648.

Source: Bildarchiv Preussischer Kulturbesitz/Art Resource, NY

12. The image is an example of which of the following developments in early modern history?
   (A) Protestants were more violent than Catholics regarding the imposition of religious doctrine.
   (B) Minority groups often resisted the imposition of cultural values by dominant national groups.
   (C) Increased violence in warfare was the result of new weapons and the military revolution.
   (D) Increased warfare between monarchs and nobles occurred over state power and religious authority.

13. Which of the following was a long-term result of the activities depicted in the image?
   (A) The recognition of Bohemian autonomy within the Holy Roman Empire
   (B) The Holy Roman Emperor's imposition of Catholicism throughout the empire
   (C) Decline of religion as a cause for major warfare in Europe
   (D) The dissolution of the Holy Roman Empire into 39 states

Questions 14–15 refer to the image below.

The Battle of White Mountain, 1620

The Battle of White Mountain near Prague on 7–8 November 1620, painting by Pieter Snayers (1592–1667) preserved in Santa Maria della Vittoria, Rome.

Source: DEA/G. NIMATALLAH De Agostini Picture Library/Getty Images

14. The image reflects which of the following changes in European warfare?
    (A) New forms of warfare as a result of the "military revolution"
    (B) A change from legions to phalanx formations
    (C) The first time that gunpowder was used in European warfare
    (D) Increased reliance upon cavalry units and less upon infantry

15. Which of the following was a result of the changes in European warfare during this time period?
    (A) States not modernizing their militaries ceased to exist.
    (B) Many states were forced to increase taxation to finance their militaries.
    (C) Only states with absolute monarchies transformed their militaries into more efficient units.
    (D) "Balance of power" politics by stronger nations declined.

Short-Answer Question

Use the map below to answer all parts of the question.

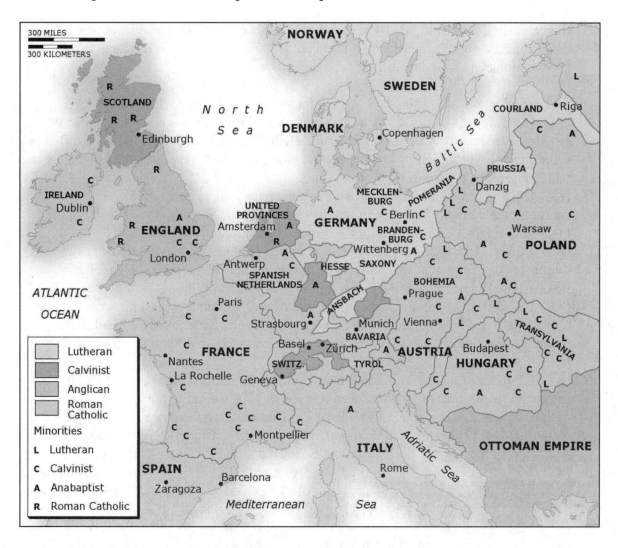

Answer a, b, and c:

1. a) Describe one cause for the religion patterns shown on the map.
    b) Explain one way in which the patterns shown on the map contributed to religious warfare during the period 1550–1650.
    c) Explain one effect of the religious wars during the period 1550–1650.

Long-Essay Question

Evaluate the extent to which politics played a role in religious warfare during the period 1550–1648.

ANSWERS AND EXPLANATIONS: AP® PRACTICE TEST

Multiple-Choice Questions

1. D (KC: 1.2.II.C; LO: Unit 2 B) Beza argues that kings rule conditionally, and when those conditions are not met, resistance is allowed, and this particular source focuses on the French monarchy's war against the Huguenots.

2. C (KC: 1.2.III.A; LO: Unit 2 C) This source was written two years after the St. Bartholomew's Day Massacre, which intensified the French religious wars.

3. A (KC: 1.2.III.D; LO: Unit 2 C) After the War of the Three Henrys concluded in 1589, Huguenot leader Henry of Navarre became Henry IV, King of France, and converted to Catholicism. Not forgetting his Protestant leanings, in 1598 he issued the Edict of Nantes which allowed a degree of religious tolerance.

4. B (KC: 1.5.III.A; LO: Unit 3 B) English Parliamentary leaders during the seventeenth century, notably many Puritans, used ideas similar to the ones expressed by Beza to justify the English Civil War, which led to the beheading of Charles I.

5. C (KC: 1.2.II.C; LO: Unit 2 B) The ideas expressed in the passage, which justify the overthrow of a ruler who advocates what the author considers to be a false religion, justified the Huguenot position during the French Wars of religion.

6. D (KC: 1.2.III.B; LO: Unit 2 C) The image's portrayal of Flanders (as a milk cow) is representative of how the European powers were involved in the Dutch revolt from Spain. Philip (riding the cow) is symbolic of the reassertion of Spanish power that led to the Dutch revolt.

7. B (KC: 1.2.III.C; LO: Unit 2 C) This image portrays the conflicts that existed among the European rulers. Many monarchs used religion as justification to pursue their own political goals. For example, Elizabeth of England (feeding the cow) assisted the Netherlands to (1) keep Philip II from invading England using the Netherlands as a base and (2) to check Spanish power and halt Spanish dominance on the continent.

8. B (KC: 1.2.III.B; LO: Unit 2 C) In the fifteen-year period prior to the creation of this image, Habsburg military forces during the reign of Philip II successfully defeated the Ottoman Empire at the Battle of Lepanto (1571), halting the Ottoman advance into Europe.

9. A (KC: 1.2.II.A; LO: Unit 1 F) In the sixteenth century, monarchs and princes often chose the religion of their realm, and Elizabeth I was not an exception to that rule. The Elizabethan Settlement was meant to appeal to both Catholics and Protestants, as many members of the House of Lords were Catholic and many in the House of Commons were Protestant. The Act of Uniformity continued Henry VIII's policy of monarchical control of religion.

10. D (KC: 1.2.II.A; LO: Unit 1 F) Monarchs such as Elizabeth I, among others, often initiated religious reform to gain greater control over moral issues as well as religious life. Monarchical control of religion also increased their political power.

11. C (KC: 1.2.II.A; LO: Unit 1 F) The decade or so before Elizabeth's succession was a time of religious turmoil in England. Edward VI's advisors made England more Protestant than Henry VIII had ever intended, and Mary I brought Catholicism back to England. Elizabeth was able to settle the religious turmoil with her policies of moderation and compromise. Mary, Queen of Scots was executed in 1587, nearly thirty years after the issuance of the Act of Uniformity.

12. B   (KC: 1.5.III.C; LO: Unit 3 A) The direct cause of the Thirty Years' War was the defenestration of Prague; however, there were many other causes as well. Bohemian regional identity was strong and had long been resentful of Catholic policies, and when the German Habsburg ruler Ferdinand II tried to reimpose Catholicism, the Bohemians revolted.

13. C   (KC: 1.5.II.A; LO: Unit 3 E) It was apparent that religion was less and less important as a cause for war throughout the Thirty Years' War, but especially after the French, led by Catholic Cardinal Richelieu began assisting the Protestant Swedes and later fighting the Catholic Habsburgs. As a result, this was the last major European religious war, and even the extent to which religion contributed to the war at all is debated among historians.

14. A   (KC: 1.5.II.B; LO: Unit 3 F) The "military revolution" consisted of advances in military technology including better firearms, mobile cannons, and increasing number of infantry.

15. B   (KC: 1.5.II.B; LO: Unit 3 F) One result of the changes shown in the image was that the states that began to use this new technology required heavier taxation. For example, Frederick William the Great Elector established an excise tax in Brandenburg-Prussia in order to finance his military buildup.

Short-Answer Question
(KC: 1.2; LO: Unit 2 C)

Possible responses for part a) include:
- Lutheranism spread to northern Germany as princes sought to eliminate Catholic authority from their realms. This is also true of Denmark, Sweden, and Norway.
- The spread of Calvinism was the most dynamic, as its Protestant work ethic ideas appealed to the middle class in various countries.
- Henry VIII's desire for an annulment of his marriage to Catherine of Aragon prompted him to leave the Catholic Church and create the Church of England.
- The Roman Catholic Church remained strongest in France, Italy, Spain, and the southern part of the Holy Roman Empire, in part, due to the Catholic Reformation.
- Anabaptists often renounced temporal authority and remained a relatively small minority in various regions.

Possible responses for part b) include:
- The conflict between Catholic factions (Valois and Guise) and Bourbon Huguenots led to decades of civil war in France.
- The existence of Calvinism within the Spanish Habsburg Empire under Philip II led to the Dutch Revolt against Spanish authority.
- The religious division of the Holy Roman Empire between Lutherans and Catholics led to decades of warfare between the League of Schmalkalden and the HRE. The Habsburg-Valois Wars played a role in this conflict as well.
- The continued religious divisions within the Holy Roman Empire led to the Thirty Years' War, first between Calvinists in Bohemia and the HRE, and later between Lutherans and the HRE.
- Philip II's desire to return England to Catholicism led to the spectacular failure of the Spanish Armada in 1588.
- Religious conflict between Anglican royalists and Puritan and Presbyterian Calvinists in Parliament led to the English Civil War.

Possible responses for part c) include:
- The Wars of Religion resulted in the permanent division of the German states and the demise of the Holy Roman Empire.
- The Netherlands and Switzerland won their independence as a result of the Thirty Years' War.
- France resolved its civil wars with the ascension of Henry IV to the throne and the Edict of Nantes.
- France emerged as the most powerful European state by the end of the Thirty Years' War.
- Oliver Cromwell established a Puritan dictatorship in England after the English Civil War.

Long-Essay Question

(KC: 1.2.II, 1.2.III; LO: Unit 2 B, C)

Evaluate the extent to which politics played a role in religious warfare during the period 1550–1648.

Possible responses regarding politics include:

- Political ambitions of the Valois, Bourbon, and Guise factions in France led to the French Civil Wars.
- Dutch and Belgian leaders sought political autonomy from Philip II's Spanish empire.
- Philip II sought to increase his political influence over England through the Spanish Armada of 1588.
- Political goals led France to support Protestant forces against the Catholic Holy Roman Empire during the Thirty Years' War.
- Political conflicts between King Charles I and Calvinists in the House of Commons led to the English Civil War.

Other possible responses regarding other factors include:

- Religious issues resulted in religious warfare
  - Spain under Philip II sought to turn England back to Catholicism
  - Philip II sought to maintain Catholic unity in his empire by attacking Calvinists in the Netherlands.
  - Religious differences between Calvinist nobles and Catholic HRE authorities led to the onset of the Thirty Years' War in Bohemia
  - Religious differences between Calvinist members of Parliament and King Charles I led to the English Civil War.
- Economic issues: The Protestant work ethic in countries where Calvinists exerted significant influence led to conflict with Catholic authorities.
  - Dutch burghers sought to maintain their capitalist economy in the face of Philip II's threats.
  - Calvinists in Parliament sought to protect their rights against the absolutist ambitions of Charles I

CHAPTER 5

European State Consolidation in the Seventeenth and Eighteenth Centuries

In the seventeenth century, England and France moved in different political directions—one toward a constitutional form of government, and the other toward monarchy rule.

THE NETHERLANDS: GOLDEN AGE TO DECLINE

- The United Provinces of the Netherlands were the only new state to appear in Europe during the early modern period. A formal republic, the Netherlands central government exercised its authority through cooperation with the provinces.
- Dutch life was marked by religious toleration and an economic prosperity that derived from the country's extensive trade and overseas commercial empires and its urban consolidation. The highly advanced Dutch capital system financed economic life throughout Europe.

AP® FRAMEWORK
TOPIC # 3.5; LO: UNIT 3 D
KC:
2.1.II.B The Dutch Republic, established by a Protestant revolt against the Habsburg monarchy, developed an oligarchy of urban gentry and rural landholders to promote trade and protect traditional rights.

TWO MODELS OF EUROPEAN POLITICAL DEVELOPMENT

- Monarchy: England's monarchs' efforts to get new sources of income threatened the country's political and economic stability. In France, Louis XIV made the French nobility dependent upon his patronage, but he allowed the Parlement of Paris to oversee his royal decrees and regional parlements to administer local taxation.
- Religion: In England, the Protestant religious movement of **Puritanism** opposed the Stuart monarchy and sought to limit its powers. In France, Louis XIV, with the support of Roman Catholics, crushed the Protestant dissident movement to create religious unity.
- Government: The English system of a **parliamentary monarchy** remained ingrained in the political culture, even if it was not the strong institution it would become by the end of the seventeenth century. The parliamentary government in England involved nobility and large landowners trying to limit the power of the monarch to interfere on a local level. The French nobility preferred to support Louis XIV's **political absolutism** and to benefit from his patronage. In France, the Estates General was not an institutional base for political reform.

AP® FRAMEWORK
TOPIC # 3.1; LO: UNIT 3 A
KC:
1.5.III The competition for power between monarchs and corporate and minority language groups produced different distributions of governmental authority in European states.
2.1.I In much of Europe, absolute monarchy was established over the course of the 17th and 18th centuries.
2.1.II Challenges to absolutism resulted in alternative political systems.

CONSTITUTIONAL CRISIS AND SETTLEMENT IN STUART ENGLAND

- King James I was an outsider, a Scot who advocated the divine right of kings. James angered many of his subjects by his decision to maintain and augment Anglican episcopacy. He enforced a series of levies on his subjects—new custom duties known as *impositions* that were unpopular with Parliament. In 1620, a group of Puritan separatists left England and founded the Plymouth Colony in Cape Cod Bay in North America. Another group left a few years later and founded the Massachusetts Bay Colony.

- Charles I forced more unpopular levies and taxes on the English people and stationed troops en route to war with Spain in private homes. Parliament forced Charles to agree to the Petition of Right, a document that required the monarch to gain consent of Parliament before levying taxes or quartering soldiers in private homes. In 1629, Parliament declared that Charles's levying of taxes without consent was an act of treason.

- In 1641, Parliament presented Charles with the Grand Remonstrance, a summary of grievances. Charles invaded Parliament with his soldiers, and Parliament began to raise an army of its own, bringing about the civil war (1642–1646) of England. Oliver Cromwell (1599–1658) led the reorganized parliamentary army, known as the New Model Army, into victory against Charles I's forces and his execution in 1649. England became a Puritan republic from 1649 until 1660, led by the military dictator Cromwell, who ruled as "Lord Protector" until his death in 1658. By then, the exiled Charles II was permitted to return and to bring peaceful rule back to England.

- Charles II's rule is known as the Stuart Restoration because it brought England back to the conditions of the 1640s, when an Anglican Church was at the fore of religion, and the monarch had little or no responsibility to call Parliament.

- James II renewed fears of a Catholic England by openly appointing Catholics to high positions in the court and in the army. In 1688, after James fled to France in the face of William of Orange's superior army, William and Mary were declared the new monarchs of England. This bloodless accession was known as the **Glorious Revolution**, and the subsequent Bill of Rights, which William and Mary recognized, limited the powers of the monarchy, prohibited Roman Catholics from occupying the throne, and guaranteed the role of Parliament in government.

AP ® KEY CONCEPTS AP® FRAMEWORK
TOPIC # 3.2; LO: UNIT 3 B
KC:
1.5.III.A The English Civil War—a conflict among the monarchy, Parliament, and other elites over their respective roles in the political structure—exemplified the competition for power among monarchs and competing groups.
2.1.II.A The outcome of the English Civil War and the Glorious Revolution protected the rights of gentry and aristocracy from absolutism through assertions of the rights of Parliament.

- Louis XIV ("The Sun King") successfully suppressed discontent among the nobility and landowners through absolute monarchy and strict Catholic rule. His motto was "one king, one law, one faith," and he sought glory for France in an aggressive series of foreign wars. Louis XIV was helped early in his reign by Cardinal Mazarin, who continued Richelieu's policy of centralization of government.

- Louis XIV was a master of propaganda and the cultivation of his public image. He believed himself to have a divine right to his royal authority and was contented to be unbound by the rules of princes and parliaments. He is famous for his alleged outburst, "L'état c'est moi" ("I am the state").

- Louis XIV's palace court and permanent residence at Versailles were symbolic of his majesty. Louis supported religious conformity and helped to suppress the rise of the **Jansenists**, a group of Catholics opposed to the influence of Jesuits on Catholic theology.

- During Louis XIV's reign, France was superior to other European countries in its administrative bureaucracy, military, and national unity. Jean-Baptiste Colbert, controller general of finances, helped Louis XIV consolidate France's wealth and create an economic base for funding wars. Colbert's close government control of the economy (known as mercantilism) aimed to maximize exports and internal stores of bullion.

- In 1685, Louis revoked the Edict of Nantes, which resulted in the immediate closure of Protestant churches and schools, the expulsion of Protestant ministers, the forced conversion of the laity, and the voluntary emigration of more than a quarter million French people, who joined resistance to France throughout the world.

AP® FRAMEWORK
TOPIC # 3.7; LO: UNIT 3 E, G
KC:

2.1.I.A Absolute monarchies limited the nobility's participation in governance but preserved the aristocracy's social position and legal privileges.

2.1.I.B Louis XIV and his finance minister, Jean-Baptiste Colbert, extended the administrative, financial, military, and religious control of the central state over the French population.

2.1.III.C Louis XIV's nearly continuous wars, pursuing both dynastic and state interests, provoked a coalition of European powers opposing him.

Central and eastern Europe were less economically advanced than their western European rivals, and their economies were more agrarian than maritime in nature.

- Charles XII of Sweden came to the throne and led a strong campaign against the Russians in the Great Northern War (1700–1721), but he was ultimately defeated. He exhausted Swedish military and economic resources and lost a section of the Baltic coast.

- The Ottoman Empire was overextended by the end of the seventeenth century, and its economy was dependent on the loyalty of local rulers in far-flung provinces. Russia began to extend its territory into the Ottoman Empire, and the Turks made a treaty with the Habsburgs and surrendered their control of revenues from Hungary, Transylvania, Croatia, and Slavonia.

- King John Sobieski (r. 1674–1696) struggled against a nobility that refused to submit to authority. Poland couldn't collect taxes or build an army without unity in the legislative body, the *Sejm*.

- The Austrian Habsburgs consolidated their political power in the modern Czech Republic, Slovakia, Moravia, Silesia, Hungary, Croatia, and Transylvania. In the early eighteenth century, the Habsburgs received the former Spanish Netherlands, Lombardy, and the kingdom of Naples. These inherited territories faced problems of Magyar resistance in Hungary.

- The Hohenzollerns of Brandenburg-Prussia acquired a collection of land holdings and transformed them into a single unit. Frederick William (r. 1640–1688) forged these disparate areas by breaking up nobles' estates and organizing a royal bureaucracy. Known as the Great Elector, Frederick imposed taxes to build up a strong military, members of which took an oath of loyalty to him. Frederick I (the Great Elector's son) built palaces, patronized the arts, and eventually was rewarded for putting his army at the disposal of the Habsburg Holy Roman Emperor with the title of King of Prussia. Frederick I's son, Frederick William I, was a disciple of military discipline, and he built up the size of his army to more than 80,000 in 1740. The army became a great symbol of Prussian power.

AP® FRAMEWORK
TOPIC # 3.6, 3.7, 4.6; LO: UNIT 3 E, G, H; UNIT 4 H
KC:
2.1.I.A Absolute monarchies limited the nobility's participation in governance but preserved the aristocracy's social position and legal privileges.
2.1.III.A As a result of the Holy Roman Empire's limitation of sovereignty in the Peace of Westphalia, Prussia rose to power, and the Habsburgs, centered in Austria, shifted their empire eastward.
2.I.III.B After the Austrian defeat of the Turks in 1683 at the Battle of Vienna, the Ottomans ceased their westward expansion.
2.1.III.C Louis XIV's nearly continuous wars, pursuing both dynastic and state interests, provoked a coalition of European powers opposing him.

RUSSIA ENTERS THE EUROPEAN POLITICAL ARENA

- The reign of Ivan the Terrible ended with a period of anarchy known as the Time of Troubles.
- In 1613, Michael Romanov was elected tsar by Russian nobles. This dynasty would rule Russia until 1917.
- In 1682, Peter the Great ascended the Russian throne as co-ruler with his half-brother, Ivan V. They rose to power under the *streltsy,* the guards of the Moscow garrison. Peter ruled personally, navigating between the jealousy of the *boyars* (nobles) and the greed of the *streltsy.* Peter's determination to Westernize Russia had five main goals: controlling the *boyars* and *streltsy,* gaining secular control of the church, reorganizing governmental administration, growing the economy, and building a major army and navy.

AP® FRAMEWORK
TOPIC # 3.7; LO: UNIT 3 G
KC:
2.1.I.A Absolute monarchies limited the nobility's participation in governance but preserved the aristocracy's social position and legal privileges.
2.1.I.E Peter the Great 'westernized' the Russian state and society, transforming political, religious, and cultural institutions; Catherine the Great continued this process.

Multiple-Choice Questions

Questions 1–2 refer to the passage below.

"With our own ears we heard the general complaint of our people, that they were barred from all lawful recreation and exercise upon the Sunday's afternoon, after the ending of all divine service, which cannot but produce two evils: the one the hindering of the conversion of many [Roman Catholic subjects]…persuading them that no honest mirth or recreation is lawful or tolerable in our religion…the other inconvenience is, that this prohibition barreth the common and meaner sort of people from using such exercises as may make their bodies more able for war, when we or our successors shall have occasion to use them… For when shall the common people have leave to exercise, if not upon the Sundays and holy days, seeing they must apply their labor and win their living in all working days?… [A]s for our good people's lawful recreation, our pleasure likewise is, that after the end of divine service our good people be not disturbed,… or discouraged from any lawful recreation, such as dancing… archery for men, leaping, vaulting, or any other such harmless recreation… and other sports therewith used…"

King James I, declaration to the English clergy, 1618

Source: Henry Bettenson, ed., *Documents of the Christian Church*, 2nd ed. (London: Oxford University Press, 1963), pp. 400–403.

1. The passage most clearly shows the influence of which of the following trends in early modern Europe?
   (A) Religious disputes that justified challenges to monarchies
   (B) The close relationship between the Catholic and Anglican churches
   (C) The influence of Anabaptist doctrine on the Puritan lifestyle
   (D) The growth of the temperance movement

2. The conflict described in the passage contributed to which of the following?
   (A) Charles I's acceptance of the Petition of Right
   (B) James I signing the English Bill of Rights
   (C) The English Civil War
   (D) The formation of the Whigs and the Tories

Questions 3–6 refer to the passage below.

"We, Friedrich Wilhelm…. Do hereby proclaim and make known to all…that since the cruel persecutions and rigorous ill-treatment…of the Evangelical-Reformed faith have for some time past been subjected in the Kingdom of France, have caused many families to remove themselves and to betake themselves out of the said Kingdom into other lands, We now… have been moved graciously to offer them through this Edict… a secure and free refuge in all Our Lands and Provinces.…

Since Our Lands are not only well and amply endowed with all things necessary to support life, but also very well-suited to the reestablishment of all kinds of manufactures and trade and traffic by land and water, We permit, indeed, to those settling therein free choice to establish themselves where it is most convenient for their profession and way of living.…

The personal property which they bring with them, including merchandise and other wares, is to be totally exempt from any taxes, customs dues, licenses, or other imposts of any description, and not detained in any way.…

As soon as these Our French co-religionists of the Evangelical-Reformed faith have settled in any town or village, they shall be admitted to the domiciliary rights and craft freedoms customary there, gratis and without payments of any fee; and shall be entitled to the benefits, rights, and privileges enjoyed by Our other, native, subjects, residing there.…"

Friedrich Wilhelm [Frederick William], The Great Elector of Brandenburg-Prussia, proclamation to Protestant refugees from France, 1685

Source: C. A. Macartney, ed., *The Habsburg and Hohenzollern Dynasties in the Seventeenth and Eighteenth Centuries* (New York: Walker, 1970), pp. 270–273.

3. The passage above was a result of which of the following?
   (A) Cardinal Richelieu's persecution of the Huguenots, which led to a mass emigration from France to Prussia.
   (B) Louis XIV's revocation of the Edict of Nantes, which ensured monarchical control over religion and restored Catholicism as the one true religion in France.
   (C) The French Civil Wars of religion, which led to Henry of Navarre converting to Catholicism in order to unify France.
   (D) Friedrich Wilhelm, the Great Elector's, enlightened policies as a result of his correspondence with the *philosophes*.

4. The Evangelical-Reformed faith is a refererence to adherents of which of the folloiwng religious beliefs?
   (A) Lutherans
   (B) Calvinists
   (C) Anabaptists
   (D) Catholics

5. Which of the following events led to Brandenburg-Prussia's rise to power?
    (A) The Peace of Westphalia limited the sovereignty and power of the Holy Roman Emperor.
    (B) Austria was defeated by the Ottoman Empire in 1683.
    (C) Friedrich Wilhelm allied with Sweden during the Thirty Years' War.
    (D) Poland was partitioned among three eastern European empires.

6. The ideas expressed in the passage show which of the following trends in seventeenth- century Europe?
    (A) The development of a consumer culture in Europe
    (B) The development of the putting-out system
    (C) Increasing freedom from traditional economic constraints enacted by governments
    (D) The abandonment of mercantilism in favor of capitalism

Questions 7–8 refer to the map below.

The First Three Wars of Louis XIV

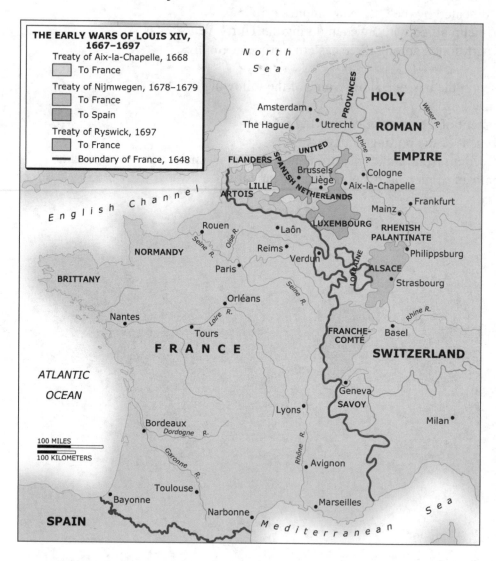

7. Which of the following contributed to the trends shown on the map?
   (A) Louis XIV sought to spread Catholicism into the Netherlands.
   (B) The intendant system allowed Louis XIV to conscript peasant soldiers.
   (C) The Peace of Westphalia resulted in territorial gains for France.
   (D) Louis, with the aid of his finance and war ministers, successfully built up his military.

8. The trends shown on the map resulted in which of the following?
   (A) France annexed the Austrian Netherlands and the Dutch Republic.
   (B) A coalition of nations opposed French expansion to maintain an effective balance of power.
   (C) New territories enriched the French treasury.
   (D) French became the "lingua franca" of seventeenth-century Europe.

72

Questions 9–12 refer to the passage below.

"…. The prince need render account of his acts to no one. "I counsel thee to keep the king's commandment, and that in regard of the oath of God. Be not hasty to go out of his sight; stand not on an evil thing for he doeth whatsoever pleaseth him. Where the word of a king is, there is power; and who may say unto him What doest thou? Whoso keepeth the commandment shall feel no evil thing" [Eccles. 8:2–5]. Without this…authority the king could neither do good nor repress evil. It is necessary that his power be such that no one can hope to escape him, and finally, the only protection of individuals against the public authority should be their innocence…"

Bishop Jacques-Bénigne Bossuet, Politics Drawn from the Very Words of Holy Scripture, 1679
(published in 1709)

Source: *Politics Drawn from the Very Words of Holy Scripture*, James Harvey Robinson, ed., *Readings in European History*, Vol. 2 (Boston: Athenaeum, 1906), pp. 275–276.

9. Bossuet's ideas regarding the power of a prince are most clearly exemplified in which of the following?
   (A) Absolute Monarchies
   (B) Constitutional Monarchies
   (C) Republicanism
   (D) Dictatorships

10. A king influenced by the ideas of the passage would most likely try to enforce which of the following?
    (A) Limited political involvement of the nobility
    (B) Increased taxation of the nobility
    (C) Frequent and regular meetings of a legislative body such as a Parliament
    (D) John Locke's idea of a "social contract"

11. All of the following monarchs enacted policies that support the ideas expressed in the passage EXCEPT?
    (A) Peter the Great of Russia
    (B) Louis XIV of France
    (C) Charles II of England
    (D) Elizabeth I of England

12. The monarchies of which of the following states were unable to implement policies that were supportive of the ideas of the passage?
    (A) Poland
    (B) Russia
    (C) France
    (D) Prussia

Questions 13–15 refer to the passage below.

"Man being born… with a title to perfect freedom, and an uncontrolled enjoyment of all the rights and privileges of the law of nature, equally with any other man, or number of men in the world, hath by nature a power, not only to preserve his property, that is, his life, liberty and estate, against the injuries and attempts of other men; but to judge of, and punish the breaches of that law in others, as he is persuaded the offence deserve….

Hence it is evident, that absolute monarchy, which by some men is counted the only government in the world, is indeed inconsistent with civil society, and so can be no form of civil government at all; for the end of civil society, being to avoid, and remedy those inconveniencies of the state of nature, which necessarily follow from every man's being judge in his own case, by setting up a known authority, to which every one of that society may appeal upon any injury received, or controversy that may arise, and which every one of the society ought to obey; wherever any persons are, who have not such an authority to appeal to, for the decision of any difference between them, there those persons are still in the state of nature; and so is every absolute prince, in respect of those who are under his dominion."

John Locke, *Two Treatises of Government,* 1690

Source: John Locke, *Of Civil Government*, paragraphs 87, 89, 90, 91 in *Two Treatises of Government*, a new ed. (London: 1824), pp. 179–183.

13. Which of the following would be the historical context in which Locke published this passage?
    (A) The English Civil War
    (B) The Glorious Revolution
    (C) The American Revolution
    (D) The French Revolution

14. Based on the ideas of the passage, it can be inferred that Locke believed
    (A) that people should give up their natural rights in return for the state providing order
    (B) in the principles of mercantilism
    (C) that the individual was more important than the state
    (D) that the state was more important than the individual

15. The ideas of the passage most influenced which of the following movements?
    (A) The Scientific Revolution
    (B) Italian humanism
    (C) The Protestant Reformation
    (D) The Enlightenment

Short-Answer Question

Answer a, b, and c:
1. a) Explain one way in which Peter the Great's rule reflected <u>changes</u> in Russian politics and/or society.
   b) Explain one way in which Peter the Great's rule reflected <u>continuities</u> in Russian politics and/or society.
   c) Explain one factor that led to Peter the Great's changes in Russia in the late-seventeenth and early-eighteenth centuries.

Long-Essay Question

Evaluate the extent to which absolutism in France differed from absolutism in Russia during the late-seventeenth and early-eighteenth centuries.

ANSWERS AND EXPLANATIONS: AP® PRACTICE TEST

Multiple-Choice Questions

1. **A** (KC: 1.2.II.C; LO: Unit 2 B) Many non-noble, upper-class English people adopted the ideas of Puritans, who sought to purify the Anglican church of Catholic influences. Much of the House of Commons was made up of Puritans and they perceived James I and Charles I as too Catholic-friendly. Furthermore, they wanted more political power. Religious issues often became the basis for a direct challenge of monarchial control such as in England prior to the Civil War.

2. **C** (KC: 1.5.III.A; LO: Unit 3 B) The conflict between the monarchy and Parliament ultimately led to the English Civil War, fought from 1642–1649. Puritan rule afterwards lasted until the restoration of the monarchy in 1660.

3. **B** (KC: 2.1.I.B; LO: Unit 3 G) Louis XIV issued the Edict of Fontainebleau in 1685, which revoked the Edict of Nantes, which had given Huguenots in France basic rights including the freedom to worship. Historians estimate at least 200,000 Huguenots left France (some estimate closer to 1 million). Many settled in Prussia and approximately 4,000 moved to the New World.

4. **B** (KC: 2.3.IV.B; LO: Unit 4 D) The Evangelical-Reformed faith referenced by Friedrich Wilhelm, the Great Elector, were the Huguenots, or French Calvinists. The Hohenzollerns were also Calvinist and certainly welcomed the economic benefit of an increased population.

5. **A** (KC: 2.1.III.A; LO: Unit 4 H) The Peace of Westphalia divided the Holy Roman Empire into approximately 300 independent states, seriously weakening the effectiveness of the Habsburg emperor. In 1640, Friedrich Wilhelm inherited a scattered collection of territories known as Brandenburg-Prussia and built up his military as one of the great European powers, thus competing with Austria for dominance among the German states.

6. **C** (KC: 2.2.I.A; LO: Unit 3 C) Friedrich Wilhelm's economic incentives (discussed in the passage) to attract the Huguenots to Prussia show his willingness to foster economic growth by reducing restrictions that would hinder economic growth. This pattern was repeated in many areas of Europe during this time period.

7. **D** (KC: 2.1.I.B; LO: Unit 3 G) Louis XIV was able to build Europe's most powerful military during the late sixteenth century, mostly due to Colbert's economic policies as well as the military tactics of his Minister of War, the Marquis de Louvois, who dramatically increased the size of the French army during Louis' reign. As a result, Louis' armies were involved in four major wars in the late-17th and early-18th centuries.

8. **B** (KC: 2.1.III.C; LO: Unit 3 E) Louis' wars ultimately led to a number of countries successfully containing French expansion and upholding the balance of power. These nations included England and the Netherlands.

9. **A** (KC: 2.1.I.A; LO: Unit 3 G) Bossuet's ideas clearly advocate that people should accept the rule of a king—a foundation of absolutism. He was an advocate of the "divine right of kings" and was court preacher for Louis XIV.

10. A (KC: 2.1.I.A; LO: Unit 3 G) One of the characteristics of 17th-century absolute monarchies was limited political participation of the nobility. In France, not only did Louis XIV continue Cardinal Richelieu's *intendant* system, but he also built Versailles, in part, to keep the nobility busy with intricacies of court life in order to maintain their social standing. Nobles still retained privileges such as the *corvé* and banalités (feudal dues).

11. C (KC: 1.2.II.A and 2.1.I.A; LO: Unit 1 F, Unit 3 G) Historians consider both Louis XIV and Peter the Great to be absolute monarchs, and both rulers enacted policies that would have supported the idea of the passage. Although Elizabeth I ruled with Parliament, she only called it into session nine times in 44 years and was able to use Parliament to her advantage. Although Charles II privately promised Louis XIV that he was going to Catholicize England and may have believed in some absolutist tendencies, he was in fact more pragmatic than idealistic and allowed Parliament to legislate religious issues in England during his reign.

12. A (KC: 2.1.I.D; LO: Unit 3 E) Poland was unable to implement absolutist policies successfully. In fact, Polish kings often had less power than members of the nobility and members of the *sejm* had a considerable amount of power. Ultimately, the lack of monarchical power led to the partitioning of Poland in the late-18th century.

13. B (KC: 2.1.II.A; LO: Unit 3 B) Locke began work on his *Two Treatises on Government* during the period in which Parliament was debating whether to exclude James II from the English throne or whether to keep the hereditary monarchy intact. This work was published, during the time period of the Glorious Revolution and the passage of the English Bill of Rights.

14. C (KC: 2.3.I.B; LO: Unit 4 D) Locke believed people were born with a *tabula rasa,* or clean slate, meaning they were basically good. He also believed that the consent of those governed should be the driving force behind government and that states had a duty to rule in the interest of the people. This "social contract" allowed for the people to overthrow the government if the government failed to govern in their interest.

15. D (KC: 2.3.I; LO: Unit 4 D) Locke's ideas about liberty and natural rights were later spread through the Enlightenment *philosophes. Philosophes* such as Rousseau also believed in a social contract between those who govern and those who are governed. These ideas later became the basis for the French Revolution.

Short-Answer Question
(KC: 2.1.I.E; LO: Unit 3 G)

Possible responses for part a) include:
- Peter instituted absolute rule in Russia.
- Peter built Russia's navy and significantly expanded Russia's army.
- Peter sought to create a service nobility through the Table of Ranks.
- Peter sought to modernize society by requiring the nobles dress in modern fashion.
- Peter imported technical experts from Western Europe to help modernize Russia's military and improve manufacturing.
- Peter built St. Petersburg from scratch after defeating Sweden in the Great Northern War.
- Peter expanded Russia's influence in the Black Sea Region by defeating the Ottoman Empire.

Possible responses for part b) include:
- Russian rule had been largely autocratic, although not absolute. Peter's rule was autocratic.
- Serfdom remained a core component of Russian society.
- Russia remained an agricultural society with a powerful nobility.

Possible responses for part c) include:
- Russia had fallen far behind the West militarily. Peter sought to strengthen Russia in the Baltic region and in the Black Sea region.
- Peter was fascinated with Western European innovation and its modern society. He visited the West as a young ruler.
- Peter was influenced by the Baroque grandeur of Versailles and sought to recreate it with the Peterhof in St. Petersburg.

Long-Essay Question
(KC: 2.1.I.A, 2.1.I.B: LO: Unit 3 G)

Evaluate the extent to which absolutism in France differed from absolutism in Russia during the late-seventeenth and early-eighteenth centuries.

Possible differences might include:
- Louis XIV enforced religious uniformity to a larger extent through the Edict of Fontainebleu and his suppression of Jansenists.
- Louis exercised greater control of the nobility of the sword by requiring they spend time at Versailles every year.
- Louis utilized the middle class and robe nobles in the *intendant* system as the backbone of absolutism in France.
- Serfdom was far less prevalent in France than in Russia.
- France was technologically and economically superior to Russia.
- Louis' territorial ambitions were thwarted to a larger degree than Peter's.
- Peter did not emphasize "divine right" of kings in the way that Louis did.

Possible similarities might include:
- Both exercised increased influence over their nobles.
- Both emphasized military power.
- Both sought to enhance their power through grand architecture.
- Both built up their physical power centers: Peter in St. Petersburg and Louis at Versailles.

CHAPTER 6

New Directions in Thought and Culture in the Sixteenth and Seventeenth Centuries

This period saw a total transformation in the scientific understanding of the universe—a transformation that affected all aspects of daily life, including other branches of scientific thought, philosophy, and faith.

THE SCIENTIFIC REVOLUTION

- The **Scientific Revolution** was not a unified event, but rather a gradual movement that involved around a few hundred brilliant scientists laboring independently over many years in different countries. This new science, and especially the many significant discoveries in the field of astronomy, captured the public's imagination and enabled scientific discovery and knowledge to gain cultural authority.
- Nicholas Copernicus (1473–1543) is famous for questioning the geocentric view of the **Ptolemaic system** (in which the earth was believed to be at the center of the universe). In his work *On the Revolutions of Heavenly Spheres,* Copernicus argued on behalf of a heliocentric view of the universe.
- Tycho Brahe (1546–1601) spent much of his life advocating a geocentric view of the universe, but he made more extensive observations of the planets than any of his predecessors. Brahe's assistant, Johannes Kepler (1571–1630), used Brahe's research findings to advance a heliocentric view and demonstrate that planets orbited around the sun in an elliptical fashion in his book *The New Astronomy* (1609).
- Galileo Galilei (1564–1642) was one of the first astronomers to view the sky with the telescope. He popularized a Copernican interpretation of the heavens using the empirical, rational evidence that he found in his research.
- Isaac Newton (1642–1727), an English scientist, published his famous *Principia Mathematica* in 1687. In it he asserted—and proved mathematically—that planets and other physical objects moved through mutual attraction, or gravity.

AP® FRAMEWORK
TOPIC # 4.2; LO: UNIT 4 B
KC:
1.1.IV.A New ideas and methods in astronomy led individuals, including Copernicus, Galileo, and Newton to question the authority of the ancients and traditional knowledge, and to develop a heliocentric view of the cosmos.

PHILOSOPHY RESPONDS TO CHANGING SCIENCE

The revolution in scientific thought extended to the philosophy of the era, which came to see the world in terms of its mechanical principles.

- The image of God as a divine watchmaker came into vogue at this time, and a new emphasis on mathematics and a mechanical understanding of nature pervaded all fields.
- Francis Bacon (1561–1626) urged his peers to continue their search for the truth in the natural world. In his *Novum Organum* and *The Advancement of Learning,* Bacon attacked the belief that everything had already been discovered, and he encouraged experimentation.
- René Descartes (1596–1650) developed a scientific method that relied on deduction more than it did on empirical study and induction. In his 1637 *Discourse on Method,* Descartes endorsed the idea that all thought should be founded on a mathematical model, and he rejected outright any thought not postulated on reason.
- Thomas Hobbes (1588–1679) was supportive of the scientific movement and befriended Descartes and Galileo. Hobbes's *Leviathan* (1651) portrays human beings as materialistic, egotistical, and hedonistic. Hobbes believed human beings were constantly in a state of conflict. He felt that rulers should have no limits on their power.
- John Locke (1632–1704) was critical of Hobbes's views of absolutism and helped lay a foundation for European liberal political philosophy. In his *First Treatise of Government,* Locke rejected the idea of absolute government based on the concept of a patriarchal model of fathers ruling over a family. In his *Second Treatise of Government,* Locke argued for a government that was both accountable for and alert to the needs of the government. He believed that human beings were basically creatures of goodwill that entered into a social contract to preserve their existing liberties and rights.

AP® FRAMEWORK
TOPIC # 4.2, 4.3; LO: UNIT 4 B, C, D
KC:
1.1.IV.B Anatomical and medical discoveries by physicians, including William Harvey, presented the body as an integrated system, challenging the traditional humoral theory of the body and of disease espoused by Galen.
1.1.IV.C Francis Bacon and René Descartes defined inductive and deductive reasoning and promoted experimentation and the use of mathematics, which would ultimately shape the scientific method.
2.3.I.B Locke and Rousseau developed new political models based on the concept of natural rights and the social contract.
2.3.III.A Political theories, including John Locke's, conceived of society as composed of individuals driven by self-interest and argued that the state originated in the consent of the governed (i.e., a social contract) rather than in divine right or tradition.

THE NEW INSTITUTIONS OF EXPANDING NATURAL KNOWLEDGE

- Galileo angered the Catholic Church because he interpreted scripture in accord with the new science. For his disobedience, Galileo was put on trial and forced to live under house arrest.
- Blaise Pascal (1623–1662) was a French mathematician who saw religion as separate from reason and science; he believed that religion required a "leap of faith." He allied himself with the Jansenists. Pascal's famous wager with the skeptics was that it was better to believe that God exists and stake everything on his benevolence than not to do so.
- Faith in a rational God was an element in the English approach to the new science. Scientific advances came to be interpreted as a fulfillment of God's plan for mankind.

AP® FRAMEWORK
TOPIC # 4.2, 4.3; LO: UNIT 4 B, D
KC:
1.1.IV.A New ideas and methods in astronomy led individuals, including Copernicus, Galileo, and Newton to question the authority of the ancients and traditional knowledge, and to develop a heliocentric view of the cosmos.
2.3.I Enlightenment thought, which focused on concepts such as empiricism, skepticism, human reason, rationalism, and classical sources of knowledge, challenged the prevailing patterns of thought with respect to social order, institutions of government, and the role of faith.

CONTINUING SUPERSTITION

- From 1400 to 1700, an estimated 70,000–100,000 people were sentenced to death for magic and witchcraft. Growing religious and political tensions of the age made use of theology that portrayed demons and the devil as powerful. Cunning folk were believed to possess special powers. Over time, these abilities came into conflict with the sacred rituals of the Christian church, like the sacraments, and the exorcism of demons. The church declared that only its priests could possess legitimate magical abilities and that those who practiced magic outside the church were infernally inspired.

AP® FRAMEWORK
TOPIC # 4.2; LO: UNIT 4 B
KC:
1.1.IV.A Alchemy and astrology continued to appeal to elites and some natural philosophers, in part because they shared with the new science the notion of a predictable and knowable universe. At the same time, many people continued to believe that the cosmos was governed by spiritual forces.

Multiple-Choice Questions

Questions 1–3 refer to the image below.

Copernican model of the universe, 1543

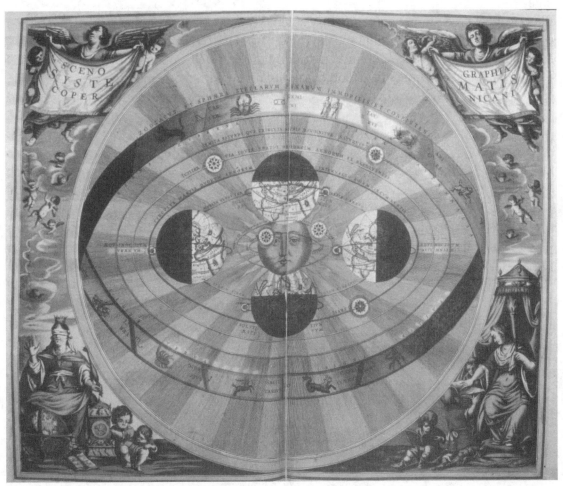

Source: British Library, London, UK© British Library Board. All Rights Reserved/Owner/Bridgeman Art Library.

1. The idea expressed in the image represents which of the following?
   (A) The development of a geocentric view of the universe
   (B) The development of a heliocentric view of the universe
   (C) The influence of antiquity on the development of the new science
   (D) The influence of superstition on the development of the new science

2. The idea expressed in the image was further explained by which of the following scientific thinkers?
   (A) René Descartes
   (B) Andreas Vesalius
   (C) Galileo Galilei.
   (D) Margaret Cavendish

3. Which of the following best explains why people were opposed to the idea expressed in the image?
   (A) Plato was revered among contemporary scientists and Copernican theory directly contradicted his ideas regarding the universe.
   (B) Newton's law of universal gravitation directly undermined Copernican theory.
   (C) The idea expressed in the image could not be proven with mathematics.
   (D) Most people believed that divine forces best explained ideas regarding the universe.

Questions 4–6 refer to the passage below.

"The only way to establish a common power that can defend them from the invasion of foreigners and the injuries of one another, and thereby make them secure enough to be able to nourish themselves and live contentedly through their own labours and the fruits of the earth, is to confer all their power and strength on one man, or one assembly of men, so as to turn all their wills by a majority vote into a single will. That is to say: to appoint one man or assembly of men to bear their person; and everyone to own and acknowledge himself to be the author of every act that he who bears their person performs or causes to be performed in matters concerning the common peace and safety, and all of them to submit their wills to his will, and their judgments to his judgment. This is more than mere agreement or harmony; it is a real unity of them all. They are unified in that they constitute one single person, created through a covenant of every man with every other man, as though each man were to say to each of the others:

I authorize and give up my right of governing myself to this man, or to this assembly of men, on condition that you surrender to him your right of governing yourself, and authorize all his actions in the same way."

Thomas Hobbes, *Leviathan,* 1651

Source: LEVIATHAN By Thomas Hobbes 1651 LEVIATHAN OR THE MATTER, FORME, & POWER OF A COMMON-WEALTH ECCLESIASTICAL AND **CIVIL** Thomas Hobbes of Malmesbury Printed for Andrew Crooke, at the Green Dragon in St. Paul's Churchyard, 1651.

4. An historian could best use the ideas of the excerpt as evidence to support the conditions that led to which of the following?
    (A) The Glorious Revolution in England
    (B) The French Revolution
    (C) The monarchy of Elizabeth I
    (D) The monarchy of Louis XIV

5. Which of the following would have been most opposed to the ideas expressed in the excerpt?
    (A) James I of England
    (B) Klemens von Metternich
    (C) John Locke
    (D) Martin Luther

6. The ideas of Hobbes, as expressed in the excerpt, were not supported by the Christian churches for which of the following reasons?
    (A) Hobbes did not recognize the authority of God and the church in his political beliefs.
    (B) Christian churches believed in a more democratic form of government than Hobbes.
    (C) Hobbes's political philosophy was a result of his belief in deism.
    (D) Hobbes condemned the power structure of John Calvin's Geneva.

Questions 7–8 refer to the passage below.

"Art has intoxicated so many men's brains, and wholly imployed their thoughts and bodily actions about phaenomena, or the exterior figure of objects, as all better Arts and Studies are laid aside…. But though there be numerous Books written of the wonder of these [experimental optical] Glasses, yet I cannot perceive any such; at best, they are but superficial wonders, as I may call them. But could Experimental Philosophers find out more beneficial Arts then our Fore-fathers have done, either for the better increase of Vegetables and brute Animals to nourish our bodies, or better and commodious contrivances in the Art of Architecture to build us houses, or for the advancing of trade and traffick… it would not only be worth their labour, but of as much praise as could be given to them: But, as Boys that play with watry Bubbles… are worthy of reproof rather than praise, for wasting their time with useless sports; so those that addict themselves to unprofitable Arts, spend more time than they reap benefit thereby."

Margaret Cavendish, *Observations Upon Experimental Philosophy,* 1666

Source: Margaret Cavendish, *Observations Upon Experimental Philosophy*, to which is added, *The Description of a New Blazing World* (London, 1666), pp. 10–11, as quoted in Anna Battigelli, *Margaret Cavendish and the Exiles of the Mind* (Lexington: University of Kentucky Press, 1998), p. 94.

7. Based on the ideas of the excerpt and your own knowledge, Cavendish would most likely advocate which of the following?
    (A) Science should be concerned primarily with knowledge for its own sake.
    (B) Experimentation leads to false conclusions.
    (C) Observation and experimentation should be concerned with practical applications.
    (D) Optics is not a science but an art.

8. The ability of Margaret Cavendish to read and write in seventeenth-century Europe was most likely the result of which of the following?
    (A) Greater acceptance of females into scientific academies
    (B) Enlightenment thinkers' views that women should have the same natural rights as men
    (C) Increasing literacy rates amongst the peasantry
    (D) Increasing debates about female literacy during the Reformation

Questions 9–12 refer to the passage below.

"My speculations were indeed truly pleasing to me…As soon, however, as I had acquired some general notions regarding physics…I believed that I could not keep them hidden without grievously sinning against the law which lays us under obligation to promote, as far as in us lies, the general good of all mankind. For they led me to see that it is possible to obtain knowledge highly useful in life…knowing the force and the actions of fire, water, air, and of the stars, of the heavens, and of all the bodies that surround us…we may in the same fashion employ them in all the uses for which they are suited… for the preservation of health, which is, without doubt, of all blessings in this life, the first of all goods and the foundation on which the others rest. For the mind is so dependent on the temper and disposition of the bodily organisms that if any means can ever be found to render men wiser and more capable than they have hitherto been, I believe that it is in the science of medicine that the means must be sought…."

René Descartes, *Discourse on Method,* 1637

Source: René Descartes, *Discourse on Method*, in Norman Kemp Smith, ed., *Descartes's Philosophical Writings* (New York: The Modern Library, 1958), pp. 130–131.

9. Which of the following contributed to the ideas expressed in this excerpt?
   (A) Newton synthesized inductive and deductive reasoning.
   (B) The Jesuits opened new schools that supported scientific studies.
   (C) Humanist scholars emphasized the importance of the individual.
   (D) Christian humanist scholars emphasized translating the Bible into the vernacular.

10. The ideas expressed in the passage regarding the "general good of all mankind" had the greatest influence on which of the following?
    (A) Robert Boyle's study of the heart
    (B) The development of utopian societies
    (C) Rousseau's emphasis on the concept of natural rights
    (D) *Philosophe* acceptance of deist teachings

11. Descartes is best known for the use of which of the following to the scientific method?
    (A) Inductive reasoning
    (B) Deductive reasoning
    (C) Heliocentric theory
    (D) Anatomical studies

12. Descartes' ideas as expressed in the passage exemplified which of the following changes in seventeenth-century Europe?
    (A) A new emphasis on observation, experimentation, and the use of mathematics that challenged existing views
    (B) The general acceptance by European society of the views of the ancients such as Aristotle
    (C) A renewed emphasis on constitutional forms of government based on the general will of the people
    (D) The beginning of the European witch hunts in response to religious uncertainty

Questions 13–15 refer to the passage below.

"The patriarchal theories of late-Renaissance Europe played an important role in determining which groups of women became victims of these obsessions. Accused witches were disproportionately widows, while infanticide defendants were single women; both groups lived outside direct male supervision in this age of reinforced patriarchal nuclear families. Their "unnatural" position aroused suspicion and sometimes fear; neighborhood enemies did the rest."

William Monter, *Protestant Wives, Catholic Saints, and the Devil's Handmaid: Women in the Age of Reformations,* 1977

Source: Monter, William, "Protestant Wives, Catholic Saints, and the Devil's Handmaid: Women in the Age of Reformations." In *Becoming Visible: Women in European History*. Eds. Renate Bridenthal, et al. (Boston: Houghton Mifflin, 1987) pp. 201–19.

13. The author's conclusion regarding the significance of the European witch hunts challenges which of the following historical interpretations of witch hunts?
    (A) Witchcraft accusations increased because of uncertainty regarding the interaction with the indigenous peoples in the Americas.
    (B) Witchcraft accusations increased because the absence of Carnival and other Catholic practices led to religious revolts in Protestant areas.
    (C) Witchcraft accusations increased due to religious warfare and economic uncertainty during the sixteenth and seventeenth centuries.
    (D) Witchcraft accusations increased due to the return of the plague and the introduction of new diseases from the Americas during the sixteenth and seventeenth centuries.

14. Which of the following undermines the author's assertion in the excerpt regarding the witch hunts?
    (A) Nuclear families did not exist until the twentieth century.
    (B) Most widows remarried within two years and were rarely accused of witchcraft.
    (C) Approximately 65 percent of those accused of witchcraft were single older women.
    (D) Approximately 20 percent of those accused of witchcraft were males.

15. Which of the following led to the end of the European witch hunts?
    (A) Humanist focus on the classics during the Renaissance
    (B) Protestant emphasis on spiritual equality during the Reformation
    (C) The Scientific Revolution's emphasis on reasoning and experimentation
    (D) The abolition of capital punishment in most western European countries

Short-Answer Question

Use the following images to answer the question below.

Image 1

The Hall of Mirrors, Palace at Versailles

Source: Russell Kord/Alamy

<u>Image 2</u>

Bernini designed the elaborate Baldacchino that stands under the dome of St. Peter's Basilica. It is one of the major examples of baroque interior decoration.

Source: Scala/Art Resource, NY

Answer a, b, and c:
1. a) Describe how Baroque art and architecture, such as the examples above, had an impact on organized religion.
   b) Describe how Baroque art and architecture, such as the examples above, had an impact on politics.
   c) Explain one way in which Baroque art and architecture was different from Renaissance art and architecture.

Long-Essay Question

Evaluate the extent to which the Renaissance led to the Scientific Revolution.

ANSWERS AND EXPLANATIONS: AP® PRACTICE TEST

Multiple-Choice Questions

1. **B** (KC: 1.1.IV.A; LO: Unit 4 B) The Copernican model of the universe represented a shift from the geocentric model of the universe, in which all heavenly bodies revolve around the earth, to a heliocentric model of the universe in which the earth and all heavenly bodies revolve around the sun.

2. **C** (KC: 1.1.IV.A; LO: Unit 4 B) Copernican theory was later refined by Johannes Kepler, who showed that the heavenly bodies did not revolve in perfect circles but rather revolved in elliptical orbits. Galileo Galilei further explained Copernican theory by use of mathematics and observed planetary motion through the use of a telescope.

3. **D** (KC: 1.1.IV.D; LO: Unit 4 B) Although the new science encouraged the use of reasoning and mathematics, many Europeans believed that the universe was governed by spiritual forces. This view was reinforced by the opposition of the Catholic Church to heliocentrism.

4. **D** (KC: 2.1.I.B; LO: Unit 3 G) The passage argues that a strong government would protect people from "injuries of one another." The Fronde, an aristocratic uprising in seventeenth-century France, led to a brief period of chaos. Although unsuccessful, it did lead to Louis XIV's creating an even more centralized government in France.

5. **C** (KC: 2.3.I.B; LO: Unit 4 C) Both Thomas Hobbes and John Locke advocated the idea of a "social contract" between those who are governed and those who govern. However, the idea of the "social contract" differed between the two writers. Hobbes believed that a strong leader was necessary for order because of the brutish nature of humans, whereas Locke believed that humans were not brutish by nature and if a ruler did not meet the needs of the people, they had the right to revolt.

6. **A** (KC: 1.2.II.B; LO: Unit 2 B) Hobbes was criticized by both Catholics and Protestants because he did not recognize God as important in his political philosophy. Many of his contemporaries accused him of being an atheist.

7. **C** (KC: 1.1.IV; LO: Unit 4 A) Margaret Cavendish was the only seventeenth-century woman who was allowed to visit a meeting of the Royal Society of London; she had, at one time, actually criticized the society for not using the new science to solve practical problems.

8. **D** (KC: 1.4.IV.B; LO: Unit 2 E) The Protestant Reformation encouraged individuals to interpret the Bible for themselves. As a result, increased debates emerged regarding the extent of female education and the role of women in general during this time period. Because Cavendish came from a wealthy family and was highly educated, she benefited from these debates.

9. **C** (KC: 1.1.I.A; LO: Unit 1 B) The Scientific Revolution came about, in part, because of Renaissance ideas of individuality and secularism. Unlike scholasticism, humanists often wrote about the perfectibility of humans.

10. **C** (KC 2.3.I.B; LO: Unit 4 C) Descartes's reference to the general good of all mankind is very similar to Rousseau's emphasis on the general will of the people. Enlightenment thinkers were often influenced by Scientific Revolution concepts and applied these to the political and social order of the eighteenth century.

11. B   (KC: 1.1.IV.C; LO: Unit 4 B) Descartes is best known for the use of deductive reasoning, exemplified by his famous phrase, "I think, therefore I am." Newton later synthesized both Descartes's deductive reasoning with Bacon's inductive reasoning in developing the scientific method.

12. A   (KC: 1.1.IV.C; LO: Unit 4 B) Descartes's ideas were part of a growing change away from explanations based on antiquity and the Church and toward a new reliance upon experimentation and mathematics.

13. C   (KC: 1.4.V.C; LO: Unit 2 E) The author asserts that the existing patriarchal system was a major factor in the increase of witch hunts in Europe during the sixteenth and seventeenth centuries. Another leading theory that the author does not address is economic uncertainty due to the religious wars and the Price Revolution.

14. D   (KC: 1.4.V.C; LO: Unit 2 E) The author's assertion regarding the patriarchal system could be undermined by the fact that roughly 20% of those accused of witchcraft were males. Some historians estimate that in some areas, notably Russia, the majority of the victims were male.

15. C   (KC: 1.1.IV.C; LO: Unit 4 B) The Scientific Revolution's emphasis on reasoning was one of several reasons for the end of the witch hunts.

Short-Answer Question
(KC: 1.1.III.C; LO: Unit 2 F)

Possible responses to part a) include:
- Baroque art and architecture were meant to show the power and grandeur of the Catholic Church, as in the Bernini image.
- Baroque art and architecture were used during the Counter-Reformation and clearly contrasted with the art and architecture used in Protestant churches.

Possible responses to part b) include:
- Baroque art and architecture were used by monarchs to display the grandeur of the crown, such as the Hall of Mirrors built by Louis XIV at Versailles.
- Baroque art and architecture were used by monarchs to show the power of the monarchy over the nobility. Louis XIV summoned much of his nobility to Versailles.
- Some monarchs used baroque art and architecture to demonstrate absolutism, such as Louis XIV's Palace of Versailles. Peter the Great built Peterhof outside of St. Petersburg and his successors contributed to its prominence.

Possible responses to part c) include:
- Baroque art focused more on showing emotion than Renaissance art. Many Renaissance sculptures, such as Michelangelo's *David,* did not show activities such as prayer or getting ready for battle that we see in Bernini's sculptures.
- Baroque paintings often emphasized more movement and color than traditional Renaissance paintings, such as in the work of Peter Paul Rubens.

93

Long-Essay Question
(KC: 1.1.IV; LO: Unit 4 A)

Evaluate the extent to which the Renaissance led to the Scientific Revolution.

Possible responses for the Renaissance leading to the Scientific Revolution include:
- The Renaissance introduced new ways of thinking, which induced curiosity.
- Leonardo da Vinci's ideas contributed to advances in anatomy and botany.
- The Renaissance encouraged secularism and individualism, leading to more people questioning the teachings of both antiquity and the Catholic Church.
- Renaissance humanists' emphasis on questioning "how and why" encouraged many thinkers to focus on observation and experimentation.
- A new emphasis on education brought about a desire to learn more about the natural world.

Possible responses for other factors leading to the Scientific Revolution or how the Renaissance did not lead to the Scientific Revolution include:
- The Protestant Reformation led to a spirit of rebellion against Catholic Church practices and ideas that allowed for scientists to experiment more openly.
- The European discovery of new lands increased inquisitiveness about the natural world.
- Increased availability of works after the fall of Constantinople led to increased education.
- Humanists often favored studying the liberal arts rather than the study of science.
- Christian humanists also favored the study of biblical works.
- The invention of the printing press allowed for the spread of new ideas that contradicted the teachings of antiquity and the Catholic Church.

CHAPTER 7

Society and Economy under the Old Regime in the Eighteenth Century

The period known as the *ancien régime,* or the **Old Regime**, usually refers to the various political and social relationships and situations prior to the French Revolution of 1789. During this time both nobles and peasants called for the return to traditional rights, and society was fairly hierarchical.

MAJOR FEATURES OF LIFE IN THE OLD REGIME
- Tradition remained the most important factor shaping the lives of Europeans in this period. The peasants, above all, were committed to maintaining the status quo, and they were opposed to change.
- Likewise, a hierarchical society remained the accepted model. Each layer of the hierarchy had its own rights, duties, and privileges.

AP® FRAMEWORK
TOPIC # 2.6, 4.4; LO: UNIT 2 E, UNIT 4 E
KC:
1.4.I.C Established hierarchies of class, religion, and gender continued to define social status and perceptions in rural and urban settings.
2.4.I In the 17th century, small landholdings, low-productivity agricultural practices, poor transportation, and adverse weather limited and disrupted the food supply, causing periodic famines. By the 18th century, the balance between population and the food supply stabilized, resulting in steady population growth.

THE ARISTOCRACY
- Aristocrats represented a mere 5 percent of the population but controlled the majority of land, as well as social, economic, and political power. As monarchs' powers expanded, European aristocrats used existing governmental institutions to limit the power of the monarchy.
- In England, game laws gave aristocratic landowners the exclusive legal rights from 1671 to 1831 to hunt. The English aristocracy owned one-fourth of all arable land and consisted of about 400 families, many of whom controlled the House of Lords and the House of Commons.
- In France, the nobility consisted of military officers, bureaucrats, and wealthy bourgeois-individuals who purchased noble titles and became known as "nobles of the robe." French nobles fell into two groups: those who attended the court at Versailles, and those who did not.

- In eastern Europe, the nobility had more rights over peasants, compared to the nobility in western Europe. Polish aristocrats exerted total control over serfs. In Austria and Hungary, nobles were exempt from taxation. In countries like Hungary and Poland, nobles were the only ones with political representation. In Prussia, nobles had authority over serfs. In Russia, nobles became determined to resist compulsory state service. In the 1785 Charter of the Nobility, Catherine the Great defined the legal rights of nobles and their families in exchange for the nobility's voluntary service of state.

AP® FRAMEWORK
TOPIC # 3.7, 4.4; LO: UNIT 3 G, UNIT 4 E
KC:
2.1.I.A Absolute monarchies limited the nobility's participation in governance but preserved the aristocracy's social position and legal privileges.
2.4.I.A By the middle of the 18th century, higher agricultural productivity and improved transportation increased the food supply, allowing populations to grow and reducing the number of demographic crises (a process known as the Agricultural Revolution).

THE LAND AND ITS TILLERS

- More than three-quarters of all Europeans lived in the country in the eighteenth century; many of them were very poor peasants who lived by subsistence agriculture.
- In Great Britain, farmers had legal rights of English citizens, but the courts were run by landowners. French peasants had to pay feudal dues and were responsible for a certain amount of forced labor, known as *corvée*.
- In Prussia and Austria, landlords exercised almost complete control over serfs. The condition of serfs in Russia was worst; serfs had no legal rights and were effectively slaves. Russia experienced numerous peasant revolts between 1762 and 1769, a period culminating in Pugachev's Rebellion between 1773 and 1775. Southeastern European peasants were free, but only because of a scarcity of labor. Balkan peasants eventually became dependent on their Ottoman Empire landlords because they sought their protection from bandits and rebels.

AP® FRAMEWORK TOPIC # 3.7; LO: UNIT 3 G
KC:
2.1.I.A Absolute monarchies limited the nobility's participation in governance but preserved the aristocracy's social position and legal privileges.

FAMILY STRUCTURES AND FAMILY ECONOMY

- The **family economy** continued to prevail across most of Europe. Households in northwestern Europe often consisted of a married couple, children through their teens, and servants (people who were hired under contract to work for the head of the household in exchange for room, board, and wages). Households were small, usually no more than five or six people. Mortality was high, and no more than two generations lived together under one roof. Most children eventually married and formed their own households—a phenomenon known as *neolocalism*. The marriage age was in the mid-twenties for men and women.

- In eastern Europe, the marriage age was much earlier, usually before the age of twenty. Wives were often older than their husbands. Russian households often consisted of as many as three or four generations living together in one house.

AP® FRAMEWORK
TOPIC # 3.7, 4.4; LO: UNIT 2 G, UNIT 4 E
KC:
1.4.IV The family remained the primary social and economic institution of early modern Europe and took several forms, including the nuclear family.
2.4.I In the 17th century, small landholdings, low-productivity agricultural practices, poor transportation, and adverse weather limited and disrupted the food supply, causing periodic famines. By the 18th century, the balance between population and the food supply stabilized, resulting in steady population growth.

THE REVOLUTION IN AGRICULTURE

- The **agricultural revolution** began in the Netherlands, where farmers built dikes, expanded land, and experimented with new crops. English landlords popularized these Dutch innovations. Jethro Tull financed the experiments of others and conducted his own, including permitting land to be cultivated for longer periods without having to be left fallow. Robert Bakewell pioneered new methods of animal breeding. Charles Townsend learned how to use fertilizer and instituted crop rotation. By the second half of the seventeenth century, **enclosures** replaced the open-field method of farming. Enclosures commercialized agriculture, maximizing the profits of the landowner.

AP® FRAMEWORK
TOPIC #3.3, 4.4; LO: UNIT 3 C, UNIT 4 E
KC:
2.2.I.B The Agricultural Revolution raised productivity and increased the supply of food and other agricultural products.
2.4.I.A By the middle of the 18th century, higher agricultural productivity and improved transportation increased the food supply, allowing populations to grow and reducing the number of demographic crises (a process known as the Agricultural Revolution).
2.4.IV.A The Agricultural Revolution produced more food using fewer workers; as a result, people migrated from rural areas to the cities in search of work.

THE INDUSTRIAL REVOLUTION OF THE EIGHTEENTH CENTURY

- The second half of the eighteenth century witnessed the industrialization of the European economy, which made possible the production of more goods and services than ever before: the **consumer revolution**. New machinery was invented that enabled this industrialization, including the **spinning jenny**, the **water frame**, and the steam engine. Iron production during this era was essential to the manufacturing of machinery. The **Industrial Revolution,** with its emphasis on heavy machinery that was often run by men, forced women, who had earlier spun thread and farmed, into cottage industries that paid women lower wages and resulted in the workplaces of men and women becoming more separate.

AP® KEY CONCEPTS AP® FRAMEWORK
TOPIC #3.3, 3.4, 6.1; LO: UNIT 3 C, UNIT 6 A
KC:
2.2.I.C The putting-out system, or cottage industry, expanded as increasing numbers of laborers in homes or workshops produced for markets through merchant intermediaries or workshop owners.
2.2.II.C Overseas products and influences contributed to the development of a consumer culture in Europe.
3.1.I Great Britain established its industrial dominance through the mechanization of textile production, iron and steel production, and new transportation systems in conjunction with uniquely favorable political and social climates.

THE GROWTH OF CITIES

- Between 1650 and 1700, cities that grew most in population were capitals and ports; the urban Industrial Revolution, overseas trade, and governmental bureaucracy came to control European economies. New cities began to emerge in the middle of the eighteenth century; improved agricultural production enabled the growth of nearby urban centers that gave farmers access to consumer goods. Social divisions were marked between the upper classes, middle class, artisans, and peasants.

AP® FRAMEWORK
TOPIC #4.4, 4.5; LO: UNIT 4 E,F
KC:
2.4.II The consumer revolution of the 18th century was shaped by a new concern for privacy, encouraged the purchase of new goods for homes, and created new venues for leisure activities.
2.4.IV.A The Agricultural Revolution produced more food using fewer workers; as a result, people migrated from rural areas to the cities in search of work.
2.4.IV.B The growth of cities eroded traditional communal values, and city governments strained to provide protection and a healthy environment.
2.4.IV.C The concentration of the poor in cities led to a greater awareness of poverty, crime, and prostitution as social problems, and prompted increased efforts to police marginal groups.

THE JEWISH POPULATION: THE AGE OF THE GHETTO

- The majority of Jews lived in Eastern Europe, with the Netherlands being a notable exception. The Jewish population was concentrated in Lithuania, Poland, and the Ukraine.
- Catherine the Great was intolerant of the Jewish population in Russia and discouraged their settlement there. Jews were often victims of intolerance in the countries where they settled.

AP® FRAMEWORK
TOPIC #4.6; LO: UNIT 4 G
KC:
2.3.IV.C By 1800, most governments in western and central Europe had extended toleration to Christian minorities and, in some states, civil equality to Jews.

Multiple-Choice Questions

Questions 1–2 refer to the passage below.

"In times when industry and the arts flourish, men are kept in perpetual occupation, and enjoy, as their reward, the occupation itself, as well as those pleasures which are the fruit of their labour. The mind acquires new vigour; enlarges its powers and faculties; and by an assiduity in honest industry, both satisfies its natural appetites, and prevents the growth of unnatural ones, which commonly spring up, when nourished by ease and idleness…

The more these refined arts advance, the more sociable men become…. They flock into cities; love to receive and communicate knowledge; to show their wit or their breeding; their taste in conversation or living, in clothes or furniture. Curiosity allures the wise; vanity the foolish, and pleasure both. Particular clubs and societies are everywhere formed: Both sexes meet in an easy and sociable manner: and the tempers of men, as well as their behaviour, refine apace. So that, beside the improvements which they receive from knowledge and the liberal arts, it is impossible but they must feel an encrease of humanity, from the very habit of conversing together, and contributing to each other's pleasure and entertainment…But industry, knowledge, and humanity are not advantageous in private life alone: They diffuse their beneficial influence on the public, and render the government as great and flourishing as they make individuals happy and prosperous..."

David Hume, "Of Refinement in the Arts," 1752

Source: David Hume, "Of Refinement in the Arts (1752)," in *Essays: Moral, Political and Literary* (Indianapolis, IN: Liberty Classics, 1985), pp. 270–272.

1. The flourishing of industry, as described in the passage, reflects which of the following eighteenth-century trends?
   (A) Increased value of labor because of resurgence of bubonic plague
   (B) An increase in the number of women in the workplace
   (C) Increasing economic freedom from government and traditional restrictions
   (D) The use of railroads to transport goods between towns and cities

2. The social trends that Hume describes in the passage were most likely written in the context of the
   (A) Scientific Revolution
   (B) French Revolution
   (C) Renaissance
   (D) Enlightenment

Questions 3–6 refer to the image below.

A feather adornment workshop

Source: Bpk, Berlin/Art Resource, NY

3. An historian could use this image to best illustrate which of the following eighteenth-century developments?
   (A) The Industrial Revolution
   (B) The Consumer Revolution
   (C) Increased economic opportunities for women
   (D) Social and economic dislocation during the eighteenth century.

4. The trends depicted in the image contributed to which of the following developments?
   (A) Increased prestige for women who worked outside of the home
   (B) The mechanization of the textile industry
   (C) The diminishing importance of the guild system
   (D) A decline in commercial wealth

5. Which of the following economic activities occurred during the same time period of the events depicted in the image?
   (A) The development of the putting-out system
   (B) The development of the factory system
   (C) Increasing government control over economic activities
   (D) A decrease in enclosure movements in rural areas

6. Which of the following was necessary for eighteenth-century economic trends such as the one depicted in the image?
   (A) The development of an extensive railway system for better transportation
   (B) The acquisition of territories in Africa and Asia
   (C) The transatlantic slave trade
   (D) Changes in banking and financial practices

Questions 7–9 refer to the passage below.

"Mr. Taylor, If you don't discharge James Hobson from the House of Correction we will burn your House about your Ears for we have sworn to stand by one another and you must immediately give over any more Mashen [machine] Work for we are determined there shall be no more of them made use of in the Trade and it will be madness for you to contend with the Trade as we are combined by Oath to fix Prices…therefore mind you comply with the above or by God we will keep our Words with you we will make some rare Bunfires in this Countey and at your Peril to call any more Meetings mind that we will make the Mosney Pepel shake in their Shoes we are determined to destroy all Sorts of Masheens for…our Meetings are legal for we want nothing but what is honest and to work for selvs and familers and you want to starve us but it is better for you and a few more which we have marked to die…"

Manchester's Calico Printers Protest the Use of New Machinery

Source: *London Gazette*, 1786, p. 36, as reprinted in Douglas Hay, ed., *Albion's Fatal Tree* (New York: Pantheon Books, 1975), p. 318.

7. The technological trends described by the Manchester printers best reflect which of the following developments?
   (A) The power of labor unions in early modern Europe
   (B) Technological advances that evolved from the advances of the Scientific Revolution
   (C) The growth of industry in Britain and the development of the factory system
   (D) The spread of industrialism from the continent to Britain

8. The Manchester printers would have supported which of the following nineteenth-century movements?
   (A) Conservative movements
   (B) Nationalistic movements
   (C) Feminist groups
   (D) Labor unions

9. All of the following would have advanced the interests of British business owners and industrialists during the late-eighteenth and early-nineteenth centuries EXCEPT
   (A) the growth of the cottage industry of producing textiles
   (B) abundant coal and iron ore resources
   (C) parliamentary policies that favored industrialization
   (D) an able supply of laborers

Questions 10–11 refer to the passage below.

"Another heavy discouragement to the industry of women is the inequality of the reward of their labor, compared with that of men; an injustice which pervades every species of employment performed by both sexes. In employments which depend on bodily strength, the distinction is just; for it cannot be pretended that the generality of women can earn as much as men…but it is a subject of great regret, that this inequality should prevail even where an equal share of skill and application is exerted. Male stay-makers, mantua-makers, and hair-dressers, are better paid than female artists of the same professions; but surely it will never be urged as an apology for this disproportion, that women are not as capable of making stays, gowns, dressing hair, and similar arts, as men…. Besides these employments which are commonly performed by women, and those already shown to be suitable for such persons as are above the condition of hard labor, there are some professions and trades customarily in the hands of men, which might be conveniently exercised by either sex. Watchmaking requiring more ingenuity than strength, seems peculiarly adapted to women…. Pastry and confectionery appear particularly consonant to the habits of women, though generally performed by men; perhaps the heat of the ovens, and the strength requisite to fill and empty them, may render male assistants necessary; but certain women are most eligible to mix up the ingredients, and prepare the various kinds of cakes for baking…"

Priscilla Wakefield, *Reflections on the Present Condition of the Female Sex, 1798*

Source: Priscilla Wakefield, *Reflections on the Present Condition of the Female Sex* (1798) (London, 1817), pp. 125–127, as quoted in Bridget Hill, ed., *Eighteenth-Century Women: An Anthology* (London: George Allen & Unwin, 1984), pp. 227–228.

10. In the context of her own society, Wakefield's ideas about women's work would have been considered
    (A) reactionary
    (B) typical
    (C) progressive
    (D) militant

11. Which of the following would have most disagreed with Wakefield's ideas about women's work?
    (A) Mary Wollstonecraft
    (B) Jean Jacques Rousseau
    (C) John Stuart Mill
    (D) Marquis de Condorcet

Questions 12–15 refer to the images below.

Image 1

Thomas Gainesborough, Mr. and Mrs. Andrews, c. 1750

Source: National Gallery, London/Art Resource, NY

Image 2

Louis and Antoine Le Nain, Peasant Family, c. 1650

Source: Kimbell Art Museum, Fort Worth, Texas / Art Resource, NY

12. The activities depicted in the images are best explained by which of the following?
    (A) Societal expectations based upon class and social status continued to exist through the outbreak of the French Revolution.
    (B) Both aristocratic and peasant families could afford to hire professional artists.
    (C) Aristocratic families were responsible for hunting food while peasant families were responsible for farming.
    (D) Compulsory education in western Europe affected rural lifestyle.

13. Image 1 could be used as evidence to support which of the following legislation in Britain?
    (A) The Ten Hours Act
    (B) The Gin Act
    (C) The Reform Acts
    (D) The Game Laws

14. Image 1 best reflects which of the following changes in Britain?
    (A) The Enclosure Movement
    (B) The Agricultural Revolution
    (C) The Open Field Method
    (D) A new system of crop rotation

15. Which of the following developments in eighteenth-century art history is shown in Image 1?
    (A) Romanticism focused on nature and emotion
    (B) Realism focused on everyday life
    (C) Eighteenth century art often reflected the values of Enlightenment ideals
    (D) Eighteenth century art often reflected the values of aristocratic society

Short-Answer Question

Answer a, b, and c:

1. a) Describe how one technological factor in the eighteenth century contributed to the Agricultural Revolution in Great Britain.
    b) Describe how one political factor in the eighteenth century contributed to the Agricultural Revolution in Great Britain.
    c) Explain how the Agricultural Revolution changed Great Britain's economy during the period 1750–1815.

Long-Essay Question

Evaluate the extent to which the Consumer Revolution changed family and private life during the period 1700–1815.

Multiple-Choice Questions

1. C (KC: 2.2.I.A; LO: Unit 3 C) One of the many reasons that the European economy was transformed in the seventeenth and eighteenth centuries was the transition from mercantilist economic practices to capitalist economic practices. Consequently, traditional restrictions on commerce were lifted and economic prosperity ensued.

2. D (KC: 2.3.II.A; LO: Unit 4 D) The *philosophes* often gathered at private homes (salons) to discuss many of the political and social ideas that were part of the Enlightenment. Many of the salons were hosted by women and both genders freely mixed.

3. B (KC: 2.4.II; LO: Unit 4 F) Shops such as the one in the image were the product of the Commercial Revolution of the 1700s, in which consumer goods were produced on a much larger scale than before.

4. B (KC: 3.1.I; LO: Unit 6 A, B) The Commercial Revolution led to an increased demand for goods that helped to spark the Industrial Revolution. An important factor was the mechanization of the textile industry.

5. A (KC: 2.2.I.C; LO: Unit 3 C) Another economic development that occurred during the same time as the trend shown in the image was the "cottage industry" or putting out system. This also increased the demand for goods, as both peasant families and middle-class entrepreneurs had extra income to spend.

6. D (KC: 1.4.I.A, 2.2.I.D; LO: Unit 1 M, Unit 3 C) There was an increase in the number of businesses and shops, such as the one in the image, that were made possible by changes in banking and financial practices. This made it easier for entrepreneurs to engage in merchant activity.

7. C (KC: 3.1.III.A; LO: Unit 6 C) The increasing use of machinery would contribute to the growth of industry and the advancement of the factory system.

8. D (KC: 3.3.III.B; LO: Unit 6 I) It is very likely that the Manchester printers would have later supported labor unions because unions generally promoted reforms that would help the working class.

9. A (KC: 3.1.I; LO: Unit 6 K) An abundance of natural resources including coal and iron ore, a business minded Parliament that promoted economic development, as well as an able supply of laborers due to Enclosure movements and the Agricultural Revolution, all contributed to the Industrial Revolution in Great Britain.

10. C (KC: 2.3.I.C; LO: Unit 4 C) At this time, women had begun to work in new mechanized industries, as well as filling more traditional roles alongside their husbands. Her demands were, therefore, ahead of their time, but they would not have been considered militant.

11. B (KC: 2.3.I.C; LO: Unit 4 C) Wakefield's assertions regarding women in the workplace would have been most opposed by Jean-Jacques Rousseau, who believed in the idea of separate spheres for women and men. The other three thinkers disagreed with Rousseau's beliefs.

12. A (KC: 1.4.I.C; LO: Unit 2 E) The images essentially show the hierarchy that existed and the social and cultural customs of the two different classes.

13. D (KC: 1.4.I.C; LO: Unit 2 E) The first image could be used as evidence to support the English Game Laws which gave landholders exclusive hunting rights.

14. A (KC: 2.4.I; LO: Unit 4 E) The Enclosure movement could also be reflected in the first image. In the eighteenth century, English landlords enclosed their estates in order to increase agricultural production, often disrupting traditional communities and forcing small farmers off of the land. The image shows the wheat that the landowner would be selling on the market. The landowners were members of Parliament and often enacted legislation such as the Enclosure Laws that would benefit themselves.

15. D (KC: 2.3.V.B; LO: Unit 4 F The painting can be used as evidence of eighteenth-century art reflecting the values of commercial society including gender roles and economics (note the wheat).

Short-Answer Question
(KC: 2.4.I.A; LO: Unit 4 E)

Possible responses to part a) include:
- Enclosure of common lands
- Crop-rotation
- Selective breeding of livestock
- Drainage of swamps
- Jethro Tull's seed drill

Possible responses to part b) include:
- Wealthy landowners such as the country gentry exercised significant influence on Parliament to pass enclosure laws.
- The Corn Laws enriched agricultural landowners while adversely affecting the majority of the English population.
- Game Laws protected flora and fauna of landowners from use by the peasantry.

Possible responses to part c) include:
- Commercialization of agriculture
- Enclosure laws that drove peasants off the common lands
- Rise of cottage industries as peasants looked for new ways of economic survival
- Increase of population that created a work force for the Industrial Revolution
- Entrepreneurs, frustrated with inconsistencies of the cottage industry, who developed factories to better control production

Long-Essay Question
(KC: 2.2.II.C/D; LO: Unit 3 C)

Evaluate the extent to which the Consumer Revolution changed family and private life during the period 1700–1815.

Possible changes might include:
- Improved health and life expectancy due to increased availability of various foods
- Increased access to cheaper clothing such as cotton underwear for the masses
- Increased demand for goods leading to an increase of the cottage industry where families often worked together
- Gradually decreasing child mortality leading to closer relations between parents and children

Possible continuities might include:
- Many western European peasants lived in abject poverty and did not share in the fruits of the Consumer Revolution.
- Peasants in eastern Europe had little access to consumer goods.

CHAPTER 8

The Transatlantic Economy, Trade Wars, and Colonial Rebellion

PERIODS OF EUROPEAN OVERSEAS EMPIRES

- First era: the period of exploration, conquest, settlement. Completed by 1600.
- Second era: the era of mercantile empires. Marked by increased contact with Africa, and the development and peak of the slave trade. This period saw the independence of Europe's American colonies.
- Third era: the period of increasing colonization in Africa and Asia.
- Fourth era: decolonization of the mid-twentieth century.

AP® FRAMEWORK
TOPIC # 2.6, 4.4; LO: UNIT 2 E, UNIT 4 E
KC:
2.2.II.A European states followed mercantilist policies by drawing resources from colonies in the New World and elsewhere.
2.2.II.B The transatlantic slave-labor system expanded in the 17th and 18th centuries as demand for New World products increased.

MERCANTILE EMPIRES

- The Treaty of Utrecht (1713) established the boundaries of empire until the 1750s.
- **Mercantilism** was the economic theory behind the system of acquiring colonies, and it involved governments heavily regulating trade and commerce in hope of increasing national wealth. During this period, the economic well-being of the home country was the primary concern; colonies provided markets and resources for the industries of the home country, which would help administer and defend the colony. Home countries and colonies had navigation laws, tariffs, and bounties to encourage production and to prohibit trade with neighboring countries or colonies controlled by other empires.
- The West Indies and the Indian subcontinent were great sources of rivalry among European powers because they had resources that appealed to many of these powers.

AP® FRAMEWORK
TOPIC # 3.4, 3.6, 5.3; LO: UNIT 3 C, E, UNIT 5 C
KC:
2.2.II.A European states followed mercantilist policies by drawing resources from colonies in the New World and elsewhere.

2.1.III.C Louis XIV's nearly continuous wars, pursuing both dynastic and state interests, provoked a coalition of European powers opposing him.

2.1.III.D Rivalry between Britain and France resulted in world wars fought both in Europe and in the colonies, with Britain supplanting France as the greatest European power.

THE SPANISH COLONIAL SYSTEM

- Spanish control of the Americas was subject to few limitations. Colonial political structures existed to buoy Spanish commercial interests. Spain used the *flota* system to control supplies and bullion that went to and from its colonies. Trade outside the *flota* was forbidden.

- The French Bourbons replaced the Spanish Habsburgs, leading to some increased royal involvement and administrative changes in the Spanish colonies. Charles III (r. 1759–1788) abolished some of the Spanish monopolies, opened more South American ports to trade and commerce, and attempted to increase tax collection and end corruption. He introduced the *intendant* into the Spanish empire. These reforms stimulated the Spanish economy and brought the empire more fully under Spanish control.

AP® FRAMEWORK
TOPIC # 1.7, 3.4; LO: UNIT 1 I, UNIT 3 C
KC:
1.3.III.B The Spanish established colonies across the Americas, the Caribbean, and the Pacific, which made Spain a dominant state in Europe in the 16th century.

2.2.II.A European states followed mercantilist policies by drawing resources from colonies in the New World and elsewhere.

1.3 Europeans explored and settled overseas territories, encountering and interacting with indigenous populations.
   III. Europeans established overseas empires and trade networks through coercion and negotiation.
2.2 The expansion of European commerce accelerated the growth of a worldwide economic network.
   II. The European-dominated worldwide economic network contributed to the agricultural, industrial, and consumer revolutions in Europe.

BLACK AFRICAN SLAVERY, THE PLANTATION SYSTEM, AND THE ATLANTIC ECONOMY

- Slave labor became a fundamental aspect of empire building. Labor shortages led Europeans settling in the New World to exploit Native Americans; however, disease killed many of them, so Europeans turned to the labor of imported African slaves. Slave markets in central West Africa, Sierra Leone, the Gold Coast, and other areas were sources for slaves.
- Slavery exploded in Brazil and in the Caribbean, thanks to the cultivation of sugar on plantations and the growing consumer demand for the product. High rates of mortality led to the constant need for a fresh influx of slaves.

AP® FRAMEWORK
TOPIC # 1.9, 3.4; LO: UNIT 1 L, UNIT 3 C
KC:

1.3.IV.C Europeans expanded the African slave trade in response to the establishment of a plantation economy in the Americas and demographic catastrophes among indigenous peoples.
2.2.II.B The transatlantic slave-labor system expanded in the 17th and 18th centuries as demand for New World products increased.

MID–EIGHTEENTH-CENTURY WARS

- Spain and England disagreed over British rights to the Spanish market in the West Indies, and during a 1731 coastal patrol of an English vessel, Spaniards cut off the ear of an English captain named Robert Jenkins. The War of Jenkins's Ear began in 1739, when Robert Walpole responded to pressure to stop Spanish intervention in trade.
- In December of 1740, Frederick II of Prussia seized Silesia, an Austrian province belonging to the Habsburg Dynasty. Cardinal Fleury, minister to Louis XV, supported the Prussian aggression against Austria. This move threatened Britain, which wanted the Low Countries to remain in possession of Austria rather than France. In 1744, the British-French conflict expanded beyond Europe as France supported Spain against Britain in the Americas. The War of the Austrian Succession ended in a stalemate in 1748.
- The Diplomatic Revolution of 1756 involved a series of alliances that set the stage for a larger European conflict. Britain and Prussia signed the Convention of Westminster, an alliance aimed at preventing the entry of foreign troops into Germany. Britain aligned itself with the enemy of its former ally, Austria. Austria and France allied, with the goal of crushing Prussia.
- The Seven Years' War (1756–1763) began with Frederick II's invasion of Saxony, which led to France, Austria, Sweden, Russia, and smaller German states agreeing to destroy Prussia. Prussia and Russia made peace, and Frederick II held off Austria and France. William Pitt used the continental wars to leverage England's position in America. Pitt used an unprecedented number of soldiers in the American colonies, India, and Canada to dominate against the French in every theater of battle and to gain English possessions.
- In the Treaty of Paris of 1763, Britain received all of Canada, the Ohio River Valley, and the eastern half of the Mississippi River Valley. Britain returned Pondicherry and Chandernagore in India and the West Indian islands of Guadeloupe and Martinique to the French. Great Britain emerged a world power as a result of its international efforts. A quest to pay the war debt had consequences in the British colonies of North America.

AP® FRAMEWORK
TOPIC # 4.6, 5.3; LO: UNIT 4 H, UNIT 5 C
KC:
2.1.III.A As a result of the Holy Roman Empire's limitation of sovereignty in the Peace of Westphalia, Prussia rose to power, and the Habsburgs, centered in Austria, shifted their empire eastward.
2.1.III.D Rivalry between Britain and France resulted in world wars fought both in Europe and in the colonies, with Britain supplanting France as the greatest European power.

THE AMERICAN REVOLUTION AND EUROPE

- The revolt of British colonies in North America was a reaction to perceived unfairness in revenue collection. The British wanted the colonies to pay for their protection and administration. The 1764 Sugar Act and the Stamp Act of 1765 were rejected as unfair by the American colonists, who argued that they were not represented in Parliament.
- In March 1770, the Boston Massacre occurred, further inflaming colonists against Britain. The famous Boston Tea Party episode of 1773 escalated the conflict. By April 1775, battles between colonials and British regiments had begun at Lexington and Concord.
- A colonial army and navy were established, and in 1776, the Continental Congress opened American ports to trade with all nations. On July 4, 1776, the Continental Congress adopted the Declaration of American Independence. The American Revolutionary War continued until 1781, when George Washington defeated Lord Cornwallis at Yorktown.
- France and Spain came to the aid of the colonies. The 1783 Treaty of Paris concluded the conflict, and the American colonies established their independence. The American Revolution had a broad impact on Continental views of government and established the idea of a government based on popular consent rather than on divine law or monarchy.

AP® FRAMEWORK
TOPIC # 5.3, 5.4; LO: UNIT 5 C, 5 D
KC:
2.1.III.D Rivalry between Britain and France resulted in world wars fought both in Europe and in the colonies, with Britain supplanting France as the greatest European power.
2.1.IV.A The French Revolution resulted from a combination of long-term social and political causes, as well as Enlightenment ideas, exacerbated by short-term fiscal and economic crises.

Multiple-Choice Questions

Questions 1–3 refer to the image below.

Return of Columbus From the New World, painted sometime between 1850–1900.

Source: Library of Congress Prints and Photographs Division

1. Which of the following was a result of the event portrayed in the image?
   (A) Portugal became a major trading power in Europe during the sixteenth century.
   (B) The Portuguese established Mexico as their most important colony in the Americas.
   (C) Spain became the leading state in Europe during the sixteenth century.
   (D) The Spanish established colonies along the African coast.

2. The event portrayed in the image changed the European economy by
   (A) shifting the center of economic power from the Mediterranean states to the Atlantic seaboard states
   (B) leading to a steep drop in prices due to the import of massive amounts of gold and silver from the New World
   (C) the European states' abandonment of mercantilist policies
   (D) states eliminating protective tariffs and encouraging free trade policies

3. The event portrayed in the image had which of the following long-term effects?
   (A) The mass importation of African and Indian slaves to Europe accelerated.
   (B) Spain was able to unify the Iberian Peninsula under Ferdinand and Isabella.
   (C) Portugal ended the slave-trade in Brazil due to the influence of Enlightenment thinkers.
   (D) The Columbian Exchange occurred, an exchange of plants, animals, and diseases between the Old and New Worlds.

Questions 4–6 refer to the image below.

Pedro Cieza de León, Potosi, *the first image of the Peruvian silver mines of Potosi in Europe, 1553*

Source: INTERFOTO/Alamy Stock Photo

4. The importation of precious metals from mining areas such as the one portrayed in the image had which of the following effects on the European economy?
   (A) The influx of precious metals into Europe led to the Commercial Revolution in the sixteenth century.
   (B) The influx of precious metals into Europe during the sixteenth century led to a period of sustained inflationary growth.
   (C) The influx of precious metals into Europe during the sixteenth century led to a more prosperous lifestyle for the majority of Europeans.
   (D) The influx of precious metals into Europe during the sixteenth century led to the beginnings of the cottage industry in western Europe.

118

5. Based on the image, we can infer that which of the following was an important motivation for the Spanish to create settlements in the Americas?
   (A) The growing population of Spain needed increasing amounts of food supplies imported from the Americas
   (B) The acquisition of sugar because of its importance to the European elite
   (C) Competition with Portugal, England, and France for colonial lands
   (D) The spread of Christianity to the indigenous peoples of the Americas

6. A historian could use the image as evidence to support which of the following?
   (A) The rise of capitalism
   (B) The influence of mercantilist ideas
   (C) The importance of warfare to subdue indigenous peoples
   (D) The influence of the triangular trade

Questions 7–8 refer to the map below.

The Slave Trade, 1400–1860

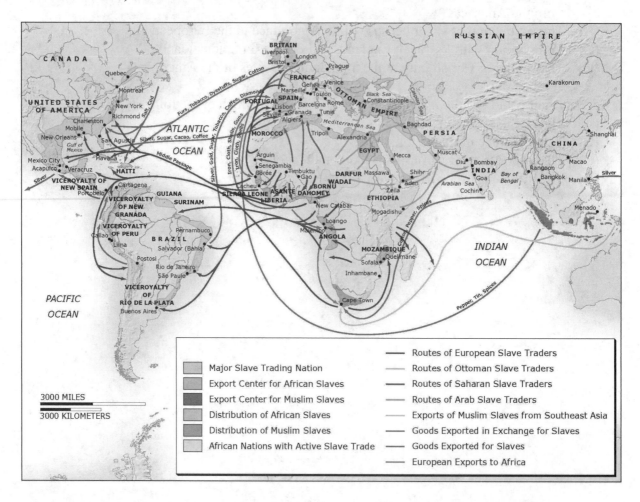

7. Which of the following contributed most to the trends displayed on the map regarding African slaves?
   (A) Deadly diseases such as smallpox that killed nearly 90% of native-American population
   (B) Social Darwinist theories advocated by Herbert Spencer
   (C) A need for labor in the New World as a result of Pope Paul III's condemnation of the *encomienda* system
   (D) Ferdinand and Isabella's *Reconquista* of Muslim lands in southern Spain

8. Which of the following is true regarding the slave-labor system in the Americas during the seventeenth and eighteenth centuries?
   (A) Increased demand in Europe for products from the Americas led to an expansion of the slave trade.
   (B) Reform movements developed that advocated returning African slaves to Africa.
   (C) The majority of slaves transported from Africa were brought to North America.
   (D) The slave trade declined due to a high birthrate among slaves already in the Americas.

Questions 9–12 refer to the passage below.

"In December 1740, only seven months after becoming king of Prussia, Frederick II (r. 1740–1786) opportunistically seized the Austrian province of Silesia in eastern Germany. The new Habsburg ruler, Maria Theresa (r. 1740–1780), had only occupied the throne herself for two months, was only twenty-three, and was a woman whose control of the dynasty's holdings had yet to be established. The invasion shattered the provisions of the Pragmatic Sanction and upset the continental balance of power. The young king of Prussia had treated the House of Habsburg simply as another German state rather than as the leading power in the region. Silesia was a valuable possession, and Frederick was determined to keep his ill-gotten prize"

Source: Donald Kagan, *The Western Heritage, 11th edition (*Boston: Pearson Education, 2016), p. 291

9. Which of the following seventeenth-century events precipitated the rivalry described in the passage?
   (A) The Peace of Augsburg gave the German princes independence from the Habsburg emperor.
   (B) Prussia's alliance with the French during the Thirty Years' War led to Austria's acquisition of Silesia.
   (C) The Peace of Westphalia limited the sovereignty of the Holy Roman Emperor, leading to the rise of Austria and Prussia.
   (D) Conflict arose from the Austro-Prussian alliance that took part in the partitions of Poland.

10. Which of the following best exemplified Habsburg military power during the seventeenth century?
    (A) The return of Catholicism to the northern German states
    (B) The defeat of France during the Thirty Years' War
    (C) The defeat of Sweden in the Great Northern War
    (D) The halting of Ottoman expansion at the Battle of Vienna

11. Which of the following best explains why Frederick II was able to successfully seize Silesia as described in the passage?
    (A) Military aid from Great Britain doubled the size of Prussia's army.
    (B) Frederick William I left his son, Frederick II, one of the largest armies in Europe.
    (C) Maria Theresa was unable to gain support from the non-German minorities in Austria.
    (D) Frederick II conscripted serfs to raise an army.

12. Which of the following was a result of the conflict described in the passage?
    (A) Prussia's alliance with Britain resulted in the disintegration of the Habsburg Empire.
    (B) Russia's withdrawal from the war resulted in a Prussian victory.
    (C) Austria regained Silesia and then conquered Galicia.
    (D) Britain, allied with Austria, fought Prussia's ally France in North America.

Questions 13–15 refer to the passage below.

"America would have flourished as much, and probably much more, had no European power taken any notice of her. The commerce by which she hath enriched herself are the necessaries of life, and will always have a market while eating is the custom of Europe....

But the injuries and disadvantages which we sustain by that connection, are without number; and our duty to mankind at large, as well as to ourselves, instruct us to renounce the alliance: because, any submission to, or dependence on, Great Britain, tends directly to involve this Continent in European wars and quarrels, and set us at variance with nations who would otherwise seek our friendship, and against whom we have neither anger nor complaint. As Europe is our market for trade, we ought to form no partial connection with any part of it.

But Britain is the parent country, say some. Then the more shame upon her conduct. Even brutes do not devour their young, nor savages make war upon their families...Europe, and not England, is the parent country of America. This new World hath been the asylum for the persecuted lovers of civil and religious liberty from every part of Europe. Hither have they fled, not from the tender embraces of the mother, but from the cruelty of the monster; and it is so far true of England, that the same tyranny which drove the first emigrants from home, pursues their descendants still."

Thomas Paine, *Common Sense,* 1776

Source: *The Political Writings of Thomas Paine*, New York 1830, Vol I, pp. 75–92. Reprinted in *The Annals of America, Vol 3, 1784–1796: Organizing the New Nation* (Chicago: Encyclopedia Britannica, Inc. 1976)

13. Which of the following countries would eventually support the colonies in the conflict with Britain, but not necessarily support the ideas of the passage?
    (A) Prussia
    (B) Italy
    (C) Sweden
    (D) France

14. Which of the following British policies would have contributed to the conflict Paine describes in the passage?
    (A) British enforcement of mercantilist policies regarding the colonies
    (B) British promotion of free trade throughout its empire
    (C) Britain's policy of salutary neglect regarding the colonies
    (D) The small percentage of British citizens who had the right to vote

15. Which of the following would be most supportive of Paine's ideas expressed in the passage?
    (A) Louis XIV
    (B) Thomas Hobbes
    (C) John Locke
    (D) Edmund Burke

Short-Answer Question

Use the image below to answer all parts of the question.

David Livingstone: *Narrative of an Expedition to the Zambesi and Its Tributaries, and of the Discovery of the Lakes Shirwa and Nyassa, 1858–1864.* **London: John Murray, 1865.**

Source: North Wind Picture Archives

Answer a, b, and c:
1. a) Describe one cause of the activities illustrated in the image.
   b) Briefly explain one demographic effect of the activities illustrated in the image.
   c) Briefly explain one economic effect of the activities illustrated in the image.

Long-Essay Question

Evaluate the extent to which commercial rivalries influenced European warfare during the eighteenth century prior to the French Revolution.

ANSWERS AND EXPLANATIONS: AP® PRACTICE TEST

Multiple-Choice Questions

1. C (KC: 1.3.III.B; LO: Unit 1 I) Columbus's first journey to the New World and subsequent visits led to Spanish colonization in the Americas. As a result of Spanish conquests, Spain acquired raw materials and was able to build a substantial military during the sixteenth century becoming Europe's dominant power.

2. A (KC: 1.3.IV.A; LO: Unit 1 J) During and after the conquest of the Americas by the European powers, there was a shift in economic power from the Mediterranean states to the Atlantic states because of their geography. Also contributing to this shift was the downfall of the Byzantine Empire in 1453 and the decline of the Italian city-states.

3. D (KC: 1.3.IV.B; LO: Unit 1 J) The meeting between the two worlds resulted in the Columbian Exchange, an exchange of plants, animals, and diseases that transformed both the economics and the ecology of the world.

4. B (KC: 1.4.II.B; LO: Unit 1 M) The influx of precious metals from the New World along with a population explosion contributed to the Price Revolution of the sixteenth century, a time of sustained inflation that greatly affected the European economy.

5. D (KC: 1.3.I.C; LO: Unit 1 H) The image features several prominent Christian churches scattered throughout the mining village showing the importance of the spread of Christianity.

6. B (KC: 1.3.I.B, 2.2.II.A; LO: Unit 1 H, Unit 3 C) An historian could use the image as evidence of the importance of mineral wealth from the Americas to Europe that gave rise to the mercantilism, an economic theory that encouraged the growth of colonies as well as the acquisition of bullion into state treasuries.

7. A (KC: 1.3.IV.C; LO: Unit 1 L) The development of plantation economies in the New World led to a demand for labor. However, indigenous populations did not have resistance to European diseases, resulting in the death of approximately 90% of the native population by 1600. Consequently, African slaves were imported to work in inhumane conditions in the Americas.

8. A (KC: 2.2.II.B; LO: Unit 3 C) As Europe experienced a Consumer Revolution in the seventeenth and eighteenth centuries, there was an increased demand for products such as sugar and coffee from the New World. This demand led to the expansion of the slave-labor system and the movement of approximately 12 million Africans to the New World.

9. C (KC: 2.1.III.A; LO: Unit 4 H) The defeat of the Habsburgs in the Thirty Years' War and the provisions of the Peace of Westphalia in 1648 led to the disintegration of the Holy Roman Empire and the creation of more than 300 independent German states. The Habsburgs then focused their attention on the eastern parts of their empire, including Austria, Hungary, and Bohemia.

10. D (KC: 2.1.III.B; LO: Unit 3 E) Habsburg defeat of the Ottoman Turks in 1683 at the Battle of Vienna maintained an Austrian presence in central Europe and halted the Ottomans' westward expansion.

11. B (KC: 2.1.III.A; LO: Unit 4 H) Frederick II's father, Frederick William I, built the Prussian army into the third or fourth largest army in Europe during his lifetime. Despite building up this large army, Frederick William I did not use it so when Frederick II became king, he inherited a state that some historians say existed for the military as well as a having well-funded military.

12. D (KC: 2.1.III.D; LO: Unit 5 C) Frederick II's invasion of Silesia initiated the War of the Austrian Succession. Britain allied with Austria, and France, along with Spain, allied with Prussia. Furthermore, the British and the French also fought the war in North America where it became known as King George's War.

13. D (KC: 2.1.III.D; LO: Unit 5 C) The competition with Great Britain ultimately drove France into the American Revolution fighting against the British. Although the French supported American independence, the absolute government of Louis XVI would not have supported Paine's beliefs regarding civil liberties.

14. A (KC: 2.2.II.A; LO: Unit 3 C) After the Seven Years' War, Britain went from a policy of salutary neglect regarding the 13 North American colonies to trying to enforce mercantilist policies regarding trade and taxes with the 13 colonies that seemed unfair to those in the colonies.

15. C (KC: 2.3.III.A; LO: Unit 4 D) John Locke's philosophy that states originate in the consent of those that are governed would seem to be most supportive of the American independence movement advocated by Paine in the passage.

Short-Answer Question
(KC: 1.3.IV, 1.3.IV.C, 2.2.II; LO: Unit 1 J, L, Unit 3 C)

Possible responses to part a) might include:
- The production of sugar for the Atlantic trade led to the demand for slave labor in the New World.
- The death of 90% of the American Indian population resulted in a shortage of labor in the New World for Europeans seeking to profit from sugar and mining of precious metals.
- The Commercial Revolution led to colonization of the New World and the growth of the Atlantic trade.

Possible responses to part b) might include:
- Millions of Africans were forcibly transported to the New World.
- Africa experienced a significant decline in its population.
- African slaves mixed with American Indians and whites, resulting in racial mixing and the emergence of a caste system in the New World.

Possible responses to part c) might include:
- European global empires emerged that incorporated the African slave trade and enriched merchants.
- Brazil became the largest sugar-producing colony in the New World.
- Other European countries established sugar colonies in the Caribbean.
- Slavery spread to North America beginning in the seventeenth century for the production of tobacco and indigo, and later, cotton in the eighteenth century.

Long-Essay Question

(KC: 2.1.III.D, 2.2.III; LO: Unit 5 C, J)

Evaluate the extent to which commercial rivalries influenced European warfare during the eighteenth century prior to the French Revolution.

Possible responses for larger extent include:
- Four world wars between England and France between 1689 and 1763 included battles in North America and India over resources: War of the League of Augsburg, War of the Spanish Succession, War of Austrian Succession, and the Seven Years' War.
- Spain lost control of the *asiento* to Britain as a result of the War of the Spanish Succession.
- The American Revolution led to Spain and the Netherlands joining the war on the American-French side to weaken Britain's colonial empire.

Possible responses for lesser extent include:
- Balance of power diplomacy led to numerous wars between Britain and France that were not sparked by colonial considerations.
- The War of the Spanish Succession was the result of dynastic considerations and fears of Bourbon domination of Spain.
- The War of Austrian Succession began due to Prussia's invasion of Austria, not commercial rivalries.
- The Seven Years' War began over issues of Austrian land conquered by Prussia in the previous war rather than commercial rivalries.

CHAPTER 9

The Age of Enlightenment: Eighteenth-Century Thought

The eighteenth-century sentiment that economic and political reforms were possible was a novel conviction that was fostered by people and ideas of the Enlightenment. The intellectuals, writers, and critics who championed this reform in the emerging print culture were known as philosophes. The philosophes were interested in greater freedoms and liberties, and they sought rational improvement on many levels of society.

FORMATIVE INFLUENCES ON THE ENLIGHTENMENT

- Isaac Newton's determining the role of gravitation in the relationship between objects enabled other Europeans to realize that much remained to be discovered. His use of empirical support for general laws became an important feature of Enlightenment thought.
- John Locke's view of psychology—that all humans begin life as a *tabula rasa,* or blank page—gave Enlightenment thinkers grounds for arguing that the human condition could be improved by modifying the surrounding social and political environment.
- Britain's domestic stability, religious toleration, freedom of the press, small army, unregulated domestic life, and the political sovereignty of Parliament all suggested to Enlightenment thinkers that absolutist monarchy might not be the best path.
- Louis XIV's heavy taxation, absolute monarchy, religious persecution, and large standing army were perceived by philosophes as obstacles to reform. Voltaire suggested reforms in his book, *Letters on the English,* that he believed could improve French life, modeling his theories on the English system. In *Candide* he attacked war and religious persecution.
- The emergence of a print culture during the Enlightenment helped spread the ideas of philosophes like Voltaire. The public became more literate during this era, a process that enabled these printed materials to be more influential in shifting public opinion.

AP® FRAMEWORK
TOPIC # 4.2, 4.3; LO: UNIT 4 B, C, D
KC:
1.1.IV.A New ideas and methods in astronomy led individuals, including Copernicus, Galileo, and Newton, to question the authority of the ancients and traditional knowledge, and to develop a heliocentric view of the cosmos.
2.3.I.A Intellectuals, including Voltaire and Diderot, began to apply the principles of the Scientific Revolution to society and human institutions.
2.3.I.B Locke and Rousseau developed new political models based on the concept of natural rights and the social contract.

2.3.III.A Political theories, including John Locke's, conceived of society as composed of individuals driven by self-interest and argued that the state originated in the consent of the governed (i.e., a social contract) rather than in divine right or tradition.

THE PHILOSOPHES

- Those thinkers who help to mold the Enlightenment are known as philosophes. Generally, they were independent scholar and writers, usually working towards reform.
- Philosophes depended on patrons, often royal. Sometimes there existed close personal and intellectual relations between philosophes and their patrons.

AP® FRAMEWORK
TOPIC # 4.3; LO: UNIT 4 C, D
KC:
2.3.I.A Intellectuals, including Voltaire and Diderot, began to apply the principles of the Scientific Revolution to society and human institutions.
2.3.I.B Locke and Rousseau developed new political models based on the concept of natural rights and the social contract.
2.3.II.A A variety of institutions, including salons, explored and disseminated Enlightenment culture.
2.3.III.A Political theories, including John Locke's, conceived of society as composed of individuals driven by self-interest and argued that the state originated in the consent of the governed (i.e., a social contract) rather than in divine right or tradition.

THE ENLIGHTENMENT AND RELIGION

- Many philosophes were critical of Christianity. Voltaire's famous slogan "Crush the Infamous Thing" summed up their general attitude. Philosophes felt that Christianity focused attention on the world to come to the detriment of the present condition. Philosophes also objected to the power structure of the old regime, which gave special rights to clergy.
- **Deism**, or the belief that religion and reason could be combined, was popular among some of the philosophes, who believed that God must be rational and that religion should be so as well. Deists believed that God existed and could be empirically justified in the study of nature.
- Toleration and appreciation of other religions grew in this period. Gotthold Lessing's *Nathan the Wise* is perhaps the best example, arguing for greater toleration of Judaism. This toleration was by no means universal, and Christian views and values remained dominant in Europe.
- In the same period, Jewish scholars such as Baruch Spinoza applied a similar critique of their own religion that Voltaire had applied to Christianity.

AP® FRAMEWORK
TOPIC # 4.3; LO: UNIT 4 C, D
KC:
2.3.IV.A Intellectuals, including Voltaire and Diderot, developed new philosophies of deism, skepticism, and atheism.
2.3.IV.B Religion was viewed increasingly as a matter of private rather than public concern.

THE ENLIGHTENMENT AND SOCIETY

- Assembled by Denis Diderot and Jean le Rond d'Alembert, the *Encyclopedia* was a major undertaking by Enlightenment thinkers. The book was the product of writing by more than 100 authors, and it survived many attempts at censorship. It included the most advanced ideas of the day, secularized learning, and was, in part, a plea for freedom of expression.
- The philosophes were concerned with the application of laws of reason to the social condition. The Italian philosophe, Cesare Beccaria (1738–1794), attacked torture and capital punishment in his work *On Crimes and Punishments*, and he used critical analysis to address the problem of making punishments just and effective.
- Many philosophes believed that economic policy could be reformed in a way that was consistent with the operation of natural laws. These reformers, known as physiocrats, believed that mercantilist policies hampered the expansion of trade. Their leaders included François Quesnay and Pierre Dupont de Nemours.
- The English economist Adam Smith believed that economic liberty was the foundation for a natural economic system, and he urged that the mercantilist system of England be abolished. Smith believed that individuals should be able to pursue their own economic interests, and he is widely credited as being the founder of *laissez-faire* economic thought and policy. Smith's four-stage theory of human social and economic development enabled Europeans to see themselves dwelling at the highest level of achievement, which served as a major justification for their economic and imperial domination of the world.

AP® FRAMEWORK
TOPIC # 4.3; LO: UNIT 4 C, D
KC:
2.3.I.A Intellectuals, including Voltaire and Diderot, began to apply the principles of the Scientific Revolution to society and human institutions.
2.3.III.B Mercantilist theory and practice were challenged by new economic ideas, including Adam Smith's, which espoused free trade and a free market.

POLITICAL THOUGHT OF THE PHILOSOPHES

- In his 1748 book, *Spirit of the Laws*, Baron de Montesquieu held up the British constitution as an example of the wisest model for regulating the power of government. A political conservative, Montesquieu championed the aristocracy as being an important part of improving the French political regime.
- In *The Social Contract* (1762), Jean-Jacques Rousseau envisioned a society in which each individual could maintain personal freedom while participating as a loyal member in a larger community. He saw human beings as enmeshed in social relationships, and he believed that loyalty to the community should be encouraged.

AP® FRAMEWORK
TOPIC # 4.3; LO: UNIT 4 C, D
KC:
2.3.I.A Intellectuals, including Voltaire and Diderot, began to apply the principles of the Scientific Revolution to society and human institutions.

2.3.I.B Locke and Rousseau developed new political models based on the concept of natural rights and the social contract.

2.3.III.A Political theories, including John Locke's, conceived of society as composed of individuals driven by self-interest and argued that the state originated in the consent of the governed (i.e., a social contract) rather than in divine right or tradition.

WOMEN IN THE THOUGHT AND PRACTICE OF THE ENLIGHTENMENT

- Women helped promote the careers of philosophes by giving them access to their social and political contacts and providing a forum for them to circulate their ideas. Louis XV's mistress, the marquise de Pompadour, helped the Encyclopedia overcome censorship efforts. Madame de Tencin promoted Montesquieu's Spirit of the Laws by purchasing it and circulating it among friends. The philosophes were by no means ardent feminists; Mary Wollstonecraft addressed their shortcomings and critiqued Rousseau in A Vindication of the Rights of Woman, in 1792.In his 1748 book, *Spirit of the Laws*, Baron de Montesquieu held up the British constitution as an example of the wisest model for regulating the power of government. A political conservative, Montesquieu championed the aristocracy as being an important part of improving the French political regime.

AP® FRAMEWORK
TOPIC # 4.3; LO: UNIT 4 C, D
KC:
2.3.I.C Despite the principles of equality espoused by the Enlightenment and the French Revolution, intellectuals such as Rousseau offered controversial arguments for the exclusion of women from political life.

2.3.II.A A variety of institutions, including salons, explored and disseminated Enlightenment culture.

ROCOCO AND NEOCLASSICAL STYLES IN EIGHTEENTH-CENTURY ART

- The **Rococo** style can be seen as a development and culmination of the Baroque style. It is marked by lavish decoration in architecture, and scenes of rural frivolity in painting.
- By contrast, the **Neoclassical** style was marked by greater restraint, drawing its inspiration from the classical Greek and Roman past and from Enlightenment thought. Painters tended to draw their subjects from Roman history.

AP® KEY CONCEPTS AP® FRAMEWORK
TOPIC # 4.5; LO: UNIT 4 F
KC:
2.3.V.B Eighteenth-century art and literature increasingly reflected the outlook and values of commercial and bourgeois society. Neoclassicism expressed new Enlightenment ideals of citizenship and political participation.

ENLIGHTENED ABSOLUTISM

- The phrase "enlightened absolutism" refers to the phenomenon (observed during the last third of the eighteenth century) of several European rulers' embrace of the reforms set out by the philosophes. Monarchs most closely associated with this phenomenon included Frederick II of Prussia, Joseph II of Austria, and Catherine II of Russia. These monarchs pushed for innovations that would increase their revenue.

AP® KEY CONCEPTS AP® FRAMEWORK
TOPIC # 4.6; LO: UNIT 4 G
KC:
2..1.I.C In the 18th century, a number of states in eastern and central Europe experimented with enlightened absolutism.
2.3.IV.C By 1800, most governments in western and central Europe had extended toleration to Christian minorities and, in some states, civil equality to Jews.

Multiple-Choice Questions

Questions 1–4 refer to the passage below.

"My goal is not to write for all sorts of social orders and all sorts of people; all ranks are not susceptible to the same kind of happiness. I write only for those who are called people of quality, that is to say, for those who are born with a fortune already made, more or less distinguished, more or less opulent, but such that they can maintain their station without being ashamed, and they are perhaps not the easiest to make happy....

Undeniably, the love of study is much less necessary to the happiness of men than it is to that of women. Men have infinite resources for their happiness that women lack. They have many means to attain glory.... But women are excluded, by definition, from every kind of glory, and when, by chance, one is born with a rather superior soul, only study remains to console her for all the exclusions and dependencies to which she finds herself condemned by her place in society."

Émilie du Châtelet, *Discourses on Happiness*, c. 1740s

Source: Emilie Du Châtelet, *Selected Philosophical and Scientific Writings*, edited by Judith Zinsser, translated by Isabelle Bour and Judith Zinsser (Chicago: University of Chicago Press, 2009), pp. 349–351, 357.

1. The ideas expressed in the passage reflect which of the following aspects of early modern Europe?
   (A) Continued debates about women's role in society
   (B) Enlightenment changes regarding social mobility
   (C) Enlightenment thinkers' support of female education
   (D) Changes to the system of patriarchy in family life

2. The ideas expressed in the passage would have found support from many Enlightenment thinkers because they believed that
   (A) women were the equals of men
   (B) learning and knowledge were important for the betterment of society
   (C) true knowledge was obtainable only through faith
   (D) education should be restricted only to the upper classes

3. Which of the following would have been least receptive to the activities suggested in the second paragraph of the passage?
   (A) Voltaire
   (B) Baron de Montesquieu
   (C) Marquis de Condorcet
   (D) Rousseau

4. The increasing number of writings with ideas similar to those expressed in the passage was most likely the result of which of the following?
   (A) Growing support for female suffrage
   (B) Increasing literacy rates
   (C) Universal elementary education
   (D) Enlightenment support for mass democracy

Questions 5–7 refer to the passage below.

"In the system of laws which has been established for the management of our American and West Indian colonies the interest of the home-consumer has been sacrificed to that of the producer…great empire has been established for the sole purpose of raising up a nation of customers who should be obliged to buy from the shops of our different producers, all the goods with which these could supply them. For the sake of that little enhancement of price which this monopoly might afford our producers, the home-consumers have been burdened with the whole expense of maintaining and defending that empire…in the two last wars, more than two hundred millions have been spent, and a new debt of more than a hundred and seventy millions has been contracted over and above all…It cannot be very difficult to determine who have been the contrivers of this whole…system; not the consumers… whose interest has been entirely neglected; but the producers, whose interest has been so carefully attended to; and among this latter class our merchants and manufacturers have been by far the principal architects.

The importation of gold and silver is not the principal much less the sole benefit which a nation derives from its foreign trade…By opening a more extensive market…it encourages them to improve its productive powers and to augment its annual produce to the utmost, and thereby to increase the real revenue and wealth of the society."

Adam Smith, *The Wealth of Nations*, 1776

Source: Adam Smith, *The Wealth of Nations*, (London, 1776), pp. 342, 346, 348–349, 424, 444–445.

5. Which of the following is Smith criticizing in the passage?
   (A) The transatlantic slave trade
   (B) The continued supremacy of the domestic system
   (C) The guild system
   (D) The mercantilist economy

6. Which of the following advocated economic ideas similar to Smith's?
   (A) Jean Baptiste Colbert
   (B) Sir Robert Walpole
   (C) François Quesnay
   (D) George III

7. The two wars that Smith refers to in the first paragraph of the passage were
   (A) King George's War and the Seven Years' War between Great Britain and France
   (B) wars between the United States and Great Britain during the American Revolution and the War of 1812
   (C) the War of the Spanish Succession and the War of Jenkins's Ear between Great Britain and Spain
   (D) warfare between Great Britain and the Netherlands over control of Indian trade routes

8. Smith's ideas regarding the economy reflects the emerging ideas of which of the following developments of this period?
   (A) Economic nationalism
   (B) Economic protectionism
   (C) Capitalism
   (D) Socialism

136

Questions 9–11 refer to the image below.

CAPTION: All mortals are equal; it is not birth but virtue that makes the difference.

Voltaire, *Mahomet* [play from which the caption is taken, 1736]

Source: Bridgeman-Giraudon/Art Resource, NY

9. The image provides evidence for which of the following features of the Enlightenment era?
   (A) Colonial encounters with non-European peoples encouraged the philosophes to support the ideas of European biological supremacy.
   (B) Colonial encounters with non-European peoples provoked debates among intellectuals over colonial acquisition and control.
   (C) Most Europeans continued to support the Atlantic slave trade during this era.
   (D) Europe began to trade with the Ottoman Empire after their defeat by the Austrians in 1683.

10. The image reflects which of the following about eighteenth-century art?
   (A) Eighteenth-century artists often created works that incorporated elements of mannerism.
   (B) Eighteenth-century artists often created works constructed on the realities of daily life.
   (C) Eighteenth-century artists often created works based on a utopian outlook for the future.
   (D) Eighteenth-century artists often created works that reflected the concerns of bourgeois society.

11. The image refutes which common European assumption regarding colonization of areas outside of Europe?
   (A) Colonization is beneficial because it provides raw materials, markets, and labor to the European countries.
   (B) Non-European individuals and societies are not as advanced as those from Europe.
   (C) Non-Europeans profit from European colonization because of the technology introduced by Europeans.
   (D) Non-Europeans benefit from European colonization because of the better educational system introduced by Europeans.

Questions 12–15 refer to the maps below

Map 1
Expansion of Russia, 1689–1796

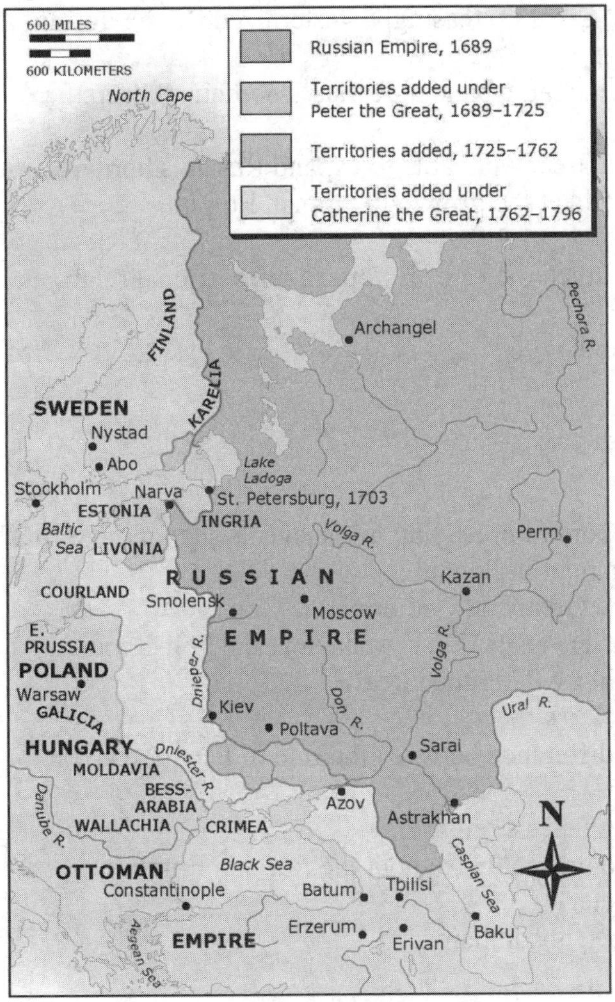

Map 2
Partitions of Poland, 1772, 1793, 1795

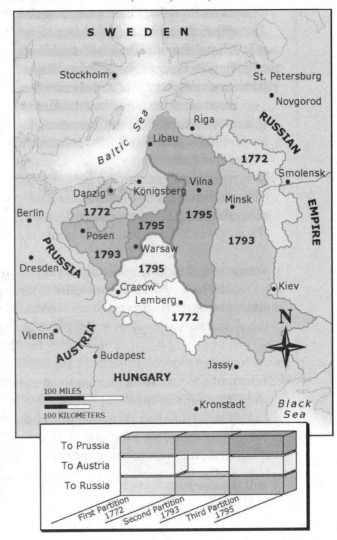

12. The geographic trends on Map 1 are best understood in the context of which of the following developments during the late-seventeenth and early-eighteenth centuries?
    (A) Both Peter the Great and Catherine the Great continued Ivan IV's policies of conquering land formerly controlled by the Mongols.
    (B) Both Peter the Great and Catherine the Great increasingly westernized Russia during their respective reigns.
    (C) Both Peter the Great and Catherine the Great expanded Russia's borders to keep the *boyars* content.
    (D) Both Peter the Great and Catherine the Great were able to expand Russia's borders because of an alliance with Austria aimed at the growing Ottoman Empire.

13. Both maps reflect which of the following characteristics of European international relations during this era?
    (A) Uninterrupted warfare between 1689 and 1796
    (B) The emergence of nationalism
    (C) Balance of power politics
    (D) Economic competition between nations

14. Which of the following factors was most important in leading to the events shown on Map 2?
    (A) The lack of a strong centralized government in Poland
    (B) The bitter rivalry between Frederick the Great and Catherine the Great
    (C) Austria's victory over Poland in the Seven Years' War weakening the Polish military
    (D) The strong Russian navy originally built by Peter the Great

15. Which of the following reflects the greatest difference between the rule of Peter the Great and Catherine the Great?
    (A) The *boyars* had increased power during Peter's reign.
    (B) Peter introduced the idea of religious tolerance throughout the Russian Empire.
    (C) Catherine was more militaristic than Peter.
    (D) Catherine experimented with enlightened absolutism.

Short-Answer Question

Use the passage below to answer all parts of the question.

"More than any other ruler of the age, Frederick the Great of Prussia embodied enlightened absolutism. Drawing upon the accomplishments of his Hohenzollern forebears, he forged a state that commanded the loyalty of the military, the Junker nobility, the Lutheran clergy, a growing bureaucracy recruited from an educated middle class, and university professors. Because the authority of the Prussian monarchy and the military were so strong and because the nobles, bureaucracy, clergy, and professors were so loyal, Frederick had the confidence to permit a more open discussion of Enlightenment ideas and to put into effect more Enlightenment values, such as extensive religious toleration, than any other continental ruler."

Donald Kagan, *The Western Heritage, 11th edition,* (Boston: Pearson Education, 2016)

Answer a, b, and c:
1. a. Explain how one piece of evidence <u>supports</u> Kagan's argument regarding how Frederick the Great's rule embodied enlightened absolutism.

   b. Explain how one piece of evidence <u>undermines</u> Kagan's argument regarding how Frederick the Great's rule embodied enlightened absolutism.

   c. Explain the policies of another monarch from during the period 1740 to 1800 that embodied enlightened absolutism.

Long-Essay Question
Evaluate the extent to which the ideas of the Enlightenment contributed to change in Europe during the period 1700–1815.

ANSWERS AND EXPLANATIONS: AP® PRACTICE TEST

Multiple-Choice Questions

1. A (KC: 2.3.I.C; LO: Unit 4 C) The passage suggests that during this time, women had few of the opportunities that were available to men. Women's role in society, politics, economic, and educational opportunity had been an ongoing intellectual debate since the Renaissance and Reformation.

2. B (KC: 2.3.I; LO: Unit 4 C, D) Enlightenment thinkers often challenged the existing social order and believed that education based on reason and scientific empiricism would create a better world.

3. D (KC: 2.3.I.C; LO: Unit 4 C) The second paragraph of the passage suggests that women could be superior. Rousseau argued that men and women should have separate spheres and distinct social roles and that the "whole education of women ought to relate to men."

4. B (KC: 2.3.II.B; LO: Unit 4 F) During the eighteenth century there were several new writings, pamphlets, treatises, newspapers and periodicals that were produced for an increasingly literate public. It is estimated that literacy rates reached 60% in England and 50% in France by the mid-eighteenth century.

5. D (KC: 2.3.III.B; LO: Unit 4 D) In *The Wealth of Nations*, Adam Smith criticizes mercantilist practices towards tariffs and colonies, among others. The passage describes how only the British producers are benefiting from the current economy; Smith advocates a policy of free trade and free markets.

6. C (KC: 2.3.III.B; LO: Unit 4 D) Adam Smith's ideas were expressed during the Enlightenment by a group known as the physiocrats. Physiocrats led by François Quesnay and Pierre Dupont de Nemours were also opposed to mercantilist economic practices.

7. A (KC: 2.1.III.D; LO: Unit 5 C) The two wars to which Smith refers in the first paragraph are the wars between Great Britain and France prior to the American Revolution. British-French rivalry led to the War of the Austrian Succession (also known as King George's War) and the Seven Years' War (also known as the French and Indian War). Both wars were fought in Europe, the Americas, and India.

8. C (KC: 2.3.III.B; LO: Unit 4 D) Smith's ideas regarding supply and demand, free trade, and free markets reflect the ideas of capitalism which continued to develop during this period.

9. B (KC: 3.5.III.B; LO: Unit 7 I) Although most of the Enlightened thinkers still favored European expansion and colonialism, partly to spread ideals of "western civilization," there were some thinkers of this time period that questioned expansion and enslavement, notably Denis Diderot and Immanuel Kant.

10. D (KC: 2.3.V.B; LO: Unit 4 F) Most philosophes and intellectuals of the era were from the upper classes, notably the bourgeoisie. As a result, artists and writers tended to create works based on concerns of the upper classes.

11. B (KC: 2.3.II.C; LO: Unit 4 F) Many Europeans favored colonialism because they believed European culture was superior to indigenous cultures in other parts of the world. This was true even among many who were educated in Enlightenment thought because of the Enlightenment's emphasis on progress and reason. The image shows non-Europeans as equals.

12. B (KC: 2.1.I.E; LO: Unit 3 G) Both Peter the Great and Catherine the Great are known for their policies of westernization in Russia. Peter mostly sought westernization as a means to build up his military, while Catherine introduced many elements of Enlightenment culture into Russia.

13. C (KC: 2.1.III; LO: Unit 3 E) Both maps reflect balance of power theory. During Peter's reign, Russia was most concerned about Swedish domination of the Baltic Sea, whereas during Catherine's reign, Russia was very concerned about the expansion of both Prussia and Austria into Eastern Europe.

14. A (KC: 2.1.I.D; LO: Unit 3 D) The Polish monarchy was elected by the Polish nobility and was therefore unable to build a strong absolutist state during this era. The king was also at the mercy of the nobles in order to raise an army and as a result, Poland ceased to exist after the three partitions by Russia, Prussia, and Austria (who only participated in two).

15. D (KC: 2.1.I; LO: Unit 3 H) See explanation for #12.

Short-Answer Question
(KC: 2.1.I.C; LO: Unit 4 G)

Possible responses to part a) include:
- Frederick saw himself as the "first servant of the state."
- Frederick ended serfdom on crown lands.
- Religious toleration for Christians increased (although not as much toleration for Jews).
- Education in schools and universities was promoted.
- Frederick codified and streamlined laws.
- He reduced censorship.
- He abolished capital punishment (but not in the army).
- He encouraged industrial and agricultural growth.

Possible responses to part b) include:
- Frederick spent the first 23 years of his rule at war, including attacking and conquering lands belonging to Austria (Silesia).
- Most of Frederick's reforms were intended to increase the power of the state.
- Freeing of serfs on crown lands resulted in these peasants being conscripted into the Prussian army.
- The social structure in Prussia remained heavily stratified.

Possible responses to part c) include:
- Reforms of Catherine the Great:
  - She imported Western culture into Russia.
  - She supported the rise of printing presses in Russia.
  - She supported the opening of some schools for noble girls.
  - She restricted the use of torture.
  - She allowed a degree of religious toleration.
- Reforms of Joseph II of Austria:
  - He abolished serfdom and feudal dues.
  - He allowed freedom of religion to Protestants and Jews.
  - He allowed freedom of the press to a certain degree.
  - He reformed the judicial system and sought to make it equal for all citizens.
  - He abolished torture and ended the death penalty.
  - He established state schools.

Long-Essay Question

(KC: 2.1.IV, 2.3.I, 2.3.II, 2.3.III, 2.3.IV; LO: Unit 4 C, D, Unit 5 J)

Evaluate the extent to which the ideas of the Enlightenment contributed to change in Europe during the period 1700–1815.

Possible responses for larger extent include:
- The Enightenement helped popularize the Scientific Revolution and promote a secular world view.
- Deism emerged among the upper classes as a naturalistic religion.
- The influence of the Catholic Church throughout western Europe continued to decline.
- John Locke's ideas profoundly influenced the development of classical liberalism.
- The Enlightenent led to Enlightened despotism in Prussia, Russia, and Austria (and France under Napoleon after 1799).
- The Enlightenement contributed to the French Revolution.
- Adam Smith's capitalist ideas influenced economic policy in Britain and France.
- In France, women played a leading role in the salon movement.
- Female writers such as Olympe de Gouge and May Wollstonecraft published works that were widely read.

Possible responses for smaller extent include:
- Most of society (except for the bourgeoisie and nobility) were not exposed much to Enlightenment ideas.
- Women saw few gains in rights.
- Warfare remained frequent and violent throughout the period.
- Countries such as Spain and Italy saw limited influence of Enlightenment philosophy.
- Absolutism remained entrenched in countries that embraced Enlightened despotism (except for France after 1789).

The French Revolution

THE CRISIS OF THE FRENCH MONARCHY

- The French monarchy emerged from the Seven Years' War defeated and in debt; support of the American Revolution further endangered its financial stability. Louis XV and Louis XVI were unable to solve taxation disputes with the *parlements*.
- Jacques Necker issued a report blaming the aristocratic government for France's financial troubles. In 1786, Charles Alexandre de Calonne proposed new taxes, like the gabelle on salt and a new tax on landowners, regardless of status. An Assembly of Notables met with Calonne and claimed they had no authority to consent to new taxes; only the Estates General had that right. In 1788, Louis XVI agreed to convene the Estates General in 1789.

AP® FRAMEWORK
TOPIC # 5.4; LO: UNIT 5 D
KC:
2.1.IV.A The French Revolution resulted from a combination of long-term social and political causes, as well as Enlightenment ideas, exacerbated by short-term fiscal and economic crises.

THE REVOLUTION OF 1789

- The Estates General consisted of the First Estate (the clergy), the Second Estate (the nobility), and the **Third Estate** (wealthy members of the professional middle class). The organization of the Estates General was a source of initial debate. After the calling of the Estates General, new conflicts between aristocrats and the bourgeoisie emerged.
- The Cahiers de Doléances were lists of grievances presented to the monarch. The Third Estate petitioned the king for equality of rights among the king's subjects. After a standoff, the Third Estate invited the clergy and nobles to join them in creating a new legislative body. On June 17, the body declared itself the National Assembly. Members pledged their loyalty in the Tennis Court Oath and renamed their group the National Constituent Assembly.
- On July 14, more than 800 Parisians stormed the Bastille in search of weapons for the citizen militia they had formed in response to the presence of royal troops in the city and their frustrations with Louis XVI. The crowd stormed the fortress, released prisoners, and killed troops as well as the governor.
- The "Great Fear" that swept the countryside was driven by peasants who felt that they were reclaiming what was rightfully theirs but what had been lost to aristocrats over time.
- In August of 1789, the Assembly set forth the Declaration of the Rights of Man and Citizen, a document that claimed all men were "born and remain free and equal in rights." Louis XVI was forced by a group of women to return from Versailles to Paris.

AP® FRAMEWORK
TOPIC # 5.4; LO: UNIT 5 D
KC:
2.1.IV.B The first, or liberal, phase of the French Revolution established a constitutional monarchy, increased popular participation, nationalized the Catholic Church, and abolished hereditary privileges.

THE RECONSTRUCTION OF FRANCE

- The National Constituent Assembly declared that only "active citizens"—men paying annual taxes equal to three days of local labor were allowed to vote for electors, who, in turn, voted for members of the legislature. Women could not vote or hold office. This law transferred power from aristocratic wealth to anyone with accumulated land or property.
- In local and judicial administration, eighty-three *départements* replaced ancient provinces.
- The National Constituent Assembly suppressed guilds, liberated the grain trade, and established the metric system.
- The Roman Catholic Church was reconstructed by the Assembly into a branch of the secular state by the issuance of the Civil Constitution of the Clergy.
- Disgruntled aristocrats known as émigrés left France and resettled in areas near the French border where they plotted counterrevolution.

AP® FRAMEWORK
TOPIC # 5.4; LO: UNIT 5 D
KC:
2.1.IV.B The first, or liberal, phase of the French Revolution established a constitutional monarchy, increased popular participation, nationalized the Catholic Church, and abolished hereditary privileges.
2.1.IV.E Women enthusiastically participated in the early phases of the revolution; however, while there were brief improvements in the legal status of women, citizenship in the republic was soon restricted to men.

THE END OF THE MONARCHY: A SECOND REVOLUTION

- A group of deputies from the Third Estate, called **Jacobins**, pressed for more radical reform. In the Legislative Assembly, a group of Jacobins known as Girondists ordered the émigrés to return or suffer loss of property and demanded that clergy who had refused to take the oath to support the Civil Constitution do so or lose their state pensions. Louis XVI vetoed both acts.
- In August of 1792, a Parisian crowd invaded the Tuileries Palace and forced Louis XVI and Marie Antoinette to take refuge in the Legislative Assembly. Louis effectively lost his power, which was now in the hands of the Paris Commune, a committee of representatives from wards of Paris. During the September Massacres, the Paris Commune murdered about 1,200 people in jails, many of whom were aristocrats or priests. Following these acts, the Convention, a new assembly, declared France a republic. In December of 1792, Louis XVI was executed; one month later, France was at war with England, Holland, Spain, and Prussia.

147

AP® Key Concepts AP® Framework
Topic # 5.4; LO: Unit 5 D
KC:
2.1.IV.C After the execution of Louis XVI, the radical Jacobin republic led by Robespierre responded to opposition at home and war abroad by instituting the Reign of Terror, fixing prices and wages, and pursuing a policy of de-Christianization.

EUROPE AT WAR WITH THE REVOLUTION

- Edmund Burke, a British statesman and Irish-born writer, condemned the Revolution for its extreme measures in *Reflections on the Revolution in France* (1790). Other European leaders, like William Pitt in England, and rulers in Prussia and Russia, discouraged popular uprisings.

AP® Framework
Topic # 5.4, 5.5; LO: Unit 5 D, E
KC:
2.1.IV.C After the execution of Louis XVI, the radical Jacobin republic led by Robespierre responded to opposition at home and war abroad by instituting the Reign of Terror, fixing prices and wages, and pursuing a policy of de-Christianization.
2.1.IV.G While many were inspired by the revolution's emphasis on equality and human rights, others condemned its violence and disregard for traditional authority.

THE REIGN OF TERROR

- War brought new challenges for the Republic of France. The revolutionary government established a series of committees to protect its new creation. The Committee of General Security and the Committee of Public Safety were created to carry out executive duties of the government. A *levée en masse,* or military conscription, for all males in the population was mobilized to defend the country. This citizen army led to the **Reign of Terror**, a period marked by quasi-judicial executions from autumn 1793 to mid-summer 1794. The Christian calendar, with its religious holidays, was replaced by a secular calendar, and other places of worship were "de-Christianized."
- Executions were increasingly arbitrary, with sans-culottes revolutionaries serving as victims as well as persecutors. Marie Antoinette and other members of the royal family were the first victims. Maximilien Robespierre, a powerful member of the Committee for Public Safety, who established the "Cult of the Supreme Being," a civic religion modeled after the views of Rousseau, had encouraged the execution of key republican political figures, including his Committee colleague Jacques Danton. Robespierre also became a victim of the terror he had helped create and was executed. The Reign of Terror claimed more than 25,000 victims.

AP® FRAMEWORK
TOPIC # 5.4; LO: UNIT 5 D
KC:
2.1.IV.C After the execution of Louis XVI, the radical Jacobin republic led by Robespierre responded to opposition at home and war abroad by instituting the Reign of Terror, fixing prices and wages, and pursuing a policy of de-Christianization.
2.1.IV.D Revolutionary armies, raised by mass conscription, sought to bring the changes initiated in France to the rest of Europe.
2.1.IV.E Women enthusiastically participated in the early phases of the revolution; however, while there were brief improvements in the legal status of women, citizenship in the republic was soon restricted to men.

THE THERMIDORIAN REACTION

- The **Thermidorian Reaction** carried out political reconstruction and abandoned the Constitution of 1793. In its place, the Convention issued the Constitution of the Year III, which provided for a legislature of two houses. The upper body, or Council of Elders, consisted of men over forty who were husbands or widowers. The lower Council of Five Hundred consisted of men of at least thirty years old who were either married or single. The executive body was a five-person Directory, chosen by the Elders from a list submitted by the Council of Five Hundred.

AP® FRAMEWORK
TOPIC # 5.4; LO: UNIT 5 D
KC:
2.1.IV.C After the execution of Louis XVI, the radical Jacobin republic led by Robespierre responded to opposition at home and war abroad by instituting the Reign of Terror, fixing prices and wages, and pursuing a policy of de-Christianization.

Multiple-Choice Questions

Questions 1–3 refer to the passage below.

Cahier
Third Estate of Versailles, 1789

Of the grievance, complaints, and remonstrance of the members of the third estate of the bailliage of Versailles.

1. The power of making laws resides in the King and the nation.
2. The nation being too numerous for a personal exercise of this right, has confided its trust to representatives freely chosen from all classes of citizens. These representatives constitute the national assembly.
3. Frenchmen should regard of laws of the Kingdom those alone which have been prepared by the national assembly and sanctioned by the King.
4. Succession in the male line and primogeniture are usages as ancient as the monarchy, and ought to be maintained and consecrated by solemn and irrevocable enactment.
5. The laws prepared by the Estates General and sanctioned by the King shall be binding upon all classes of citizens and upon all provinces of the Kingdom. They shall be registered literally and accurately in all courts of law. They shall be open for consultation at all seats of municipal and communal government; and shall be read at sermon time in all parishes.
6. That the nation may not be deprived of that portion of legislation which is its due, and that the affairs of the Kingdom may not suffer neglect and delay, the Estates General shall be convoked at least every two or three years.

A Cahiers de Doléances, 1789

Source: Cahiers de Doleances Versailles Merrick Whitcombe, ed. "Typical Cahiers of 1789" in Translations and Reprints From The Original Sources of European History (Philadelphia: Dept. of History, Univ. of Pennsylvania, 1898) vol. 4, no. 5.

1. Which of the following was most likely a cause of the content in the passage?
    (A) Recent fiscal and economic crises
    (B) Oppression by the Catholic Church
    (C) Game laws aimed at the peasantry
    (D) Disproportionate share of taxation paid by the aristocracy

2. The passage was most likely written just prior to the
   (A) Thermidorian Reaction
   (B) Directory
   (C) liberal phase of the Revolution
   (D) death of Louis XV

3. Which of the following most likely influenced the content in the passage?
   (A) The Great Awakening
   (B) The emergence of Methodism
   (C) The development of pietism
   (D) The Enlightenment

Questions 4–5 refer to the passage below.

"The National Assembly completely abolishes the feudal regime. It decrees that, among the rights and dues… all those originating in real or personal serfdom, personal servitude, and those which represent them, are abolished without indemnification; all other are declared redeemable, and that the price and mode of redemption shall be fixed by the National Assembly….

2. The exclusive right to maintain pigeon-houses and dove-cotes is abolished….
3. The exclusive right to hunt and to maintain unenclosed warrens is likewise abolished….
4. All manorial courts are suppressed without indemnification.
5. Tithes of every description and the dues which have been substituted for [them]… are abolished on condition, however, that some other method be devised to provide for the expenses of divine worship, the support of the officiating clergy, the relief of the poor, repairs and rebuilding of churches and parsonages, and for all establishments, seminaries, schools, academies, asylums, communities, and other institutions, for the maintenance of which they are actually devoted….
6. The sale of judicial and municipal offices shall be suppressed forthwith….
7. Pecuniary privileges, personal or real, in the payment of taxes are abolished forever…
8. All citizens, without distinction of birth, are eligible to any office or dignity, whether ecclesiastical, civil or military…."

French National Assembly, Decrees, August 4, 1789

Source: Frank Maloy Anderson, ed. And trans. *The Constitutions and Other Select Documents Illustrative of the History of France, 1789–1907, 2nd ed., rev. and enl.* (Minneapolis, MN: H.W. Wilson, 1908), pp. 11–13.

4. Which of the following groups experienced the biggest change in their social status as a result of the laws in the passage?
   (A) The working class
   (B) Peasants
   (C) Civil servants
   (D) Parish priests

5. Which of the following saw a significant decline in its influence as a result of the laws in the passage?
   (A) Bourgeoisie
   (B) *Sans culottes*
   (C) The nobility
   (D) The *Énrages*

"Remaining to this day under the oppression of the white colonists, we dare hope that we do not ask the National Assembly in vain for the rights, which it has declared, belong to every man.

In our just protests, if the troubles, the calumnies that you have witnessed until today under the legislation of white colonists, and finally, if the truths which we had the honor of presenting yesterday to the bar of the Assembly do not overcome the unjust pretensions of the white colonial legislators who want to [proceed] without our participation, we beg the Assembly not to jeopardize the little remaining liberty we have, that of being able to abandon the ground soaked with the blood of our brothers and of permitting us to flee the sharp knife of the laws they will prepare against us.

If the Assembly has decided to pass a law which lets our fate depend on twenty-nine whites [in the colonial Assembly], our decided enemies, we demand to add an amendment to the decree which would be rendered in this situation, that free men of color can emigrate with their fortunes so that they can be neither disturbed nor hindered by the whites.

Mr. President, this is the last recourse which remains for us to escape the vengeance of the white colonists who menace us for not having given up our claims to the rights which the National Assembly has declared belong to every man."

Julian Raymond, Petition to the French National Assembly, 1791

Source: Laura Mason and Tracey Rizzo, *The French Revolution: A Document Collection* (Boston: Houghton Mifflin Company, 1999), p. 109.

6. The author of the passage is most likely from which of the following?
    (A) The United States
    (B) Algeria
    (C) Brazil
    (D) Haiti

7. Which of the following would most likely support the content of the passage?
    (A) Louis XVI
    (B) Jean-Jacques Rousseau
    (C) Cardinal Richelieu
    (D) Jean-Baptiste Colbert

Questions 8–10 refer to the passage below.

"A government of the nature of that set up at our very door has never been hitherto seen, or ever imagined in Europe…. France, since her revolution, is under the sway of a sect, whose leaders have deliberately, at one stroke, demolished the whole body of that jurisprudence which France had pretty nearly in common with other civilized countries….

Its foundation is laid in regicide, in Jacobinism, and in atheism, and it has joined to those principles a body of systematic manners, which secures their operation….

Jacobinism is the revolt of the enterprising talents of a country against its property. When private men form themselves into associations for the purpose of destroying the pre-existing laws and institutions of their country; when they secure to themselves an army, by dividing amongst the people of no property the estates of the ancient and lawful proprietors, when a state recognizes those acts; when it does not make confiscations for crimes, but makes crimes for confiscations; when it has its principal strength, and all its resources, in such a violation of property…—I call this Jacobinism by establishment."

Edmund Burke, *Reflections on the Revolution in France,* 1790

Source: *The Works of the Right Honourable Edmund Burke* (London: Henry G. Bohn, 1856) 5, pp. 206–208.

8. Which of the following conclusions best reflects the content in the passage?
    (A) Burke prefers a republican form of government rather than a constitutional monarchy.
    (B) Burke believes the king of France should be executed.
    (C) Burke believes the French are foolishly abandoning traditional authority.
    (D) Burke believes Britain should adopt some French reforms.

9. Based on the content of the passage, which of the following groups does Burke most likely support?
    (A) The First Estate
    (B) The Second Estate
    (C) The Third Estate
    (D) The Fourth Estate

10. Which of the following would most likely disagree with the ideas expressed in the passage?
    (A) Marie Antoinette
    (B) Joseph de Maistre
    (C) The *Émigrés*
    (D) Maximilien Robespierre

Questions 11–13 refer to the passage below.

Rise! Yes, rise all! Arrest all enemies of tour revolution and all suspects. Exterminate pitilessly all conspirators unless we wishto be exterminated ourselves….

Let the departments,districts, municipalities, and all patriotic societies unite and agree to appeal to the Convention; to send a rain of petitions formally demanding the instant recall of all the unfaithful members who have failed in their duty in not desiring the tyrant's death, and particularly against those who have led astray so many of their colleagues. *Such delegates are traitors, royalists, or idiots.* The Republic condemns the friends of kings…

Let us all equally uniteto demand that the thunder of decrees of accusation be loosed against treacherous generals prevaricating ministers, functionaries, and on all faithless agents of the government. This is our best means of defence; but let us defeat the traitors and tyrants.

Here is the heart of the conspiracy: it is in Paris that our perfidious enemies wish to complete their crime. Paris, the cradle and bulwark of liberty, is, doubt it not, the place where they have sworn to bury the holy cause of humanity under the corpses of patriots."

Paris Jacobin Club Circular, 1793

Source: *Revolution from 1789 to 1906, Documents Selected and edited with Notes and Introduction by R.W Postgate* (Boston and New York: Houghton Mifflin Company 1921).

11. Which of the following was most likely a cause of the sentiments expressed in the passage?
    (A) Warfare against other European countries
    (B) Anger at the passage of the Civil Constitution of the Clergy
    (C) Anger concerning the execution of Louis XVI
    (D) A severe economic recession

12. All of the following events occurred as a result of the ideas expressed in the passage EXCEPT
    (A) de-Christianization
    (B) the Reign of Terror
    (C) passage of the *Declaration of the Rights of Man and Citizen*
    (D) mass conscription.

13. Which of the following was a consequence of the ideas expressed in the passage?
    (A) The reinstitution of guilds and labor unions
    (B) Increased rights for women by 1800
    (C) The overthrow of the Committee of Public Safety by members of the nobility
    (D) The fixing of prices and wages

Questions 14–15 refer to the image below.

The caption is: "To Versailles, to Versailles, October 5, 1789"

Source: Bridgeman-Giraudon/Art Resource, New York

14. Which of the following was a cause for the event shown in the image?
    (A) The marchers believed they were best suited to take over the French government.
    (B) The marchers were frustrated at the lack of legal rights they received from the National Assembly.
    (C) The marchers were inspired by the "September Massacres" and supported the creation of a Republic.
    (D) The marchers were frustrated by food shortages brought on by continued economic crises.

15. Which of the following occurred within a decade of the events shown in the image?
    (A) Women saw little to no participation in popular movements in the 1790s.
    (B) Women saw brief improvements in their legal status but were soon denied citizenship rights.
    (C) Women saw significant increases in suffrage and property rights.
    (D) Women oversaw the government's violent policies during the Reign of Terror.

Short-Answer Question

Answer a, b, and c:
a) Describe one way that Enlightenment philosophy influenced the French Revolution.
b) Describe one way in which class conflict influenced the French Revolution.
c) Explain one way in which the French Revolution changed French society.

Long-Essay Question

Evaluate the extent to which the French Revolution transformed France during the period 1789 to 1799.

ANSWERS AND EXPLANATIONS: AP® PRACTICE TEST

Multiple-Choice Questions

1. A (KC: 2.1.IV.A; LO: Unit 5 D) On the eve of the French Revolution, the government was on the verge of bankruptcy. Louis XVI sought revenue through increased taxes that the nobility refused to pay, even though French nobles paid far lower taxes than British nobles. The bourgeoisie resented its tax burden and the benefits and exemptions the nobility enjoyed.

2. C (KC: 2.1.IV.B; LO: Unit 5 D) Prior to the meeting of the Estates General in 1789, each of the three estates was asked to submit a list of grievances for discussion—*cahiers de doléances*. Frustrations among the middle class and the support of a few liberal nobles and clergymen led to the creation of the National Assembly in June 1789. This marks the beginning of the liberal phase of the Revolution.

3. D (KC: 2.1.IV.A; LO: Unit 5 D) The Enlightenment profoundly influenced the leaders of the French Revolution. John Locke argued that all men have natural rights that the government is duty-bound to protect. Voltaire criticized the intolerance of the Catholic Church and advocated for religious toleration. Rousseau wrote that good government should reflect the "general will" of the people by increasing democratic practices. And Montesquieu suggested that government should be organized into three separate branches, each of which checks the power of the other two.

4. B (KC: 2.1.IV.C; LO: Unit 5 D) Peasants revolted against their noble lords in the summer of 1789—a wave that came to be known as the "Great Fear." In response, the National Assembly abolished feudalism in August. As a result, peasants gained much land at the expense of the nobles and retained most of these lands in perpetuity. While other groups, such as the working class and women, saw some gains during the early years of the Revolution, many of the gains were wiped out during the Reign of Terror or the Directory.

5. C (KC: 2.1.IV.B; LO: Unit 5 D) The nobility and the monarchy were the two biggest casualties of the Revolution prior to 1793. Noble lands were taken over by peasants during the Great Fear and thousands of nobles fled the country in fear for their lives.

6. D (KC: 2.1.IV.F; LO: Unit 5 D) Certain Haitian leaders were inspired by the ideals of the French Revolution and demanded increased rights for free Haitians. Eventually, large-scale slave revolts in Haiti in the 1790s and early 1800s led to Haitian independence in 1804.

7. B (KC: 2.3.I.B; LO: Unit 4 C) As a French *philosophe* who championed Enlightenment ideals, Rousseau believed in natural rights for all men. He opposed slavery in the French empire.

8. C (KC: 2.1.IV.G; LO: Unit 5 E) Burke wrote the quintessential work on conservatism in the late-eighteenth century in which he criticized the French Revolution's attack on the nobility. Burke believed the natural progression of society over the centuries had led to the existing system where strong monarchies and a powerful nobility provided stability. The French Revolution, in his view, threatened to permanently overthrow the old system.

9. B (KC: 2.1.IV.A; LO: Unit 5 D) Since the Middle Ages, French society had been organized into three estates: the First Estate represented the Clergy, the Second Estate represented the Nobility, and the Third Estate represented the rest of the population.

10. D (KC: 2.1.IV.C; LO: Unit 5 D) As the most powerful Jacobin in France, Robespierre detested the hereditary privileges of the nobility and oversaw their arrest and execution in the thousands.

11. A (KC: 2.1.IV.C; LO: Unit 5 D) Fearing potential Austrian and Prussian invasions of France, the Legislative Assembly and National Convention waged war against those countries beginning in 1792. Britain joined the effort against France. War hysteria accelerated the radicalism of the Revolution leading to the 1792 "September Massacres," the removal of the king from power that same month, and the king and queen's execution in 1793.

12. C (KC: 2.1.IV.C; LO: Unit 5 D) The *Declaration of the Rights of Man and Citizen* was created a blueprint for a new constitution during the first year—or liberal phase—of the revolution. It called for the creation of a constitutional monarchy that protected the natural rights of the people. The other answer choices occurred during the Reign of Terror under Robespierre in 1793 and 1794.

13. D (KC: 2.1.IV.C; LO: Unit 5 D) During wartime, the Committee of Public Safety regulated the economy to a hitherto unprecedented degree in European history. Maximum prices were established to ensure that people could afford necessities such as bread. Wages were frozen to combat the high inflation that wracked the French economy. While these measures were Draconian, they did stabilize the economy to some extent.

14. D (KC: 2.1.IV.B; LO: Unit 5 D) Although the liberal phase of the Revolution had occurred earlier in 1789 and the king had been forced to accept a constitutional monarchy, bread shortages and other challenges continued to wrack the French economy. In October, urban women who were part of the *sans culottes* marched to Versailles demanding that the king remedy food shortages. The marchers forced the royal family to relocate to Paris and killed some of the royal family's guards.

15. B (KC: 2.1.IV.E; LO: Unit 5 E) While women enjoyed increased public participation during the early years of the French Revolution, they saw a decline in participation as the Revolution became more radical in 1793 with the creation of the Committee of Public Safety. They received few lasting rights during the 1790s and saw their public roles diminished further when Napoleon took control in 1799.

Short-Answer Question
(KC: 2.1.IV.A, 2.1.IV.B, 2.1.IV.C, 2.1.IV.G; LO: Unit 5 D, E)

Possible responses for a) include:
- Locke's views of natural rights influenced the *Declaration of the Rights of Man and Citizen*
- Voltaire's views on the Catholic Church and religious toleration inspired revolutionaries to nationalize the Church and eventually, de-Christianize the country.
- Rousseau's views of the "general will" led to the institution of elements of democracy to varying degrees during the period.

Possible responses for b) include:
- The middle class resented its lack of privileges and influence and took over the government through the National Assembly.
- The *sans culottes* drove the Revolution forward through the storming of the Bastille, the women's march of Versailles, and the September Massacres.
- Nobles were largely forced to flee France, opening the door to government by non-nobles.

Possible responses for c) include:
- Peasants took over lands from nobles during the Great Fear and largely retained those lands during and after the Revolution.
- France became a constitutional monarchy and later, a Republic.
- The government established *assignats* as currency and later fixed prices and wages.
- Women saw some gains during the liberal phase of the Revolution, although many of the gains would be reversed by 1799.

Long-Essay Question
(KC: 2.1.IV; LO: Unit 5 D, E)

Evaluate the extent to which the French Revolution transformed France during the period 1789 to 1799.

Possible examples of achieving revolutionary goals include:
- Creation of a constitutional monarchy during the liberal phase of the Revolution
- The abolition of feudalism
- The nationalization of the Catholic Church
- Increased suffrage for men
- Creation of a Republic

Possible examples of failure to achieve goals include:
- The excesses of the Reign of Terror
- The excesses of de-Christianization
- Economic instability

CHAPTER 11

The Age of Napoleon and the Triumph of Romanticism

THE RISE OF NAPOLEON BONAPARTE

- Napoleon Bonaparte (1769–1821) rose to power in the aftermath of the Thermidorian Reaction by defending the new regime against a rebellion on October 5, 1795.
- In November of 1799, Napoleon overthrew the Directory through a *coup d'état,* issued the Constitution of Year VIII, which effectively established him as ruler, and formed a new government: the Consulate.

AP® FRAMEWORK
TOPIC # 5.6; LO: UNIT 5 F
KC:
2.1.V.A As first consul and emperor, Napoleon undertook a number of enduring domestic reforms while often curtailing some rights and manipulating popular impulses behind a façade of representative institutions.

THE CONSULATE IN FRANCE (1799–1804)

- The **Consulate** was composed of three Consuls, but Napoleon retained all of the power as First Consul. His constitution was overwhelmingly approved in a plebiscite.
- Bonaparte quickly made peace with France's enemies and restored peace and order at home, requiring loyalty from those he employed from every political faction. He was also ruthless and efficient in suppressing opposition. Napoleon made peace with the Catholic Church in the Concordat of 1801. In 1802, a plebiscite raified Napoleon as consul for life, and Napoleon began the codification of French law by producing the Civil Code of 1804—also known as the Napo leonic Code.

AP® FRAMEWORK
TOPIC # 5.6; LO: UNIT 5 F
KC:
2.1.V.A As first consul and emperor, Napoleon undertook a number of enduring domestic reforms while often curtailing some rights and manipulating popular impulses behind a façade of representative institutions.

NAPOLEON'S EMPIRE (1804–1814)

- In 1804, Napoleon crowned himself Napoleon I. He proceeded to conquer much of Europe in a series of military campaigns that transformed the map of the continent.
- Citizen loyalty and a *levée en masse* gave Napoleon virtually limitless resources of soldiers to wage war. Napoleon sent an army to restore the rebellious colony of Haiti to French rule.
- William Pitt the Younger formed the Third Coalition, persuading Austria and Russia to move against French aggression in Germany. In 1805, the British defeated Napoleon's navy at the Battle of Trafalgar, which ended to Napoleon's plans to invade the British Isles.
- In his greatest victory, Napoleon defeated Austrian and Russian forces at Austerlitz in 1805. The subsequent treaty with Austria gave Napoleon major concessions and recognized him as king of Italy. In 1806, Napoleon organized the Confederation of the Rhine, enabling the dissolution of the Holy Roman Empire.

AP® FRAMEWORK
TOPIC # 5.6; LO: UNIT 5 F
KC:
2.1.V.A As first consul and emperor, Napoleon undertook a number of enduring domestic reforms while often curtailing some rights and manipulating popular impulses behind a façade of representative institutions.
2.1.V.B Napoleon's new military tactics allowed him to exert direct or indirect control over much of the European continent, spreading the ideals of the French Revolution across Europe.

EUROPEAN RESPONSE TO THE EMPIRE

- The Napoleonic Code was established in the territories that French forces had conquered, and Enlightenment attitudes of liberalism and nationalism spread to nations throughout Europe.
- When Napoleon deposed the Spanish Bourbons and put his brother on the throne, a rebellion arose, which began a guerilla war that was consummated when British and Spanish forces under the Duke of Wellington drove the French out.
- Napoleon resolved to invade Russia after Alexander I withdrew from the Continental System in 1812, which prohibited trade with Britain. Napoleon had superior manpower, but the Russians burned crops and villages, destroying all food and supplies as they retreated. Napoleon captured Moscow, but ordered his army to retreat; many of his soldiers perished during this ill-fated attempt at domination. Napoleon abdicated his throne in 1814 and was exiled to Elba, an island off the Italian coast.

AP® FRAMEWORK
TOPIC # 5.6; LO: UNIT 5 G
KC:
2.1.V.C Napoleon's expanding empire created nationalist responses throughout Europe.

THE CONGRESS OF VIENNA AND THE EUROPEAN SETTLEMENT

- The Congress of Vienna took more than a year to conclude, and England, Prussia, Russia, and Austria dominated the discussions. All the powers agreed that France should not be allowed to dominate Europe again. However, to pacify France, the leaders restored the French Bourbon monarchy and worked out a boundary settlement that was not overly punitive.
- Napoleon returned from exile and was restored to power for 100 days before the Duke of Wellington defeated him at the Battle of Waterloo. Thereafter, Napoleon lived on Saint Helena. The Quadruple Alliance among England, Austria, Prussia, and Russia was renewed. The purpose of the alliance was to serve as a coalition for peace and to maintain the balance of power, while suppressing revolutionary ideas of nationalism.

AP® FRAMEWORK
TOPIC # 5.7; LO: UNIT 5 H
KC:
2.1.V.D After the defeat of Napoleon by a coalition of European powers, the Congress of Vienna (1814–1815) attempted to restore the balance of power in Europe and contain the danger of revolutionary or nationalistic upheavals in the future.

THE ROMANTIC MOVEMENT

- **Romanticism** was a reaction against much of the thought of the Enlightenment. Romantic writers rejected the ideas of the philosophes and sought to interpret nature in terms of their experience with it and reaction to it, rather than through mechanical terms or categories.
- Romanticism elevated the role of the individual and the importance of individual cultures. A new spirit of nationalism developed across Europe, partly in reaction to the new importance placed on individual feeling and experience.

AP® FRAMEWORK
TOPIC # 5.8; LO: UNIT 5 I
KC:
2.3.VI.A Rousseau questioned the exclusive reliance on reason and emphasized the role of emotions in the moral improvement of self and society.
2.3.VI.B Romanticism emerged as a challenge to Enlightenment rationality.

THE ROMANTIC QUESTIONING OF THE SUPREMACY OF REASON

- Some of the intellectuals affiliated with the Romantic movement were influenced by the work of Jean-Jacques Rousseau. Rousseau's *Émile* focuses on the importance of letting children grow and learn by trial and error. This concept of human development appealed to Romantics who believed that people should grow in accord with their individual natures.
- Immanuel Kant's works of philosophy endorsed his belief in human freedom, immortality, and existence in God. Many Romantics believed his work refuted the rational focus of the Enlightenment, which negated the importance of imagination and feeling.

AP® Framework

Topic # 5.8, 7.8; LO: Unit 5 I, Unit 7 J
KC:2.3.VI.A Rousseau questioned the exclusive reliance on reason and emphasized the role of emotions in the moral improvement of self and society.

2.3.VI.B Romanticism emerged as a challenge to Enlightenment rationality.

3.6.I.A Romantic artists and composers broke from classical artistic forms to emphasize emotion, nature, individuality, intuition, the supernatural, and national histories in their works.

ROMANTIC LITERATURE

- Romantic authors wrote works that did not conform to classical rules and that made use of the imagination. This kind of literature was represented by Victor Hugo in France and Goethe and Schlegel in Germany. English Romantics tended to be absorbed by the idea of the imagination, how it was affected by nature, and the mystical elements of experience. William Blake, Samuel Taylor Coleridge, William Wordsworth, and Lord Byron were some of the most important English Romantics.

AP® Framework

Topic # 7.8; LO: Unit 7 J
3.6.I.B Romantic writers expressed similar themes while responding to the Industrial Revolution and to various political revolutions.

ROMANTIC ART

- As in literature, painters and architects were inspired by the culture of the Middle Ages. At the same time, the landscapes of John Constable and Caspar David Friedrich focused on natural forces.

AP® Framework

Topic # 7.8; LO: Unit 7 J
3.6.I.A Romantic artists and composers broke from classical artistic forms to emphasize emotion, nature, individuality, intuition, the supernatural, and national histories in their works.

RELIGION IN THE ROMANTIC PERIOD

- Many Romantics believed in the supremacy of the imagination for perceiving nature and the world, and they were drawn to the medieval Christianity and spiritual mysteries of all kinds, believing that religion and their beliefs were compatible. **Methodism**, a faith that stressed inward, heartfelt religion was founded by John Wesley in England.

AP® Framework

Topic # 5.8; LO: Unit 5 I
2.3.VI.C Consistent with the Romantic Movement, religious revival occurred in Europe and included notable movements such as Methodism, founded by John Wesley.

ROMANTIC VIEWS OF NATIONALISM AND HISTORY

- Nationalism and Romanticism were essentially distinct movements but with important mutual influences.
- In Germany and Italy, nationalism assisted the formation of new nations.
- In viewing other cultures, Christian Europeans veered between a fondness for tales of Crusader victories over Muslims and romanticized views of Muslim leaders.
- The French Egyptian campaign and translations of Persian classics led to a new appreciation of Middle Eastern culture, especially the ancient past.

AP® FRAMEWORK
TOPIC # 5.8; LO: UNIT 5 I
2.3.VI.D Revolution, war, and rebellion demonstrated the emotional power of mass politics and nationalism.

CHAPTER 11: AP® PRACTICE TEST

Multiple-Choice Questions

Questions 1–2 refer to the passage below.

"On my return to Paris, I found a division reigning amongst all the constituted authorities. There was no agreement but on this single point—that the constitution was half destroyed, and could by no means effect the salvation of our liberties. All the parties came to me... and demanded my support. I refused to be a man of any party. A council of elders invited me, and I answered to their call. [Their] plan demanded a calm and liberal examination, free from every influence and every fear. The council of elders resolved, in consequence, that the sittings of the legislative body should be removed to St. Cloud, and charged me with the disposition of the force necessary to secure its independence, I owed it, my fellow-citizens, to the soldiers who are perishing in our armies, and the national glory, acquired at the price of their blood, to accept of this command.. Frenchmen! you will recognize, without doubt, in this conduct, the zeal of a soldier of liberty, and of a citizen devoted to the republic. The ideas of preservation, protection, and freedom, immediately resumed their places on the dispersion of the faction who wished to oppress the councils, and who, in making themselves the most odious of men, never cease to be the most contemptible."

Napoleon Bonaparte, First Consul of France, 1799

Source: *The Annual Register, or, A View of the History, Politics, and Literature for the Year 1799* (London: Otridge & Sons, 1801), p. 253.

1. Which of the following conclusions best reflects the content of the passage?
   (A) Napoleon sought to create an absolute monarchy.
   (B) Napoleon disagreed with the liberal phase of the French Revolution.
   (C) Napoleon sought to defend the ideals of the French Revolution.
   (D) Napoleon sought to conquer Europe.

2. Which of the following is a result of the ideas expressed in the passage?
   (A) Napoleon further reduced the influence of the Catholic Church.
   (B) Napoleon returned to the nobles most of the lands they had lost during the Revolution.
   (C) Napoleon introduced a number of mercantilist principles.
   (D) Napoleon undertook a series of domestic reforms.

Questions 3–4 refer to the map below.

The Continental System, 1806–1810

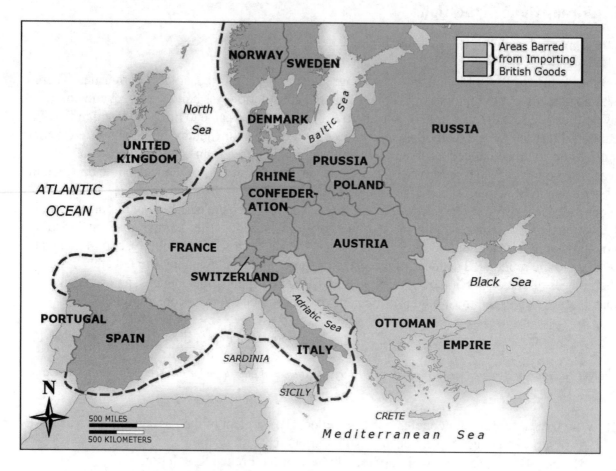

3. Which of the following conclusions best reflects the map?
   (A) Napoleon cultivated a trade relationship with Great Britain.
   (B) Napoleon asserted direct or indirect control of much of Europe.
   (C) Napoleon sought to enforce laissez faire principles to Europe's economic system.
   (D) Napoleon sought to create a balance of power on the Continent.

4. Which of the following was a result of the system illustrated in the map?
   (A) Nationalist responses against Napoleon's policies intensified.
   (B) The United States entered the war against France.
   (C) Napoleon created an alliance of European countries against Russia.
   (D) Other countries in Europe adopted the French *assignat* as part of their national economies.

Questions 5–6 refer to the passage below.

"Fired with enthusiasm, the people rose [against Napoleon], "with God for King and Fatherland." Among the Prussians there was only one voice, one feeling, one anger and one love, to save the Fatherland and to free Germany…. War, war, sounded the cry from the Carpathians to the Baltic, from the Niemen to the Elbe. War! cried the nobleman and landed proprietor who had become impoverished. War! that peasant who was driving his last horse to death…. War! the citizen who was growing exhausted from quartering soldiers and paying taxes. War! the widow who was sending her only son to the front. War! the young girl who, with tears of pride and pain, was leaving her betrothed…. Even young women, under all sorts of disguises, rushed to arms; all wanted to drill, arm themselves and fight and die for the Fatherland….

The most beautiful thing about all this holy zeal and happy confusion was… that the one great feeling for the Fatherland, its freedom and honor, swallowed all other feelings, caused all other considerations and relationships to be forgotten."

Ernst Moritz Arndt, German Writer, 1913

Source: Louis L., Snyder, trans., *Documents of German History*. Copyright © 1958 by Rutgers, the State University.

5. Which of these notable consequences of Napoleon's conquests is illustrated in the passage?
   (A) Enlightenment philosophy
   (B) Conservatism
   (C) Nationalism
   (D) Liberalism

6. Which of the following is a result of the ideas expressed in the passage?
   (A) Nationalist forces dominated the European political system up until 1850.
   (B) Prussia unified the German states shortly after the Napoleonic Wars.
   (C) Napoleon was defeated by a coalition of European powers.
   (D) Liberal monarchies emerged in Continental Europe due to Napoleon's influence.

169

Questions 7–8 refer to the image below.

CAPTION: "The Natives Revolt in Haiti"

RÉVOLTE DES NOIRS A SAINT-DOMINGUE.

Source: Pantheon/Superstock

7. Which of the following best explains the events in the image?
   (A) The decline of sugar prices on the world market
   (B) The spread of French revolutionary ideals
   (C) Haitian anger at the institution of the Lycée system
   (D) The impact of the Mexican Revolution on Caribbean countries

8. Which of the following would have supported the events in the image?
   (A) Toussaint L'Ouverture
   (B) Lazare Carnot
   (C) Duke of Enghien
   (D) Louis XVIII

Questions 9–11 refer to the passage below.

"The Congress has been criticized for failing to recognize and provide for the great forces that would stir the nineteenth century—nationalism and democracy. Such criticism is inappropriate. At the time nationalist pressures were relatively rare; the general desire was for peace. The settlement, like all such agreements, aimed to solve past ills, and in that it succeeded. The statesman at Vienna could not have anticipated future problems and understandably refused to yield to forces of which they disapproved and that they believed threatened international peace and stability. The measure of the success of the Vienna settlement is that it remained essentially intact for almost half a century and prevented general war for a hundred years."

Source: Donald Kagan, *The Western Heritage*, 11th edition (Boston: Pearson Education, 2016), p. 413.

9. Which of the following did the Congress of Vienna embrace?
   (A) Balance of power
   (B) Self-determination
   (C) Secularism
   (D) Realpolitik

10. Which of the following conclusions best reflects the passage?
    (A) The Congress of Vienna supported romantic ideals.
    (B) The Congress of Vienna supported classical liberalism.
    (C) The Congress of Vienna supported Enlightened despotism.
    (D) The Congress of Vienna supported conservatism.

11. Based on the passage, the members of the Congress of Vienna would most likely support which of the following?
    (A) Religion has no role in public policy.
    (B) Human nature is not perfectible.
    (C) War is inevitable.
    (D) Stratification of society by classes is undesirable.

Questions 12–15 refer to the passage below.

"If we do not admit that the empire of literature has been divided between paganism and Christianity, the north and the south, antiquity and the middle ages, chivalry and the institutions of Greece and Rome, we shall never succeed in forming a philosophical judgment of ancient and of modern taste. Some French critics have asserted that German literature is still in its infancy; this opinion is entirely false:... [German writers,] their character, their habits, and their modes of reasoning, have led them to prefer that which is founded on the recollection of chivalry, on the wonders of the middle ages, to that which has for its basis the mythology of the Greeks. Classic poetry, before it comes home to us, must pass through our recollections of paganism; that of the Germans is the Christian era of the fine arts; it employs our personal impressions to excite strong and vivid emotions... The new school maintains the same system in the fine arts as in literature, and affirms that Christianity is the source of all modern genius; the writers of this school also characterize, in a new manner, all that in Gothic architecture agrees with the religious sentiments of Christians.... It is only of consequence to us, in the present silence of genius, to lay aside the contempt which has been thrown on all the conceptions of the middle ages."

Madame de Staël, *Concerning Germany,* 1813

Source: From Madame de Staël, *Concerning Germany* (London: John Murray, 1813) as quoted in Howard E. Hugo, ed., The Romantic Reader (New York: Viking, 1957), pp. 64–66.

12. The passage most likely favors which of the following philosophies?
    (A) Humanism
    (B) Secularism
    (C) Romanticism
    (D) Neoclassicism

13. The passage most likely rejects which of the following?
    (A) Enlightenment philosophy
    (B) Medieval legends
    (C) Glorification of nature
    (D) Human emotion

14. Which of the following would the passage most likely embrace?
    (A) The Scientific Revolution
    (B) Nationalism
    (C) Positivism
    (D) Rationalism

15. The ideas in the passage later led to the philosophy's
    (A) embrace of the Congress of Vienna
    (B) support for Realism
    (C) embrace of Marxism
    (D) criticism of the Industrial Revolution

Short-Answer Question

Answer a, b, and c:

1. a) Describe one reason why Romantics rejected Enlightenment philosophy.
   b) Describe one way that Romantics embraced Enlightenment philosophy.
   c) Explain how Romanticism supported or influenced political movements in Europe.

Long-Essay Question

Evaluate the extent to which Napoleon embraced the ideals of the French Revolution.

ANSWERS AND EXPLANATIONS: AP® PRACTICE TEST

Multiple-Choice Questions

1. **C** (KC: 2.1.V.A; LO: Unit 5 F) In this statement, Napoleon presented himself as the savior of France and of the Revolution. He vowed to maintain republican principles.

2. **D** (KC: 2.1.V.A; LO: Unit 5 F) Napoleon saw himself as a "child" of the Enlightenment and he instituted a number of reforms including the Code Napoleon, the Bank of France, and the Concordat of 1801 with the Catholic Church.

3. **B** (KC: 2.1.V.B; LO: Unit 5 F) Napoleon sought to freeze his arch-enemy, Great Britain, out of Europe's trade network. He hoped that his Continental System would weaken Britain economically. The blockade on Britain only served to increase frustration among Prussia, Austria, and Russia regarding their limited trade opportunities with Europe's most powerful economy.

4. **A** (KC: 2.1.V.C; LO: Unit 5 G) The German States, Prussia, Austria, and Russia grew weary of Napoleon's heavy-handed approach in dominating the European economy. In Germany, nationalist resentment against French control led to increased resistance to Napoleon's policies. Austria, Prussia, and Russia eventually joined Great Britain in a coalition that defeated Napoleon in 1814–1815.

5. **C** (KC: 2.1.V.C; LO: Unit 5 G) See explanation to Question 4.

6. **C** (KC: 2.1.V.D; LO: Unit 5 H) See explanation of Question 4.

7. **B** (KC: 2.1.IV.F; LO: Unit 5 E) Haitian revolutionaries in the 1790s and early 1800s revolted against their French colonial masters. They were inspired by Enlightenment natural rights philosophy that permeated the liberal and radical phases of the French Revolution.

8. **A** (KC: 2.1.IV.F; LO: Unit 5 E) Toussaint L'Ouverture led the Haitian Revolution against the French. The large-scale slave rebellion prevailed in 1804 when Napoleon reluctantly granted Haiti its independence.

9. **A** (KC: 2.1.V.D; LO: Unit 5 H) The Congress of Vienna sought to prevent another major war from destabilizing Europe as the Napoleonic Wars had done. The four victors in the war—Britain, Prussia, Austria, and Russia—established a new international order that would check French aggression: the Concert of Europe.

10. **D** (KC: 3.3.I.C; LO: Unit 6 F) The Congress of Vienna, led by leaders such as Austrian minister Klemens von Metternich, sought to return to the society of the "Old Regime" governed by absolute rulers who placed nobles in preferred positions of influence. In their view, the French Revolution represented the mortal dangers of liberalism. They resolved to prevent such revolutions from occurring in the future by suppressing liberalism and nationalism throughout Europe.

11. **B** (KC: 3.3.I.C; LO: Unit 6 F) Enlightenment philosophers, most notably John Locke, believed human beings were essentially good in a state of nature. Through progress—largely the result of education—humans were capable of creating a more perfect society. On the other hand, the members of the Congress of Vienna embraced conservatism. They believed human beings were not capable of self-rule and they pointed to the excesses of the French Revolution as proof. The Congress of Vienna sought to restore "old regime" society where the noble class would dominate politically and socially while middle-class influence would be reduced.

12. C (2.3.VI.B, 3.6.I.A; LO: Unit 5 I, Unit 7 J) The passage promotes chivalry and faith, two important features of the Medieval period that Romantics embraced. While the Enlightenment favored the classical past—ancient Greece and Rome—the Romantics preferred the medieval past.

13. A (2.3.VI.B, 3.6.I.A; LO: Unit 5 I, Unit 7 J) While the Enlightenment emphasized science, rationalism, and deism, Romantics rejected the Enlightenment's deemphasis of human emotion and Christianity.

14. B (3.6.I.A; LO: Unit 7 J) Romanticism in Germany, France, and Italy supported nationalistic goals during the Revolutions of 1830 and 1848. Romantics also embraced aspects of liberalism such as constitutionalism, natural rights of the individual, and self-determination.

15. D (3.6.I.B; LO: Unit 7 J) Romantics glorified nature and its majesty and unpredictability. They lamented the impact of the Industrial Revolution on the natural landscape. Moreover, Romantics opposed the dehumanizing aspects of the Industrial Revolution on the working class.

Short-Answer Question
(KC: 2.3.VI.B, 3.3.I.F, 3.6.I; LO: Unit 5 I, Unit 7 B, J)

Possible responses for a) include:
- Romantics embraced faith (including Christianity)
- Romantics embraced human emotion while rejecting the rationalism of the Enlightenment
- Romantics glorified nature while the Enlightenment saw nature as something to be studied and enjoyed.

Possible responses for b) include:
- Romantics embraced the natural rights philosophy of the Enlightenment as well as its emphasis on constitutionalism and religious toleration.

Possible responses for c) include:
- Romantics supported Greece's successful war for independence against the Ottoman Empire.
- Romantics supported nationalist movements in 1830 and 1848, such as the Italian, Hungarian, and Polish attempts at independence.
- Romantics opposed conservative authoritarianism and supported liberal revolutions such as the overthrow of Charles X in France in 1830 and the overthrow of Louis-Philippe in 1848.

Long-Essay Question
(KC: 2.1.V.A; LO: Unit 5 F)

Evaluate the extent to which Napoleon embraced the ideals of the French Revolution.

Possible responses arguing in favor of Napoleon embracing revolutionary ideas include:
- His promotion of social equality
- The institution of the Code Napoleon
- The continuation of the Revolutionary Calendar
- The *Lycée* system
- Liberal economic reforms
- Religious toleration

Possible responses arguing against Napoleon embracing revolutionary ideas include:
- His crowning himself emperor
- His use of a secret police
- His suspension of democratic practices

CHAPTER 12

The Conservative Order and the Challenges of Reform (1815–1832)

Nationalism was the most powerful political ideology of nineteenth- and twentieth-century European affairs.

THE CONSERVATIVE ORDER

- After the Congress of Vienna, the major European powers—the **Concert of Europe**—met informally to discuss their differences in what was known as the Concert of Europe. This system functioned well for the first few years, until 1820, when the Bourbon Ferdinand VII of Spain violated his promise to govern according to a written constitution. At this time, revolution occurred in Naples. Metternich was especially concerned about the events in Italy that threatened to spread to Austria. The other powers were divided on the proper course of action.
- Nineteenth-century **conservatism** was dominated by monarchies, landed aristocracies, and established churches that united over their resistance to any change of the social order. These groups cooperated to slow the progress of nationalism and liberalism.

AP® FRAMEWORK
TOPIC # 6.5; LO: UNIT 6 F
KC:
3.3.I.C Conservatives developed a new ideology in support of traditional political and religious authorities, which was based on the idea that human nature was not perfectible.
3.4.I. The Concert of Europe (or Congress System) sought to maintain the status quo through collective action and adherence to conservatism.
3.4.I.A Metternich, architect of the Concert of Europe, used it to suppress nationalist and liberal revolutions.
3.4.I.B Conservatives reestablished control in many European states and attempted to suppress movements for change and, in some areas, to strengthen adherence to religious authorities.

THE EMERGENCE OF NATIONALISM AND LIBERALISM

- Early nineteenth-century nationalists opposed the Congress of Vienna because it did not allow for individual representation of ethnic groups, but rather upheld monarchies and dynasties in its redistribution of land. Many issues of nationalism arose during this era.

- Nineteenth-century European conservatives defined as *liberal* anything or anyone that challenged their own political, social, or religious values. Nineteenth-century liberals were influenced by Enlightenment writers and the French Revolution, and they sought to gain legal equality, religious toleration, and freedom of speech. Many liberals had economic goals of being able to enrich themselves without governmental interference. The economic ideas of Adam Smith were popular among economic liberals.
- Nationalism was sometimes associated with liberalism, but it could also occur alongside conservatism.

AP® FRAMEWORK
TOPIC # 6.7, 7.2; LO: UNIT 6 H, UNIT 7 B
KC:
3.3.I.A Liberals emphasized popular sovereignty, individual rights, and enlightened self-interest but debated the extent to which all groups in society should actively participate in its governance.
3.3.I.E Nationalists encouraged loyalty to the nation in a variety of ways, including romantic idealism, liberal reform, political unification, racialism with a concomitant anti-Semitism, and chauvinism justifying national aggrandizement.

CONSERVATIVE RESTORATION IN EUROPE
- Austrian Prince Metternich embodied conservatism more than any other nineteenth-century statesman. Metternich feared that recognizing minority rights would destroy his empire.
- Frederick III of Prussia reneged on his pledge to create a constitutional government, and he resisted aspirations by German nationalists to dissolve the conservative order.
- Students in the southern German states Baden, Bavaria, and Württemberg reacted against the lack of popular sovereignty and formed *Burschenschaften,* or student associations, to address their goal of a unified Germany.
- In England, the Tory ministry of Lord Liverpool focused on the issues of landowners and the elite rather than on the average citizens. Unruly meetings of reformers resulted in Parliament's passage of the Coercion Act of March 1817, which suspended the rights of *habeas corpus* and discouraged free speech. By 1819, a liberal crowd gathered in Manchester at Saint Peter's Fields, and when the militia moved into the audience, it set off a mass panic. Eleven people were killed, many more were injured; the event is known as the Peterloo Massacre. Parliament went on to pass laws called the Six Acts, which were designed at intimidating agitators and limiting their free speech.
- A Bourbon restoration in France brought Louis XVIII to the throne after Napoleon's abdication. He issued a constitution known as the Charter that gave the monarch greater control over government leaders, maintained the Declaration of the Rights of Man and Citizen, and did not challenge the property rights of lands confiscated from aristocrats and the Church. Louis XVIII's moderate Charter angered royalists who carried out attacks against Napoleon's allies. In 1820, the assassination of the duke of Berri gave royalists an excuse to persecute liberal politicians. Louis XVIII responded with more repressive measures that gave royalists and conservatives greater power.
- Metternich sought the help of Prussia and Russia, and unofficial groups from Britain and France assisted in suppressing of Italian nationalism. They issued the Protocol of Troppau, which stated that stable governments could intervene in countries experiencing revolution to help restore order. All of the interventions that occurred through the congress system sought to maintain the international order achieved at the Congress of Vienna.

179

AP® FRAMEWORK
TOPIC # 6.5; LO: UNIT 6 F
KC:
3.4.I.A Metternich, architect of the Concert of Europe, used it to suppress nationalist and liberal revolutions.

3.4.I.B Conservatives reestablished control in many European states and attempted to suppress movements for change and, in some areas, to strengthen adherence to religious authorities.

THE CONSERVATIVE ORDER SHAKEN IN EUROPE

- Other movements for independence—such as that of the Greek Revolution of 1821 and the 1830 fight for Serbian independence—demonstrated the growing issues of nationalism and liberalism coming into conflict with conservatism.

- Political discontent spread to Europe in the mid-1820s. In Russia, Russian officers who had fought Napoleon were exposed to ideas of the Enlightenment, and they developed reformist sympathies. Two secret societies, the Northern Society and the Southern Society, united forces in 1825 to carry out a coup d'état in 1826. When the Russian army was required to swear its allegiance to the new Tsar Nicholas, the Moscow regiment refused, and Nicholas had the artillery attack them. This so-called Decembrist Revolt came to symbolize to Russian liberals the oppressive conditions of life under the tsars. Nicholas reasserted his conservative authority when Poland nationalists agitated for change.

- In France in 1830, Charles X was the new king, and he favored aristocrats and ultra-royalists. He restored the rule of primogeniture, supported the Catholic Church, and gave special rights to the descendants of émigrés. Liberals gained enough seats in the Chamber of Deputies in 1827 to override some of Charles's new laws. When this happened again after the elections of 1830, Charles attempted a royalist seizure of power of the Chamber of Deputies. Parisians responded by staging massive protests, and Charles X turned troops against them before departing in August for exile. The July Monarchy, as Louis Philippe's ascension was called, focused on his role as a king of the French people.

- In Britain, the Great Reform Bill was passed in 1832. It represented a compromise between liberal and conservative factions. Catholic emancipation was a triumph for Irish nationalists, but it was passed as a means of avoiding unrest.

AP® FRAMEWORK
TOPIC # 6.6; LO: UNIT 6 G
KC:
3.4.I.C In the first half of the 19th century, revolutionaries attempted to destroy the status quo.

THE WARS OF INDEPENDENCE IN LATIN AMERICA

- Wars of independence in Latin America included efforts by Haiti, Brazil, and the present-day lands of Venezuela, Mexico, Paraguay, Uruguay, and Argentina to shed their colonial ties to Europe and gain their sovereignty.

AP® FRAMEWORK
TOPIC # 6.6; LO: UNIT 6 G
KC:
3.4.I.C In the first half of the 19th century, revolutionaries attempted to destroy the status quo.

Multiple-Choice Questions

Questions 1–5 refer to the passage below.

"The essential characteristics of a nationality are common ideas, common principles and a common purpose. A nation is an association of those who are brought together by language, by given geographical conditions or by the role assigned them by history, who acknowledge the same principles and who march together to the conquest of a single definite goal under the rule of a uniform body of law.

The life of a nation consists in harmonious activity (that is, the employment of all individual abilities and energies comprised within the association) towards this single goal....

If nationality is to be inviolable for all... it must be regarded inside a country as holy, like a religion, and outside a country as a grave mission. It is necessary too that the ideas arising within a country grow steadily, as part of the general law of Humanity which is the source of all nationality...These ideas, a necessary component in the order of universal destiny, must retain their originality even as they enter harmoniously into mankind's general progress.

The people must be the basis of nationality; its logically derived and vigorously applied principles its means; the strength of all its strength; the improvement of the life of all and the happiness of the greatest possible number its results; and the accomplishment of the task assigned to it by God its goal. This is what we mean by nationality."

Giuseppe Mazzini, Italian nationalist, 1835

Source: Herbert H. Rowen, ed., *From Absolutism to Revolution, 1648–1848*, 2nd ed. (Upper Saddle River, NJ: Prentice Hall, 1969), pp. 277–280. © 1969.

1. Based upon the ideas of the passage, Mazzini would have been most opposed to the influence of which of the following in Italy?
   (A) The Catholic Church
   (B) The military
   (C) Liberals
   (D) Austria

2. The ideas of the last paragraph of the passage reference which of the following nineteenth century ideologies?
   (A) Socialism
   (B) Communism
   (C) Liberalism
   (D) Conservatism

3. Which of the following European leaders would have been most opposed to the ideas expressed in the passage?
   (A) Louis XVIII
   (B) Klemens von Metternich
   (C) Giuseppe Garibaldi
   (D) Maximilien Robespierre

4. Ideas such as those expressed in the passage resulted in which of the following?
   (A) Successful independence movements in Poland and Algeria during the first half of the nineteenth century
   (B) Repeated attempts by revolutionaries to put an end to the status quo during the first half of the nineteenth century
   (C) The creation of constitutional monarchy in the Austrian Empire after the Revolutions of 1830
   (D) Papal support of Italian unification after the Revolutions of 1830

5. Which of the following was a response to ideas such as those expressed in the passage?
   (A) Conservatives attempted to suppress revolutionary movements that inspired change.
   (B) Conservatives supported independence movements in Poland and Greece.
   (C) Conservatives accepted nationalistic ideals after the Revolutions of 1830.
   (D) The Concert of Europe intervened to prevent Latin American independence from Spain.

Questions 6–9 refer to the passages below.

Source 1

"Women are so brought up, as not to be able to subsist in the mere physical sense, without a man to keep them: they are so brought up as not to be able to protect themselves against injury or insult, without some man on whom they have a special claim, to protect them, they are so brought up, as to have no vocation or useful office to fulfil in the world. . ..

There is no natural inequality between the sexes; except perhaps in bodily strength; even that admits of doubt: and if bodily strength is to be the measure of superiority, mankind are no better than savages. . ..

If nature has not made men and women unequal, still less ought the law to make them so. . .. A woman ought not to be dependent on a man, more than a man on a woman, except so far as their affections make them so. . ..
The first and indispensable step, therefore, towards the enfranchisement of woman, is that she be so educated, as not to be dependent either on her father or her husband for subsistence: a position which in nine cases out of ten, makes her either the plaything or the slave of the man who feeds her; and in the tenth case, only his humble friend…."

John Stuart Mill, British philosopher, Letters *On Marriage*, c. 1830s

Source: John Stuart Mill, "On Marriage," *The Collected Works of John Stuart Mill*, ed. John M. Robson (Toronto: University of Toronto Press, 1984), volume XXI, pp. 41–44.

Source 2

"There is equality in nothing now—all the pleasures such as there are being men's, and all the disagreeables and pains being women's…. Women are educated for one single object, to gain their living by marrying…. To be married is the object of their existence and that object being gained they do really cease to exist as to anything worth calling life or any useful purpose…. I have no doubt that when the whole community is really educated, tho' the present laws of marriage were to continue[,] they would be perfectly disregarded, because no one would marry. The widest and perhaps the quickest means to do away with its evils is to be found in promoting education—as it is the means of all good….

At this present time, in this state of civilization, what evil could be caused by, first placing women on the most entire equality with men, as to all rights and privileges, civil and political, and then doing away with all laws whatever relating to marriage? Then if a woman had children she must take charge of them, women would not then have children without considering how to maintain them. Women would have no more reason to barter person for bread, or for anything else, than men have—public offices being open to them alike, all occupations would be divided between the sexes in their natural arrangement…"

Harriet Taylor Mill, British philosopher, Letters *On Marriage*, c. 1830s

Source: Harriet Taylor Mill, "On Marriage," in *The Complete Works of Harriet Taylor Mill*, edited by Jo Ellen Jacobs (Bloomington, IN: Indiana University Press, 1998), 22–23.

6. Both sources agree with which of the following?
   (A) The most important duty for a woman is to bear children.
   (B) Women should be able to receive an education.
   (C) Women are inferior to men and should have no active role in society other than being a homemaker.
   (D) Women and men should be paid equal wages in the workforce.

7. The ideas expressed by John Stuart Mill (Source 1) may have been influenced by which of the following?
   (A) Radical beliefs during the early nineteenth century that encouraged women's suffrage
   (B) Utopian socialist ideas that called for gender equality and a redistribution of wealth and power
   (C) Protestant reformer views that encouraged spiritual equality for men and women
   (D) Liberal ideas that encouraged individual rights and self-interest

8. Which of the following is most similar to the ideas expressed by Harriet Taylor (Source 2)?
   (A) The Women's March on Versailles during the early stages of the French Revolution
   (B) The Napoleonic Code's emphasis on gender equality
   (C) Brief improvements in the legal status of women during the early stages of the French Revolution
   (D) The imposition of universal suffrage during the radical stage of the French Revolution

9. Which of the following philosophers would have been most opposed to the ideas expressed in both passages?
   (A) The Marquis de Condorcet
   (B) Olympe de Gouge
   (C) Mary Wollstonecraft
   (D) Jean Jacques Rousseau

Questions 10–11 refer to the 1820s painting below.

The French Bourbon Restoration (1815–1830)

Source: Bpk Bildagentur/Art Resource, NY

10. Which of the following best explains the historical context of the painting above?
    (A) The Bourbons used the French victory during the Napoleonic wars to gain support of commoners.
    (B) Bourbon kings in the nineteenth century made no attempt to reinstate absolute rule in France.
    (C) France's return to absolute monarchy after Napoleon's abdication included the dissolution of the Chamber of Deputies.
    (D) The Congress of Vienna attempted to return Europe to the conservative ideals of the pre-Revolutionary period.

11. Policies enacted during Bourbon rule after the Napoleonic period resulted in
    (A) revolutionaries overthrowing the Bourbon king in 1830
    (B) Charles X reluctantly accepting his role as a constitutional monarch
    (C) an end to monarchy in France and the establishment of the Second French Republic
    (D) the Belgian declaration of independence from French rule

185

Questions 12–13 refer to the passage below.

"Regarding University Life

1. There shall be appointed for each university a special representative of the ruler of each state, the said representatives to have appropriate instructions and extended powers, and they shall have their place of residence where the university is located….

2. The confederated governments mutually pledge themselves to eliminate from the universities or any other public educational institutions all instructors who shall have obviously proved their unfitness for the important work entrusted to them by openly deviating from their duties, or by going beyond the boundaries of their functions, or by abusing their legitimate influence over young minds, or by presenting harmful ideas hostile to public order or subverting existing governmental instructions….

Any instructor who has been removed in this manner becomes ineligible for a position in any other public institution of learning in another state of the Confederation.

3. The laws that have for some time been directed against secret and unauthorized societies in the universities shall be strictly enforced…. The special representatives of the government are enjoined to exert great care in watching these organizations.

The governments mutually agree that all individuals who shall be shown to have maintained their membership in secret or unauthorized associations, or shall have taken membership in such associations, shall not be eligible for any public office."

The Carlsbad Decrees of the German Confederation, 1819

Source: P. A. G. von Meyer, *Corpus juris confoederationis Germanicae*, 2nd ed., Vol. 2 (Frankfort on Main, 1833), pp. 138 ff., as quoted and translated in Louis L. Snyder, ed., *Documents of German History* (New Brunswick, NJ: Rutgers University Press, 1958), pp. 158–160.

12. The ordinances of the passage were a reaction against which of the following?
    (A) New ideologies that developed during the French Revolution and Napoleonic era
    (B) Student protests regarding the restoration of the Holy Roman Empire
    (C) The failure of the Frankfurt Assembly to create a German Empire
    (D) Unsanitary conditions in cities as a result of industrialization

13. Ordinances such as the Carlsbad Decrees reflect which of the following trends in Europe during the period 1815–1850?
    (A) Attempts by governments to embrace nationalism through authoritative control
    (B) The creation of new legislative bodies in absolute monarchies
    (C) Government policies that suppressed movements advocating change
    (D) The denial of suffrage to persons who did not own a significant amount of property

Questions 14–15 refer to the map below.

Centers of Revolution, 1820–1831

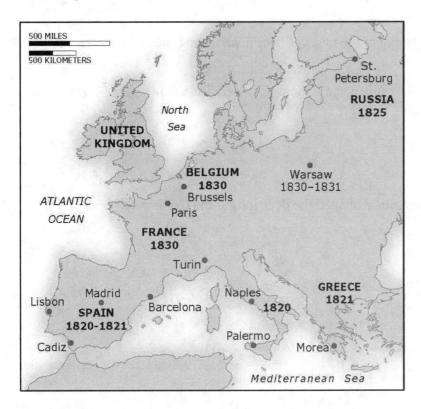

14. The events depicted on the map were influenced by which of the following?
    (A) Communism
    (B) Liberalism
    (C) Socialism
    (D) Anarchism

15. The events depicted on the map were mostly unsuccessful because of
    (A) the collective action of the Concert of Europe
    (B) the military power of the Russian Empire
    (C) Great Britain's leadership involving continental warfare
    (D) the failure of revolutionary groups to gain popular support from the people

187

Short-Answer Question

1. a) Describe one significant <u>continuity</u> in the ideas of liberalism during the early nineteenth century.

    b) Describe one significant <u>change</u> in the ideas of liberalism during the early nineteenth century.

    c) Explain one way in which liberalism and nationalism were linked during the early nineteenth century.

Long-Essay Question

Evaluate the extent to which conservatism shaped the decisions at the Congress of Vienna (1814–1815).

ANSWERS AND EXPLANATIONS: AP® PRACTICE TEST

Multiple-Choice Questions

1. D (KC: 3.3.I.F; LO: Unit 7 B) Like many fervent nationalists, Mazzini wanted his country to be free of any foreign control. During this time period, the Austrian government dominated much of Italy.

2. C (KC: 3.3.I.A; LO: Unit 6 H) Mazzini's ideas are representative of both nationalism and liberalism during the period after the Congress of Vienna. During the first part of the nineteenth century, many people who supported the ideas of nationalism also supported the ideas of liberalism. In fact, Mazzini sought to create a Roman republic during the Revolutions of 1848.

3. B (KC: 3.4.I.A; LO: Unit 6 F) Mazzini's ideas regarding both liberalism and nationalism were most opposed by Klemens von Metternich, the architect of the Vienna settlement and chief minister of the Austrian Empire. It would have been folly for Metternich to support liberalism and nationalism considering the absolute nature and the multiethnic character of the Austrian Empire.

4. B (KC: 3.4.I.C; LO: Unit 6 G) Despite efforts to slow its growth by conservative leaders, both liberalism and nationalism continued to grow during the nineteenth century. A new generation of revolutionaries challenged European governments during the first half of the century, most notably in 1830 and 1848. However, by the second half of the century, both liberalism and nationalism became more mainstream and accepted in some Western European countries.

5. A (KC: 3.4.I.B; LO: Unit 6 F) The Congress System usually attempted to thwart revolutionary movements in the early part of the nineteenth century because they feared another era of rapid change and chaos similar to the French Revolutionary period.

6. B (KC: 3.3.III.C; LO: Unit 6 I) Both authors argue that women should be better educated, so that they can work, and are capable of being independent.

7. D (KC: 3.3.I.A; LO: Unit 6 H) John Stuart Mill, known for his tract, *On Liberty*, was very typical of early-nineteenth-century liberals. It is likely that liberal ideas that encouraged basic rights would have influenced his viewpoint toward women; however, his very liberal view toward women was often debated, and women's rights did not become a mainstream issue until the end of the century.

8. C (KC: 2.1.IV.E; LO: Unit 5 E) The very brief improvement in women's legal status during the early phase of the French Revolution is somewhat similar to Harriet Taylor's ideas in Source 2. Taylor's ideas, broader than ideas and events during the early Revolutionary period regarding women, were somewhat based on the Revolutionary idea of legal equality.

9. D (KC: 2.3.I.C; LO: Unit 4 C) Jean-Jacques Rousseau argued that men and women inhabited "separate spheres," and he believed in a patriarchal society. He also believed that women should be excluded from politics.

10. D (KC: 3.4.I.B; LO: Unit 6 F) After the Napoleonic Wars, the goal of the Concert of Europe was to maintain the legitimacy of the pre-Revolutionary monarchies through conservative actions that would help to ensure stability. One of the consequences of the Congress of Vienna was the restoration of the Bourbons to the French throne under Louis XVIII.

11. A (KC: 3.4.I.C; LO: Unit 6 G) Louis XVIII, ever mindful of his brother's fate, ruled as a constitutional monarch; however, his brother Charles X, leader of the Ultraroyalists, attempted to limit the rights of the bourgeoisie and after issuing the July Ordinances [Four Ordinances] was forced to abdicate during the July Revolution in 1830.

12. A (KC: 3.3.I.F; LO: Unit 7 B) After the defeat of Napoleon, nationalism continued to grow in the German states. Students formed Burschenschaften (student organizations) that advocated for a unified German state. Urged by Austrian minister Klemens von Metternich, the Carlsbad Decrees were created to suppress nationalist sentiment at universities.

13. C (KC: 3.4.I.B; LO: Unit 6 F) Many conservative governments in Europe attempted to turn back the clock to the period prior to the French Revolution. Conservative governments in countries such as Austria and Russia made laws that censored citizens and suppressed nationalistic tendencies.

14. B (KC: 3.3.I.A; LO: Unit 6 H) The events on the map, including uprisings, revolutions, and independence movements, were generally influenced by the liberal ideas that spread throughout Europe during the French Revolution and Napoleonic era.

15. A (3.4.I.C; LO: Unit 6 G) Many of the revolts (but not all) were failures because of the collective action of the Concert of Europe, a system in which the Quintuple Alliance of Great Britain, Austria, Russia, Prussia, and France met to discuss international problems and oppose revolutionary activity. Note that the Greek and Belgian revolutions were supported by the major European powers, and they gained independence in 1829 and 1830, respectively.

Short-Answer Question

(KC: 3.3.I.A, 3.3.I.F; LO: Unit 6 H, Unit 7 B)

Possible responses to part a) include:
- Classical liberals believed in laissez faire, constitutionalism, and the protection of individual rights.
- Classical liberals opposed the absolutism of the "Old Regime" and the autocratic nature of the Congress of Vienna after the Napoleonic Wars.

Possible responses to part b) include:
- Some liberals, such as Jeremy Bentham and Edwin Chadwick, urged government intervention to improve the harsher aspects of urbanization.
- The Reform Bill of 1832, Factory Act of 1833, and repeal of the Corn Laws in 1846 demonstrate a new type of liberalism that favored some degree of government intervention in the economy and the increase in suffrage.

Possible responses to part c) include:
- Liberals often favored self-determination of peoples oppressed by foreign powers, such as in the Greek revolt for independence, Belgian independence, and the attempts at independence in Italy from Austrian rule in 1830 and 1848.
- French liberalism and nationalism played a role in the July Revolution in 1830 and the February Revolution in 1848.

Long-Essay Question
(KC: 2.1.V.D, 3.4.I; LO: Unit 5 H, Unit 6 F)

Evaluate the extent to which conservatism shaped the decisions at the Congress of Vienna (1814–1815).

Possible responses for conservatism shaping decisions:
- The leaders of the Quadruple Alliance sought to eliminate the influence of liberalism and nationalism in Europe in response to the traumas of the French Revolution and Napoleonic Wars.
- The Congress of Vienna restored families to power in various countries who had been removed by Napoleon including France, Spain, and Italy.
- A new balance of power emerged to maintain conservative rule throughout Europe and to prevent France from threatening other countries.
- Members of the Quadruple Alliance received lands at the expense of the French Empire as compensation for sacrifices in defeating Napoleon.

Possible responses for conservatism not shaping decisions:
- Although the Bourbons were restored to power in France, the French government became a constitutional monarchy—a more liberal form of government.
- French control of the Netherlands was removed and the country once again assumed a republican form of government.
- Napoleon's elimination of serfdom in the German states remained intact.

CHAPTER 13

Economic Advance and Social Unrest (1830–1850)

TOWARD AN INDUSTRIAL SOCIETY

- Through its textile industry, Britain achieved economic stability that led to its dominance in the world in the nineteenth century.
- As industrialization spread, the population of Europe continued to grow, and more people chose to live in cities. Migration from the countryside put new pressures on urban infrastructure: Poor harvests from 1845 to 1847 caused massive emigration to cities.
- The explosion of railway building in the 1830s and 1840s and the improvement of canals and roads made transportation to urban centers easier and increased industrialization.

AP® FRAMEWORK
TOPIC # 6.1, 6.2; LO: UNIT 6 A, B
KC:
3.1.I: Great Britain established its industrial dominance through the mechanization of textile production, iron and steel production, and new transportation systems in conjunction with uniquely favorable political and social climates.
3.1.I.B: Economic institutions and human capital such as engineers, inventors, and capitalists helped Britain lead the process of industrialization, largely through private initiative.
3.1.II.A: France moved toward industrialization at a more gradual pace than Great Britain, with government support and with less dislocation of traditional methods of production.
3.2 The experiences of everyday life were shaped by industrialization, depending on the level of industrial development in a particular location.
3.2.II Europe experienced rapid population growth and urbanization, leading to social dislocations.
3.2.V Because of the continued existence of more primitive agricultural practices and landowning patterns, some areas of Europe lagged in industrialization while facing famine, debt, and land shortages.

THE LABOR FORCE

- The nineteenth-century workforce was extremely varied; conditions differed from country to country and decade to decade.
- Artisans and factory workers alike underwent a process of proletarianization, whereby they entered into a wage economy and gradually lost significant ownership of the means of production. This process occurred rapidly wherever the factory system existed.
- The economic security of factory workers was often better than that of urban artisans. By the nineteenth century, it became more difficult for artisans to exercise control over their trades; European liberals disapproved of and banned labor and guild organizations.

- Some workshops began the practice known in France as *confection,* which involved the production of goods in standard sizes and styles rather than by special orders, in order to compete with larger establishments or machine production.
- In 1836, William Lovett and other radical London artisans formed the London Working Men's Association, and in 1838 they demanded six specific reforms in a charter: universal male suffrage, annual election of the House of Commons, the secret ballot, equal electoral districts, abolition of property qualifications for members of the House of Commons, and payment of salaries to members of the House of Commons. **Chartism**, as this movement was called, failed as a national faction, but many of the six points were enacted into law.

AP® FRAMEWORK
TOPIC # 6.1; LO: UNIT 6 A
KC:
3.2 The experiences of everyday life were shaped by industrialization, depending on the level of industrial development in a particular location.
3.2.I Industrialization promoted the development of new classes in the industrial regions of Europe.
3.3 Political revolutions and the complications resulting from industrialization triggered a range of ideological, governmental, and collective responses.
3.3.I Ideologies developed and took root throughout society as a response to industrial and political revolutions.

FAMILY STRUCTURES AND THE INDUSTRIAL REVOLUTION

- Prior to the Industrial Revolution, home life and economic life occurred in the same place; thereafter, these worlds were increasingly distinct.
- Factory wages for skilled adult males enabled some families to rely solely on the male breadwinner's income. As machines became less complex and required fewer skilled operators, more women and children maintained them, earning reduced salaries compared to their adult male counterparts.
- The shift from the domestic system of production to the factory system brought with it profound shifts in family life. Often, adult males could earn enough to support their entire family.
- As child labor was gradually curtailed, and public education expanded, the role of parents in educating and training their children shrank.

AP® FRAMEWORK
TOPIC # 6.4; LO: UNIT 6 E
KC:
3.2.III.A Bourgeois families became focused on the nuclear family and the cult of domesticity, with distinct gender roles for men and women.
3.2.III.B By the end of the century, higher wages, laws restricting the labor of children and women, social welfare programs, improved diet, and increased access to birth control affected the quality of life for the working class.

WOMEN IN THE EARLY INDUSTRIAL REVOLUTION

- As more husbands were able to support their families on one salary, more wives came to be associated with domestic duties, such as housekeeping, food preparation, and cottage industries. By the 1820s, more unmarried women became employed in factories, tending machines that required little skilled labor. These women were usually young, single, or widowed.
- The largest groups of working women were found in domestic service or in agricultural work.
- The English Factory Act of 1833 prohibited the employment of children under the age of nine, limited the workday for children, and required that children receive two hours of daily education at the factory owner's expense. The wage economy meant that families were not spending as much time together as they had before.

AP® FRAMEWORK
TOPIC # 6.4; LO: UNIT 6 E
KC:
3.2.III.A Bourgeois families became focused on the nuclear family and the cult of domesticity, with distinct gender roles for men and women.
3.2.III.B By the end of the century, higher wages, laws restricting the labor of children and women, social welfare programs, improved diet, and increased access to birth control affected the quality of life for the working class.

PROBLEMS OF CRIME AND ORDER, AND POVERTY

- Cities became associated with crime as the Industrial Revolution expanded.
- Propertied members of society strove to improve the crime situation during this time via prison reform and better systems of police. Professional police forces helped an orderly European society emerge.
- Prison reform was undertaken in France and in Britain in the 1840s. Isolation was a common feature. Transportation of criminals to remote locations (such as Australia) was abandoned by the British, but used by the French into the twentieth century.
- Most economists followed the *laissez-faire* thought of Adam Smith's *Wealth of Nations,* and urged that economic decisions be made through the mechanism of the marketplace. They emphasized thrift, competition, and personal industry, all of which appealed to the middle class.
- Thomas Malthus (1766–1834) published his *Essay on the Principle of Population,* in which he argued that population would eventually outstrip food supply. He encouraged chastity and discouraged the raising of families. David Ricardo (1772–1823) argued his theory of "the iron law of wages," based on Malthus's principles, that if wages were raised, more children would be produced, which would cause wages to fall and working people to produce fewer children, which would then cause wages to rise, in a continuous cycle.

195

AP® FRAMEWORK
TOPIC # 4.3, 6.4, 6.10; LO: UNIT 6 E, K
KC:
2.3.III.B Mercantilist theory and practice were challenged by new economic ideas, including Adam Smith's, which espoused free trade and a free market.
3.2.II.B With migration from rural to urban areas in industrialized regions, cities experienced overcrowding, while affected rural areas suffered declines in available labor as well as weakened communities.
3.3.II Governments, at times based on the pressure of political or social organizations, responded to problems created or exacerbated by industrialization.

EARLY SOCIALISM

- Early socialists were in favor of the new productive capacity of industrialism. A group of writers known as the **utopian socialists** questioned the structures and values of the existing capitalistic framework.
- Other important forms of socialism, including Saint-Simonianism, Owenism, Fourierism, Anarchism, and Marxism developed during this period.

AP® FRAMEWORK
TOPIC # 6.7; LO: UNIT 6 H
KC:
3.3.I.D Socialists called for the redistribution of society's resources and wealth and evolved from a utopian to a Marxist scientific critique of capitalism.
3.3.I.E Anarchists asserted that all forms of governmental authority were unnecessary and should be overthrown and replaced with a society based on voluntary cooperation.
3.6.II.C Marx's scientific socialism provided a systematic critique of capitalism and a deterministic analysis of society and historical evolution.

1848: YEAR OF REVOLUTIONS

- A series of liberal and nationalist revolutions exploded across the Continent in 1848. Political liberals were the chief advocates of reforms. In France, a "Second Republic" emerged with Napoleon's nephew, Louis Napoleon Bonaparte, at the helm. In 1851, he seized power and became emperor in 1852, returning France to a dictatorship. The Habsburg lands saw unrest, and there were revolts in Hungary and Austria. Czech nationalists rebelled and the Pan-Slavic Congress—which consisted of Poles, Ruthenians, Czechs, Slovaks, Croats, Slovenes, and Serbs—called for national equality of Slavs and protested the repression of all Slavic peoples. Other revolts in Italy and Germany were suppressed, the liberal era ended, and the European middle class ceased to be revolutionary.

AP® FRAMEWORK
TOPIC # 6.1, 6.6; LO: UNIT 6 A, G
KC:

3.3 Political revolutions and the complications resulting from industrialization triggered a range of ideological, governmental, and collective responses.

3.3.I Ideologies developed and took root throughout society as a response to industrial and political revolutions.

3.4.I.D The revolutions of 1848, triggered by economic hardship and discontent with the political status quo, challenged conservative politicians and governments and led to the breakdown of the Concert of Europe.

Multiple-Choice Questions

Questions 1–5 refer to the map below.

European Railroads in 1850

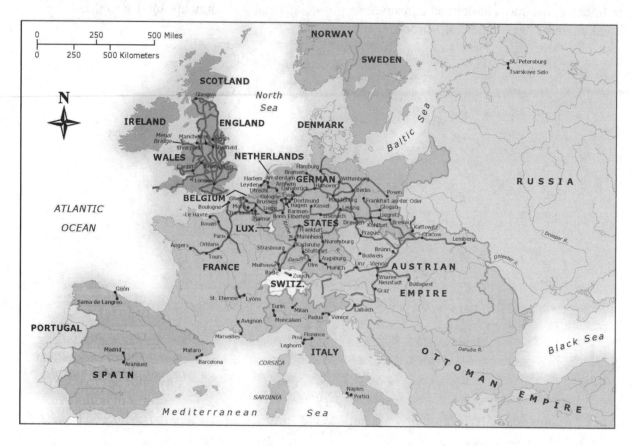

1. Which of the following contributed most to the overall trend shown on the map?
   (A) Great Britain's dominance in the cottage industry
   (B) Improvements in agricultural production in the Mediterranean countries
   (C) The growth of the Industrial Revolution in western Europe
   (D) Government control of the railroad industry

2. The trends shown on the map first developed in which of the following countries?
   (A) Great Britain
   (B) France
   (C) Prussia
   (D) The Netherlands

3. Which of the following best explains the trend shown on the map in eastern and southern Europe?
   (A) Eastern and southern European nations were not as centralized as those in western Europe.
   (B) Lack of resources and the continuation of traditional agricultural practices hindered the development of railroads in eastern and southern Europe.
   (C) The Ottoman Empire's dominance of eastern and southern Europe prevented these regions from adopting western innovations.
   (D) The growth of socialism in eastern and southern Europe hindered industry and innovation.

4. How were the origins of the trend shown on the map different in Great Britain from on the Continent?
   (A) Britain had the most extensive rail network by mid-century, and their railroads were largely built through private initiative.
   (B) Great Britain was the only country to have both coal and iron resources.
   (C) Great Britain's mercantilist economy was dependent upon building a better infrastructure to encourage domestic production.
   (D) Great Britain's Parliament completely funded the railroad industry, minimizing any risk to investors.

5. The trends shown on the map had which of the following effects in western Europe?
   (A) Increased emigration to Great Britain
   (B) Increased emigration to the United States
   (C) A surplus of consumer goods
   (D) The growth of cities

Questions 6–8 refer to the letter to the editor below.

"Sir,

Living as we do, in the densely populated manufacturing districts…and most of us belonging to that class of females who earn their bread either directly or indirectly by manufactories, we have looked with no little anxiety for your opinion on the Factory Bill…. You are for doing away with our services in manufactories altogether. So much the better, if you had pointed out any other more eligible and practical employment for the surplus female labour, that will want other channels for a subsistence. If our competition were withdrawn, and short hours substituted, we have no doubt but the effects would be as you have stated, "not to lower wages, as the male branch of the family would be enabled to earn as much as the whole had done," but for the thousands of females who are employed in manufactories, who have no legitimate claim on any male relative for employment or support, and who have, through a variety of circumstance, been early thrown on their own resources for a livelihood, what is to become of them?

In this neighbourhood, hand-loom has been almost totally superseded by power-loom weaving, and no inconsiderable number of females, who must depend on their own exertions, or their parishes for support, have been forced, of necessity into the manufactories, from their total inability to earn a livelihood at home.

The Female Operatives of Todmorden, Letter to the Editor—The Examiner, 1832

Source: *The Examiner*, February 26, 1832, as quoted in Ivy Pinchbeck, *Women Workers and the Industrial Revolution, 1750–1850* (New York: Augustus M. Kelley, 1969), pp. 199–200.

6. Which of the following contributed to the events described in the passage?
   (A) The growth of the women's suffrage movement
   (B) Innovations in the cottage industry
   (C) The mechanization of the textile industry
   (D) Population decreases during the early nineteenth century

7. The events described in the passage occurred in context with which of the following?
   (A) Increasing opportunities for women in clerical and sales positions
   (B) Encouraging a new conservatism in which women should earn their own income
   (C) Women gaining full citizenship in most western European countries
   (D) Newly married women leaving the workforce and living on their husbands' earnings

8. The attitudes that the content of the letter addresses reflect which of the following?
   (A) A belief that women should only work in industrial occupations
   (B) Increased industrialist demand for workers in factories
   (C) Increasingly distinct gender roles for men and women
   (D) Fears that women will demand equal pay in the factories

Questions 9–12 refer to the passage below.

"The history of all hitherto existing society is the history of class struggles....

Our epoch, the epoch of the bourgeoisie, possesses, however, this distinctive feature: it has simplified the class antagonisms. Society as a whole is more and more splitting up into two great hostile camps, into two great classes directly facing each other: Bourgeoisie and Proletariat....

Each step in the development of the bourgeoisie was accompanied by a corresponding political advance of that class....

The bourgeoisie, wherever it has gotten the upper hand, has put an end to all feudal, patriarchal, idyllic relations. It has pitilessly torn asunder the motley feudal ties that bound man to his "natural superiors," and has left remaining no other nexus between man and man than naked self-interest, than callous "cash payment."...

The proletariat goes through various stages of development. With its birth begins its struggle with the bourgeoisie....

But with the development of industry the proletariat not only increases in number; it becomes concentrated in greater masses, its strength grows, and it feels that strength more. The various interests and conditions of life within the ranks of the proletariat are more and more equalized, in proportion as machinery obliterates all distinctions of labour, and nearly everywhere reduces wages to the same low level...."

Karl Marx and Friedrich Engels, philosophers, *The Communist Manifesto*, 1848

Source: Karl Marx and Friedrich Engels, *The Communist Manifesto*, in Lawrence H. Simon, ed., *Karl Marx, Selected Writings* (Indianapolis, IN: Hackett Publishing Company, Inc., 1994), pp. 158, 159, 160, 161, 165, 166–167, 168, 169, 186. © 1994 International Publishers Co.

9. Marx and Engels's ideas reflect which of the following nineteenth-century economic characteristics?
   (A) Agricultural continuities in eastern Europe reinforced the existing class structure.
   (B) The division of labor created new classes during the Industrial Revolution.
   (C) Urban factory workers had developed into a robust middle class.
   (D) Reform movements were mostly based on laissez-faire economics.

10. Most likely, Marx and Engels were influenced by the development of
    (A) Anarchism
    (B) Liberal Democracy
    (C) Republicanism
    (D) Constitutionalism

11. Marx and Engels would have been most opposed to the ideas of
    (A) Henry de Saint-Simon
    (B) Robert Owen
    (C) Adam Smith
    (D) Maximilien Robespierre

12. *The Communist Manifesto* was
    (A) a critique of society based upon the liberal ideas of the Enlightenment and French Revolution
    (B) an analysis of industrial society that led almost immediately to legislation introducing social-welfare reform
    (C) a scientific critique of capitalism that had profound effects throughout the rest of the nineteenth and twentieth centuries
    (D) a succinct condemnation of industrial Europe with very little impact

Questions 13–15 refer to the passage below.

"The events of February 1848 in Paris immediately reverberated throughout the Habsburg domains. The empire was susceptible to revolutionary challenge on every score. Its government rejected liberal institutions. Its borders cut across national lines that more people found meaningful than ever before. Its society perpetuated serfdom. In 1848, the regime confronted rebellions in Vienna, Prague, Hungary, and its Italian holdings. The disturbances that broke out in many German cities also threatened Habsburg predominance. In the initial months, rebels appeared to work together in their demands for reform. By the fall, however, fundamental differences in their priorities became apparent. While some demands focused on national autonomy, others concerned liberal political priorities, like a constitution. Workers' interest in radical social and economic change was not shared by liberal revolutionaries."

Donald Kagan, *The Western Heritage* 8th edition *(*Boston, Pearson Education, 2010)

13. The events in Paris in February 1848 were caused by which of the following?
    (A) Issuance of the July Ordinances by Charles X
    (B) Discontent with the monarchy of Louis Philippe
    (C) Nationalist uprisings throughout the city
    (D) The Storming of the Bastille

14. The Hungarian rebellion mentioned in the passage was most influenced by which of the following ideologies?
    (A) Nationalism
    (B) Imperialism
    (C) Socialism
    (D) Communism

15. The Revolutions of 1848 resulted in which of the following changes in Europe?
    (A) New liberal regimes in Eastern Europe
    (B) The Frankfurt Assembly and the creation of a unified Germany
    (C) The proclamation of the Kingdom of Italy
    (D) The beginning of the breakdown of the Concert of Europe

Short-Answer Question

Use the image below to answer all parts of the question below.

New Lanark: Robert Owen, a Scottish industrialist, created an ideal community at New Lanark, Scotland.

Source: Chronicle/Alamy Stock Photo

Answer a, b, and c:
1. a) Describe how one economic trend in the early nineteenth century contributed to reform movements such as the one illustrated above.
   b) Describe how one demographic trend in the early nineteenth century contributed to reform movements such as the one illustrated above.
   c) Explain how reform movements such as the one illustrated above reflected changing ideas about government's responsibility towards the working class.

Long-Essay Question

Evaluate the extent to which the spread of liberal ideas led to the Revolutions of 1848.

ANSWERS AND EXPLANATIONS: AP® PRACTICE TEST

Multiple Choice Questions

1. C (KC: 3.1; LO: Unit 6 A) Beginning in late-eighteenth-century Britain, the Industrial Revolution spread to the European continent during the first half of the nineteenth century. The need for a better infrastructure combined with technological improvements during the Industrial Revolution ultimately contributed to railroad building that allowed for more efficiency transporting raw materials and finished products.

2. A (KC: 3.1.I.A; LO: Unit 6 B) The Industrial Revolution began in Great Britain and the first railways were built there.

3. B (KC: 3.1.II.C; LO: Unit 6 B) Eastern and southern Europe, still dominated by the landed elites, had limited industrialization during the first half of the nineteenth century. Railroads were not built with the same urgency as in western Europe because they were not vital to eastern and southern European national economies.

4. A (KC: 3.1.I.B; LO: Unit 6 B) For the most part, British industrialization relied more upon human capital and private initiative than on the Continent, partly because continental industrialization was less advanced than British industrialization. As a result, Britain had the most extensive rail network by 1850.

5. D (KC: 3.1.III.B; LO: Unit 6 C) The growth of the railroad industry had several long-term effects including the development of national economies, increased urbanization, and increasing globalization.

6. C (KC: 3.1.III.A; LO: Unit 6 C) The authors of this petition were responding to ideas that factory laws should limit and possibly even eliminate women's employment. Women were already losing employment opportunities due to new innovations and inventions in the textile industry that led to mechanization and the factory system.

7. D (KC: 3.2.III.C; LO: Unit 6 E) As a result of increasing urbanization, options for marriage increased for women, and arranged marriages began to decline in industrialized areas. Often it was expected that married women would leave the workplace and live on their husbands' earnings, thus reflecting the continued values of a patriarchal society despite increasing numbers of single women working.

8. C (KC: 3.2.III.A; LO: Unit 6 E) See explanation for question 7.

9. B (KC: 3.2.I.A; LO: Unit 6 E) Marx and Engels were influenced by the idea of class conflict as a moving force in history. They believed labor was the source of all wealth. This led to their belief that the new division of labor into the bourgeoisie and the proletariat would inevitably lead to a revolution of the masses.

10. D (KC: 3.3.I.D; LO: Unit 6 H) Socialist theories, which called for both reform and a redistribution of both wealth and resources, greatly influenced the ideas of *The Communist Manifesto,* which predicted the violent overthrow of bourgeois industrialists by the working class.

11. C (KC: 3.6.II.C; LO: Unit 6 H) *The Communist Manifesto* expressed views that were hostile to the economic conditions of the time period, namely capitalism, a philosophy espoused by Adam Smith.

12. C   (KC: 3.3.I.D, 3.6.II.C; LO: Unit 6 H) Marx's scientific claim and use of empirical analysis of economics contributed to Marxism's having a profound impact in Europe for the next 150 years or more. His writings later influenced Vladimir Lenin and Joseph Stalin, as well as numerous world leaders, and would contribute to the Cold War.

13. B   (KC: 3.4.I.D; LO: Unit 6 G) General discontent with the policies of Louis Philippe and his Chief Minister François Guizot, especially increased censorship and their appeal to the elite, enraged many liberals and workers, leading to Louis Philippe's flight to Britain in February 1848. It also led to the establishment of the Second French Republic, albeit for four years only.

14. A   (KC: 3.3.I.F, 3.4.I.A, 3.6.II.C; LO: Unit 6 F, H, Unit 7 B) In large parts of Austria, nationalism played an important role both during and after the Revolutions of 1848. In 1848, the Hungarians, led by Louis Kossuth, declared independence and nearly succeeded in achieving it. Hungarians failed to get support from other nationalities within the empire, as well as Russia, leading to the end of Kossuth's brief Hungarian regime. Nevertheless, Hungarians received the same rights as German Austrians in 1867.

15. D   (KC: 3.4.I.D; LO: Unit 6 G) The Revolutions of 1848 led to the breakdown of the Concert of Europe. By 1853, former members of the Quintuple Alliance were at war with each other. The Kingdom of Italy (answer choice "C") would not become completely unified until 1871.

Short Answer Question
(KC: 3.3.I, 3.3.II; LO: Unit 6 H, 6 J)

Possible responses for part a) include:
- Industrialization was seen by many as dehumanizing and inspired reformers to create alternative societies.
- Factory work could be dangerous, and many reformers saw the conditions within the factories as less than favorable.
- Child labor was prevalent with children as young as seven years old working long hours. Physical punishment was frequent.
- All workers worked long hours. Many workers often awoke before dawn and returned home after dusk with perhaps an hour for supper.

Possible responses for part b) include:
- The challenges of urbanization and overcrowding inspired reformers to create alternative societies.
- Family life suffered as a result of factory work. Family members often worked different shifts and during the week might only see each other in passing.
- As the average life span slowly increased, older workers often had no recourse if they were unable to perform their work satisfactorily.
- Increased migration from rural to urban areas kept wages very low due to the large number of unskilled workers.

Possible responses for part c) include:
- Liberal reformers urged increased government intervention to remedy problems that included poor sanitation, overcrowding, vagrancy, and crime.
- The British Parliament commissioned reports on the workplace such as the Sadler report that led to Parliamentary legislation regulating women and children in the workplace.
- Poor conditions in cities and factories led to the growth of socialist parties that championed the working classes.
- By the end of the century, some politicians would advocate for trade unions.

Long-Essay Question
(KC: 3.4.I; LO: Unit 6 G)

Evaluate the extent to which the spread of liberal ideas led to the Revolutions of 1848.

Possible responses to larger extent might include:
- Liberalism played an important role in the February Revolution in France where King Louis Philippe was removed, as the bourgeoisie feared he was moving in an increasingly conservative direction.
- Liberalism, along with nationalism, played a role in Italy as revolutionaries created a short-lived republic before being defeated by Austrian forces.
- Liberalism, along with nationalism, played a role in Germany where the Frankfurt Parliament sought to create a united Germany with Prussia as the leading force.
- A degree of liberalism, coupled with strong nationalism, played a role in driving Hungarian revolutionaries in Austria toward autonomy before being defeated by Austrian forces.

Possible responses to smaller extent might include:
- Nationalism played a much larger role in the Hungarian revolution and in the Frankfurt Parliament's call for a unified Germany.
- Socialism played a major role in the June Days' Revolution in France, where the working class rebelled against the domination of the bourgeois government.

CHAPTER 14

The Age of Nation-States

THE CRIMEAN WAR (1853–1856)

- The Crimean War grew out of the rivalry between the Ottoman Empire and Russia. A war among the major European states ensued with France and Britain declaring war on Russia, and Austria and Prussia remaining neutral. Russia fell to the French and British, who settled the matter in 1856 at the Treaty of Paris.
- The Crimean War broke the Concert of Europe, marking a new era in European politics.

AP® FRAMEWORK
TOPIC # 7.3; LO: UNIT 7 C
KC:
3.4.II.A The Crimean War demonstrated the weakness of the Ottoman Empire and contributed to the breakdown of the Concert of Europe, thereby creating the conditions in which Italy and Germany could be unified after centuries of fragmentation.

REFORMS IN THE OTTOMAN EMPIRE

- The *Tanzimat*, or "reorganization" of the empire, was inspired by European models. The reorganization widened the toleration of other religions. A constitution was promulgated in 1876.
- Balkan wars weakened the Ottoman Empire.

AP® FRAMEWORK
TOPIC # 7.3; LO: UNIT 7 C
KC:
3.4.II.A The Crimean War demonstrated the weakness of the Ottoman Empire and contributed to the breakdown of the Concert of Europe, thereby creating the conditions in which Italy and Germany could be unified after centuries of fragmentation.

ITALIAN UNIFICATION

- Nationalists hoped for Italian unification, but Italian statesmen disagreed about how to accomplish it.
- Romantic republican nationalism was led by Giuseppe Mazzini (1805–1872), who founded the Young Italy Society to drive Austria from the peninsula. Mazzini and Giuseppe Garibaldi (1807–1882) led insurrections in the 1830s through the 1850s.
- Between 1852 and 1860, Italy was transformed into a nation-state governed by a constitutional monarchy. Full unification remained elusive.

AP® FRAMEWORK

TOPIC # 7.3; LO: UNIT 7 C

KC:

3.4.II.A The Crimean War demonstrated the weakness of the Ottoman Empire and contributed to the breakdown of the Concert of Europe, thereby creating the conditions in which Italy and Germany could be unified after centuries of fragmentation.

3.4.III.A Cavour's diplomatic strategies, combined with the popular Garibaldi's military campaigns, led to the unification of Italy.

GERMAN UNIFICATION

- The construction of a unified Germany was one of the most important political developments in Europe between 1848 and 1914 because it altered the international balance of power.

- In 1862, William I of Prussia turned to Otto von Bismarck (1815–1898), who moved against the liberal Parliament and sought support for unifying Germany through a war with Denmark.

- Bismarck supported the duchies of Schleswig and Holstein in their efforts to avoid getting incorporated into Denmark. Together, Prussia and Austria defeated Denmark in 1864, which elevated Bismarck's prestige and led to a conflict between the two countries in 1865.

- Bismarck then provoked war with Austria over the administration of Schleswig and Holstein. The Seven Weeks' War led to the defeat of Austria in 1866 and established Prussia as the only major power among the German states. In 1867, the North German Confederation formed with Bismarck representing the King of Prussia as president. Germany had become a military monarchy, crushing Prussian liberalism.

- The Franco-Prussian War (1870–1871) enabled Bismarck to bring the states of southern Germany into the confederation. Bismarck orchestrated the war by provoking France against Prussia, and the southern German states joined Prussia against Napoleon III's armies. The Germans beat the French army, captured Napoleon III, besieged Paris, and proclaimed the German Empire.

AP® FRAMEWORK

TOPIC # 7.3; LO: UNIT 7 C

KC:

3.4.II.A The Crimean War demonstrated the weakness of the Ottoman Empire and contributed to the breakdown of the Concert of Europe, thereby creating the conditions in which Italy and Germany could be unified after centuries of fragmentation.

3.4.III.B Bismarck used Realpolitik, employing diplomacy, industrialized warfare, weaponry, and the manipulation of democratic mechanisms to unify Germany.

FRANCE: FROM LIBERAL EMPIRE TO THE THIRD REPUBLIC

- The provinces and Paris differed on how to handle a settlement with the Prussians. The National Assembly was dominated by monarchists and led by Adolphe Thiers, who agreed in the Treaty of Frankfurt that France would pay an indemnity, and that Prussians would occupy France until it was paid. Alsace and part of Lorraine were granted to the Prussians.
- Parisians who had suffered under the Prussian siege rebelled against the Treaty of Frankfurt, and elected a new, short-lived municipal government on March 28, 1871, called the Paris Commune, which was created to administer Paris separately from the rest of France. On May 8, the National Assembly bombarded the city and broke through defenses on May 21. Troops restored order to Paris, killing 20,000 Parisians in the process and ending the Commune.
- In 1875, the National Assembly adopted a new republican political system that provided for a chamber of deputies elected by universal male suffrage, a senate chosen indirectly, and a president elected by the two legislative houses. Following the 1879 resignation of President Marshal MacMahon, Republicans gained control of the national government. The Dreyfus Affair, a case involving the trumped-up case of a Jewish captain, was the major crisis.

AP® FRAMEWORK
TOPIC # 7.2; LO: UNIT 7 B
KC:

3.3.I.F Nationalists encouraged loyalty to the nation in a variety of ways, including romantic idealism, liberal reform, political unification, racialism with a concomitant anti-Semitism, and chauvinism justifying national aggrandizement.

3.4.II.B A new generation of conservative leaders, including Napoleon III, Cavour, and Bismarck, used popular nationalism to create or strengthen the state.

THE HABSBURG EMPIRE

- The Habsburg domains had remained primarily absolutist after the revolutions of 1848.
- In 1861, Francis Joseph issued the February Patent, which set up a bicameral imperial parliament or *Reichsrat,* with an upper chamber appointed by the emperor and an indirectly elected lower chamber. The Magyars refused to recognize this system, but the February Patent ruled the empire for six years. In 1867, Francis Joseph transformed the Habsburg Empire into Austria-Hungary to satisfy the desires of Magyars to maintain their lands separately from Austria while sharing the same monarch. The unrest of the many nationalities in the Habsburg Empire caused instability throughout Europe.

AP® FRAMEWORK
TOPIC # 7.2; LO: UNIT 7 B
KC

3.4.II.C The creation of the dual monarchy of Austria-Hungary, which recognized the political power of the largest ethnic minority, was an attempt to stabilize the state by reconfiguring national unity.

RUSSIA: EMANCIPATION AND REVOLUTIONARY STIRRINGS

- Alexander II restructured Russian society after Russia's defeat in the Crimean War, ushering in some of the much-needed reforms, including the abolition of serfdom in 1861. Alexander II became known as the Tsar Liberator, but he was never popular with his noble subjects, who resented his control over policy.
- In the 1870s, young Russians drew on the ideas of Alexander Herzen and formed a populism movement, which sought social revolution based on the communal life of the Russian peasants.

AP® FRAMEWORK
TOPIC # 6.6; LO: UNIT 6 G
KC:
3.4.II.D In Russia, autocratic leaders pushed through a program of reform and modernization, including the emancipation of the serfs, which gave rise to revolutionary movements and eventually the Russian Revolution of 1905.

GREAT BRITAIN: TOWARD DEMOCRACY

- Britain took a step toward democracy in the reform bill sponsored by Benjamin Disraeli (1804–1881), a House of Commons leader, in 1867. By the time the measure had passed, the number of voters had been almost doubled from 1,430,000 to 2,470,000.
- William Gladstone ushered in many liberal reforms, including opening more institutions to the public and people from other classes and religious denominations. The Education Act of 1870 made the government responsible for administering elementary schools. Gladstone was forced to confront the Irish question during his administration.

AP® FRAMEWORK
TOPIC # 6.8; LO: UNIT 6 A
KC:
3.3.III.A Mass-based political parties emerged as sophisticated vehicles for social, economic, and political reform.

Multiple-Choice Questions

Questions 1–5 refer to the passage below.

"Russia demanded the right of protection over all Greek Christians living in the Turkish Empire, of whom there were several millions. The demand was loosely expressed and might possibly, if granted, grow into a constant right of intervention by Russia in the internal affairs of Turkey, ultimately making that country a kind of vassal of the former…War therefore broke out between the two powers…in 1853. Russia expected that the war would be limited to these two. In this she was shortly undeceived, for England [Britain] and France and later Piedmont [Sardinia], came to the support of the Turks. England went to war because she feared an aggressive and expanding Russia, feared for the route to India; France because Napoleon III wished to pay back old grudges against Russia, wished revenge for the Moscow campaign of Napoleon I, wished also to tear up the treaties of 1815, which sealed the humiliation of France. Piedmont went to war merely to win the interest of England and France for Cavour's plan…

Charles Downer Hazen, Professor of History at Columbia University,
Modern European History 1917

Source: Charles Downer Hazen, *Modern European History*, New York, Henry Holt and Company, 1917), pp. 543–544.

1. The causes of the Crimean War, referenced in the passage, directly contributed to which of the following?
   (A) Bismarck's Alliance System
   (B) The breakup of the Austro-Hungarian Empire
   (C) The breakup of the Ottoman Empire
   (D) The breakdown of the Concert of Europe

2. Based on the passage and historical context, which of the following best explains Britain's motivation for entering the war?
   (A) Russia threatened to take India from British control.
   (B) Britain wanted to assert its power to deter future German aggression in the eastern Mediterranean.
   (C) Britain wanted to maintain a balance of power in the eastern Mediterranean region.
   (D) Britain wanted to isolate both Russia and the Ottoman Empire from European affairs.

3. The author's assertion that France wanted to "tear up the treaties of 1815" is a reference to French discontent with which of the following?
   (A) Peace of Westphalia
   (B) Treaty of Utrecht
   (C) Congress of Vienna
   (D) Treaty of Aix-la-Chappelle

4. "Cavour's plan" in the last sentence of the passage is a reference to which of the following?
   (A) Cavour's plan to take Rome from the Pope
   (B) Cavour's plan to create an Italian state under the leadership of Victor Emmanuel II
   (C) Cavour's plan to unite with Garibaldi to create an Italian republic
   (D) Cavour's plan to obtain Nice and Savoy from France

5. Cavour and Napoleon III were similar in which of the following ways?
   (A) Both were conservative leaders who used nationalism to strengthen their states.
   (B) Both used liberalism as a way to unite their countries.
   (C) Both were hereditary monarchs.
   (D) Both leaders lost territory to the Austrians as a result of warfare.

214

Questions 6–7 refer to the passage below.

"Italians! The Sicilians are fighting against the enemies of Italy and for Italy. To help them with money, arms, and especially men, is the duty of every Italian.

Let the Marches, Umbria, Sabine, the Roman Campagna, and the Neapolitan territory rise, so as to divide the enemy's forces.

If the cities do not offer a sufficient basis for insurrection, let the more resolute throw themselves into the open country. A brave man can always find a weapon. In the name of Heaven, hearken not to the voice of those who cram themselves at well served tables. Let us arm. Let us fight for our brothers; tomorrow we can fight for ourselves.

A handful of brave men, who have followed me in battles for our country, are advancing with me to the rescue. Italy knows them; they always appear at the hour of danger. Brave and generous companions, they have devoted their lives to their country; they will shed their last drop of blood for it, seeking no other reward than that of a pure conscience.

"Italy and Victor Emmanuel!"—that was our battle cry when we crossed the Tincino; it will resound into the very depths of Aetna [the volcanic mountain]. As this prophetic battle-cry re-echoes from the hills of Italy to the Tarpeian Mount, the tottering thrones of tyranny will fall to pieces, and the whole country will rise like one man."

Giuseppe Garibaldi, Italian guerilla fighter and republican, speech in Naples, Italy, 1860

Source: "History," *The Annual Register… 1860* (London, 1861), p. 221, as quoted in Raymond Phineas Stearns, *Pageant of Europe: Sources and Selections from the Renaissance to the Present Day* (New York: Harcourt, Brace & Company, 1948), pp. 583–584.

6. The ideas expressed in the speech would most appeal to which of the following?
   (A) Liberals
   (B) Nationalists
   (C) Socialists
   (D) Conservatives

7. The emotional appeal of Garibaldi's speech is similar to which of the following intellectual movements?
   (A) The Enlightenment
   (B) Realism
   (C) Romanticism
   (D) Humanism

8. Garibaldi contributed to Italian unification in which of the following ways?
   (A) He was the architect of the movement who carefully planned every step of unification.
   (B) He successfully convinced Cavour to accept the creation of Italy as a republic.
   (C) He and his Red Shirts successfully conquered southern Italy, ceding it to Victor Emmanuel II.
   (D) His invasion of Rome led to papal acceptance of the new Italian state.

Questions 9–11 refer to the passage below.

"The sense of justice to Germany demands the lessening of France….

In view of our obligation to secure the peace of the world, who will venture to object that the people of Alsace and Lorraine do not want to belong to us?...These territories are ours by the right of the sword, and we shall dispose of them in virtue of a higher right—the right of the German nation, which will not permit its lost children to remain strangers to the German Empire. We Germans, who know Germany and France, know better than these unfortunates themselves what is good for the people of Alsace…. Against their will we shall restore them to their true selves…

At all times the subjection of a German race to France has been an unhealthy thing; today it is an offence against the reason of history—a vassalship of free men to half-educated barbarians….

The people of Alsace are already beginning to doubt the invincibility of their nation, and at all events to divine the mighty growth of the German Empire. Perverse obstinacy, and a thousand French intrigues creeping in the dark, will make every step on the newly conquered soil difficult for us: but our ultimate success is certain, for on our side fights what is stronger than the lying artifices of the stranger—nature herself and the voice of common blood."

Heinrich von Treitschke, German historian, newspaper article, *What We Demand from France*, 1870

Source: From Heinrich von Treitschke, "What We Demand from France" (1870), in Heinrich von Treitschke, *Germany, France, Russia and Islam* (New York: G. P. Putnam's Sons, 1915), pp. 100, 102, 106, 109, 120, 122, 134–135, 153, 158.

9. Which of the following best summarizes Von Treitschke's rationale for the annexation of Alsace-Lorraine?
   (A) He promotes the idea of national self-determination, because the people of Alsace-Lorraine wish to join Germany.
   (B) He is a nationalist and he believes that Germany should reclaim her former territory of Alsace-Lorraine.
   (C) He is a liberal and because Alsace-Lorraine is mostly German, it should be a part of the newly formed German Empire.
   (D) He believes that language should dictate political boundaries.

10. Von Treitschke's reference to the "subjection of a German race to France" was a result of which of the following?
   (A) Charles V's defeat at the Battle of Pavia that led to French control of German lands in Italy
   (B) Napoleon I's overthrow of the Hohenzollern king of Prussia during the Napoleonic wars
   (C) French rejection of a German king for the throne of Spain prior to the Franco-Prussian war
   (D) The Holy Roman Emperor's loss of sovereignty over the German states due to French victory in the Thirty Years' War

216

11. Which of the following led to the "mighty growth of the German Empire" as described in the passage?
    (A) Bismarck's acceptance of liberal policies ensured the support by German people for a strong empire after the Franco-Prussian War.
    (B) Bismarck's use of *Realpolitik* and warfare created a conservative German Empire after the Franco-Prussian War.
    (C) An alliance between Prussia and Austria defeated France, annexed Alsace-Lorraine, and declared the German Empire at Versailles in 1871.
    (D) Bismarck's acceptance of the Frankfurt Assembly's constitution during the early 1860s encouraged German states to support Bismarck's war against France in 1870–71.

Questions 12–13 refer to the passage below.

The matter of the liberation of the serfs, which has been submitted for the consideration of the State Council, I consider to be a vital question for Russia, upon which will depend the development of her strength and power. I am sure that all of you…are just as convinced as I am of the…necessity of this measure. I have another conviction, which is that this matter cannot be postponed… that this matter should be finished right away.

For four years now it has dragged on and has been arousing various fears and anticipations among both the estate owners and the peasants. Any further delay could be disastrous to the state….Although the apprehensions of the nobility are to a certain extent understandable…I have not forgotten and shall never forget that the approach to the matter was made on the initiative of the nobility itself…I hope, gentlemen, that on inspection of the drafts presented to the State Council, you will assure yourselves that all that can be done for the protection of the interests of the nobility has been done; if on the other hand you find it necessary in any way to alter or to add to the present work, then I am ready to receive your comments; but I ask you only not to forget that the basis of the whole work must be the improvement of the life of the peasants—an improvement not in words alone or on paper but in actual fact.

Tsar Alexander II, *Address to the State Council,* St. Petersburg, Russia, 1861

Source: George Vernadsky, Ralph T. Fisher, Jr., Alan D. Ferguson, Andrew Lossky and Sergei Pushkarev ed., A Source Book for Russian History From Early Times to 1917 (New Haven: Yale University Press, 1972), III, pp. 599–600.

12. Alexander II's attitude toward freeing the serfs is most likely a result of which of the following?
    (A) Russia's defeat by the western powers during the Crimean War
    (B) Increased pressure by Russian reformers for humanitarian reasons
    (C) Russia following the lead of Prussia and Austria who had freed their serfs in 1848
    (D) Alexander II's desire to convince the boyars they must submit to his authority

13. Alexander II's ideas regarding Russian reform is most clearly influenced by which of the following ideas?
    (A) Balance of Power
    (B) *Realpolitik*
    (C) Marxism
    (D) Socialism

Questions 14–15 refer to the image below.

Painting depicting the assassination of Tsar Alexander II, 1881

Source: bpk Bildagentur/Art Resource, NY

14. The painting above reflects which of the following?
    (A) That even moderate politicians accepted violence as a legitimate way to express dissatisfaction with the status quo
    (B) The growth of the Bolshevik party in Russia during the second half of the nineteenth century
    (C) Radical revolutionary movements that encouraged violence and terrorist tactics
    (D) The immediate cause of the Russian Civil War

15. The Russian government's failure to address issues such as those that led to the events shown in the painting resulted in which of the following?
    (A) The Decembrist Revolt
    (B) The assassination of Archduke Franz Ferdinand
    (C) World War I
    (D) The Russian Revolution of 1905

Short-Answer Question

Use the passage below to answer all parts of the question.

"The…results of the 1848 revolutions were stunning. Never in a single year had Europe known so many major uprisings. The French monarchy fell, and other thrones were shaken. Yet the revolutions proved to be a false spring for progressive Europeans. Without exception, the revolutions failed to establish genuinely liberal or national states. The conservative order proved stronger and more resilient than anyone had expected. Moreover, the liberal middle-class political activists in each country discovered they could no longer push for political reform without also raising the social question. The liberals refused to follow political revolution with social reform and thus isolated themselves from the working classes. Once separated from potential mass support, the liberal revolutions became easy prey for the armies of the reactionary classes."

Donald Kagan, *The Western Heritage 8th edition* (Boston, Pearson Education, 2010)

Answer a, b, and c:
1. a) Explain how one piece of evidence <u>supports</u> Kagan's argument regarding the effects of the Revolutions of 1848.
   b) Explain how one piece of evidence <u>undermines</u> Kagan's argument regarding the effects of the Revolutions of 1848.
   c) Explain one way in which conservative politicians after 1848 used nationalism to strengthen the state.

Long-Essay Question

Evaluate the extent to which the unification of Italy and the unification of Germany were different.

ANSWERS AND EXPLANATIONS: AP® PRACTICE TEST

Multiple-Choice Questions

1. D (KC: 3.4.II.A; LO: Unit 7 C) The outbreak of the Crimean War confirmed the end of the Concert of Europe. The Quintuple Alliance was broken as Britain and France declared war on Russia. Both Prussia and Austria chose to remain neutral. In particular, Austrian neutrality led to a period of diplomatic isolation as all of the belligerents were unhappy with its response to the war.

2. C (KC: 3.4.II.A, 3.5.III.A; LO: Unit 7 C, I) Britain distrusted Russia's intentions in the Balkans and eastern Mediterranean region and preferred to prop up the weakening Ottoman Empire to maintain stability as well as to keep Russian power in check.

3. C (KC: 2.1.V.D; LO: Unit 5 H) The author makes the assertion that the French wanted to tear up the treaties that were signed at the Congress of Vienna back in 1815. This is debatable; however, most historians do agree that Napoleon III involved France in the Crimean War in order to bolster France's position as a great power.

4. B (KC: 3.4.II.B; LO: Unit 7 B) "Cavour's plan" is a reference to his plan to expel Austria from northern Italy and to create a constitutional monarchy under Piedmont-Sardinia's leadership.

5. A (KC: 3.4.II.B; LO: Unit 7 B) Both Cavour and Napoleon III were conservative by nature; however, both utilized *Realpolitik* using nationalism to strengthen their states. Cavour was able to unite Italy under a constitutional monarchy while Napoleon III was able to gain the support of the French people for his authoritative rule.

6. B (KC: 3.3.I.F; LO: Unit 7 B) This is an appeal based primarily on nationalist sentiments.

7. C (KC: 3.6.I.A; LO: Unit 7 J) Nationalism and Romanticism were often linked during the nineteenth century. Both movements emphasized emotion, self-determination, and national histories and were often influenced by the other.

8. C (KC: 3.4.III.A; LO: Unit 7 C) Garibaldi and his Red Shirts, a guerilla force of about 1000 men, successfully conquered southern Italy. Cavour, nervous about Garibaldi's republican background, sent troops to prevent him from trying to conquer Rome. Garibaldi accepted Cavour's wishes and ceded southern Italy to King Victor Emmanuel II. The Kingdom of Italy was proclaimed in 1861, initially without Venice and Rome. Cavour died shortly thereafter, Austria gave up Venice in 1866, and Rome was annexed by Italy in 1870.

9. B (KC: 3.3.I.F; LO: Unit 7 B) In this article, von Treitschke, a German nationalist, argues that Alsace was historically German, and should return to Germany, regardless of the fact that most of the inhabitants resist because they are French and do not speak German. France ceded Alsace-Lorraine to Germany as part of the treaty that ended the Franco-Prussian war. The regions reverted to France after World War I, to Germany in 1940, and again to France at the end of World War II.

10. D (KC: 1.5.I.B, 2.1.III.A; LO: Unit 2 C, Unit 4 H) French victory in the Thirty Years' War led to a period of French hegemony in continental affairs, particularly in the German states. Provisions of the Peace of Westphalia allowed for French interference in German issues and effectively removed most political power of the German Habsburg emperor. Afterwards, Habsburg rulers began to focus their rule on Austria and the non-German regions of central Europe including Hungary and Bohemia.

11. B (KC: 3.4.III.B; LO: Unit 7 C) Bismarck's use of *Realpolitik* encouraged both diplomacy and warfare in order to unite Germany. Provisions of the treaties that ended the 1866 Seven Weeks' War included southern German states allying with Prussia if faced with war with a non-German state. Bismarck's alteration of the Ems Dispatch led to Napoleon III's declaration of war. Germany's subsequent quick victory over the French ensured German support for the declaration of Empire at Versailles in January 1871.

12. A (KC: 3.4.II.A, 3.4.II.D; LO: Unit 7 C, Unit 6 G) Russia's defeat by the western powers during the Crimean War resulted in major reform movements by Alexander II. This was the first war that Russia had lost in almost 150 years. Alexander, who became tsar toward the end of the war in 1855, recognized that the extent to which the western powers had grown economically contributed to Russia's defeat. Influenced by *Realpolitik*, Alexander was interested in reform insofar as it served the state, thus, began a period of modernization and the imposition of some liberal reforms, which included the emancipation of the serfs, creation of *zemstvos*, and easing up of censorship and repressive measures.

13. B (KC: 2.3.I.A, 2.3.I.B; LO: Unit 4 C) See explanation for question 12.

14. C (KC: 3.4.II.B; LO: Unit 7 B) Extreme measures were becoming common for radical and revolutionary groups that advocated the overthrow of the existing regime. *The People's Will* was one such group in Russia who were successful in assassinating Alexander II, but not in overthrowing the Russian monarchy. Revolutionary movements such as the one illustrated would eventually lead to revolutions in both 1905 and 1917 in Russia.

15. D (KC: 3.4.II.D; LO: Unit 6 G) See explanation for question 14.

Short-Answer Question

(KC: 3.4.I, 3.4.II, 3.4.III; Unit 6 F, Unit 7 A, B, C)

Possible responses for part a) include:

- The "June Days" Revolution in France weakened the new Second Republic and led to the emergence of the Second French Empire under Napoleon III in 1852.
- Although Italy temporarily defeated Austrian forces and established the Roman Republic in 1849, its success was short lived as Austrian forces reasserted control later that year.
- The Hungarian revolution against Austria in 1848 failed to achieve its goal of autonomy from Austrian rule.
- German nationalists who sought to unify the German states under Prussian leadership failed to achieve their goals.

Possible responses for part b) include:

- The February Revolution in France resulted in the overthrow of King Louis Philippe and the establishment of the Second Republic that lasted four years under Louis Napoleon.

Possible responses for part c) include:

- Cavour used nationalism to gradually unify the Italian state starting in the late-1850s.
- Bismarck used nationalism to engineer German unification starting in the mid-1860s.
- Austrian leaders had to compromise in 1867 with Hungarians in the creation of the Dual Monarchy.
- Napoleon III used nationalism as a means of strengthening his control of the Second Empire.

Long-Essay Question
(KC: 3.4.III.A, 3.4.III.B; Unit 7 C)

Evaluate the extent to which the unification of Italy and the unification of Germany were different.

Possible responses for differences might include:
- Italy sought unification by removing foreign rulers while Bismarck sought unification among sovereign German states.
- Bismarck initiated major wars with Austria and France to achieve unification while Cavour opportunistically used alliances, diplomacy, and less grand military engagements against Austria.
- Garibaldi's liberation of southern Italy from Spanish rulers and his subsequent consent to allow King Victor Emmanuel to rule the entire country was different from Germany, where Prussia drove the entire unification process.

Possible responses for similarities might include:
- Both Cavour and Bismarck used *realpolitik* to achieve their unification goals.
- Both Cavour and Bismarck used nationalism to achieve their goals.
- Both countries utilized military conflicts to advance their goals.
- Both Bismarck and Cavour were conservatives who incorporated aspects of liberalism to achieve their goals, such as establishing constitutional monarchies (in theory).

CHAPTER 15

The Building of European Supremacy: Society and Politics to World War I

POPULATION TRENDS AND MIGRATION

- European population, with respect to world population, was at its all-time high in 1900—one-fifth of the world was European at that time. After that time, birth and death rates leveled off in Europe and grew in other areas, which led in turn to the divide between the developed and the less developed world (which is still characterized by differences in industrial and technological advancements).
- More than 50 million Europeans migrated away from their continent between 1846 and 1932. This outflow of people relieved social and population pressures on the continent and spread European culture throughout the world. Combined with Europe's economic and technological superiority, the migration contributed to the dominant role Europe continues to play in the world.

AP® FRAMEWORK
TOPIC # 6.3, 6.4; LO: UNIT 6 C, E
KC:
3.1.III.B New technologies and means of communication and transportation—including railroads—resulted in more fully integrated national economies, a higher level of urbanization, and a truly global economic network.
3.2.II.B With migration from rural to urban areas in industrialized regions, cities experienced overcrowding, while affected rural areas suffered declines in available labor as well as weakened communities.

THE SECOND INDUSTRIAL REVOLUTION

- Continental industries caught up to those of Britain toward the end of the nineteenth century, and the expansion of railroad systems on the Continent helped to spur economic growth and enable new industries to emerge. This phase of development, which accelerated the production of steel, chemicals, electricity, and oil, is known as the Second Industrial Revolution.
- Several inventions were essential in this period: Henry Bessemer's process for manufacturing steel; the Solway process of alkali production enabled the recovery of more chemical by-products; the application of electrical energy to production and to homes and transportation; and the invention of the internal combustion engine (which eventually gave birth to the automobile) were the major developments during this period. Machines that required petroleum created a great need for oil.

225

AP® FRAMEWORK
TOPIC # 6.3; LO: UNIT 6 C, D
KC:
3.1.II.B Industrialization in Prussia allowed that state to become the leader of a unified Germany, which subsequently underwent rapid industrialization under government sponsorship.
3.1.III During the Second Industrial Revolution (c. 1870–1914), more areas of Europe experienced industrial activity, and industrial processes increased in scale and complexity.
3.1.III.A Mechanization and the factory system became the predominant modes of production by 1914.
3.2.IV.B New, efficient methods of transportation and other innovations created new industries, improved the distribution of goods, increased consumerism, and enhanced quality of life.

THE MIDDLE CLASSES IN ASCENDANCY

- The middle class was at its height in the sixty years prior to World War I: They defined consumer taste and were no longer associated with the radical revolutions of the 1840s, but rather they were identified with a desire to protect their assets. The middle class grew more diverse as it came to encompass more people—some were industrialists, others were entrepreneurs and professionals who had sufficient income for private homes and some basic domestic luxuries.

AP® FRAMEWORK
TOPIC # 6.4; LO: UNIT 6 E
KC:
3.2.I.A In industrialized areas of Europe (i.e., western and northern Europe), socioeconomic changes created divisions of labor that led to the development of self-conscious classes, including the proletariat and the bourgeoisie.
3.2.I.C Class identity developed and was reinforced through participation in philanthropic, political, and social associations among the middle classes, and in mutual aid societies and trade unions among the working classes.

LATE NINETEENTH-CENTURY URBAN LIFE

- Europe became more urbanized as migration to the cities continued. From 1850 to 1911, urban dwellers grew from 25 percent to 44 percent of the population in France and from 30 percent to 60 percent of the population in Germany. Rural migrants frequently lived in unhealthy conditions and experienced widespread discrimination.
- Cities were redesigned to accommodate the changes in urban living. While central urban areas had always been places for people of all social classes, urban planners transformed these areas into business and government centers, but not residential dwelling spaces.
- Sanitation improvements were made following concerns with health and housing after the cholera epidemics of the 1830s and 1840s. New water and sewer systems were constructed to improve conditions, which led to a reduction of the mortality rate. Suburbs became popular for both middle and working classes, and improved transit eased this transformation.

AP® FRAMEWORK
TOPIC #6.3, 6.4, 6.9; LO: UNIT 6 C, E, J
KC:
3.1.III.B New technologies and means of communication and transportation—including railroads—resulted in more fully integrated national economies, a higher level of urbanization, and a truly global economic network.
3.2.II.B With migration from rural to urban areas in industrialized regions, cities experienced overcrowding, while affected rural areas suffered declines in available labor as well as weakened communities.
3.3.II.B Reforms transformed unhealthy and overcrowded cities by modernizing infrastructure, regulating public health, reforming prisons, and establishing modern police forces. The reforms were enacted by governments motivated by such forces as public opinion, prominent individuals, and charity organizations.

VARIETIES OF LATE NINETEENTH-CENTURY WOMEN'S EXPERIENCES

- Women remained second-class citizens in the nineteenth century. Through marriage, many women lost their individual legal identities and suffered tremendous disadvantages that limited their freedom to work, to save, and to move from one location to another.
- Although jobs available for single women expanded during the Second Industrial Revolution, middle class notions of patriarchy prevailed and more married women withdrew from the workforce. The jobs available to women were usually low-paying jobs that did not require training or skills. New cultural ideas that connected prosperity with women not working outside the home took root in the middle classes.

AP® FRAMEWORK
TOPIC # 6.4, 6.7, 6.8; LO: UNIT 6 E, H, I
KC:
3.2.III.A Bourgeois families became focused on the nuclear family and the cult of domesticity, with distinct gender roles for men and women.
3.2.III.C Economic motivations for marriage, while still important for all classes, diminished as the middle-class notion of companionate marriage began to be adopted by the working classes.
3.3.I.B Radicals in Britain and republicans on the continent demanded universal male suffrage and full citizenship without regard to wealth and property ownership; some argued that such rights should be extended to women.
3.3.III.C Feminists pressed for legal, economic, and political rights for women as well as improved working conditions.

JEWISH EMANCIPATION

- Jews saw gains in political equality and social status in the nineteenth century, but changes came slowly. The conditions for Jews improved after the Revolutions of 1848, especially in western Europe. Jews and Christians were granted roughly equal laws by Joseph II in 1782, and in France, the National Assembly recognized Jews as French citizens in 1789. Traditional prejudices against Jews continued in eastern Europe until World War I; in Russia, Jews were treated as foreigners and were restricted in all aspects of their daily lives.
- Despite improved conditions, anti-Semitism increased in the late-nineteenth century, as critics attributed economic stagnation to Jewish bankers and financial institutions.

AP® FRAMEWORK
TOPIC # 7.2; LO: UNIT 7 B
KC:

3.3.I.F Nationalists encouraged loyalty to the nation in a variety of ways, including romantic idealism, liberal reform, political unification, racialism with a concomitant anti-Semitism, and chauvinism justifying national aggrandizement.

3.3.I.G While during the 19th century western European Jews became more socially and politically acculturated, Zionism, a form of Jewish nationalism, developed late in the century as a response to growing anti-Semitism throughout Europe.

LABOR, SOCIALISM, AND POLITICS TO WORLD WAR I

- After 1848, workers turned to new institutions and ideologies to seek change. Trade unions emerged in the latter part of the nineteenth century, and through them some workers attempted to gain an overall improvement in wages and working conditions. Most European workers were not represented by unions during this period, but unions did help those workers they represented bargain collectively for improvements to their employment.
- Universal male suffrage was extended during this era in many countries, so the voices of lower-class workers carried more political weight than they had previously. Political parties made efforts to appeal to the working classes and socialist movements of many kinds emerged throughout Europe.
- Karl Marx spoke at the First International (International Working Men's Association) of 1864, a group of radicals, socialists, anarchists, and Polish nationalists organized by a group of British and French trade unionists.
- From the activities of the First International, Marxism emerged as a new kind of socialism, and it became popular in Germany. In Britain, Fabianism and early welfare programs took root. French and German socialists emerged at this time, forming the Socialist Party and the German Social Democratic Party, respectively. A Social Democratic party emerged in Russia as well as more radical organizations such as the Bolsheviks.

AP® FRAMEWORK
TOPIC # 6.4, 6.7. 6.8; LO: UNIT 6 E, H, I
KC:

3.2.I.A In industrialized areas of Europe (i.e., western and northern Europe), socioeconomic changes created divisions of labor that led to the development of self-conscious classes, including the proletariat and the bourgeoisie.

3.2.I.C Class identity developed and was reinforced through participation in philanthropic, political, and social associations among the middle classes, and in mutual aid societies and trade unions among the working classes.

3.3.I.D Socialists called for the redistribution of society's resources and wealth and evolved from a utopian to a Marxist scientific critique of capitalism.

3.3.III.B Workers established labor unions and movements promoting social and economic reforms that also developed into political parties.

3.6.II.C Marx's scientific socialism provided a systematic critique of capitalism and a deterministic analysis of society and historical evolution.

Multiple-Choice Questions

Questions 1–4 refer to the maps below.

European Industrialization in 1860

 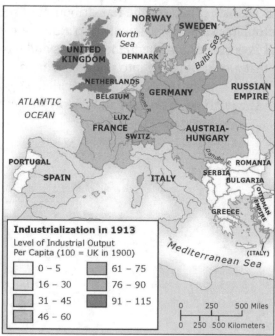

1. Which of the following best explains the trends shown on the maps regarding the Industrial Revolution in Europe?
   (A) The Zollverein was ineffective at best, delaying German industrialization until later in the nineteenth century and contributing to early British industrial power.
   (B) Britain relied upon food imports from the continent to feed its people resulting in a population of landless peasants migrating to cities to look for work.
   (C) British political stability with its parliamentary system during the early nineteenth century allowed it to develop its industrial might earlier than the rest of the continent.
   (D) Serfdom in France, Spain, and Italy prior to the Napoleonic period hindered the growth of industry in those countries, which contributed to early British industrial dominance.

2. Which of the following best explains the lack of industrial output in eastern and southern Europe?
   (A) Continued reliance on the cottage industry in those areas
   (B) Strong socialist movements in those areas that did not allow industry to develop
   (C) Traditional social structures that did not encourage industrial change in those areas
   (D) Dry climate and a lack of navigable waterways in those areas that hindered industrial development

3. Which of the following best explains how industrialization differed in Britain and France?
   (A) France had to import coal and iron ore resources whereas Britain had a ready supply.
   (B) France industrialized at a more gradual pace with more government intervention than in Britain.
   (C) The Napoleonic period led to greater industrial self-sufficiency in France than in Britain.
   (D) France promoted free trade policies whereas Britain was a proponent of protective tariffs.

4. Which of the following developments in the period through 1914 is most surprising considering the trends shown on the map?
   (A) The rapid industrialization of Germany
   (B) The rapid industrialization of Russia
   (C) The growth of the railroad industry in Britain and France
   (D) The development of a strong middle class in the Ottoman Empire

Growth of Major European Cities

GROWTH OF MAJOR EUROPEAN CITIES
(FIGURES IN THOUSANDS)

	1850	1880	1910
Berlin	419	1,122	2,071
Birmingham	233	437	840
Frankfurt	65	137	415
London	2,685	4,470	7,256
Madrid	281	398	600
Moscow	365	748	1,533
Paris	1,053	2,269	2,888
Rome	175	300	542
Saint Petersburg	485	877	1,962
Vienna	444	1,104	2,031
Warsaw	160	339	872

5. The trend shown on the table was most directly a result of all of the following EXCEPT
   (A) the Industrial Revolution
   (B) longer life expectancy
   (C) lower infant mortality rates
   (D) new methods of birth control

6. The trends shown on the table resulted in which of the following changes to European cities?
   (A) Governments created ethnic enclaves to ease tension among migrant workers.
   (B) Governments subsidized public housing for those unable to afford high rents in urban areas.
   (C) Government reforms improved sanitary conditions and modernized urban areas.
   (D) Governments created Poor Laws to stop vagrancy and provide relief for those unable to find employment.

7. The trends shown on the table contributed to which of the following?
    (A) The end of serfdom in eastern Europe
    (B) Reforms that regulated public health
    (C) reforms that encouraged universal health care
    (D) The legalization of women's suffrage in large urban areas

8. An historian could use this table as evidence to support which of the following assertions?
    (A) While there was greater industrialization in western Europe, urbanization occurred proportionately throughout most of the continent.
    (B) Western European cities grew more rapidly than those in southern and eastern Europe due to liberal government policies that encouraged urbanization.
    (C) French urbanization increased due to their economic rivalry with Germany after the Franco-Prussian war.
    (D) France's industrial output ranked second only to Britain by the outbreak of the First World War.

Questions 9–10 refer to the passage below.

"…I was appointed to the Committee on Technical Education, the one woman admitted to this committee. I learned that the Manchester Technical College, called the second best in Europe, spending thousands of pounds annually for technical training, had practically no provision for training women. Even in classes where they might easily have been admitted, bakery and confectionary classes and the like, the girls were kept out because the men's trades unions objected to their being educated for such skilled work. It was rapidly becoming clear to my mind that men regarded women as a servant class in the community, and that women were going to remain in the servant class until they lifted themselves out of it. I asked myself many times in those days what was to be done. I had joined the Labour Party, thinking that through its councils something vital might come, some such demand for the women's enfranchisement that the politicians could not possibly ignore. Nothing came."

Emmeline Pankhurst, British suffragette and reformer, *Suffragette, The Autobiography of Emmeline Pankhurst*, 1914

Source: *From Emmeline Pankhurst, My Own Story (*New York: Hearst International Library, 1914)

9. Based on the passage, which of the following can be safely inferred about Pankhurst's beliefs?
    (A) She believed in greater access to birth control.
    (B) She believed that women should serve in the military forces.
    (C) She believed that suffrage would enable women to better their condition.
    (D) She believed in increased social welfare legislation.

10. Pankhurst's ideas were finally achieved partly as a result of which of the following?
    (A) Growing pressure from Britain's allies during the First World War
    (B) The growth of the Labour party
    (C) The influential communist movement in Britain
    (D) Women's contributions to the war effort during the First World War

Questions 11–13 refer to the passage below.

"Social conditions have not developed to such an acute opposition of things and classes as is depicted in the [Communist] Manifesto…. The number of members of the possessing classes is today not smaller but larger. The enormous increase of social wealth is not accompanied by a decreasing number of large capitalists but by an increasing number of capitalists of all degrees….

In all advanced countries we see the privileges of the capitalist bourgeoisie yielding step by step to democratic organizations….

The conquest of political power by the working classes, the expropriation of capitalists, are not ends in certain aims and endeavours….

Universal franchise is, from two sides, the alternative to a violent revolution. But universal suffrage is only a part of democracy, although a part which in time must draw the other parts after it as the magnet attracts to itself the scattered portions of iron. It certainly proceeds more slowly than many would wish, but in spite of that it is at work….

Is there any sense… in maintaining the phrase of the "dictatorship of the proletariat" at a time when in all possible places representatives of social democracy have placed themselves practically in the arena of Parliamentary work, have declared for the proportional representation of the people, and for direct legislation—all of which is inconsistent with a dictatorship."

Eduard Bernstein, German Revisionist Marxist philosopher and politician,
Evolutionary Socialism, 1899

Source: Eduard Bernstein, Evolutionary Socialism: A Criticism and Affirmation, 1899 (New York: Schocken Books, 1961), pp. xxiv–xxv, xxix,

11. The ideas expressed in the passage are similar to Marx's ideas because
    (A) both Bernstein and Marx are supportive of the idea of violent revolution against the bourgeoisie
    (B) both Bernstein and Marx are supportive of the idea of violent revolution against the proletariat
    (C) both Bernstein and Marx are supportive of the goals of the bourgeoisie as opposed to the proletariat
    (D) both Bernstein and Marx are supportive of the goals of the proletariat as opposed to the bourgeoisie

12. Bernstein's assertion regarding communist revolution in the passage was likely influenced by which of the following changes in the second half of the nineteenth century?
    (A) The development of mass-based political parties in most western European countries
    (B) The extension of universal suffrage in virtually all European countries
    (C) The creation of an effective German legislature after Bismarck's dismissal by Wilhelm II
    (D) Nationalistic euphoria over a united German Empire at peace with itself

13. Bernstein would have been most opposed to the political philosophy of
    (A) Henri de Saint-Simon
    (B) Friedrich Engels
    (C) Otto von Bismarck
    (D) V.I. Lenin

Questions 14–15 refer to the passage below.

"…Rioting and disturbances in the capitals and in many localities of Our Empire fill Our heart with great and heavy grief. The well-being of the Russian Sovereign is inseparable from the well-being of the nation, and the nation's sorrow is his sorrow…

… We are obliged to use every resource of wisdom and of Our authority to bring a speedy end to unrest that is dangerous to Our state. We have ordered the responsible authorities to take measures to terminate direct manifestations of disorder, lawlessness, and violence and to protect peaceful people who quietly seek to fulfill their duties…

We require the government dutifully to execute our unshakeable will:

(1.) To grant to the population the essential foundations of civil freedom, based on the principles of genuine inviolability of the person, freedom of conscience, speech, assembly and association.

(2.) Without postponing the scheduled elections to the State Duma, to admit to participation in the duma (insofar as possible in the short time that remains before it is scheduled to convene) of all those classes of the population that now are completely deprived of voting rights; and to leave the further development of a general statute on elections to the future legislative order.

(3.) To establish as an unbreakable rule that no law shall take effect without confirmation by the State Duma and that the elected representatives of the people shall be guaranteed the opportunity to participate in the supervision of the legality of the actions of Our appointed officials."

Tsar Nicholas II, The October Manifesto, October 1905

Source: http://academic.shu.edu/russianhistory/index.php/Manifesto_of_October_17th,_1905 Translated by Daniel Field.

14. Which of the following long-term factors led to the conditions in which Nicholas was forced to issue *The October Manifesto*?
    (A) The return of serfdom in Russia contributed to revolutionary movements that encouraged industrialization and universal manhood suffrage.
    (B) Alexander II's reform movements inadvertently gave rise to revolutionary movements that called for political representation and other liberal reforms.
    (C) The perceived influence of Rasputin caused Russian elites to demand political representation and the creation of a Duma.
    (D) Nicholas II believed that mild concessions such as those in the *Manifesto* would gain support for the government to prevent the return of Lenin and radical revolution.

15. Which of the following was a long-term effect of *The October Manifesto*?
    (A) Nicholas II ignored most provisions; as a result, he was forced to abdicate during the Revolution of 1917.
    (B) Russia achieved a degree of stability that would last until Lenin overthrew Nicholas during the radical phase of the Russian revolution.
    (C) The tsar's government gained enough support to successfully industrialize over the next ten years.
    (D) Nicholas denied political and financial support to the Russian Orthodox Church in order to gain the confidence of former revolutionaries.

Short-Answer Question

Answer a, b, and c:

1. a). Describe one way in which European Jews became more *politically* acculturated during the nineteenth century.
    b). Describe one way in which European Jews became more *socially* acculturated during the nineteenth century.
    c). Explain one way anti-Semitism increased during the second half of the nineteenth century.

Long-Essay Question

Evaluate the extent to which urban life was transformed during the second half of the nineteenth century.

238

ANSWERS AND EXPLANATIONS: AP® PRACTICE TEST

Multiple-Choice Questions

1. C (KC: 3.1.I.C; LO: 6 B) Britain's early start to industrialization was due to a number of factors including a stable government that avoided the warfare and revolutions that took place on the continent as well as a parliament that represented business interests.

2. C (KC: 3.1.II.C; LO: 6 B) Traditional social structures in eastern Europe, most notably a strong landed class and the persistence of serfdom, did not encourage changes that would lead to industrialization.

3. B (KC: 3.1.II.A; LO: 6 B) Compared with Britain, France's pace of industrialization was more gradual while smaller factories tended to be family-owned. The British government often promoted laissez faire policies and was generally opposed to tariffs (largely because competition was limited) whereas the French government subsidized the infrastructure and enacted tariffs, despite pursuing trade agreements with other countries.

4. A (KC: 3.1.II.B; LO: 6 D) By 1860 there was little industry in Germany. The Zollverein (a German trade agreement led by Prussia) had contributed to the advance of industry prior to 1860, but at a very slow pace. After German unification in 1871, German industry rapidly developed. Many historians believe that Germany was the dominant economic power in Europe by the outbreak of World War I.

5. D (KC: 3.2.II; LO: 6 A) Urbanization increased rapidly in the late-nineteenth century for a number of reasons including factories being built in urban centers, better transportation, increased availability of foodstuffs, and better medicines and antiseptics. New methods of birth control became available during this time and were not a direct cause of the growth of cities.

6. C (KC: 3.1.II.B; LO: 6 D) Due to the massive influx of population European cities, governments were forced to enact public health reforms in urban areas to stop the spread of disease and improve life. Governments also redesigned cities such as Paris and Vienna to provide more leisure activities, create a sense of pride, and control military insurrections.

7. B (KC: 3.3.II.B, 3.3.IIC; LO: 6 J) Due to industrialization and urbanization, reformers were more successful in achieving their goals to better society for the public good such as the British Public Health Act of 1875, which was enacted to prevent filthy urban conditions and halt the spread of diseases.

8. A (KC: 3.2.II; LO: 6 A) Although western Europe experienced more rapid industrialization and urbanization, with few exceptions, cities grew proportionately throughout the continent. For instance, London was still by far the largest city in 1850 and again in 1910 with a growth rate similar to Berlin, Paris, and most other cities.

9. C (KC: 3.3.III.C; LO: 6 I) Pankhurst led the Women's Social and Political Union in Britain (WSPU), a group that advocated strongly for women's suffrage. In addition to women's suffrage, women's groups during this time period also advocated for legal and economic rights and improved working conditions. Pankhurst believed that earlier, more peaceful methods had failed and began a more militant movement that, along with women's contribution to the war effort, contributed to partial suffrage in Britain after the First World War.

10. D (KC: 4.4.II.A; LO: 8 M) See explanation for question 9.

11. D (KC: 3.2.I.A, 3.6.II.C; LO: 6 E, H) In broad terms, both Bernstein and Marx agreed with proletariat goals that would lead to better living and working conditions for the working classes. A key point of disagreement between Bernstein and Marx was that Bernstein did not believe a violent revolution was necessary

12. A (KC: 3.3.III.A; LO: 6 I) The development of mass-based political parties gave the average worker a say in many European countries, something that did not exist when Marx wrote *The Communist Manifesto* in 1848. Bernstein believed that this new "evolutionary socialism" could be achieved through the democratic process.

13. C (KC: 3.4.II.B; LO: 7 B) As chancellor of Germany, Bismarck tried to silence the Social Democratic Party (of which Bernstein was a member) through a variety of methods. Interestingly, Bismarck enacted some social welfare legislation in hopes that workers would become more loyal to the government and less to the SPD; nevertheless, the SPD continued to grow as Germany continued to industrialize.

14. B (KC: 3.4.II.D; LO: 6 G) Alexander II's reforms did not go far enough for many, leading to the formation of more radical groups such as *The People's Will* who were responsible for his assassination. Other groups were also unhappy with the weak government and after losses in the Russo-Japanese war and the events of Bloody Sunday, a full-scale revolution began in Russia. Unable to end the violence, Nicholas II reluctantly agreed to grant representation through universal manhood suffrage and the election of a Duma.

15. A (KC: 4.2.I.A; LO: 8 E) As the Duma lost power in the years leading up to World War I, Nicholas reverted to his old absolutist tendencies. Combined with staggering losses during the First World War, another revolution began in 1917 which ended 300-plus years of Romanov rule.

Short-Answer Question
(KC: 3.3.I.F, 3.3.I.G; LO: 7 B)

Possible responses for part a) include:
- The European Jewish population gained full citizenship in many of the German states, Italy, Belgium, and the Netherlands after the revolutions of 1848.
- Jewish politicians served in high offices in many states including British prime minister Benjamin Disraeli. (1868, 1874–1880)

Possible responses for part b) include:
- In many western European countries including Britain, Italy, France, and Germany, legal discrimination of Jews ended.
- Intermarriage with non-Jews became more frequent in the second half of the century and many countries repealed laws that had banned such marriages.

Possible responses for part c) include:
- Jewish bankers were often blamed for economic downturns during the last two decades of the century.
- As nationalism increased throughout the continent, many ardent nationalists began to see Jews as non-European, even those that had fully assimilated.

Long-Essay Question
(KC: 3.2.II.B, 3.3.II.B; LO: 6 E, J)

Evaluate the extent to which urban life was transformed during the second half of the nineteenth century.

Possible responses for ways in which urban life was transformed include:
- Many cities including Paris and Vienna were redesigned. New city centers were no longer mostly residential and instead areas where business, government functions, department stores, and leisure activities were predominant.
- Streets were widened both for beauty and to prevent unruly activity. Wide boulevards allowed for quicker troop movements to put down any type of rebellion or disturbance.
- Suburbs were developed for both the middle and working classes.
- Public transportation was improved with the creation of subways and streetcars.
- Efforts were made to clean up the cities and improve public health. New sewer systems were created.

Possible responses for way in which urban life remained the same include:
- Neighborhoods remained mostly segregated according to class. For example, even though both working and middle classes moved to the suburbs, they continued to reside in districts with people of their class.
- Some cities did not see improvements to water systems until into the twentieth century.
- Despite attempts at improving, the housing problem for the working class was not fully addressed until early in the twentieth century.

CHAPTER 16

The Birth of Modern European Thought

THE NEW READING PUBLIC

- By 1900, 85 percent of people could read in Britain, France, Belgium, the Netherlands, Germany, and Scandinavia, thanks largely to improvements in primary education. Improvements in literacy led to greater secondary education opportunities in many countries.
- The amount of printed matter available to the public increased dramatically during this time; some of the materials catered to the marginally literate or the lowest levels of public taste.
- Literacy enabled Europeans to gain knowledge and improve their social situations.

AP® FRAMEWORK
TOPIC # 6.10; LO: UNIT 6 K
KC:
3.3.II Governments, at times based on the pressure of political or social organizations, responded to problems created or exacerbated by industrialization.

SCIENCE AT MIDCENTURY

- The philosophy of **positivism** of Auguste Comte (1798–1857) influenced the field of science.
- Charles Darwin's 1859 book, *The Origin of Species,* formulated the principle of **natural selection**, which explained how species evolved over time. In his 1871 work, *The Descent of Man,* Darwin explored the principle of natural selection and the application of evolutionary theory to humans.
- Many philosophers during this time period used Darwin's theories to legitimize racism and western superiority, a philosophy that came to be known as **Social Darwinism**.

AP® FRAMEWORK
TOPIC # 7.4, 7.5; LO: UNIT 7 E, F
KC:
3.6.II.A Positivism, or the philosophy that science alone provides knowledge, emphasized the rational and scientific analysis of nature and human affairs.
3.6.II.B Charles Darwin provided a scientific and material account of biological change and the development of human beings as a species, and inadvertently, a justification for racialist theories that became known as Social Darwinism.

- Historical scholarship in the nineteenth century attacked Christianity on many grounds. David Friedrich Strauss in *The Life of Jesus* questioned the historical evidence of Jesus's existence. Julius Wellhausen, Ernst Renan, and William Robertson argued that human authors had written and edited the books of the Bible.
- The progress of science undermined the Christian underpinning of the doctrine of Creation by determining the actual age of the earth. Other scientists proposed that religious thought was just like any other phenomena, not spiritually inspired nor did it reveal "the truth."
- Friedrich Nietzsche also attacked Christianity, accusing it of promoting weakness and not glorifying strength.
- There was more conflict between church and state throughout Europe at this time. In England, there was increased hostility between the Anglican Church and other Protestant denominations; in France, where the Catholic Church was frequently at odds with the Third Republic, the Ferry Laws (sponsored by Jules Ferry) replaced religious instruction in the public schools with civil training. In Germany, Bismarck removed Catholic and Protestant clergy from overseeing local education in Prussia. He instituted the May Laws of 1873, which demanded that priests be educated in German schools and universities and gave control of the appointment of priests to the state. This ***Kulturkampf,*** or "cultural struggle," failed, and Bismarck retreated from his policies.

AP® FRAMEWORK
TOPIC # 7.2, 7.5; LO: UNIT 7 B, F
KC:
3.4.II.B A new generation of conservative leaders, including Napoleon III, Cavour, and Bismarck, used popular nationalism to create or strengthen the state.
3.6.III.A Philosophy largely moved from rational interpretations of nature and human society to an emphasis on irrationality and impulse, a view that contributed to the belief that conflict and struggle led to progress.

TOWARD A TWENTIETH-CENTURY FRAME OF MIND

- The scientists Ernst Mach, Henri Poincaré, and Hans Vaihinger urged that scientists consider their theories hypothetical constructs of the physical world. Scientists like Wilhelm Roentgen, Henri Becquerel, J.J. Thompson, Marie Curie, and Ernest Rutherford established the important properties and uses of radioactive materials. Albert Einstein researched relativity, and Werner Heisenberg published his uncertainty principle.
- In literature, realism and naturalism became dominant themes. Flaubert used realism to portray life without adornment in his *Madame Bovary,* and Zola set forth realism as a movement. Henrik Ibsen and George Bernard Shaw brought realism into the depiction of domestic life and romantic ideals.
- From the 1870s onward, a new movement of **modernism** was captured in works by artists trying to break away from traditional forms. Igor Stravinsky broke from tradition with his Rite of Spring musical composition, Picasso brought the art world to modernism with cubist forms, and members of the Bloomsbury Group, including Virginia Woolf challenged the structure of traditional literature and the assumptions of Victorian culture.

- Marcel Proust, James Joyce, Thomas Mann, and T.S. Eliot were just a few of the important literary modernists of this era.
- Sigmund Freud (1856–1939) introduced psychoanalysis to the modern period. He became interested in the idea that dreams expressed the repressed desires of everyday life, and he developed a theory of infantile sexuality. Freud's former student, Carl Jung, advanced his own ideas of the collective unconscious.
- The influential German sociologist Max Weber advanced his belief in noneconomic factors that might account for major developments in history and his faith in the role of the individual in society. Weber differed from many of his peers, who considered collective behavior more of a social factor. These scientists included Émile Durkheim, Georges Sorel, Gustave LeBon, Vilfredo Pareto, and Graham Wallas.
- Racial thinking in this century supported the ideas of superior and inferior races (in Europe and beyond) and led to racist ideology. One example of this ideology was anti-Semitism.

AP® FRAMEWORK
TOPIC # 7.5, 7.9, 8.10; LO: UNIT 7 F, K, UNIT 8 M
KC:
3.6 European ideas and culture expressed a tension between objectivity and scientific realism on one hand, and subjectivity and individual expression on the other.
3.6.II Following the revolutions of 1848, Europe turned toward a realist and materialist worldview.
3.6.III.B Freudian psychology offered a new account of human nature that emphasized the role of the irrational and the struggle between the conscious and subconscious.
4.3.II.A The challenge to the certainties of the Newtonian universe in physics opened the door to uncertainty in other fields by undermining faith in objective knowledge while also providing the knowledge necessary for the development of nuclear weapons and power.

WOMEN AND MODERN THOUGHT
- The biological role of women as mothers became more entrenched in social views of women during this century. Misogyny was not uncommon in the fiction and art of this period.
- Women were excluded from the scientific community, as their alleged "inferiority" made them ineligible for participation. Freud's views helped perpetuate these ideas, and his theories were later debunked by distinguished psychoanalysts such as Melanie Klein and Karen Horney.
- Feminists of this era supported wider sexual freedom for women and advocated contraception. Some women became active in socialist groups; others sought to carve out careers for themselves in professions that had previously been unavailable to them.

AP® FRAMEWORK
TOPIC # 6.8, 7.5; LO: UNIT 6 I, UNIT 7 F
KC:
3.3.III Political movements and social organizations responded to the problems of industrialization.
3.3.III.C Feminists pressed for legal, economic, and political rights for women as well as improved working conditions.
3.6.III.B Freudian psychology offered a new account of human nature that emphasized the role of the irrational and the struggle between the conscious and subconscious.

CHAPTER 16: AP® PRACTICE TEST

Multiple-Choice Questions

Questions 1–4 refer to the passage below.

"History shows me one way, and one way only, in which a state of civilisation has been produced, namely, the struggle of race with race, and the survival of the physically and mentally fitter race. This dependence of progress on the survival of the fitter race, terribly black as it may seem to some of you, gives the struggle for existence its redeeming features; it is the fiery crucible out of which comes the finer metal. You may hope for a time when the sword shall be turned into the ploughshare, when American and German and English traders shall no longer compete in the markets of the world for raw materials, for their food supply, when the white man and the dark shall share the soil between them, and each till it as he lists. But, believe me, when that day comes mankind will no longer progress; there will be nothing to check the fertility of inferior stock; the relentless law of heredity will not be controlled and guided by natural selection. Man will stagnate…. The path of progress is strewn with the wreck of nations; traces are everywhere to be seen of the hecatombs of inferior races, and of victims who found not the narrow way to the greater perfection. Yet these dead peoples are, in very truth, the stepping stones on which mankind has arisen to the higher intellectual and deeper emotional life of today."

Karl Pearson, English scientist, *National Life from the Standpoint of Science*, 1907

Source: Karl Pearson, *National Life from the Standpoint of Science*, 2nd ed. (Cambridge, UK: Cambridge University Press, 1907), pp. 21, 26–27, 64.

1. Pearson's argument in the passage was most influenced by the ideas of which of the following?
   (A) Charles Darwin
   (B) Ernest Rutherford
   (C) Max Planck
   (D) Sigmund Freud

2. The ideas expressed in the passage are reflective of which of the following?
   (A) Anti-Feminism
   (B) Positivism
   (C) Social Darwinism
   (D) Skepticism

3. The ideas expressed in the passage were used
    (A) to convince the Christian churches to accept the theory of natural selection
    (B) to explain the concepts of *The Great Chain of Being* and the *Body Politic*
    (C) to justify European treatment of colonial subjects in Africa and Asia
    (D) to deny women the right to vote

4. The ideas expressed in the passage had which of the following effects?
    (A) Increasingly harsh laws against the poor and unemployed
    (B) The growth of socialist movements in western Europe
    (C) A return to serfdom in many parts of eastern Europe
    (D) An increase in anti-Semitic behaviors and actions

Questions 5–8 refer to the passage below.

"The great mistake that is made in the matter now under consideration is…that class is naturally hostile to class; that rich and poor are intended by Nature to live at war with one another. So irrational and so false is this view that the exact contrary is the truth…. Each requires the other; capital cannot do without labour, nor labour without capital. Mutual agreement results in pleasantness and good order; perpetual conflict necessarily produces confusion and outrage. Now, in preventing such strife as this, and in making it impossible, the efficacy of Christianity is marvelous and manifold…. Religion teaches the labouring man and the workman to carry out honestly and well all equitable agreements freely made; never to injure capital, or to outrage the person of an employer; never to employ violence in representing his own cause, or to engage in riot or disorder…Religion teaches the rich man and the employer that their work people are not their slaves; that they must respect in every man his dignity as a man and as a Christian; that labour is nothing to be ashamed of, if we listen to right reason and to Christian philosophy, but is an honourable employment, enabling a man to sustain his life in an upright and creditable way; and that it is shameful and inhuman to treat men like chattels to make money by, or to look upon them merely as so much muscle or physical power…"

Pope Leo XIII, *Rerum Novarum (On Capital and Labor)*, 1891

Source: F. S. Nitti, *Catholic Socialism*, trans. by Mary Mackintosh (London: S. Sonnenschein, 1895), p. 409.

5. Based on the ideas of the document and its context, Pope Leo XIII might have been influenced by which of the following?
   (A) Adam Smith's ideas regarding supply and demand
   (B) Poor living and working conditions for the working classes
   (C) Legislation passed by the Italian Parliament
   (D) Social Darwinist ideas and philosophy

6. Leo XIII's ideas were similar to the ideas of Karl Marx because both agreed with which of the following?
   (A) A social revolution would take place.
   (B) Capitalism needed to be restrained.
   (C) The existing social order was divinely sanctioned.
   (D) Wealth should be redistributed.

7. Leo XIII's ideas were different from the ideas of Karl Marx because of which of the following?
   (A) Marx believed religion could not help improve the lives of workers whereas Leo XIII believed daily prayer was the only way to improve conditions.
   (B) Marx believed improvement could only happen through violent revolution whereas Leo XIII believed improvement could happen peacefully.
   (C) Marx believed socialist governments could peacefully initiate reforms whereas Leo XIII believed governments needed church influence.
   (D) Marx believed improvement could only happen through government initiative whereas Leo XIII believed in laissez-faire economics.

8. Leo XIII most likely would have looked favorably upon which of the following?
   (A) British legislation that restricted child labor
   (B) French policies that subsidized the building of railroads
   (C) The German *Kulturkampf*
   (D) Italian national policies after unification

Questions 9–12 refer to the passage below.

"I accuse Lt-Col du Paty de Clam of having been the diabolical agent of a miscarriage of justice…and then of having defended his evil deed for the past three years through the most preposterous and most blameworthy machinations…I accuse General Billot of having had in his hands undeniable proof that Dreyfus was innocent and of having suppressed it, of having committed this crime against justice and against humanity for political purposes, so that the General Staff, which had been compromised, would not lose face. I accuse Generals de Boisdeffre and Gonse of having been accomplices to this same crime, one out of intense clerical conviction, no doubt, and the other perhaps because of the esprit de corps which makes the War Office the Holy of Holies and hence unattackable…I am fully aware that my action comes under Articles 30 and 31 of the law of 29 July 1881 on the press, which makes libel a punishable offence. I deliberately expose myself to that law. As for the persons I have accused, I do not know them: I have never seen them: I feel no rancour or hatred towards them. To me, they are mere entities, mere embodiments of social malfeasance. And the action I am taking here is merely a revolutionary means to hasten the revelation of truth and justice…. Let them dare to summon me before a court of law! Let the inquiry be held in broad daylight! I am waiting.

   Emile Zola, author and political activist, *J'Accuse*, open letter to the newspaper L'Aurore, 1898

Source: Emile Zola letter to M. Felix Faure, President of the Republic, published in L'Aurore, January 13, 1898, trans by Eleanor Levieux, in Alain Pages, ed. Emile Zola, The Dreyfus Affair: J'accuse" and Other Writings (New Haven CT Yale University Press, 1966) pp. 52–53

9. Zola's work above, *J'Accuse*, became well known because of which of the following reasons?
   (A) Universal suffrage ensured that all voters were interested in government misdeeds.
   (B) Napoleon III's censorship of the press led to a robust black market for printed materials.
   (C) The Catholic Church helped distribute the letter so that Captain Dreyfus would become free.
   (D) Many states instituted compulsory elementary education, which greatly increased literacy rates.

10. Captain Dreyfus's subsequent pardon is reflective of which of the following characteristics of this time period?
    (A) Judges in France believed that persons on trial should be presumed innocent.
    (B) Politicians were often responsive to political and social pressure due to the rise of mass-based political parties.
    (C) Legislatures often passed anti-libel laws that increasingly freed journalists from traditional restrictions.
    (D) The continued influence of Christian churches led to a new form of morality during this time period.

11. Dreyfus was accused of selling state secrets to France's greatest rival in this period, which was
    (A) Great Britain
    (B) Austria-Hungary
    (C) Germany
    (D) Russia

12. Realist writers, such as Emile Zola, were influenced by which of the following?
    (A) Romanticism, which emphasized national histories, emotion, and nature
    (B) Humanist and Classical themes that emphasized Greco-Roman works
    (C) Materialist themes that drew attention to social problems
    (D) Positivism, which emphasized that explanations should be scientific

250

Questions 13–15 refer to the image below.

Edvard Munch. The Scream. Lithograph, 1895. The Metropolitan Museum of Art. Bequest of Scofield Thayer, 1982.

Source: Edvard Munch. The Scream. Lithograph, 1895.

13. The painting is an example of which of the following developments in modern European art?
    (A) Modern artists such as Munch glorified the lower classes.
    (B) Modern artists moved toward less focused and more expressive works.
    (C) Modern artists were influenced by African art as well as Japanese artistic styles.
    (D) Modern artists moved more toward portraiture and the glorification of the individual.

251

14. The modern art movement occurred in which of the following intellectual contexts?
    (A) A movement away from reason and toward the irrational
    (B) A movement that was able to synthesize religion and science
    (C) Acceptance of Darwinism and natural selection as fact
    (D) Rejection of Darwinism and natural selection as theory.

15. Art and literature during the modern period (c. 1870s and onward), such as Munch's painting, was different from art and literature prior to this period in which of the following ways?
    (A) Realist works were influenced by increased interactions with non-Europeans.
    (B) Realist works often incorporated nationalism and were used to glorify the state.
    (C) Realist works were more influenced by Renaissance and humanist works.
    (D) Realist works often tried to portray the reality of the lives of ordinary people.

Short-Answer Question

Use the passage below to answer all parts of the question.

"The Jewish question… is a remnant of the Middle Ages, which civilized nations do not even yet seem able to shake off, try as they will…. The Jewish question exists wherever Jews live in perceptible numbers. Where it does not exist, it is carried by Jews in the course of their migrations. We naturally move to those places where we are not persecuted, and there our presence produces persecution. This is the case in every country, and will remain so, even in those most highly civilized—France itself being no exception—till the Jewish question finds a solution on a political basis….

We have honestly endeavored everywhere to merge ourselves in the social life of surrounding communities, and to preserve only the faith of our fathers. It has not been permitted to us. In vain are we loyal patriots, our loyalty in some places running to extremes; in vain do we make the same sacrifices of life and property as our fellow citizens; in vain do we strive to increase the fame of our native land in science and art, or her wealth by trade and commerce. In countries where we have lived for centuries we are still cried down as strangers, and often by those whose ancestors were not yet domiciled in the land where Jews had already made experience of suffering."

Theodore Herzl, journalist and activist, *The Jewish State*, 1896

Source: Theodor Herzl, *The Jewish State: An Attempt at a Modern Solution of the Jewish Question* (New York: Maccabæan, 1904), pp. 3–5.

Answer a, b, and c:
1. a) Describe one cause for Herzl's ideas as expressed in the passage.
   b) Describe another cause for Herzl's ideas as expressed in the passage.
   c) Explain one effect of Herzl's ideas as expressed in the passage.

Long-Essay Question

Evaluate the extent to which intellectual ideas in philosophy and science changed during the period 1871–1914.

ANSWERS AND EXPLANATIONS: AP® PRACTICE TEST

Multiple-Choice Questions

1. A (KC: 3.6.II.B; LO: 7 E) Pearson implies that older cultures died out because they were weaker or inferior, and his assertions regarding the "survival of the physically and mentally fitter race" were influenced by Charles Darwin's studies in the Galapagos Islands and his theory of natural selection.

2. C (KC: 3.5.I.C, 3.6.II.B; LO: 7 E, G) Pearson's ideas are reflective of Herbert Spencer's works and the concept of Social Darwinism.

3. C (KC: 3.5.I.C; LO: 7 G) Increased nationalism and the acceptance of Social Darwinism were later used to justify poor treatment and subjugation of people of color in European colonies. It was believed that the Europeans were racially superior, and people of color were naturally inferior.

4. D (KC: 3.3.I.F, 3.3.I.G; LO: 7 B) The same beliefs that supported European superiority toward people of color were also used, along with nationalism, to justify anti-Semitic policies in Europe. While anti-Semitism increased throughout the continent, it was harshest in Russia and Eastern Europe.

5. B (KC: 3.2.I.A, 3.2.II.B; LO: 6 E) Pope Leo XIII would most likely have been influenced by industrialization in Italy during this time period. Italy was one of the later countries to begin the process of industrialization, and the living and factory conditions for the working class were poor. Similar to Marx, he would most likely agree that capitalism would need to be restrained; however, unlike Marx, he believed that capitalism could work if modified and that progress and improvement could take place peacefully.

6. B (KC: 3.3.I.D, 3.6.II.C; LO: 6 H) See explanation to question 5.

7. B (KC: 3.3.I.D, 3.6.II.C; LO: 6 H) See explanation to question 5.

8. A (KC: 3.2.III.B; LO: 6 E) Leo XIII, interested in improving relations between the Catholic Church and the working class, would most likely have looked favorably on legislation that restricted pure capitalism and would have taken away some of the more abusive elements including child labor.

9. D (KC: 3.3.II.C; LO: 6 J) Increasing literacy rates characterized European education after 1860 because of compulsory education laws. France, for example, began funding elementary schools between 1878–1881. Greater literacy rates led to the publication of more reading materials including newspapers that were now available to the general public. Although *J'Accuse* was written in response to the Dreyfus Affair, the Catholic Church did not try to exonerate Dreyfus. In fact, leadership in the French Catholic Church was openly hostile to Dreyfus.

10. B (KC: 3.3.I.A, 3.3.II.A, LO: 6 H, J) Mass political parties that were responsive to voters' needs became the norm in western Europe. Zola was sentenced to a year in prison and later went into exile in England, which actually helped the case for Dreyfus. Responsive to public sentiment, the French authorities later pardoned Dreyfus and reinstated him in the army.

11. C (KC: 3.3.I.F; LO: 7 B) After the Franco-Prussian War, the French sought revenge against Germany as well as the return of Alsace-Lorraine. However, German Chancellor Otto von Bismarck began a series of alliances aimed at isolating France, which only increased hostility between the two countries, culminating in the First World War.

12. C (KC: 3.6.II.D; LO: 7 J) Realist writers often portrayed the lives of ordinary people and tried to address social issues. In *Germinal*, Zola emphasized the role of the working class in the coal-mining village of Montsou. Other realist authors included Charles Dickens and Leo Tolstoy.

13. B (KC: 3.6.III.D; LO: 7 J) Modern painters generally moved away from the representational and more toward the subjective and the expressive. Often, they painted their perception of a scene rather than a more detailed work. Their works often had less focus, and many artists were influenced by African art as well as Japanese styles (although that is not evident in this painting).

14. A (KC: 3.6.III; LO: 7 F) The late nineteenth century saw a movement away from the rational to an emphasis on irrationality that included the development of Freudian Psychology and Einstein's theory of relativity and the New Physics.

15. D (KC: 3.6.II.D; LO: 7 J) Realist works tended to portray the gritty realities of everyday life (see explanation for question 12).

Short-Answer Question
(KC: 3.3.I.F, 3.3.I.G; LO: 7 B)

Possible responses for parts a) and b) include:
- The growth of nationalism led to increased anti-Semitism, even in Western Europe where much of the Jewish population had assimilated.
- Savage *pogroms* in Russia wreaked havoc on Jewish communities.
- The emergence of Social Darwinism further accelerated anti-Semitic attitudes.
- Many Jewish bankers were blamed for the economic instability in the later part of the century furthering anti-Semitism.
- The Dreyfus Affair in France showed the extent of anti-Semitism in France.

Possible responses for part c) include:
- The beginnings of the Zionist movement advocated a homeland for Jews in the Middle East.
- Debate occurred amongst the Jewish community regarding the Zionist movement. Jewish opponents believed that distinguishing themselves as Jewish would lead to continued growth of anti-Semitism.

Long-Essay Question
(KC: 3.6.III; LO: 7 F)

Evaluate the extent to which intellectual ideas in philosophy and science changed during the period 1871–1914.

Possible responses to larger extent include:
- Philosophy and science largely moved from an emphasis on reason and the rational to an emphasis on the irrational.
- New theories in physics such as the works of Einstein and Planck challenged Newton's earlier works.
- Philosophers such as Nietzsche also questioned reliance upon rational thinking and reason.
- Freud's ideas about unconscious sexuality and the importance of dreams were unlike previous studies.

Possible responses to lesser extent include:
- Positivism continued to emphasize the rational and that human behavior could be scientifically measured.
- Scientific studies often continued to contradict church teachings, for example, Darwin's theory of natural selection.
- Freud was also a realist who wanted humans to rationally understand themselves.

CHAPTER 17

The Age of Western Imperialism

THE CLOSE OF THE AGE OF EARLY MODERN COLONIZATION

- The era of early modern European expansion that lasted from the late fifteenth to the late eighteenth centuries witnessed the encounter, conquest, settlement, and exploitation of the American continents by the Spanish, Portuguese, French, and English; the establishment of modest trading posts by European countries in Africa and Asia; the Dutch dominance in the East Indies (modern Indonesia); and the British domination of India.

- During these three centuries, the European powers had largely conducted their colonial rivalries within the context of the mercantilist economic assumptions discussed in Chapter 16. Each empire was, at least in theory and largely in fact, closed to the commerce of other nations. Furthermore, in the Americas, from New England to the Caribbean and then throughout Latin America, slavery was a major fact of economic life, with most slaves brought from Africa.

AP® FRAMEWORK
TOPIC # 1.6, 1.7, 1.8, 1.9, 3.4; LO: UNIT 1 G, H, I, J, L, UNIT 3 C
KC:
1.3.I.A European states sought direct access to gold, spices, and luxury goods to enhance personal wealth and state power.
1.3.I.B The rise of mercantilism gave the state a new role in promoting commercial development and the acquisition of colonies overseas.
1.3.III Europeans established overseas empires and trade networks through coercion and negotiation.
1.3.III.B The Spanish established colonies across the Americas, the Caribbean, and the Pacific, which made Spain a dominant state in Europe in the 16th century.
1.3.III.C The Atlantic nations of France, England, and the Netherlands followed by establishing their own colonies and trading networks to compete with Portuguese and Spanish dominance in the 17th century.
1.3.III.A The Portuguese established a commercial network along the African coast, in South and East Asia, and in South America in the late 15th and throughout the 16th centuries.
1.3.IV.C Europeans expanded the African slave trade in response to the establishment of a plantation economy in the Americas and demographic catastrophes among indigenous peoples.
2.2.II.A European states followed mercantilist policies by drawing resources from colonies in the New World and elsewhere.
2.2.II.B The transatlantic slave-labor system expanded in the 17th and 18th centuries as demand for New World products increased.

THE AGE OF BRITISH IMPERIAL DOMINANCE

▪ During the first half of the nineteenth century, no one doubted that Great Britain was the single power that could exert its influence virtually around the world. During this half century, Britain fostered the settlements that became the nations of Canada, Australia, and New Zealand and expanded its control of India.

▪ The early nineteenth-century British Empire also included smaller colonies and islands in the Caribbean and the Pacific and Indian Oceans. However, until the 1860s and 1870s, except in India and western Canada, Britain did not seek additional territory. Rather, it extended its influence through what historians call the **Imperialism of Free Trade**.

AP® FRAMEWORK
TOPIC # 7.6; LO: UNIT 7 G
KC:
3.5.I European nations were driven by economic, political, and cultural motivations in their new imperial ventures in Asia and Africa.

INDIA—THE JEWEL IN THE CROWN OF THE BRITISH EMPIRE

▪ Until its independence in 1947, India was the most important part of the British Empire and provided the base for British military and economic power throughout Asia. The protection of the commercial and military routes to India would be the chief concern of British imperial strategy during the nineteenth century.

▪ Other nations, particularly Russia, believed they could threaten Britain by bringing military pressure to bear on India. As we shall see later in the chapter, Britain became involved in Africa in the late nineteenth century largely to protect India.

AP® FRAMEWORK
TOPIC # 7.6; LO: UNIT 7 G
KC:
3.5.I European nations were driven by economic, political, and cultural motivations in their new imperial ventures in Asia and Africa.
3.5.I.A European national rivalries and strategic concerns fostered imperial expansion and competition for colonies.
3.5.I.B The search for raw materials and markets for manufactured goods, as well as strategic and nationalistic considerations, drove Europeans to colonize Africa and Asia, even as European colonies in the Americas broke free politically, if not economically.

THE "NEW IMPERIALISM," 1870–1914

▪ In the last third of the nineteenth century, European states expanded their control over one-fifth of the world's land and one-tenth of its population. This expansion was driven by developments in science, agriculture, technology, communication, transportation, and military weapons. This movement, known as **New Imperialism,** had numerous motives.

AP® FRAMEWORK
TOPIC # 7.6; LO: UNIT 7 H
KC:
3.5.II.A The development of advanced weaponry ensured the military advantage of Europeans over colonized areas.
3.5.II.B Communication and transportation technologies facilitated the creation and expansion of European empires.
3.5.II.C Advances in medicine enabled European survival in Africa and Asia.

MOTIVES FOR THE NEW IMPERIALISM

- The many interpretations of motives for New Imperialism include an economic theory advanced by both J. A. Hobson and Vladimir Lenin. They each viewed imperialism as a monopolistic form of capitalism. Others argue that these nonindustrialized nations had raw materials and provided markets, and still others claim that imperialism was an effort to cure the depression of 1873–1896. None of these theories has been proven. Some view this imperialism as an effort to extend European culture and Christianity to less-industrialized regions. Some advocates of imperialism viewed these regions as inferior and "backward," and they resolved to bring them culture in the form of religion and domestic reform. Some believed that the colonies would attract Europe's surplus population, but in fact European emigrants preferred areas not controlled by their home countries, including North and South America.

AP® FRAMEWORK
TOPIC # 7.6; LO: UNIT 7 G
KC:
3.5.I European nations were driven by economic, political, and cultural motivations in their new imperial ventures in Asia and Africa.
3.5.I.A European national rivalries and strategic concerns fostered imperial expansion and competition for colonies.
3.5.I.B The search for raw materials and markets for manufactured goods, as well as strategic and nationalistic considerations, drove Europeans to colonize Africa and Asia, even as European colonies in the Americas broke free politically, if not economically.
3.5.I.C European imperialists justified overseas expansion and rule by claiming cultural and racial superiority.

THE PARTITION OF AFRICA

- For almost fifty years, inter-European rivalries played out in regions far away from Europe itself and nowhere more intensely than in Africa. During the so-called "Scramble for Africa," which occurred between the late 1870s and about 1912, the European powers sought to maximize their strategic control of African territory, markets, and raw materials. Motivated by intense competition, the imperial powers eventually divided almost all the continent among themselves (see Map 17–2). The short- and long-term consequences were complex and, in most cases, devastating for the Africans. One of the long-term effects was that European control forcibly integrated largely agrarian African societies into the modern world industrial economy. In the process, new forms of agrarian production, market economies, social organizations, political structures, and religious allegiances emerged that would form the basis for the post-colonial African nations (see Map 17–3).

- The European partition of Africa was not based on a universal policy, and each power acquired and administered its new possessions in different ways. Their goals, however, were the same: to gain control, or at least dominance, through diplomacy or force and then either to place Europeans directly in charge of administering the territories or to compel local rulers to accept European "advisers" who would exercise real authority.

AP® FRAMEWORK
TOPIC # 7.6, 7.7; LO: UNIT 7 G, I
KC:
3.5.I European nations were driven by economic, political, and cultural motivations in their new imperial ventures in Asia and Africa.
3.5.I.A European national rivalries and strategic concerns fostered imperial expansion and competition for colonies.
3.5.I.B The search for raw materials and markets for manufactured goods, as well as strategic and nationalistic considerations, drove Europeans to colonize Africa and Asia, even as European colonies in the Americas broke free politically, if not economically.
3.5.I.C European imperialists justified overseas expansion and rule by claiming cultural and racial superiority.
3.5.III.A Imperialism created diplomatic tensions among European states that strained alliance systems.

RUSSIAN EXPANSION IN MAINLAND ASIA

- The British presence in India was intimately related to Russian expansion across mainland Asia in the nineteenth century, which eventually brought huge territories and millions of people of a variety of ethnicities and religions under tsarist rule.

AP® FRAMEWORK
TOPIC # 7.6; LO: UNIT 7 G
KC:
3.5.I European nations were driven by economic, political, and cultural motivations in their new imperial ventures in Asia and Africa.
3.5.I.A European national rivalries and strategic concerns fostered imperial expansion and competition for colonies.
3.5.I.B The search for raw materials and markets for manufactured goods, as well as strategic and nationalistic considerations, drove Europeans to colonize Africa and Asia, even as European colonies in the Americas broke free politically, if not economically.

WESTERN POWERS IN ASIA

- While merchants had established the British interest in India and south Asia, French interest in Indochina arose because of the activity of Roman Catholic missionaries. The French domain in Indochina eventually consisted of Vietnam, Cambodia, and Laos.

- In 1853, a U.S. naval squadron under Commodore Matthew C. Perry (1794–1858) arrived in Japanese waters to open Japanese markets to American goods. In 1867, American interest in the Pacific again manifested itself when the United States bought Alaska from Russia. For the next twenty-five years, the United States assumed a fairly passive role in foreign affairs, but it had established its presence in the Pacific.
- From late 1899 through the autumn of 1901, a Chinese group called The Righteous and Harmonious Society of Fists, better known in the West as the Boxers, attempted to resist the Western incursions. The Boxers, who were supported by a faction at the Qing court, hated missionaries whom they saw as agents of the imperial powers and killed thousands of their Chinese converts.

AP® FRAMEWORK
TOPIC # 7.6, 7.7; LO: UNIT 7 G, I
KC:
3.5.I European nations were driven by economic, political, and cultural motivations in their new imperial ventures in Asia and Africa.
3.5.I.A European national rivalries and strategic concerns fostered imperial expansion and competition for colonies.
3.5.I.B The search for raw materials and markets for manufactured goods, as well as strategic and nationalistic considerations, drove Europeans to colonize Africa and Asia, even as European colonies in the Americas broke free politically, if not economically.
3.5.III.C Especially as non-Europeans became educated in Western values, they challenged European imperialism through nationalist movements and by modernizing local economies and societies.

TOOLS OF IMPERIALISM
- The domination that Europe and peoples of European descent came to exert over the entire globe by 1900 is extraordinary. It had not existed a century earlier and would not exist a century later. At the time, many Europeans, as well as Americans who worked their way across the North American continent in what many regarded as manifest destiny, saw this domination as evidence of cultural or racial superiority.
- Western domination was based on distinct and temporary technological advantages, what one historian called the "tools of empire." These tools gave Westerners the capacity to conquer and dominate vast areas of the world. Steamboats, the conquest of tropical diseases, and the technological advantage of Western firearms, can all be considered "tools of imperialism."

AP® FRAMEWORK
TOPIC # 7.6; LO: UNIT 7 G, H
KC:
3.5.I.C European imperialists justified overseas expansion and rule by claiming cultural and racial superiority.
3.5.II.A The development of advanced weaponry ensured the military advantage of Europeans over colonized areas.
3.5.II.B Communication and transportation technologies facilitated the creation and expansion of European empires.
3.5.II.C Advances in medicine enabled European survival in Africa and Asia.

THE MISSIONARY FACTOR

- The modern Western missionary movement, which continues to the present day, originated in Great Britain in the late eighteenth century as a direct outgrowth of the rise of evangelical Christianity. Evangelicalism, which influenced Protestant communities from central Europe to the United States, emphasized the authority of the Bible, the importance of a personal conversion experience, and the duty to spread the Gospel. Many Evangelicals were also concerned about preparing the world for the Second Coming of Jesus by carrying the message of Christian redemption to peoples who had not heard it. British Evangelicals first looked to unchurched groups in their own nation as the primary field for bearing Christian witness, but by the close of the eighteenth century, in a largely new departure for Protestants, small groups of Evangelicals began to be active in the non-Western world. Roman Catholics later copied these early Protestant missionary efforts. The result of this widespread nineteenth-century missionary campaign was the establishment of large Christian communities in Africa and Asia, which today thrive and continue to expand.

AP® FRAMEWORK
TOPIC # 7.6; LO: UNIT 7 G
KC:
3.5.I.C European imperialists justified overseas expansion and rule by claiming cultural and racial superiority.

SCIENCE AND IMPERIALISM

- The early modern European encounter with the non-Western world from the fifteenth-century voyages of discovery onward had been associated with the expansion of natural knowledge. The same would be true of Western imperialism in the nineteenth and early twentieth centuries. Starting in 1768, Captain James Cook (1728–1779) took his famous voyages to the South Pacific under the patronage of the Royal Society of London to observe the transit of the planet Venus. Sir Joseph Banks (1744–1820), later president of the Royal Society, went with him to collect specimens of plants and animals unknown in Europe. Other British, French, and Spanish naval expeditions also carried scientists with their crews.
- Scientific societies often cooperated with military forces to carry out their research. For example, dozens of French scholars accompanied Napoleon's invasion of Egypt in 1798.

AP® FRAMEWORK
TOPIC # 7.7; LO: UNIT 7 I
KC:
3.5.III Imperial endeavors significantly affected society, diplomacy, and culture in Europe and created resistance to foreign control abroad.
3.5.III.B Imperial encounters with non-European peoples influenced the styles and subject matter of artists and writers and provoked debate over the acquisition of colonies.

Multiple-Choice Questions

Questions 1–3 refer to the passage below

"…after a long period of commercial intercourse, there appear among the crowd of barbarians [that is, foreigners trading in China] both good persons and bad, unevenly. Consequently there are those who smuggle opium to seduce the Chinese people and so cause the spread of the poison to all provinces… His Majesty the Emperor, upon hearing of this, is in a towering rage. .

. . The wealth of China is used to profit the barbarians…. By what right do they then in return use the poisonous drug to injure the Chinese people?… Let us ask, where is your conscience? I have heard that smoking of opium is very strictly forbidden by your country; that is because the harm caused by opium is clearly understood. Since it is not permitted to do harm to your own country, then even less should you let it be passed on to the harm of other countries—how much less to China! Of all that China exports to foreign countries, there is not a single thing which is not beneficial to people….

Even if you do not sell opium, you still have this threefold profit. How can you bear to go further, selling products injurious to others in order to fulfill your insatiable desire? . . ."

Lin Tse- hsü, Chinese official writing on behalf of the emperor,
Letter to Queen Victoria of Great Britain, 1839

Source: Ssu-yü Teng and John K. Fairbank, *China's Response to the West: A Documentary Survey, 1939–1923* (Cambridge, MA: Harvard University Press, 1954), pp. 24–27.

1. Which of the following conclusions best represents the content of the passage?
    (A)   Britain sought cultural imperialism over China.
    (B)   Britain sought territorial conquest of Chinese lands.
    (C)   Britain sought to expand its access to markets in Asia.
    (D)   Britain sought to send British migrants to colonize China.

2. In contrast to European encounters in Africa in the late-nineteenth century, Britain's policies in China during the mid-nineteenth century focused primarily on
    (A)   nationalist goals
    (B)   trade with Chinese people
    (C)   extracting raw materials
    (D)   missionary activity

3. Based on the content of the passage, Britain's actions in mid-nineteenth century China MOST resembled
    (A)   Portugal's relations with Brazil in the seventeenth century
    (B)   Britain's relations with India in the eighteenth century
    (C)   Spain's relations with Mesoamerica in the sixteenth century
    (D)   France's relations with St. Domingue in the eighteenth century

Questions 4–6 refer to the passage below.

…More important…is the consideration that a people which has been led to the pinnacle of political power, can succeed in maintaining its historic position only for as long as it…asserts itself as the bearer of a cultural mission. This is…the only way of ensuring the continuance and growth of the national prosperity…The days are past when Germany's share in carrying out the tasks of our century consisted almost exclusively in intellectual and literary activity…But political power, when it forces itself into the foreground as an end in itself among a nation's aspirations, leads to cruelty… if it is not ready and willing to fulfil the cultural tasks of its age, ethical, moral and economic…

There has admittedly often been talk…of "the declining power of Britain". Those who can only estimate the power of a State in terms of the size of its standing army…may well regard this opinion as justified. But those who let their gaze wander over the globe…to them this talk will seem the reasoning of an ignoramus. That Britain, moreover, maintains her world-wide possessions, her position of predominance over the seas of the world, with the aid of troops whose numbers scarce equal one quarter of the armies of one of the military States of our continent, constitutes not only a great economic advantage, but also the most striking testimony to the solid power and the cultural strength of Britain….It would…be advisable for us Germans to learn from…and begin to emulate them in peaceful competition. When, centuries ago, the German Reich stood at the head of the States of Europe, it was the foremost trading and seagoing Power. If the new German Reich wishes to entrench and preserve its regained power for long years to come, then it must regard that power as a cultural mission…

Friedrich Fabri, German Protestant theologian, *Does Germany Need Colonies?*, 1879

Source: Original German text and English translation reprinted in Friedrich Fabri, Bedarf Deutschland der Colonien? / Does Germany Need Colonies? Eine politische-ökonomische Betrachtung von D [r. Theol.] Friedrich Fabri, ed., trans. and intro. by E.C.M. Breuning and M. Chamberlain, Studies in German Thought and History, no. 2. Lewiston: Edwin Mellen Press, 1998, pp. 46–59, 78–79, 82–85, 148–53, 178–81.

4. The author's purpose in the passage is most likely to
   (A) justify overseas expansion
   (B) discourage racial mixing with non-Europeans
   (C) promote eugenics
   (D) promote ideals of civilizing mission

5. Which of the following is most likely a motive behind the views expressed in the passage?
   (A) Militarism
   (B) Positivism
   (C) Nationalism
   (D) Liberalism

6. The passage implies which of the following?
   (A) Scientific Socialism
   (B) *Realpolitik*
   (C) The Social Gospel
   (D) Social Darwinism

Questions 7–8 refer to the passage below.

"Imperialism is the most recent form of barbarism, the end of the line for civilization. I do not distinguish between the two terms—imperialism and barbarism—for they mean the same thing.

We Frenchmen, a thrifty people, who see to it that we have no more children than we are able to support easily, careful of adventuring into foreign lands, we Frenchmen who hardly ever leave our own gardens, for what in the world do we need colonies? What can we do with them? What are the benefits for us? It has cost France much in lives and money so that the Congo, Cochinchina, Annam, Tonkin, Guinea, and Madagascar may be able to buy cotton from Manchester, liquors from Danzig, and wine from Hamburg. For the last seventy years France has attacked and persecuted the Arabs so that Algeria might be inhabited by Italians and Spaniards!

The French people get nothing from the colonial lands of Africa and Asia. But their government finds it profitable. Through colonial conquest the military people get promotions, pensions, and awards, in addition to the glory gained by quelling the natives. Shipowners, army contractors, and shady politicians prosper. The ignorant mob is flattered because it believes that an overseas empire will make the British and Germans green with envy.
Will this colonial madness never end?..."

Anatole France, French novelist, "The Colonial Folly," 1904

Source: Louis L. Snyder, *The Imperialism Reader: Documents and Readings on Modern Expansionism* (New York: D. Van Nostrand Company, Inc., 1962), pp. 155–156.

7. Which of the following conclusions best reflects the content of the passage?
    (A) The acquisition of colonies enhanced the prestige of European states.
    (B) France was the first European country to ease control over its colonial possessions.
    (C) The economic benefits of imperialism outweighed the costs.
    (D) Imperialism provoked debate among Europeans over the acquisition of colonies.

8. Which of the following was a result of the ideas expressed in the passage?
    (A) European nations began moving away from imperialism and focusing on alliance systems.
    (B) The growing arms race reduced national resources allocated toward imperialistic ventures.
    (C) Non-European peoples increasingly challenged European imperialism.
    (D) Trade among European nations declined in the years prior to World War I.

Questions 9–11 refer to the map below.

Partition of Africa, 1880–1914

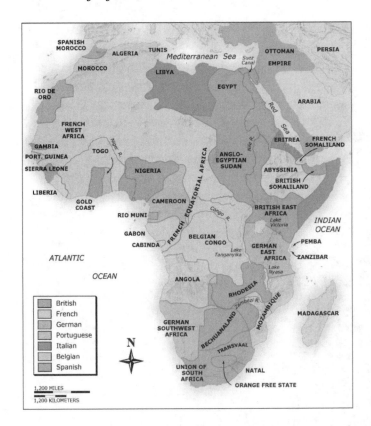

9. All of the following enabled the political situation illustrated in the map EXCEPT
   (A) advances in technology such as the caravel and arquebus
   (B) advances in medicine such as quinine
   (C) advances in communication technologies such as telegraph
   (D) advances in weaponry such as steel gunboats and machine guns

10. The political situation illustrated in the map led to which of the following?
    (A) Increased tensions in the Balkans
    (B) Diplomatic tensions that strained the balance of power
    (C) Increased European migration into central Africa
    (D) The carving up of China into separate states

11. Which of the following events had the biggest impact on the political situation illustrated in the map?
    (A) The Franco-Prussian War
    (B) The Treaty of Versailles
    (C) The Algeciras Conference
    (D) The Berlin Conference

267

Questions 12–13 refer to the cartoon below.

"The World's Plunderers," cartoon published in an American magazine, 1885

Source: Bettmann/Getty Images

12. Which of the following conclusions best represents the cartoon?
    (A) The United States aspired to emulate European nations as imperial powers.
    (B) By 1885 Germany had become the most powerful country in Africa.
    (C) Russia exercised effective control of Japan.
    (D) National rivalries fostered competition for colonies.

13. Which of the following would most likely agree with the point of view of the cartoonist?
    (A) Vladimir Lenin
    (B) Rudyard Kipling
    (C) Joseph Conrad
    (D) Otto von Bismarck

Questions 14–15 refer to the passage below.

"India has given to England wealth and fame; England has brought upon India penury and shame. Instead of being a means of civilization, English rule in India is almost an excuse to keep up barbarism in the nineteenth century. It is an attempt, by a certain class of Englishmen, to repeat in the East the regretted days of the "Conqueror" in England, when every native was a "villain" and all rights belonged to those who "came over." Instead of raising, it is degrading the people. The goods coming from it are at present remote and negative, while its immediate effects have been simply disastrous. The fiction of "England's mission" and "India's progress" is kept up by the agents of three interested industries - the military, mercantile, and missionary - aided by the co-operative journalism, in behalf of privilege and power, in which the modern Muse so sadly prostitutes herself.

….Never within the records of history have there been such widespread poverty and misery in India as her unfortunate people have had to bear since the planting of the English flag… The children of the soil are today, virtually, serfs, working away their lives for a scanty board. Free imports, which have enriched English capitalists, have killed the manufacturers of the country, maimed its industry, and made its trade pass into foreign hands, and the people have to look to Europe for the merest necessaries of life."

Amrita Lal Roy, *English Rule in India,* 1886

Source: The North American Review. Volume 142, Issue 353, April 1886.

14. Which of the following is most likely a cause for the situation described in the passage?
    (A) The British forced a socialist agenda on the Indian population.
    (B) The large British population in India took jobs away from Indians.
    (C) The British justified their rule claiming cultural and racial superiority.
    (D) The British feared increased German influence in India and exercised increased power over Indians.

15. Which of the following would most likely support the content of the passage?
    (A) Winston Churchill
    (B) J. A. Hobson
    (C) Benjamin Disraeli
    (D) Henry Morton Stanley

Short-Answer Question

Answer a, b, and c:

1. a) Explain one way that European military technology led to the "New Imperialism" between 1880 and 1914.

   b) Explain one way that either communication or transportation technologies led to the "New Imperialism" between 1880 and 1914.

   c) Explain one way that advances in medicine led to the "New Imperialism" between 1880 and 1914.

Long-Essay Question

Evaluate the extent to which the "New Imperialism" was different from imperialism in previous eras.

ANSWERS AND EXPLANATIONS: AP® PRACTICE TEST

Multiple-Choice Questions

1. C (KC: 3.5.I.B; LO: 7 G) Prior to the New Imperialism of the late-nineteenth century, Britain was primarily interested in its trade relationships in Asia and elsewhere. British colonies in south central Asia produced opium that the British sold in China. The opioid crisis that ensued in China led the emperor to demand an end to the opium trade. Britain refused and two wars ensued in the mid-nineteenth century leading to increased British influence in China.

2. B (KC: 3.5.I.B; LO: 7 G) In Africa and Asia, Britain, and other European imperial powers enjoyed trade relationships with indigenous rulers and their peoples. While these relationships, more often than not, favored Europeans, they did not always lead to the outright conquest of all regions. In China, for example, the British sold goods for profit and received Chinese goods that could be sold in Europe at a significant markup.

3. B (KC: 1.3.I.A, 2.2.III.B, 3.5.I.B, LO: 1 H, 5 B, 7 G) The British East India Company exercised increased influence in India during the eighteenth century as it sought to increase its profits. As with China, the economic relationship between India and Britain had an adverse effect on the Indian population. It was not until 1857 that the British government took control of India as an official colony. The other answer choices are more reminiscent of the New Imperialism in Africa.

4. A (KC: 3.5.I.C; LO: 7 G) Friedrich Fabri emphasized that Germany can ensure national prosperity through the acquisition of colonies. He also stressed that British power is a result of their world empire, rather than just a large army, and he insinuates that Germany needs to compete with Britain and acquire an imperial empire.

5. C (KC: 3.5.I.B; LO: 7 G) The Age of Imperialism was an extension of the Age of Nationalism during which European countries conquered new territories for prestige and national aggrandizement. European governments at times used imperialistic adventures to distract the masses from problems occurring at home.

6. D (KC: 3.5.I.C, LO: 7 G) Herbert Spencer adapted Darwin's theory of evolution to human society, arguing that Europeans represented the pinnacle of human civilization due to their superior racial and cultural attributes. Imperialists conveniently utilized Social Darwinism to justify the conquest of "lesser" peoples as part of natural law.

7. D (KC: 3.5.III.B; LO: 7 I) While imperialistic activities were for the most part popular among populations of the great powers, a rising minority of views argued against imperializing for a variety of reasons. Some, like Anatole France, saw little gain for ordinary people as a result of imperialistic activities. Others, like J. A. Hobson argued that imperialism was more costly than advantageous. Still others, like Vladimir Lenin, saw imperialism as the ultimate expression of capitalistic excess.

8. C (KC: 3.5.III.C; LO: 7 I) The debates among Europeans regarding imperialism were not lost on indigenous leaders in the colonies. Nationalist sentiments expressed by Italians and Hungarians in their drive for independence from the Austrian Empire, for example, inspired the colonies to demand their own independence. The Indian National Congress increasingly pushed for independence from Britain in the years following World War I. The ideas of Lenin and Hobson were influential in the colonies during the twentieth century.

9. A (KC: 3.5.II.A/B/C; LO: 7 H) The caravel and arquebus were sixteenth-century technologies used during the Old Imperialism. Up to the mid-nineteenth century, Europeans had great difficulty penetrating into the interior of Africa. Malaria and other tropical diseases decimated Europeans who ventured inland. European military advantages were not as decisive as they would be during the Second Industrial Revolution as evidenced by repeated foiled attempts by France to conquer Algeria prior to 1850. Eventually, the advent of the telegraph enabled Europeans in the coastal regions of Africa and Asia to communicate with the homeland after 1850, making logistical adjustments easier. Quinine became an effective prophylactic against malaria. And the development of the iron gunboat and machine gun gave Europeans overwhelming advantages over indigenous armies.

10. B (KC: 3.5.III.A; LO: 7 I) The "Scramble for Africa" heightened competition among the major European powers. Britain and France, for example, nearly came to blows over the Sudan. Germany's opposition to France's continued control of Morocco led to France creating an alliance with Britain in 1907. German diplomatic support for the Boers in South Africa infuriated Britain, who was engaged in wars with the Boers for control of the region. These tensions reconfigured alliance systems in the decades prior to World War I.

11. D (KC: 3.5.III.A; LO: 7 I) In response to the Belgian king's desire to create his own colony in the Congo, German Chancellor Otto von Bismarck organized the Berlin Conference in 1884–1885 to establish rules and guidelines for acquiring land in Africa. This ushered in the "Scramble for Africa," and all but two African countries were conquered by European nations by 1914.

12. D (KC: 3.5.I.A; LO: 7 G) Major European powers worried they might fall behind if their rivals gained strategic advantages with colonies across the globe. This drove the major powers to acquire new colonies at an accelerated pace in Africa and Asia.

13. A (KC: 3.5.III.B; LO: 7 I) At the time Thomas Nast's cartoon was published in 1885, the United States was not yet an imperial power. Nast's caption—"The World's Plunderers"—illustrated his disdain for Europe's naked aggression in the quest for new colonies. Vladimir Lenin, the leading communist in Europe after the death of Karl Marx, saw imperialism as a means through which capitalist powers enriched themselves.

14. C (KC: 3.5.I.C, LO: 7 G) Many leaders in Great Britain pointed to the need to modernize and civilize peoples in the colonies. The ideal of the "White Man's Burden" spoke to this view. The belief in European racial and cultural superiority over Africans and Asians was common during the New Imperialism.

15. B (KC: 3.5.III.B; LO: 7 I) The passage is a scathing rebuke of British rule in India. J. A. Hobson, one of the most well-known anti-imperialist voices of the era, would have supported this view.

Short-Answer Question
(KC: 3.5.II.A/B/C; LO: 7 H)

Possible responses for a) include:
* New military technologies such as the machine gun and steel gunships

Possible responses for b) include:
* Steel steam ships that enabled quicker and safer travel
* The use of telegraph that enabled improved communication between the homeland and colonial agents in Africa and Asia

Possible responses for c) include:
* Quinine enabled Europeans to penetrate to the interior of Africa with far less incidence of malaria.
* Other prophylactic measures and increased medical knowledge enabled Europeans to overcome the challenges of the African environment.

Long-Essay Question
(KC: 1.3.I, 3.3.I; LO: 1 H, 7 G)

Evaluate the extent to which the "New Imperialism" was different from imperialism in previous eras.

Differences might include:
- Europeans sought trade relationships with African and Asian peoples from the sixteenth through the nineteenth centuries. These relationships were often mutually beneficial.
- The slave trade ended in the nineteenth century while the Atlantic slave trade was a key feature of the Atlantic trade prior to the nineteenth century.

Similarities might include:
- Europeans conquered and dominated the New World.
- Spain controlled much of South America and Mesoamerica (and eventually parts of the American southwest in North America).
- England took control of the east coast of North America and its transplanted inhabitants quickly moved westward.
- Portugal dominated Brazil.

CHAPTER 18

Alliances, War, and a Troubled Peace

EMERGENCE OF THE GERMAN EMPIRE AND THE ALLIANCE SYSTEMS (1873–1890)

- In 1873, Bismarck formed the Three Emperors' League, which brought together Germany, Austria, and Russia. The league soon collapsed because of the Austro-Russian rivalry in the Balkans.
- The Congress of Berlin resulted in Russia's significant loss of territory, and a new tension arose between Germany and Russia. Germany and Austria signed the Dual Alliance, whereby they would protect each other if either country was attacked by Russia.
- Russia soon joined and renewed the Three Emperors' League in 1881. Another series of alliances between Austria, Germany, and Italy were arranged, but the rise of William II to the German throne in 1888 upset these delicate balances and led to the dismissal of Bismarck.
- New alliances and tensions led to a Franco-Russian alliance in 1894, and a new tension arose between Britain and Germany. Britain concluded agreements with the French in 1902 known as the *Entente Cordiale.*
- The Triple Entente, consisting of Britain, France, and Russia, was now posed against the Triple Alliance of Germany, Austria, and Italy. These relationships and shifting conflicts in the region pushed Europe closer to war.

AP® FRAMEWORK
TOPIC # 7.3, 7.7; LO: UNIT 7 D, I
KC:
3.4.III.C After 1871, Bismarck attempted to maintain the balance of power through a complex system of alliances directed at isolating France.
3.4.III.D Bismarck's dismissal in 1890 eventually led to a system of mutually antagonistic alliances and heightened international tensions.
3.5.III.A Imperialism created diplomatic tensions among European states that strained alliance systems.

WORLD WAR I

- A series of Balkan crises precipitated war. Both Serbia and Austria-Hungary wanted to expand into the Balkans. Austria annexed Bosnia-Herzegovina in 1908, and proceeded to alienate Russia, which sided with Serbia in the crisis. Germany joined Austria's cause to keep the Russian threat in check.

- A second crisis in Morocco occurred in 1911, when Germany protested French occupation of the region and sent the Panther gunboat to protect German interests. This action irritated Britain, which pledged its support to France. Negotiations allowed France to establish a protectorate in Morocco and gave Germany some land in the French Congo. However, the more important outcome was an increase of British fear and hostility toward Germany, and a closer alliance with France.
- The June 28, 1914, assassination of Archduke Ferdinand, Austrian heir to the throne, by a Bosnian nationalist was the spur to the outbreak of war. Serbia's involvement with the plot provoked outrage in Europe. Germany agreed to support Austria in an attack on Serbia, and war was declared in July—but not begun until August. Russia was not eager for war, but Pan-Slav nationalists demanded action, and the government ordered partial mobilization. France and Britain were not eager for war, but their alliance with Russia required their assistance.

AP® FRAMEWORK
TOPIC # 7.7, 8.2; LO: UNIT 7 I, UNIT 8 B
KC:
3.5.III.A Imperialism created diplomatic tensions among European states that strained alliance systems.
4.1.I World War I, caused by a complex interaction of long- and short-term factors, resulted in immense losses and disruptions for both victors and vanquished.
4.1.I.A A variety of factors— including nationalism, military plans, the alliance system, and imperial competition—turned a regional dispute in the Balkans into World War I.

THE RUSSIAN REVOLUTION
- In March 1917, a Russian revolution overthrew the tsarist government of Nicholas II. The war put too many demands on Russia's resources, and peasant discontent had plagued the country for many years. Strikes and worker demonstrations erupted, the tsar abdicated, the government fell to the members of the reconvened *Duma,* and a provisional government was formed composed of Constitutional Democrats with Western sympathies. This government remained loyal to the tsarist alliances and decided to continue war against Germany.
- The Bolshevik wing of the Social Democratic Party had been working against the provisional government. Vladimir Lenin demanded that political power go to the *soviets,* which were councils of workers and soldiers controlled by the Menshevik wing, a group of orthodox Marxists. With Lenin's help, Leon Trotsky organized a coup that concluded with the Bolshevik rule of Russia.

AP® FRAMEWORK
TOPIC # 6.6; 8.3 LO: UNIT 6 G, UNIT 8 D, E
KC:
3.4.II.D In Russia, autocratic leaders pushed through a program of reform and modernization, including the emancipation of the serfs, which gave rise to revolutionary movements and eventually the Russian Revolution of 1905.

4.1.I.C The effects of military stalemate, national mobilization, and total war led to protest and insurrection in the belligerent nations and eventually to revolutions that changed the international balance of power.

4.2.I The Russian Revolution created a regime based on Marxist-Leninist theory.

4.2.I.A In Russia, World War I exacerbated long-term problems of political stagnation, social inequality, incomplete industrialization, and food and land distribution, all while creating support for revolutionary change.

4.2.I.B Military and worker insurrections, aided by the revived Soviets, undermined the Provisional Government and set the stage for Lenin's long-planned Bolshevik Revolution and establishment of a communist state.

THE END OF WORLD WAR I

- In March 1918, Germany agreed to accept defeat and sought peace on the basis of Woodrow Wilson's **Fourteen Points**, which included the creation of the **League of Nations**. The Great War came to an end with some 4 million dead and 8.3 million wounded among the Central Powers and 5.4 million dead and 7 million wounded among the Allies.

AP® FRAMEWORK
TOPIC # 8.2; LO: UNIT 8 B, C, D
KC:
4.1.I World War I, caused by a complex interaction of long- and short-term factors, resulted in immense losses and disruptions for both victors and vanquished.

4.1.I.B New technologies confounded traditional military strategies and led to trench warfare and massive troop losses.

4.1.I.C The effects of military stalemate, national mobilization, and total war led to protest and insurrection in the belligerent nations and eventually to revolutions that changed the international balance of power.

4.1.I.E The relationship of Europe to the world shifted significantly with the globalization of the conflict, the emergence of the United States as a world power, and the overthrow of European empires.

THE SETTLEMENT AT PARIS

- The Paris settlement consisted of five separate treaties between victors and the defeated powers. The Soviet Union (as Russia was called after the Bolshevik victory) and Germany were not included in the peace conference.
- The League of Nations was established, and its covenant was an important part of the peace treaty. France won Alsace-Lorraine, Germany was disarmed, and the United States and Britain agreed to protect France from any future German aggression. The United States never joined the League of Nations and Germany was not allowed to join the League until 1926.
- The Austro-Hungarian Empire disappeared, giving way to five small states. Germany was required to pay $5 billion annually in reparations until 1921.

277

AP® FRAMEWORK
TOPIC # 8.2, 8.4; LO: UNIT 8 D, F
KC:

4.1.I.E The relationship of Europe to the world shifted significantly with the globalization of the conflict, the emergence of the United States as a world power, and the overthrow of European empires.

4.1.II The conflicting goals of the peace negotiators in Paris pitted diplomatic idealism against the desire to punish Germany, producing a settlement that satisfied few.

4.1.II.A Wilsonian idealism clashed with postwar realities in both the victorious and the defeated states. Democratic successor states emerged from former empires and eventually succumbed to significant political, economic, and diplomatic crises.

4.1.II.B The League of Nations, created to prevent future wars, was weakened from the outset by the nonparticipation of major powers, including the U.S., Germany, and the Soviet Union.

4.1.II.C The Versailles settlement, particularly its provisions on the assignment of guilt and reparations for the war, hindered the German Weimar Republic's ability to establish a stable and legitimate political and economic system.

4.1.VI.B The League of Nations distributed former German and Ottoman possessions to France and Great Britain through the mandate system, thereby altering the imperial balance of power and creating a strategic interest in the Middle East and its oil.

Multiple-Choice Questions

Questions 1–2 refer to the maps below.

The Balkans 1912–1913

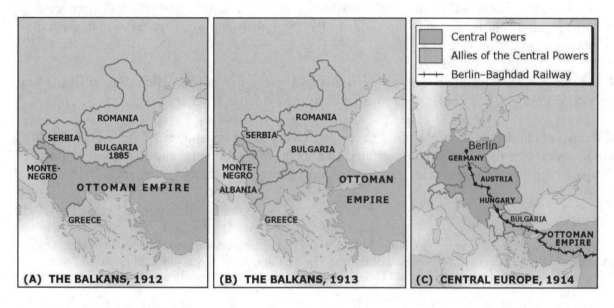

1. The crises in the Balkans in the 1910s were largely the result of changes in which of the following?
   (A) German Empire
   (B) Ottoman Empire
   (C) Austria-Hungary
   (D) France

2. The changes reflected in these maps were spurred primarily by
   (A) religious sentiment
   (B) German aggression
   (C) rising nationalism
   (D) Austrian expansion

Questions 3–4 refer to the passage below.

"The results brought out by the inquiry no longer permit the Imperial and Royal Government to maintain the attitude of patient tolerance which it has observed for years toward those agitations which center at Belgrade and are spread thence into the territories of the Monarchy. Instead, these results impose upon the Imperial and Royal Government the obligation to put an end to those intrigues, which constitute a standing menace to the peace of the Monarchy.

3. to eliminate without delay from public instruction in Serbia, everything, whether connected with the teaching corps or with the methods of teaching, that serves or may serve to nourish the propaganda against Austria-Hungary;

4. to remove from the military and administrative service in general all officers and officials who have been guilty of carrying on the propaganda against Austria-Hungary…

6. to institute a judicial inquiry against every participant in the conspiracy of the twenty-eighth of June who may be found in Serbian territory; the organs of the Imperial and Royal Government delegated for this purpose will take part in the proceedings held for this purpose;…"

Austrian ultimatum to Serbia, July 1914

Source: "The Austrian Ultimatum," in *Outbreak of the World War,* German documents collected by Karl Kautsky and ed. by Max Montgelas and Walther Schucking, trans. by the Carnegie Endowment for International Peace. Division of International Law, Supplement I (1924) (New York: Oxford University Press, 1924), pp. 604–605.

3. Which of the following was the most important cause for the provisions expressed in the passage?
   (A) Austria's creation of Albania as a means to thwart Russian ambitions in the Balkans
   (B) Serbia's refusal to return Bosnia-Herzegovina to the Austrian Empire
   (C) Russia's military mobilization against Germany
   (D) The assassination of the Austrian heir to the throne by a Pan-Slavic nationalist organization

4. Which of the following was a result of the content in the passage?
   (A) Germany issued a "blank check" of support to Austria.
   (B) Alliance systems turned a regional dispute in the Balkans into World War I.
   (C) The Triple Entente guaranteed the territorial and political sovereignty of Serbia.
   (D) The public's support of total war made a coming international conflict inevitable.

Questions 5–7 refer to the map below.

The Western Front 1914–1918

5. Which of the following conclusions best summarizes the content in the map?
   (A) The Triple Entente held the military advantage throughout the entire war.
   (B) The United States played a dominant role early in the war.
   (C) Balance of power diplomacy failed to avoid war.
   (D) New technologies undermined traditional military strategies.

6. The failure of which of the following led to the situation illustrated in the map?
   (A) The Balfour Note
   (B) The Algeciras Conference
   (C) The Schlieffen Plan
   (D) The Entente Cordiale

7. The situation illustrated in the map led to which of the following?
   (A) Insurrection and revolutions in both Germany and Austria-Hungary
   (B) German victory after the Second Battle of the Marne
   (C) Italian entry into the war on the side of the Allied powers
   (D) German surrender after the Allied powers invaded Berlin

Questions 8–9 refer to the passage below.

"At half-past eight this morning, just as I finished dressing, I heard a strange and prolonged din which seemed to come from the Alexander Bridge. I looked out: there was no one on the bridge, which usually presents such a busy scene. But, almost immediately, a disorderly mob carrying red flags appeared at the end which is on the right bank of the Neva, and a regiment came towards it from the opposite side. It looked as if there would be a violent collision, but on the contrary the two bodies coalesced. The army was fraternizing with revolt. Shortly afterwards, someone came to tell me that the Volhynian regiment of the Guard had mutinied during the night, killed its officers and was parading the city, calling on the people to take part in the revolution and trying to win over the troops who still remain loyal.

At ten o'clock there was a sharp burst of firing, and flames could be seen rising somewhere on the Liteïny Prospekt which is quite close to the embassy. Then silence... Frightened inhabitants were scattering through the streets... Soldiers were helping civilians to erect a barricade. Flames mounted from the Law Courts. The gates of the arsenal burst open with a crash. Suddenly the crack of machine-gun fire split the air: it was the regulars who had just taken up position near the Nevsky Prospekt. The revolutionaries replied. I had seen enough to have no doubt as to what was coming..."

Maurice Paléologue, an account of events in February 1917

Source: Maurice Paleologue, *An Ambassador's Memoirs,* 1924 Translated by F.A. Holt, O.B.E., 5th edition, Volume 3, (London: Hutchinson & Co. Paternoster Row), 1925.

8. Which of the following conclusions best represents the content of the passage?
   (A) The Provisional Government was on the verge of falling.
   (B) The Russian Civil War had just begun.
   (C) The tsar's government was about to fall.
   (D) Communist revolutionaries took control of the government.

9. All of the following were direct causes of the event described in the passage EXCEPT
   (A) military stalemate
   (B) imperialism
   (C) mass mobilization of armies
   (D) total war

Questions 10–11 refer to the passage below.

"Article 231

The Allied and Associated Governments affirm, and Germany accepts, the responsibility of Germany and her allies for causing all the loss and damage to which the Allied and Associated Governments and their nationals have been subjected as a consequence of the war improved upon them by aggression of Germany and her allies."

Versailles Treaty, 1919

10. The passage best reflects which of the following ideas regarding the peace treaty with Germany?
    (A) Bismarck's policy of *Realpolitik*
    (B) Wilsonian idealism
    (C) The Allied powers' desire to punish Germany for the war
    (D) Territorial gains for the Allied powers

11. This provision of the treaty eventually contributed to which of the following?
    (A) Failure of the Weimar Republic
    (B) Creation of the League of Nations
    (C) End of colonialism
    (D) Russian Civil War

Questions 12–13 refer to the map below.

World War I Peace Settlement in Europe and the Middle East

12. Which of the following conclusions best reflects the map?
    (A) The Versailles Treaty reduced the impact of imperialism.
    (B) The Ottoman Empire lost its colonial possessions to the Allies.
    (C) Countries in the Balkans failed to achieve independence.
    (D) The Ottoman Empire remained a conservative monarchy.

13. Which of the following resulted from the political situation in the map?
    (A) Self-determination prevailed in the Middle East.
    (B) Mandates altered the imperial balance of power in non-European areas.
    (C) Economic supremacy shifted from the Atlantic to the eastern Mediterranean.
    (D) Russian influence increased in the Black Sea region.

Questions 14–15 refer to the photo below.

Women munitions workers in England

Source: Hulton Archive/Stringer/Getty Images

14. The image reflects which of the following early-twentieth-century trends?
   (A) Total war
   (B) Beginning of the Second Industrial Revolution
   (C) Decreased standard of living
   (D) Gender bias

15. Which of the following was a consequence in Britain of the situation shown in the image?
   (A) Women made significant gains in industrial labor after the war.
   (B) Women were increasingly exploited in industrial occupations after the war.
   (C) Women received suffrage rights following the war.
   (D) Women increasingly rejected marriage in the decades following the war.

Short-Answer Question

Answer a, b, and c:

1. a) Explain one way that Wilsonian idealism affected the outcome of the First World War.
   b) Explain one way that French and British diplomacy affected the outcome of the First World War.
   c) Explain one way that Germany was affected by the Versailles Treaty following the end of the First World War.

Long-Essay Question

Evaluate the extent to which warfare on the Western Front during World War I was different from warfare in Europe during the nineteenth century.

ANSWERS AND EXPLANATIONS: AP® PRACTICE TEST

Multiple-Choice Questions

1. B (KC: 3.4.III.E; LO: 7 D) By the nineteenth century, the Ottoman Empire had declined significantly in its control over southeastern Europe. It became known as the "sick man of Europe." As Ottoman influence declined in the Balkans, hostilities broke out between ethnicities in the region who sought increased autonomy or independence.

2. C (KC: 3.4.III.E; LO: 7 D) Nationalism became a dominant force in European politics as the nineteenth century progressed. Nationalist sentiment spread to southeastern Europe, where ethnic groups within the Ottoman Empire demanded independence. Serbia, Romania, and Montenegro, for example, gained independence as a result of the Congress of Berlin in 1879.

3. D (KC: 4.1.I.A; LO: 8 B) On June 28, 1914, Gavrilo Princip, a nineteen-year-old Serbian nationalist and member of the Black Hand, assassinated Austrian heir Archduke Franz Ferdinand and his wife in Sarajevo, Bosnia. This event set off a chain of events that led to the outbreak of World War I.

4. B (KC: 4.1.I.A; LO: 8 B) Alliance systems among the European powers had shifted after the unification of Germany in 1871. Austria and Germany formed the nucleus of the Triple Alliance while France and Russia became allies to counter the growing strength of Germany. By 1914, Germany strongly supported Austria against Serbia after the assassination of Franz Ferdinand. Russia, an ally of Serbia, mobilized in response to Austria's aggressive stance against Serbia. Fearing a potential two-front war, Germany declared war on both Russia and France and invaded Belgium in hopes of knocking out France before the Russians had fully mobilized.

5. D (KC: 4.1.I.C; LO: 8 D) Germany's Schlieffen Plan aimed to defeat France quickly and then turn the German army's full attention against Russia. The Germans were thwarted near Paris in August 1914 by combined French and British forces, resulting in a German retreat and its fortification of positions in eastern France. What had started as a mobile war quickly became a stalemate with hundreds of miles of trenches extending from the North Sea to Switzerland. New technologies, such as the machine gun, prevented enemy forces from seizing their opponents' trenches. Mustard gas, artillery, and tanks also played important roles in four bloody years of trench warfare that ensued.

6. C (KC: 4.1.I.C; LO: 8 D) See the explanation to Question 5.

7. A (KC: 4.1.I.C; LO: 8 D) The horrific stalemate on the Western Front led to a war of attrition where societies on both sides experienced tremendous strains. Several hundred thousand German civilians, for example, starved to death as a result of the shortages caused by Britain's strangling naval blockade on the Central Powers. Revolutions in Germany and Austria severely weakened those regimes and contributed to their defeat in the war.

8. C (KC: 4.1.I.C; LO: 8 D) The First World War took a heavy toll on Russian society, leading to dissatisfaction with the tsar's leadership. In March 1917 elements of the army allied with liberal revolutionaries to overthrow the Romanovs. The Russian Revolution led to the creation of the Provisional Government that continued the war.

9. B (KC: 4.1.I.C; LO: 8 D) While imperialist competition in Africa and Asia exacerbated relations among the Great Powers, Russia was less involved in imperialist ventures, which did not play a major role in the Russian Revolution in March 1917. All of the other answer choices contributed to the Russian Revolution.

10. C (KC: 4.1.II.C; LO: 8 F) Article 231 in the Versailles Treaty forced Germany to pay $33 billion in reparations payments for its role in starting World War I. This was an enormous sum at the time that guaranteed the German economy would be hampered for years to come.

11. A (KC: 4.1.II.C; LO: 8 F) The new German Weimar Republic signed the Versailles Treaty in 1919 and was saddled with resentment by many Germans who believed the government had stabbed the nation in the back. This was a major reason for the eventual fall of the Weimar Republic. The rise of the Nazis to power in the early 1930s was due, in part, to its propaganda regarding the ill effects of the Versailles Treaty on Germany, and the Weimar Republic's acceptance of the treaty.

12. B (KC: 4.1.I.D, 4.1.I.E; LO: 8 D) As a member of the Triple Alliance, the Ottoman Empire was on the losing side of World War I and saw its empire collapse at the end of the war. Its colonies in the Middle East were taken over by Britain and France in the form of League of Nations mandates.

13. B (KC: 4.1.I.D, 4.1.I.E; LO: 8 D) The acquisition of Ottoman colonies increased the imperial power of the British and French empires. Although the peoples of the Middle East resented their lack of independence following World War I, they would begin gaining their independence in the decade following World War II.

14. A (KC: 4.1.I.C; LO: 8 D) World War I was Europe's first total war, which involved the marshaling of all of society's resources toward the war effort. During the war, European women were hired to do traditionally male jobs while tens of millions of men were off fighting the war.

15. C (KC: 4.4.I.A; LO: 8 M) Due to their indispensable role in helping Britain on the home front during the war, women 30 years of age and older gained the right to vote in 1918. Ten years later, women age 21 and older gained the right to vote.

Short-Answer Question

(KC: 4.1.II; LO: 8 F)

Possible responses for a) include:
- The Fourteen Points helped convince Germany to end the war.
- Components of the Fourteen Points were incorporated in the Versailles Treaty, such as self-determination for major European ethnic groups.
- Wilson's desire for an international collective security organization led to the creation of the League of Nations.

Possible responses for b) include:
- France and Britain sought to punish Germany for its role in starting the war.
- The negotiations for the treaty led to Italy angrily leaving the Paris Peace Conference in 1919.
- France sought to guarantee its security from a future German invasion.
- France gained Alsace-Lorraine from Germany and the demilitarization of the Rhineland.

Possible responses for c) include:
- Provisions of the Versailles Treaty regarding Germany included reparations payments, loss of German territory, loss of German colonies, French occupation and extraction of resources from the Saar region, and severe restrictions on the size of German military forces.
- The Ruhr crisis in 1923 led to France occupying the region.
- The rise of ultra-nationalist parties, such as the Nazis, reflected German dissatisfaction with the Versailles Treaty.

Long-Essay Question
(KC: 2.1.V.B, 3.4.II.A, 3.4.III.B, 4.1.I; LO: Unit 5 F, Unit 7 C, Unit 8 B)

Evaluate the extent to which warfare on the Western Front during World War I was different from warfare in Europe during the nineteenth century.

Possible differences might include:
- New technologies such as the machine gun, mustard gas, the airplane, and tanks
- Trench warfare and stalemate
- Total war
- Massive casualties

Possible similarities might include:
- Mobile warfare during the Napoleonic wars and the war on the Eastern Front during WWI
- Military alliances among the Great Powers in the Napoleonic wars and the Crimean War
- Large armies employed by Napoleon and the coalition of nations that opposed him
- The use of artillery in warfare

CHAPTER 19

The Interwar Years: The Challenges of Dictators and Depression

AFTER VERSAILLES: DEMANDS FOR REVISION AND ENFORCEMENT

- There were numerous postwar economic problems partly brought on by the many casualties of war and Europe's loss of its financial dominance. The reparations and debt structure of the peace made the economies of many European nations—even victorious ones—uncertain.
- Market and trade conditions changed radically, as much of Europe's infrastructure had been damaged or destroyed in the war. The United States also became less dependent on European production and was a major competitor. Slow postwar economic growth and an overall decline of economic activity lowered international demand for European goods. The prominence of labor during the war gave unions a greater role in national government.

AP® FRAMEWORK
TOPIC # 8.4, 8.5; LO: UNIT 8 F, G
KC:
4.1.II.B The League of Nations, created to prevent future wars, was weakened from the outset by the nonparticipation of major powers, including the U.S., Germany, and the Soviet Union.
4.1.II.C The Versailles settlement, particularly its provisions on the assignment of guilt and reparations for the war, hindered the German Weimar Republic's ability to establish a stable and legitimate political and economic system.
4.2.III.A World War I debt, nationalistic tariff policies, overproduction, depreciated currencies, disrupted trade patterns, and speculation created weaknesses in economies worldwide.
4.2.III.B Dependence on post-World War I American investment capital led to financial collapse when, following the 1929 stock market crash, the United States cut off capital flows to Europe.

TOWARD THE GREAT DEPRESSION IN EUROPE

- Reparations and war debts made international trade, capital investment, and day-to-day business difficult for European nations. After the Dawes Plan was put into effect, more American money flowed into Europe, but that changed in 1928 after the stock market crash. This triggered the **Great Depression**.
- In 1931, President Hoover put a year-long moratorium on payments of international debts. In 1932, the Lausanne Conference effectively ended all payment of reparations. Problems in agricultural commodities during this time also brought about a downturn in production and trade.

291

TOPIC # 8.4, 8.5; LO: UNIT 8 F, G
KC:

4.1.II.C The Versailles settlement, particularly its provisions on the assignment of guilt and reparations for the war, hindered the German Weimar Republic's ability to establish a stable and legitimate political and economic system.

4.2.III.A World War I debt, nationalistic tariff policies, overproduction, depreciated currencies, disrupted trade patterns, and speculation created weaknesses in economies worldwide.

4.2.III.B Dependence on post-World War I American investment capital led to financial collapse when, following the 1929 stock market crash, the United States cut off capital flows to Europe.

4.2.III.C Despite attempts to rethink economic theories and policies and forge political alliances, Western democracies failed to overcome the Great Depression and were weakened by extremist movements.

THE SOVIET EXPERIMENT

- The Bolshevik gains in Russia resulted in a communist party in the Soviet Union. Communist leaders sought to spread their ideology around the world; fear of communism and the resolve to stop its spread became a major force in Europe and the United States.

- The Bolsheviks rapidly developed authoritarian policies in response to internal and foreign military opposition. They formed the *Cheka,* a new secret police, and political and economic administrations became highly centralized. Under an economic policy of war, the Bolsheviks took control of all the major industries, financial institutions, and transportation.

- After Lenin's death in 1924, two factions emerged in struggles for leadership of the party. Leon Trotsky and Joseph Stalin were on opposite sides—with Trotsky speaking for the "left wing" and urging agricultural **collectivization**, rapid industrialization, and new revolutions in other nations. A right-wing faction emerged with Nikolai Bukharin as its chief voice and Stalin manipulating the group that called for continuation of Lenin's NEP and slow industrialization. Stalin began to amass power and in the mid-1920s, he supported Bukharin and denounced Trotsky for his vision of international revolution, endorsing the doctrine of "socialism in one country." Stalin defeated Trotsky and controlled the Soviet State.

- In 1919, the Soviet Communists founded the Third International of the European Socialist movement, known as the Comintern. In 1920, the Comintern imposed Twenty-one Conditions on any socialist party that wanted to join it. This effort to destroy democratic socialism split every major European socialist party, divided the political left, and created a vacuum of power for right-wing politicians.

TOPIC # 8.3, 8.6; LO: UNIT 8 E, I
KC:

4.2.I. The Russian Revolution created a regime based on Marxist-Leninist theory.

4.2.I.C The Bolshevik takeover prompted a protracted civil war between communist forces and their opponents, who were aided by foreign powers.

4.2.I.D.i In order to improve economic performance, Lenin compromised communist principles and employed some free-market principles under the New Economic Policy.

4.2.I.D.ii After Lenin's death, Stalin undertook a centralized program of rapid economic modernization, often with severe repercussions for the population.

4.2.I.E Stalin's economic modernization of the Soviet Union came at a high price, including the liquidation of the kulaks (the land-owning peasantry) and other perceived enemies of the state, devastating famine in the Ukraine, purges of political rivals, and, ultimately, the creation of an oppressive political system.

THE FASCIST EXPERIMENT IN ITALY

- In a response to the threat of Bolshevism, Benito Mussolini became prominent as a proponent of *fascism,* a term used to describe right-wing dictators that rose in Europe between the wars. These governments claimed to hold back Bolshevism and were antidemocratic, anti-Marxist, antiparliamentary, and often anti-Semitic. Fascist movements were nationalistic.
- In October 1922, Fascists marched on Rome, an event that became known as the Black Shirt March, and that led to Mussolini's becoming prime minister. The Fascist Party came to dominate Italy's political structure at every level.

AP® FRAMEWORK
TOPIC # 8.6; LO: UNIT 8 H
KC:

4.2.II The ideology of fascism, with roots in the pre-World War I era, gained popularity in an environment of postwar bitterness, the rise of communism, uncertain transitions to democracy, and economic instability.

4.2.II.A Fascist dictatorships used modern technology and propaganda that rejected democratic institutions, promoted charismatic leaders, and glorified war and nationalism to attract the disillusioned.

4.2.II.B Mussolini and Hitler rose to power by exploiting postwar bitterness and economic instability, using terror, and manipulating the fledgling and unpopular democracies in their countries.

GERMAN DEMOCRACY AND DICTATORSHIP

- The Weimar Republic took shape in the aftermath of World War I; its constitution was written in August of 1919. While the Weimar constitution guaranteed civil liberties and provided for direct election, it had flaws that allowed its liberal institutions to be overthrown.
- Adolf Hitler (1889–1945) arrived on the political scene around the time when the French occupation of the Ruhr sent inflation soaring, and unemployment had spread throughout Germany. Hitler affiliated with the Christian Social Party in Vienna and absorbed much of its rabid German nationalism and anti-Semitism. He moved to Munich and became involved with a small, nationalistic, anti-Semitic party known as the National Socialist German Workers' party, or the *Nazis.*

- During the chancellorship of Gustav Stresemann, Germany recovered from some of its losses. Under Stresemann, a new reparations payment plan, called the Dawes Plan, was instituted, giving Germany a flexible form of payment that varied according to the German economy. In 1925, the Locarno Agreements accepted the Franco-German border established by the Versailles Treaty, and Britain and Italy agreed to intervene against whichever side violated the frontier or if Germany sent troops into the Rhineland. No such agreement existed for Germany's eastern frontier. France supported Germany's membership in the League of Nations. The Locarno Treaty, which pleased all of the European powers, would not solve the tensions that continued to fester.
- After the Nazi party won the largest share of seats in the Reichstag in 1932, Hitler was appointed Chancellor in the ruling cabinet. Hitler consolidated his control almost as soon as he took office by crushing alternative political groups, purging his rivals in the Nazi Party, and capturing full legal authority of Germany. Hitler quickly outlawed all other political parties and arrested the leaders of offices, banks, and the newspapers of free trade unions. He effectively eliminated all institutions of opposition and began moving against the governments of individual federal states in Germany. Hitler had key SA leaders murdered to gain support from the German army officer corps. After the death of Hindenburg, Hitler combined the position of chancellor and president and became head of state and head of the government.
- Hitler oversaw the control of Germany as a police state. Police surveillance units, known as the SS *(Schutzstaffel),* terrorized much of Germany and focused their hatred against German Jews. The Nazis based their anti-Semitic views on biological racial theories rather than on religious discrimination. Jews were robbed of their citizenship, their opportunities to earn a living, and their civil liberties, and they were repeatedly persecuted and harassed. Ultimately, they were killed in Hitler's efforts to eliminate Jews in Europe. More than 6 million Jews were murdered in the Holocaust.
- Hitler effectively handled the German economic problem by subordinating all economic enterprise to the goals of the state. He instituted a massive program of spending and public works, many of which related to rearmament. In 1935, Hitler renounced the provisions of the Treaty of Versailles and began open rearmament to prepare for his next aggression.

AP® FRAMEWORK
TOPIC # 8.4, 8.6, 8.7; LO: UNIT 8 F, H, J
KC:
4.1.II.C The Versailles settlement, particularly its provisions on the assignment of guilt and reparations for the war, hindered the German Weimar Republic's ability to establish a stable and legitimate political and economic system.
4.1.III In the interwar period, fascism, extreme nationalism, racist ideologies, and the failure of appeasement resulted in the catastrophe of World War II, presenting a grave challenge to European civilization.
4.1.III.A French and British fears of another war, American isolationism, and deep distrust between Western democratic, capitalist nations and the authoritarian, communist Soviet Union allowed fascist states to rearm and expand their territory.

4.2.II The ideology of fascism, with roots in the pre-World War I era, gained popularity in an environment of postwar bitterness, the rise of communism, uncertain transitions to democracy, and economic instability.

4.2.II.A Fascist dictatorships used modern technology and propaganda that rejected democratic institutions, promoted charismatic leaders, and glorified war and nationalism to attract the disillusioned.

4.2.II.B Mussolini and Hitler rose to power by exploiting postwar bitterness and economic instability, using terror, and manipulating the fledgling and unpopular democracies in their countries.

TRIALS OF THE SUCCESSOR STATES IN EASTERN EUROPE

- The "successor states" was the name given to the lands that emerged after the breakup of the German, Austro-Hungarian, and Russian empires. Many of the postwar states (Czechoslovakia, Poland, Germany, Austria) faced major economic difficulties; except for Czechoslovakia, all of them depended on foreign loans to finance their economic rebuilding. The collapse of the old empires allowed ethnic groups to pursue nationalistic goals.

AP® FRAMEWORK
TOPIC # 8.4, 8.6; LO: UNIT 8 F, H
KC:

4.1.II.A Wilsonian idealism clashed with postwar realities in both the victorious and the defeated states. Democratic successor states emerged from former empires and eventually succumbed to significant political, economic, and diplomatic crises.

4.2.II.D After failures to establish functioning democracies, authoritarian dictatorships took power in central and eastern Europe during the interwar period.

CHAPTER 19: AP® PRACTICE TEST

Multiple-Choice Questions

Questions 1–2 refer to the passage below.

"The State will have to exercise a guiding influence on the propensity to consume partly through its scheme of taxation, partly by fixing the rate of interest, and partly, perhaps, in other ways. Furthermore, it seems unlikely that the influence of banking policy on the rate of interest will be sufficient by itself to determine an optimum rate of investment. I conceive, therefore, that a somewhat comprehensive socialization of investment will prove the only means of securing an approximation to full employment; though this need not exclude all manner of compromises and of devices by which public authority will co-operate with private initiative. But beyond this, no obvious case is made out for a system of State Socialism which would embrace most of the economic life of the community. It is not the ownership of the instruments of production which it is important for the State to assume. If the State is able to determine the aggregate amount of resources devoted to augmenting the instruments and the basic rate of reward to those who own them, it will have accomplished all that is necessary…."

John Maynard Keynes, *The Theory of Employment, Interest and* Money, 1936

Source: John Maynard Keynes, *The Theory of Employment, Interest and* Money, 1936 (London: Macmillan & Co., Ltd., 1960), p. 379.

1. Which of the following conclusions best reflects the content in the passage?
   (A) Keynes supported the emergence and dominance of the Labour party in Britain in the 1920s and 1930s.
   (B) Keynes advocated increased government spending to stimulate economies during the Great Depression.
   (C) Keynes advocated economic policies that had earlier been developed by the Popular Front.
   (D) Keynes advocated conservative policies that included imposing a moratorium on international debts.

2. The phrase, "no obvious case is made out for a system of State Socialism," is most likely a reference to Keynes's concerns about the
   (A) rise of conservative authoritarian regimes in eastern Europe
   (B) excesses of the welfare state in Great Britain
   (C) development of communism in the Soviet Union
   (D) withdrawal of the United States from the international economic system

296

Questions 3–5 refer to the poster below

This 1930 Russian propaganda poster reads, "Comrade, come join us on the collective farm!"

Source: Heritage Image Partnership Ltd/Alamy Stock Photo

3. The underlying political philosophy for the poster was developed by
   (A) Klemens von Metternich
   (B) Edouard Bernstein
   (C) Adam Smith
   (D) Karl Marx

4. Which of the following conclusions best reflects the purpose of the poster?
   (A) The Soviet government is promoting modernization.
   (B) The Soviet government is promoting the establishment of *zemstvos*.
   (C) The Soviet government is promoting an international communist revolution.
   (D) The Soviet government is promoting mass migration from cities to the countryside.

5. Which of the following would have been the policy of the Soviet government at the time the poster was published?
   (A) New Economic Policy (NEP)
   (B) De-Stalinization
   (C) Five-Year Plans
   (D) Privatization of state industries

297

Questions 6–10 refer to the passage below

"Liberalism is not the last word, nor does it represent the definitive formula on the subject of the art of government…. Liberalism is the product and the technique of the nineteenth century…. It does not follow that the Liberal scheme of government, good for the nineteenth century, for a century, that is, dominated by two such phenomena as the growth of capitalism and the strengthening of the sentiment of nationalism, should be adapted to the twentieth century, which announces itself already with characteristics sufficiently different from those that marked the preceding century….

I challenge Liberal gentlemen to tell if ever in history there has been a government that was based solely on popular consent and that renounced all use of force whatsoever. A government so constructed there has never been and never will be. Consent is an ever-changing thing…, it can never be permanent….If it be accepted as an axiom that any system of government whatever creates malcontents, how are you going to prevent this discontent from overflowing and constituting a menace to the stability of the State? You will prevent it by force… By the inexorable use of this force whenever it is necessary. Take away from any government whatsoever force—and by force is meant physical, armed force—and leave it only its immortal principles, and that government will be at the mercy of the first organized group that decides to overthrow it."

Benito Mussolini, "Force and Consent," 1923

Source: Translated in Jonathan F. Scott and Alexander Baltzly, eds., *Readings in European History Since 1814* (New York: F.S. Crofts, 1931), pp. 680–682.

6. Which of the following systems does Mussolini seem to be supporting?
   (A) Socialism
   (B) Fascism
   (C) Communism
   (D) Anarchism

7. The leaders of which of the following countries in the 1920s and 1930s would most likely have supported Mussolini's views in the passage?
   (A) Poland
   (B) France
   (C) Czechoslovakia
   (D) Great Britain

8. All of the following are means through which Mussolini achieved his objective in the passage EXCEPT
   (A) cult of personality
   (B) modern technology
   (C) tapping postwar bitterness
   (D) consent of the governed

9. Mussolini's views in the passage later led to which of the following actions in the 1930s?
   (A) Support for the League of Nations
   (B) Suppression of the Catholic Church in Italy
   (C) Intervention in the Spanish Civil War
   (D) Alliance with the Popular Front in France

10. The views expressed in the passage are most similar to those of leaders in which of the following countries in the 1930s?
    (A) Germany
    (B) Great Britain
    (C) France
    (D) The Netherlands

Questions 11–12 refer to the passage below.

"With the armistice begins the humiliation of Germany. If the Republic on the day of its foundation had appealed to the country: "Germans, stand together! Up and resist the foe! The Fatherland, the Republic expects of you that you fight to your last breath," then millions who are now the enemies of the Republic would be fanatical Republicans. Today they are the foes of the Republic not because it is a Republic but because this Republic was founded at the moment when Germany was humiliated, because it so discredited the new flag that men's eyes must turn regretfully towards the old flag.

It was no Treaty of Peace which was signed, but a betrayal of Peace.

So long as this Treaty stands there can be no resurrection of the German people: no social reform of any kind is possible! The Treaty was made in order to bring 20 million Germans to their deaths and to ruin the German nation. But those who made the Treaty cannot set it aside. At its foundation our Movement formulated three demands;

1. Setting aside of the Peace Treaty.
2. Unification of all Germans.
3. Land and soil to feed our nation…"

Adolf Hitler, speech, April 17, 1923

Source: *The Speeches of Adolf Hitler, April 1922–August 1939,* trans. by Norman H. Baynes (London and New York: Oxford University Press, 1942), pp. 56–57.

11. Which of the following conclusions best reflects the contents of the passage?
    (A) Hitler took control of Germany based on anti-Semitic ideas.
    (B) Hitler blamed the Weimar Republic for accepting war guilt.
    (C) Hitler resented Germany's exclusion from the League of Nations.
    (D) Hitler blamed the Weimar Republic for refusing to legalize the Nazi party.

12. Hitler achieved some of the goals expressed in the passage as a result of which of the following?
    (A) The Great Depression
    (B) The Ruhr Crisis
    (C) The Dawes Plan
    (D) The Locarno Pact

Questions 13–15 are based on the passage below.

"There is no escaping the fact: the old type of family has seen its day. It is not the fault of the Communist State, it is the result of the changed conditions of life. The family is ceasing to be a necessity of the State, as it was in the past; on the contrary, it is worse than useless, since it needlessly holds back the female workers from more productive and far more serious work....But on the ruins of the former family we shall soon see a new form rising which will involve altogether different relations between men and women, and which will be a union of affection and comradeship, a union of two equal members of the Communist society, both of them free, both of them independent, both of them workers. No more domestic "servitude" of women. No more inequality within the family. No more fear on the part of the woman lest she remain without support or aid with little ones in her arms if her husband should desert her. The woman in the Communist city no longer depends on her husband but on her work. It is not her husband but her robust arms which will support her. There will be no more anxiety as to the fate of her children. The State of the Workers will assume responsibility for these. Marriage will be purified of all its material elements, of all money calculations, which constitute a hideous blemish on family life in our days...."

Alexandra Kollontai, *Communism and the Family*, 1920

Source: Rudolf Schlesinger, ed. and trans., *The Family in the USSR* (London: Routledge and Kegan Paul, 1949), pp. 67–69.

13. Which of the following conclusions best reflects the content of the passage?
    (A) Women in the Soviet Union gained access to professional careers.
    (B) The birth rate in the Soviet Union declined significantly.
    (C) Absolute equality between the sexes was achieved in the Soviet Union by the 1930s.
    (D) Women achieved equality in urban areas but not in the countryside.

14. In contrast to women in the Soviet Union, women in several Western European countries received the vote after World War I due to
    (A) government policies that favored women
    (B) the efforts of feminists before and during World War I
    (C) the transition from an agricultural to an urban society
    (D) changing views of women due to the influence of movies and radio

15. In contrast to the views of women in the Soviet Union as expressed in the passage, women in Nazi Germany
    (A) received the right to vote after the Nazis seized power
    (B) were excluded from most occupations
    (C) performed most of the industrial labor during World War II
    (D) were tasked with maintaining racial purity

Short-Answer Question

Answer (a), (b), and (c):
1. a) Describe one way that the Soviet Union under Lenin or Stalin maintained Marxist ideology.
    b) Describe one way that the Soviet Union under Lenin or Stalin moved away from Marxist ideology.
    c) Explain one way that Stalin differed in his approach to governing from Lenin's approach to governing.

Long-Essay Question

Evaluate the extent to which totalitarianism in the Soviet Union differed from totalitarianism in Nazi Germany.

ANSWERS AND EXPLANATIONS: AP® PRACTICE TEST

Multiple-Choice Questions

1. B   (KC: 4.2.III.C; LO: 8 G) Keynes's *The Theory of Employment, Interest and Money* (1936) is among the most important economic works of the twentieth century. During economic recessions or depressions, Keynes argued, governments should stimulate the economy with increased government spending, as private investment was inadequate during such times. Written during the Great Depression, the book (and Keynes himself) influenced Franklin Roosevelt's New Deal in the United States and similar increases in French government spending.

2. C   (KC: 4.2.I.B; LO: 8 E) At the time Keynes published his book, many Western governments remained highly concerned about the potential spread of communism in Europe. The Bolshevik Revolution led to a "red scare" in the West in the years following World War I. Keynes seems to reassure capitalists that governments should not take over major portions of economies but rather stimulate those economies during economic downturns.

3. D   (KC: 4.2.I; LO: 8 E) Marxist-Leninist philosophy drove the 1917 Bolshevik Revolution and subsequent regimes of Vladimir Lenin and Joseph Stalin. Lenin was a staunch Marxist but modified Marx's views by arguing that a communist revolution had to be accelerated in Russia by a small, professional group of revolutionaries. He reasoned that Russia had not yet developed a proletariat large enough to initiate a socialist revolution on its own. Lenin and Stalin utilized brutal tactics to create a totalitarian society that Marx would most likely have eschewed.

4. A   (KC: 4.2.I.D; LO: 8 E) Stalin established a crash program to communize and modernize the Soviet countryside by establishing collective farms onto which peasants were forced to move. Stalin's ambitious goals for increasing agricultural production were not realized despite the enormous human cost of collectivization.

5. C   (KC: 4.2.I.D; LO: 8 E) The poster is dated 1930. Stalin emerged as the dictator of Russia by 1928, four years after Lenin's death. Stalin immediately instituted the first of his several Five-Year Plans that collectivized agriculture in Russia while marshaling the country's resources to undergo a dramatic increase in industrialization and urbanization.

6. B   (KC: 4.2.II; LO: 8 H) In the wake of World War I, the Italian economy sputtered while socialist and communist parties grew significantly. The conservative classes grew concerned that Italy might fall to communism considering recent events in Russia. Mussolini developed the fascist ideology to counter this communist threat and eventually instituted conservative authoritarianism in Italy after his March on Rome in 1922. It can be argued that Mussolini created a totalitarian regime in Italy although some historians argue Italy's government never achieved the kind of total control over its population that governments in the Soviet Union and Nazi Germany did.

7. A   (KC: 4.2.II.D; LO: 8 H) Poland suffered some of the ethnic divisions that had earlier plagued the Austrian Empire and liberal leaders were unable to create a stable government. Joseph Pilsudski eventually turned Poland into a military dictatorship based on conservative authoritarianism. Britain and France resumed their democratic systems after World War I while Czechoslovakia emerged as the only democracy in Eastern Europe during the interwar period.

303

8. D (KC: 4.2.II.A/B; LO: 8 H) In the passage, Mussolini argues that liberal governments have failed to establish order and stability and he sees democratic republican governments as throwbacks to the nineteenth century. The other answer choices were ways in which Mussolini gained power in Italy and established his fascist regime.

9. C (KC: 4.2.II.C; LO: 8 H) Mussolini in the mid-1930s gave Spanish fascist revolutionary Francisco Franco military support during the Spanish Civil War. Franco, with the help of both Italy and Nazi Germany, emerged victorious and instituted a fascist dictatorship by the late 1930s.

10. A (KC: 4.2.II.C; LO: 8 H) Adolf Hitler adopted many of Mussolini's fascist ideas to develop his own fascist ideology in the 1920s. The Nazis, however, emphasized racial superiority and anti-Semitism in addition to fascist totalitarianism.

11. B (KC: 4.1.II.C; LO: 8 F) Hitler emphasized that the Germany had been "stabbed in the back" by the Weimar Republic when it signed the Versailles Treaty in 1919 and accepted German war guilt. The Weimar government accordingly never enjoyed the support of German conservatives while the Great Depression ultimately contributed to the republic's demise.

12. A (KC: 4.2.III.C; LO: 8 G) Although the Weimar government experienced temporary successes during the mid-1920s as a result of economic recovery and the short-term resolution of the reparations issue, the Great Depression fatally weakened the government. The Nazis opportunistically seized on the misery of millions of Germans during the depression and emerged as the largest political party in the Reichstag after the elections of 1933.

13. A (KC: 4.4.II.B; LO: 9 H) Marxism embraced gender equality. The Bolsheviks led by Lenin sought to create a society that gave women the same economic opportunities that men enjoyed. By the mid-twentieth century, the Soviet Union had more female than male physicians, and women enjoyed significant access to other professional careers due to increased access to universities. Nevertheless, Russia still remained a patriarchal society outside of government and women were still expected to perform their traditional duties as wives and mothers in addition to working full time.

14. B (KC: 4.4.I.A, 4.4.II.B; LO: 8 M, 9 H) While the Soviet government believed in creating a new gender-equal communist society based on the ideas of Karl Marx, female activists in Britain, France and other countries had for decades campaigned actively for female suffrage and other rights. Their efforts saw some gains for women after the war including suffrage in Britain and Germany in 1918.

15. D (KC: 4.1.III.D; LO: 8 L) In Nazi Germany, as in fascist Italy, women were expected to breed and raise children for the benefit of the state. In Germany, Hitler emphasized racial purity. Views of women in fascist countries were far more conservative and traditional than in Communist Russia and the Western democracies. The Nazis practiced eugenics policies to reduce the births of people the regime deemed as undesirable. This included the physically handicapped as well as Jews and other non-Aryan ethnic groups.

Short-Answer Question
(KC: 4.2.I; LO: Unit 8 E)

Possible responses for a) include:
- Lenin established a society that eliminated privileges for the nobility and middle classes.
- The Soviet government took over most aspects of the Russian economy.
- Women saw increased economic opportunities but were often expected to work in traditionally-male occupations to build the new Soviet state.
- The government instituted social programs such as health care and free college education.
- Lenin favored international revolution (like Marx) through the creation of the Comintern.

Possible responses for b) include:
- Marxist-Leninist ideology led to the creation of a new government controlled by an elite cadre of revolutionaries rather than a true dictatorship of the Proletariat.
- The violence of the Lenin and Stalin regimes undermined the Marxist ideal of a society that peacefully served all its citizens.
- Lenin's NEP deviated from the Marxist ideal.
- Stalin's collectivization and industrial policies were brutal on a scale Marx would have decried.
- Marx advocated an international communist revolution while Stalin preferred "socialism in one country" prior to World War II.

Possible responses for c) include:
- Lenin's NEP included some market elements while Stalin's Five-Year Plans gave the government complete control over the economy.
- Stalin eventually purged the government of Lenin's fellow revolutionaries ("Old Bolsheviks").
- Stalin's oppression of the Soviet people, especially the kulaks, and the development of gulags, far exceeded what Lenin did in peace time.

Long-Essay Question
(KC: 4.2.I, 4.2.II; LO: Unit 8 E, H)

Evaluate the extent to which totalitarianism in the Soviet Union differed from totalitarianism in Nazi Germany.

Possible differences might include:
- Fascism in Germany vs. communism in the Soviet Union
- Racism in Germany vs. a multiethnic society in the Soviet Union
- Conservative views concerning women's roles in Germany vs. gender-equality (in theory) in the Soviet Union
- Hyper-nationalism in Germany vs. Marxist de-emphasis on nationalism (e.g. Stalin's "socialism in one country")
- Strong elements of capitalism in Germany vs. communism in the Soviet Union

Possible similarities might include:
- The use of propaganda, terror, and indoctrination to achieve totalitarian control
- Cult of personality regarding Lenin, Stalin, and Hitler
- Hatred of Western democracy

CHAPTER 20

World War II

AGAIN THE ROAD TO WAR (1933–1939)

- Hitler envisioned enlarging Germany beyond its 1914 borders and wanted to bring the entire German people, the *Volk,* into one nation.
- In 1935, Mussolini attacked Ethiopia, which engendered anger in the international community. Britain and France did not want to alienate Mussolini, but in the end he turned to Germany and in 1936 the Rome-Berlin Axis was born. Hitler marched into the demilitarized Rhineland in 1936 and seized control, registering only weak protests in the form of a policy of appeasement from Britain and France.
- Hitler and Mussolini supported Francisco Franco in his bid to take control of Spain. Hundreds of thousands of Spaniards died in the Spanish Civil War. Japan joined the Axis powers.
- Germany and Austria entered into an *Anschluss,* or union, that had profound implications for Czechoslovakia, which was surrounded by Germany. The Czechs appealed to France, England, and Russia for aid, but the British prime minister, Neville Chamberlain, was committed to the policy of appeasement and did not want Britain in another war.
- In 1939, Hitler invaded Prague, putting an end to the Czech state. Hitler began aggressive acts in Poland, and England and France considered allying with the Russians to prevent him. But in 1939, a Nazi-Soviet nonaggression pact was revealed. This pact divided Poland between the two nations and allowed Russia to occupy the Baltic states. This pact effectively led to the French and English commitment to go to war.

AP® FRAMEWORK
TOPIC # 8.6, 8.7; LO: UNIT 8 H, J
KC:
4.1.III In the interwar period, fascism, extreme nationalism, racist ideologies, and the failure of appeasement resulted in the catastrophe of World War II, presenting a grave challenge to European civilization.
4.1.III.A French and British fears of another war, American isolationism, and deep distrust between Western democratic, capitalist nations and the authoritarian, communist Soviet Union allowed fascist states to rearm and expand their territory.
4.2.II.C Franco's alliance with Italian and German fascists in the Spanish Civil War—in which the Western democracies did not intervene—represented a testing ground for World War II and resulted in authoritarian rule in Spain from 1936 to the mid-1970s.

WORLD WAR II (1939–1945)

- Germany's attack on Poland was swift—a *Blitzkrieg*—or "lightning warfare."
- Hitler invaded Denmark and Norway in 1940, and a month later, he attacked Belgium, the Netherlands, and Luxembourg. British and French armies in Belgium fled to the English Channel and escaped from the beaches of Dunkirk, saving thousands of lives. The Maginot Line, an imaginary line that ran from Switzerland to the Belgian frontier, was exposed on its left flank after Hitler remilitarized the Rhineland, and Hitler's advance through Belgium avoided French defense. Mussolini staged an invasion of southern France, and less than a week later, France, led by Marshal Pétain, asked for an armistice.
- Britain was isolated after the fall of France, but the rise to power of Prime Minister Winston Churchill ended the government's days of appeasement. Churchill established a connection with President Franklin D. Roosevelt, and the United States aided the British before it entered the war.
- Hitler invaded Britain in 1940, bombing London and destroying much of the city. British morale grew during this time and united the nation against Hitler.
- War was thrust on the Americans in 1941 when Japan, an Axis member, launched an attack on the U.S. naval base at Pearl Harbor, in Hawaii. The next day, the United States and Britain declared war on Japan; three days later, Germany and Italy declared war on the United States. In 1942, the Allies gained control of the Mediterranean Sea, and in 1943 they conquered German-controlled Italy, gaining the new leader of the government as an ally against Germany. Prior to U.S. entry, Hitler double-crossed Stalin in June 1941 when he launched a massive invasion of the Soviet Union, thus driving the Soviets into an alliance with Britain and the U.S. In the Battle of Stalingrad, fought from August 1942 through February 1943, the Russians lost more soldiers than the United States lost in combat in the entire war, but they prevailed against Germany, and Hitler's army was destroyed.
- In 1943, the American and British began a series of day and night bombings of German cities. On June 6, 1944, "D-Day," American, British, and Canadian troops landed on the coast of Normandy, France, and penetrated the German defense. France was liberated by September. The Battle of the Bulge in December of 1944 resulted in heavy Allied losses, but the Allies pushed on and crushed German resistance. By May 1, 1945, the German resistance was completely defeated and Berlin was occupied. Japan refused to surrender, and in 1945, American warplanes dropped an atomic bomb on the city of Hiroshima, killing a third of its residents. Two days later, another atomic bomb was dropped on Nagasaki. The Japanese government under Emperor Hirohito surrendered on August 14, 1945.

AP® FRAMEWORK
TOPIC # 8.8; LO: UNIT 8 K
KC:
4.1.III.B Germany's Blitzkrieg warfare in Europe, combined with Japan's attacks in Asia and the Pacific, brought the Axis powers early victories.
4.1.III.C American and British industrial, scientific, and technological power, cooperative military efforts under the strong leadership of individuals such as Winston Churchill, the resistance of civilians, and the all-out military commitment of the USSR contributed critically to the Allied victories.
4.3.II.C Military technologies made possible industrialized warfare, genocide, nuclear proliferation, and the risk of global nuclear war.

RACISM AND THE HOLOCAUST

- Hitler hoped to extinguish Jews from his new Germany, to reunite the German people of the old Habsburg Empire, and to seize land from neighboring countries—beginning with Poland and Ukraine. He also targeted other groups, including Slavs, the disabled, homosexuals, and the Roma.
- Poland had a large Jewish population that had thrived under the leadership of Jozef Pilsudski. The tendency of Nazis to equate Judaism and Bolshevism led to a large-scale attempt to kill all European Jews.

AP® FRAMEWORK
TOPIC # 8.9; LO: UNIT 8 L
KC:

4.1.III.D Fueled by racism and anti-Semitism, Nazi Germany—with the cooperation of some of the other Axis powers and collaborationist governments—sought to establish a "new racial order" in Europe, which culminated with the Holocaust.

4.4.I.B World War II decimated a generation of Russian and German men; virtually destroyed European Jewry; resulted in the murder of millions in other groups targeted by the Nazis including Roma, homosexuals, people with disabilities, and others; forced large-scale migrations; and undermined prewar class hierarchies.

THE DOMESTIC FRONTS

- In Germany, the economy remained buoyant until the army's failure to overwhelm the Russians, after which time a wartime economy took over. Germany suffered severe food shortages and demanded major sacrifices from its people. The manufacture of armaments replaced the production of consumer goods, and food rationing began in 1942. Women, teenagers, and retired men were required to work in factories, and thousands of people from conquered lands were forced to labor in Germany. Political propaganda intensified in Germany, and the role of women became important to the German ideology.
- In France, the Vichy government that followed Germany's aggression was a source of national controversy. It encouraged an intense nationalism that fostered anti-Semitism. Internal resistance to the Vichy government developed in 1942, but a large-scale movement did not arise until 1944, when General Charles de Gaulle, who had fled to Britain, urged the French people to resist their conquerors and to support the French National Committee of Liberation. In 1945, France voted to end the Third Republic, and the Fourth Republic was formed with a new constitution.

AP® FRAMEWORK
TOPIC # 8.8, 8.10; LO: UNIT 8 K, M
KC:

4.1.III.C American and British industrial, scientific, and technological power, cooperative military efforts under the strong leadership of individuals such as Winston Churchill, the resistance of civilians, and the all-out military commitment of the USSR contributed critically to the Allied victories.

4.4.II.A During the world wars, women became increasingly involved in military and political mobilization, as well as in economic production.

Preparations for Peace

- In spite of wartime cooperation, a deep rift separated the Western powers and the Soviet Union.
- In 1941, the Atlantic Charter was concluded between Roosevelt and Churchill. Based on the Fourteen Points, this agreement laid the foundation for a lasting Anglo-American understanding.
- In a series of meetings, at Tehran, Yalta, and Potsdam, the leaders of the Soviet Union, Britain, and the United States made plans for winning the war and for a postwar settlement. Key issues included plans for Eastern Europe, for a conquered Germany, and for an enduring global forum: the United Nations.

AP® Framework
Topic # 8.8, 9.3; LO: Unit 8 K, Unit 9 C
KC:

4.1.III.C American and British industrial, scientific, and technological power, cooperative military efforts under the strong leadership of individuals such as Winston Churchill, the resistance of civilians, and he all-out military commitment of the USSR contributed critically to the Allied victories.

4.1.IV.A Despite efforts to maintain international cooperation through the newly created United Nations, deep-seated tensions between the USSR and the West led to the division of Europe, which was referred to in the West as the Iron Curtain.

Multiple-Choice Questions

Questions 1–4 refer to the passage below.

"All is over. Silent, mournful, abandoned, broken, Czechoslovakia recedes into the darkness. She has suffered in every respect by her association with the Western democracies and with the League of Nations, of which she has always been an obedient servant…

The responsibility must rest with those who have had the undisputed control of our political affairs. They neither prevented Germany from rearming, nor did they rearm ourselves in time. They quarreled with Italy without saving Ethiopia. They exploited and discredited the vast institution of the league of Nations and they neglected to make alliances and combinations which might have repaired previous errors, and thus they left us in the hour of trial without adequate national defense or effective international security….

We are in the presence of a disaster of the first magnitude which has befallen Great Britain and France. Do not let us blind ourselves to that. It must now be accepted that all the countries of Central and Eastern Europe will make the best terms they can with the triumphant Nazi power. The system of alliances in Central Europe upon which France has relied for her safety has been swept away, and I can see no means by which it can be reconstituted…"

Winston Churchill, speech in Parliament, 1938

Source: *Parliamentary Debates,* 5th series, vol. 339 (1938).

1. The passage is likely referring to which of the following?
   (A) Nazi-Soviet Non-Aggression Pact
   (B) Munich Conference
   (C) London Conference
   (D) Potsdam Conference

2. The speaker would most likely criticize the Western democracies' earlier response to the
   (A) creation of the League of Nations
   (B) Great Depression
   (C) Bolshevik Revolution
   (D) remilitarization of the Rhineland

3. The passage is most likely opposed to
   (A) fascism
   (B) communism
   (C) republicanism
   (D) socialism

4. The passage reflects the speaker's disagreement with the policy of
   (A) interventionism
   (B) collective security
   (C) capitalism
   (D) appeasement

Questions 5–6 refer to the map below

Partitions of Czechoslovakia and Poland, 1938–1939

5. The status of Poland in the map was the result of which of the following?
    (A) Nazi-Soviet Non-Aggression Pact
    (B) The surrender of France
    (C) Article 231
    (D) The *Anschluss*

6. The status of Czechoslovakia in the map is most similar to which other country in the 1930s?
    (A) The Soviet Union
    (B) Hungary
    (C) Austria
    (D) Spain

Questions 7–8 refer to the map below.

Axis Europe, May 1941

7. The political status of the European continent illustrated in the map was the result of which of the following?
   (A) *Lebensraum*
   (B) *Blitzkrieg*
   (C) Collective security
   (D) *Ausgleich*

8. The Axis Powers control of territory in the map was most similar to which of the following in 1941?
   (A) The formation of Yugoslavia
   (B) Turkish conquests in the Black Sea Region
   (C) Japanese conquests in the Pacific
   (D) Soviet expansion in Asia

Questions 9–11 refer to the map below.

Yalta to the Surrender

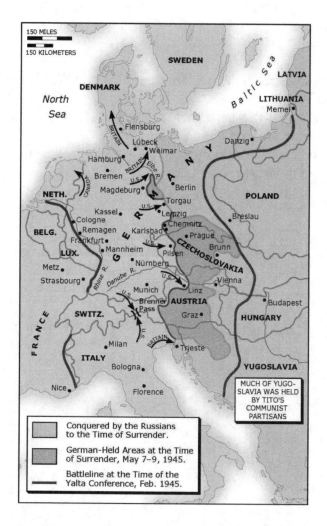

9. All of the following were causes for the military situation illustrated in the map EXCEPT
   (A) the leadership of Winston Churchill
   (B) the resistance of civilians to German forces in Nazi-occupied countries
   (C) the alliance between the United States, Britain, and the Soviet Union
   (D) the use of soldiers from colonial regions in Africa and Asia to drive back German armies

10. Which of the following was the most important reason for the military status shown in the map?
    (A)   The use of atomic bombs
    (B)   The successful resistance movement in Vichy France
    (C)   Japan's attack on Pearl Harbor, Hawaii
    (D)   Germany's construction of an Atlantic Wall

11. Which of the following represents a change in warfare on the western front in World War II when compared to the western front in World War I?
    (A)   Warfare on the western front during World War II was far more mobile.
    (B)   Casualties on the western front were more severe than during World War I.
    (C)   New technologies such as the airplane and tanks were introduced during World War II.
    (D)   The United States played a smaller role on the western front during World War II.

Questions 12–15 refer to the passage below.

"All the human culture, all the results of art, science, and technology that we see before us today, are almost exclusively the creative product of the Aryan. This very fact admits of the not unfounded inference that he alone was the founder of all higher humanity, therefore representing the prototype of all that we understand by the world "man." He is the Prometheus of mankind from whose bright forehead the divine spark of genius has sprung at all times, forever kindling anew that fire of knowledge which illumined the night of silent mysteries and thus caused man to climb the path to mastery over the other beings of this earth. Exclude him—and perhaps after a thousand years darkness will again descend on the earth, human culture will pass, and the world turn to a desert...

This self-sacrificing will to give one's personal labor and if necessary one's own life for others is most strongly developed in the Aryan..."

Adolf Hitler, *Mein Kampf,* 1923

Source: Adolf Hitler, *Mein Kampf* (Boston: English translation Houghton Mifflin Co, 1939).

12. Which of the following conclusions best explains the content in the passage?
    (A) Hitler sought to justify German imperialism in Africa.
    (B) Hitler sought to justify his destruction of France.
    (C) Hitler sought to justify the creation of the Rome-Berlin Axis.
    (D) Hitler sought to justify the creation of a new racial order.

13. Which of the following supported the ideas expressed in the passage?
    (A) Unconditional surrender
    (B) Nuremberg Laws
    (C) Enabling Acts
    (D) Locarno Pact

14. The ideas expressed in the passage ultimately led to which of the following?
    (A) The invasion of France
    (B) The *Blitz* in England
    (C) The Holocaust
    (D) Germany's withdrawal from the League of Nations

15. All of the following groups were adversely affected by the ideas expressed in the passage EXCEPT
    (A) Roma
    (B) the LBGTQ community
    (C) people with disabilities
    (D) Nordic peoples

Short-Answer Question

Answer (a), (b), and (c):

1. a) Describe one example of how European fascist countries achieved their expansionist ambitions in the 1930s.
    b) Describe one example of how the Western democracies failed to prevent fascist expansion in the 1930s.
    c) Explain one reason for why Western democracies were slow to act against fascist aggression during the 1930s.

Long-Essay Question

Evaluate the extent to which European warfare during World War II differed from European warfare during World War I.

ANSWERS AND EXPLANATIONS: AP® PRACTICE TEST

Multiple-Choice Questions

1. B (KC: 4.1.III.A; LO: Unit 8 J) In 1938, Hitler demanded Czechoslovakia turn over the Sudetenland—a region consisting of many ethnic Germans—to Germany. Czechoslovakia refused, prompting Hitler to prepare an invasion. Hoping to avoid an outbreak of war, British Prime Minister Neville Chamberlain called for a conference to resolve the crisis. In Munich, Britain and France agreed that Germany would receive the Sudetenland in exchange for Hitler's guarantee he would not make any more territorial demands. Chamberlain's willingness to give away part of Czechoslovakia became the century's most notorious example of appeasement, as it only further emboldened Hitler.

2. D (KC: 4.1.III.A; LO: Unit 8 J) Two years prior to the Munich Conference, Hitler tested the will of the League of Nations by sending troops into the German Rhineland in violation of the Versailles Treaty. While France may have been willing to act on the violation with British support, the British by the mid-1930s were less willing to risk war to enforce Versailles Treaty provisions that it now saw as excessively punitive.

3. A (KC: 4.2.II; LO: Unit 8 H) As a democracy, Britain would have disagreed with fascist dictatorships and their aggressive expansionist policies.

4. D (KC: 4.1.III.A; LO: Unit 8 J) In Britain, Churchill was the principal opponent of appeasement policies toward Nazi Germany. He assumed the position of Prime Minister several months after the war began, after Neville Chamberlain's leadership had become severely discredited.

5. A (KC: 4.1.III.A; LO: Unit 8 J) After Hitler invaded Czechoslovakia in violation of the Munich agreement, France and Britain warned that any further attempts to expand would result in war. Hoping to avoid a two-front war, Hitler secretly negotiated a deal with Joseph Stalin in August 1939 that called for the division of Poland between Germany and the Soviet Union. This would prevent a German war against the Soviets in the east while Hitler could now focus on knocking France and Britain out of the war in Western Europe.

6. C (KC: 4.1.III.A; LO: Unit 8 J) In 1938, Hitler annexed Austria without firing a shot. This event was known as the "Anschluss" (the "connection"). A year later, Hitler invaded Czechoslovakia in violation of the Munich agreement. As with Austria, the Czechs did not resist, having earlier lost strategic border defenses in the Sudetenland.

7. B (KC: 4.1.III.B; LO: Unit 8 K) In planning for a future war, the German army sought to avoid the static trench warfare that characterized the western front during World War I. *Blitzkrieg* ("lightning war") involved a massive attack on a single point on the enemy line with artillery, air power, tanks, and massed infantry. Once the enemy line had been breached, German forces would quickly move behind enemy lines and surround enemy armies. This tactic proved effective in defeating France in June 1940.

8. C (KC: 4.1.III.B; LO: Unit 8 K) Similar to Germany's aggressive territorial conquest beginning in 1939, Japan had begun its expansionist activities in 1931 when it invaded Manchuria and in 1937 when it invaded Chinese territory further south. By mid-1942, Japan had created an Asian empire through the conquests of additional countries, including Indochina, Malaysia, the Philippines, and various island nations in the Pacific.

9. D (KC: 4.1.III.C; LO: Unit 8 K) The United States and Britain did not generally utilize soldiers from their colonies to invade France and push the German army eastward. All of the other answer choices are reasons for why the Allies were successful on the western front.

10. C (KC: 4.1.III.C; LO: Unit 8 K) The United States did not enter the war until December 8, 1941, after Japan's surprise attack on Pearl Harbor. Once the U.S. entered the war, American President Franklin Roosevelt and Winston Churchill agreed to a "Hitler first" military strategy.

11. A (KC: 4.1.I.B; LO: Unit 8 C) Warfare on the western front during World War II never reached the point of stalemate as had been the case during World War I. Once the Allies broke through Normandy a month after the D-Day invasion, the Germans quickly withdrew to positions inside the German-French border. The bulk of Germany's forces were on the eastern front fighting the Red Army, leaving Germany's western border vulnerable to massive Allied armies.

12. D (KC: 4.1.III.D; LO: Unit 8 L) Hitler envisaged a new racial order where Aryans ruled the world and Slavs and Jews were eliminated. Hitler's anti-Semitic policies reflected these racial views.

13. B (KC: 4.1.III.D; LO: Unit 8 L) Hitler's anti-Semitic policies were carried out in the 1930s through the Nuremberg Laws that placed numerous restrictions on Jews living in Germany. These included loss of German citizenship, prohibition from professional occupations, and the banning of sexual relations between Jews and non-Jews.

14. C (KC: 4.1.III.D; LO: Unit 8 L) Although the discrimination against Jews in Germany was severe in Hitler's Germany in the 1930s, the wholesale murder of Jews did not begin until Germany's invasion of Poland in 1939. Jews were rounded up and sent to concentration camps and ghettos in Germany, Poland, and other countries that Germany conquered during the first three years of the war. The invasion of the Soviet Union accelerated the mass murder of Jews and in 1942 six death camps were built in Poland to murder Jews on a larger scale.

15. D (KC: 4.4.I.B; LO: Unit 8 L) The Holocaust resulted in the murder of six million Jews and six million others including Roma, Jehovah's Witnesses, political prisoners, and mentally and physically disabled persons who were deemed as inferior. Scandinavian (Nordic) peoples such as Danes and Norwegians were treated relatively well by occupying Nazi forces, as they were Germanic and seen as part of the Aryan "master race."

Short-Answer Question
(KC: 4.1.III.A; LO: Unit 8 J)

Possible responses for a) include:
- Italy's invasion of Ethiopia
- Hitler's remilitarization of the Rhineland
- Germany's takeover of Austria
- Germany's invasion of Czechoslovakia
- Germany's invasion of Poland

Possible responses for b) include:
- Failure of Britain and France to enforce the Versailles Treaty
- Failure of the League of Nations to deter or punish aggressor nations
- Appeasement policies during the 1930s (e.g., Munich Conference)

Possible responses for c) include:
- Pacifism in Britain and France due to the horrors of World War I
- The Great Depression that diverted domestic attention from international affairs
- American isolationism

Long-Essay Question
(KC: 4.1.I , 4.1.III; LO: Unit 8 B, J)

Evaluate the extent to which European warfare during World War II differed from European warfare during World War I.

Differences might include:
- New technologies during World War II such as radar, sonar, and updated weaponry, and larger and faster planes, tanks, and guns
- *Blitzkrieg* vs. trench warfare
- Massive bombing during WWII on civilian populations
- Hyper-nationalism in Germany vs. Marxist de-emphasis on nationalism (e.g. Stalin's "socialism in one country"
- Strong elements of capitalism in Germany vs. communism in the Soviet Union
- Far larger numbers of civilian casualties during WWII

Similarities might include:
- Both World Wars were fought on multiple fronts.
- Massive shipping losses occurred on the Atlantic due to submarine warfare.
- The Allies engaged in successful code-breaking.
- Air power was used against enemy positions and occasionally civilian populations (although on a far more limited scale than WWII).
- Germany fought Britain, France, and Russia in both World Wars.

CHAPTER 21

The Cold War Era, Decolonization, and the Emergence of the New Europe

THE EMERGENCE OF THE COLD WAR

- The Soviet Union and the United States entered into a tense relationship at the end of World War II. The United States pursued a policy of **containment** to prevent Soviet expansion into Eastern Europe, Asia, and Africa.
- In 1947, President Truman set forth what has been called the Truman Doctrine, and Americans also devised the **Marshall Plan**—a program that restored prosperity to Western Europe by providing broad economic aid to European states working together for their mutual benefit.
- In 1949, the Western nations formed the North Atlantic Treaty Organization, which was a commitment to mutual assistance in the event of an attack.
- The state of Israel was created in 1948, and the Arab-Israeli conflict over this disputed territory involved Europe and the United States. The Soviet Union became an ally of Arab states, and the United States continued to support Israel, further intensifying existing tensions.
- The Korean conflict in 1950 brought the United States and the Soviet Union on opposite sides of yet another international dilemma.

AP® FRAMEWORK
TOPIC # 9.2, 9.3, 9.4; LO: UNIT 9 B, C, D
KC
4.1.IV.A Despite efforts to maintain international cooperation through the newly created United Nations, deep-seated tensions between the USSR and the West led to the division of Europe, which was referred to in the West as the Iron Curtain.
4.1.IV.B The Cold War played out on a global stage and involved propaganda campaigns; covert actions; limited "hot wars" in Asia, Africa, Latin America, and the Caribbean; and an arms race with the threat of a nuclear war.
4.1.IV.C The United States exerted a strong military, political, and economic influence in Western Europe, leading to the creation of world monetary and trade systems and geopolitical alliances, including NATO.
4.2.IV.A Marshall Plan funds from the United States financed an extensive reconstruction of industry and infrastructure, and stimulated an extended period of growth in Western and Central Europe, often referred to as an "economic miracle,"
which increased the economic and cultural importance of consumerism.

THE KHRUSHCHEV ERA IN THE SOVIET UNION

- The leadership of Nikita Khrushchev led to a move away from Stalin's policies. While the Communist Party still controlled political life, somewhat more freedom of expression was allowed. In 1956, Khrushchev denounced Stalin's regime in a secret speech to the Communist Party.
- The Suez Intervention, which involved French and British intervention in the war between Egypt and Israel, proved that without U.S. support, nations of Western Europe could not use military force to impose their will on the rest of the world.
- Poland's efforts toward independence temporarily caused a crisis of Soviet troop movements in the region, but the country was still controlled by a communist—Wladyslaw Gomulka, who was approved by the Soviet Communist Party.
- After the rise to power of Imre Nagy in Hungary, Soviet troops invaded the country and deposed Nagy. The United States did not liberate Hungary as they had promised in the Truman Doctrine.

AP® FRAMEWORK
TOPIC # 9.4; LO: UNIT 9 D
KC

4.1.IV.D Countries east of the Iron Curtain came under the military, political, and economic domination of the Soviet Union within the Council for Mutual Economic Assistance (COMECON) and the Warsaw Pact.

4.2.V Eastern European nations were bound by their relationships with the Soviet Union, which oscillated between repression and limited reform, until the collapse of communist governments in Eastern Europe and the fall of the Soviet Union.

4.2.V.A Central and Eastern European nations within the Soviet bloc followed an economic model based on central planning, extensive social welfare, and specialized production among bloc members. This brought with it the restriction of individual rights and freedoms, suppression of dissent, and constraint of emigration for the various populations within the Soviet bloc.

4.2.V.B After 1956, Soviet leader Nikita Khrushchev's de-Stalinization policies failed to meet their economic goals within the Soviet Union; combined with reactions to existing limitations on individual rights, this prompted revolts in Eastern Europe, which ended with a reimposition of Soviet rule and repressive totalitarian regimes.

LATER COLD WAR CONFRONTATIONS

- The 1960 Paris Summit talks (intended to promote the peaceful coexistence of the Soviet Union and the United States) collapsed. The aborted conference produced the most difficult period of the Cold War, as the East Germans closed the wall along the border between East and West Berlin, shutting the two parts of the city off from each other.
- The Cuban Missile Crisis, which followed in 1962, tested John F. Kennedy's presidency. The threat of a Soviet ally just 100 miles from the United States was ratcheted up when it was discovered that the Soviet Union was storing nuclear weapons in Cuba. After a standoff between the United States and the Soviet Union, the Soviets backed down after a week of tense negotiations. In 1963, the Soviet Union and the United States concluded a nuclear test ban treaty that marked the beginning of reduced tensions.

AP® FRAMEWORK
TOPIC # 9.3; LO: UNIT 9 C
KC
4.1.IV.B The Cold War played out on a global stage and involved propaganda campaigns; covert actions; limited "hot wars" in Asia, Africa, Latin America, and the Caribbean; and an arms race, with the threat of a nuclear war.

THE BREZHNEV ERA

- In 1968, Leonid Brezhnev declared the right of the Soviet Union to interfere in the domestic policies of other communist countries, after the Soviet Union sent troops into Czechoslovakia to repress a more liberal form of communism. This **Brezhnev Doctrine** sought to sustain the communist governments of Eastern Europe and to prevent liberalization.
- The United States, under Richard Nixon, initiated a period of **détente**, leading to talks with the Soviet Union on arms and trade.
- In 1979, the Soviet Union invaded Afghanistan, enmeshing the Soviets in a protracted and unsuccessful war.
- In 1980 the Solidarity movement emerged in Poland, challenging communist control.
- Under Ronald Reagan, U.S. policy toward the Soviet Union included both increased diplomacy, and the characterization of the Soviet Union as the "evil empire."

AP® FRAMEWORK
TOPIC # 9.3, 9.4; LO: UNIT 9 C, D
KC
4.1.IV.B The Cold War played out on a global stage and involved propaganda campaigns; covert actions; limited "hot wars" in Asia, Africa, Latin America, and the Caribbean; and an arms race, with the threat of a nuclear war.

4.1.IV.D Countries east of the Iron Curtain came under the military, political, and economic domination of the Soviet Union within the Council for Mutual Economic Assistance (COMECON) and the Warsaw Pact.

4.2.V Eastern European nations were bound by their relationships with the Soviet Union, which oscillated between repression and limited reform, until the collapse of communist governments in Eastern Europe and the fall of the Soviet Union.

4.2.V.A Central and Eastern European nations within the Soviet bloc followed an economic model based on central planning, extensive social welfare, and specialized production among bloc members. This brought with it the restriction of individual rights and freedoms, suppression of dissent, and constraint of emigration for the various populations within the Soviet bloc.

4.2.V.B After 1956, Soviet leader Nikita Khrushchev's de-Stalinization policies failed to meet their economic goals within the Soviet Union; combined with reactions to existing limitations on individual rights, this prompted revolts in Eastern Europe, which ended with a reimposition of Soviet rule and repressive totalitarian regimes.

DECOLONIZATION: THE EUROPEAN RETREAT FROM EMPIRE

- Many European empires granted independence to their colonies after World War II, in a mass act of **decolonization** that was as much a result of war as it was a response to the nationalist movements in Africa, Asia, and the Middle East. The one exception to this rule was the Soviet Union. Many of the states that became newly independent were called the Third World, because they were aligned neither with the United States nor with the Soviet Union.

AP® FRAMEWORK
TOPIC # 9.9; LO: UNIT 9 I
KC
4.1.VI The process of decolonization occurred over the course of the century with varying degrees of cooperation, interference, or resistance from European imperialist states.
4.1.VI.C Despite indigenous nationalist movements, independence for many African and Asian territories was delayed until the mid- and even late 20th century by the imperial powers' reluctance to relinquish control, threats of interference from other nations, unstable economic and political systems, and Cold War strategic alignments.

THE TURMOIL OF FRENCH DECOLONIZATION

- France's withdrawal from Algeria was both protracted and bloody.
- France's decolonization became an important part of the Cold War, as the United States became involved in the war in Vietnam. The United States became involved from 1956 and began sending in troops in 1961. The war became a major Cold War conflict. In 1975, after American troops were withdrawn, North and South Vietnam were united.

AP® FRAMEWORK
TOPIC # 9.9; LO: UNIT 9 I
KC
4.1.VI The process of decolonization occurred over the course of the century with varying degrees of cooperation, interference, or resistance from European imperialist states.
4.1.VI.C Despite indigenous nationalist movements, independence for many African and Asian territories was delayed until the mid- and even late 20th century by the imperial powers' reluctance to relinquish control, threats of interference from other nations, unstable economic and political systems, and Cold War strategic alignments.

THE COLLAPSE OF EUROPEAN COMMUNISM

- Communism collapsed in Europe in part because of changing Soviet Union policy advanced by Mikhail Gorbachev. Gorbachev wanted to revive the Russian economy. Under the policy of **perestroika**, he proposed major reforms to the centralized economic ministries. He also abandoned traditional Marxist ideology by advocating private ownership of property and moving toward free market ideology. When these policies did not achieve all the economic gains Gorbachev desired, he pursued bold political reform, such as his policy of **glasnost**, or "openness."
- Throughout 1989, one after another Eastern European country moved toward independence. The Berlin Wall fell in 1989 as well, and in the coming months and years, communism and the Soviet Union crumbled. Gorbachev was unseated by a coup in 1991.
- As president of Russia, Boris Yeltsin dominated the post-Soviet Commonwealth of Independent States. He continued the move from communism to a market economy.

AP® FRAMEWORK
TOPIC # 9.7; LO: UNIT 9 G
KC
4.1.IV.E The collapse of the USSR in 1991 ended the Cold War and led to the establishment of capitalist economies throughout Eastern Europe. Germany was reunited, the Czechs and the Slovaks parted, Yugoslavia dissolved, and the European Union was enlarged through the admission of former Eastern bloc countries.
4.2.V.C Following a long period of economic stagnation, Mikhail Gorbachev's internal reforms of *perestroika* and *glasnost*, designed to make the Soviet system more flexible, failed to stave off the collapse of the Soviet Union and the end of its hegemonic control over Eastern and Central European satellites.

THE COLLAPSE OF YUGOSLAVIA AND CIVIL WAR

Yugoslavia, created in the wake of World War I, was an artificial entity composed of several different nationalities. Under the decades-long leadership of Marshal Josip (Broz) Tito after World War II, Yugoslavia adopted communism but remained independent of Soviet influence. In the 1980s, this union fell apart, leading to a series of bloody ethnic conflicts.

AP® FRAMEWORK
TOPIC # 9.5, 9.7; LO: UNIT 9 E, G
KC
4.1.V Nationalist and separatist movements, along with ethnic conflict and ethnic cleansing, periodically disrupted the post-World War II peace.
4.1.IV.E The collapse of the USSR in 1991 ended the Cold War and led to the establishment of capitalist economies throughout Eastern Europe. Germany was reunited, the Czechs and the Slovaks parted, Yugoslavia dissolved, and the European Union was enlarged through the admission of former Eastern bloc countries.
4.2.V.D.ii New nationalisms in Central and Eastern Europe resulted in war and genocide in the Balkans.

PUTIN AND THE RESURGENCE OF RUSSIA

- Vladimir Putin became president of the Russian Federation in 2000. He dealt harshly with Chechen separatists, reimposing Russian control of the region.
- Under Putin, the Russian economy grew stronger. Putin also sought to more strongly centralize the Russian government. He forcibly took over Ukraine's Crimean Peninsula in 2014.

AP® FRAMEWORK
TOPIC # 9.5; LO: UNIT 9 E
KC
4.1.V Nationalist and separatist movements, along with ethnic conflict and ethnic cleansing, periodically disrupted the post-World War II peace.

THE RISE OF POLITICAL ISLAMISM

- Radical Islamism spread, with long-range effects in the United States and Europe.
- Emerging as a response to secular Arab nationalism, radical Islamism looked instead to the region's Muslim traditions. The Iranian Revolution of 1979 was an example of this development. Founded on Muslim reformism, the revolution sought to establish a purified form of Islam in a modern context.
- The Soviet invasion of Afghanistan similarly sparked a **jihad** against the invaders in that country. Success in repelling the Soviet Union, and the U.S. involvement in the Persian Gulf War of 1991, turned radical Muslims' attention to the United States.

AP® FRAMEWORK
TOPIC # 9.3, 9.5; LO: UNIT 9 C, E
KC
4.1.IV.B The Cold War played out on a global stage and involved propaganda campaigns; covert actions; limited "hot wars" in Asia, Africa, Latin America, and
the Caribbean; and an arms race, with the threat of a nuclear war.
4.1.V Nationalist and separatist movements, along with ethnic conflict and ethnic cleansing, periodically disrupted the post-World War II peace.

A Transformed West

- The collapse of communism and the emergence of the European Union fundamentally altered the political, social, and economic landscape of contemporary Europe, and Europe today faces renewed challenges to its role in the world.
- The 9/11 attacks by Al Qaeda, led by Osama Bin Laden, on the United States transformed American foreign policy.
- U.S. President George W. Bush launched a "war on terrorism," and led the invasion of Afghanistan and Iraq. The Iraq war was controversial both in the United States and in Europe and challenged the long-standing alliances between the United States and European nations.

AP® FRAMEWORK
TOPIC # 9.7; LO: UNIT 9 G
KC
4.1.IV.E The collapse of the USSR in 1991 ended the Cold War and led to the establishment of capitalist economies throughout Eastern Europe. Germany was reunited, the Czechs and the Slovaks parted, Yugoslavia dissolved, and the European Union was enlarged through the admission of former Eastern bloc countries.

Multiple-Choice Questions

Questions 1–5 refer to the speech below.

"A shadow has fallen upon the scenes so lately lighted by the Allied victory. Nobody knows what Soviet Russia and its Communist international organization intends to do in the immediate future, or what are the limits, if any, to their expansive and proselytizing tendencies… From Stettin in the Baltic to Trieste in the Adriatic, an iron curtain has descended across the continent. Behind that line lie all the capitals of the ancient states of central and eastern Europe. Warsaw, Berlin, Prague, Vienna, Budapest, Belgrade, Bucharest and Sofia, all these famous cities and the populations around them lie in the Soviet sphere and all are subject, in one form or another, not only to soviet influence but to a very high and increasingly measure of control from Moscow. Athens alone, with its immortal glories, is free to decide its future at an election under British, American, and French observation."

Winston Churchill, former British Prime Minister,
speech at Westminster College, Missouri, 1946

Source: *Congressional Record,* 79th Congress, 2nd Session, pp. A1145-A1147.

1. Which of the following conclusions best reflects the ideas expressed in the speech?
   (A) Churchill is urging the United States to invade the Soviet Union.
   (B) Western Europe is in imminent danger of being invaded by Soviet forces.
   (C) The Soviet Union has violated international wartime agreements.
   (D) Greece has emerged as a major force for democracy in southeastern Europe.

2. Which of the following emerged as a result of the political situation described in the speech?
   (A) The creation of the United Nations
   (B) The creation of the Grand Alliance
   (C) The creation of International Monetary Fund
   (D) The creation of the North Atlantic Treaty Organization

3. The political situation described in the speech eventually led the Soviet Union to organize all the following EXCEPT
   (A) South East Asia Treaty Organization
   (B) Council for Mutual Economic Assistance
   (C) Warsaw Pact
   (D) Soviet Bloc

4. The American response to the situation described in the passage included which of the following?
    (A) Military support for the People's Republic of China
    (B) The Marshall Plan
    (C) The Hungarian Uprising
    (D) The Atlantic Charter

5. Which of the following resulted within a few years of the tensions described in the passage?
    (A) A nuclear arms race and threat of nuclear war
    (B) Economic stagnation in Western Europe
    (C) A final resolution to the military conflict on the Korean Peninsula
    (D) The communist takeover of West Berlin

Questions 6–9 refer to the passage below.

"Stalin acted not through persuasion, explanation, and patient cooperation with people, but by imposing his concepts and demanding absolute submission to his opinion. Whoever opposed this concept or tried to prove his viewpoint and the correctness of his position was doomed to removal from the leading collective [group] and to subsequent moral and physical annihilation....

Stalin originated the concept of "enemy of the people." This term automatically rendered unnecessary that the ideological errors of a man or men engaged in a controversy be proved; this term made possible the usage of the most cruel repression violating all norms of revolutionary legality, against anyone who in any way disagreed with Stalin, against those who were only suspected of hostile intent, against those who had bad reputations....

Lenin used severe methods only in the most necessary cases, when the exploiting classes were still in existence and were vigorously opposing the revolution, when the struggle for survival was decidedly assuming the sharpest forms, even including civil war...."

Nikita Khrushchev, secret speech to the Party Congress, 1956

Source: Congressional Record: Proceedings and Debates of the 84th Congress, 2nd Session (May 22, 1956–June 11, 1956), C11, Part 7 (June 4, 1956) pp. 9389–9402.

6. Which of the following conclusions best represents the contents of the passage?
   (A) Khrushchev sought to institute democracy within the Soviet Union.
   (B) Khrushchev sought to introduce market reforms in the Eastern European economy.
   (C) Khrushchev sought to reduce censorship within the Soviet Union.
   (D) Khrushchev sought to relax one-party rule in Eastern Bloc nations.

7. Which of the following Soviet leaders would have most supported the ideas expressed in the speech?
   (A) Leonid Brezhnev
   (B) Yuri Andropov
   (C) Konstantin Chernenko
   (D) Mikhail Gorbachev

8. The passage most likely refers to all of the following EXCEPT
   (A) gulags
   (B) *perestroika*
   (C) famine in the Ukraine
   (D) Great Purges

9. Which of the following was a consequence of the ideas expressed in the speech?
   (A) The Soviet Union saw dramatic gains in the standard of living of the average Soviet citizen.
   (B) De-Stalinization policies failed to achieve their economic goals.
   (C) Hungary and Czechoslovakia successfully moved away from one-party communist rule.
   (D) Gulags were reinstituted after attempts to eliminate them failed.

Questions 10–13 refer to the passage below.

"The colonial world is a world cut in two. The dividing line, the frontiers are shown by barracks and police stations. In the colonies it is the policeman and the soldier who are the official, instituted gobetweens, the spokesmen of the settler and his rule of oppression… In the colonial countries…the policeman and the soldier, by their immediate presence and their frequent and direct action maintain contact with the native and advise him by means of rifle butts and napalm not to budge….

The violence which has ruled over the ordering of the colonial world, which has ceaselessly drummed the rhythm for the destruction of native social forms and broken up without reserve the systems of reference of the economy, and the customs of dress and external life, that same violence will be claimed and taken over by the native at the moment when, deciding to embody history in his own person, he surges into the forbidden quarters. To wreck the colonial world is henceforward a mental picture of action which is very clear, very easy to understand and which may be assumed by each one of the individuals which constitute the colonized people."

Frantz Fanon, Algerian psychiatrist, *The Wretched of the Earth*, 1963

Source: Constance Farrington. Trans., Frantz Fanon, The Wretched of the Earth, pp. 37–41, passim. Copyright © 1963 by Presence Africaine. Grove/Atlantic, Inc.

10. Which of the following conclusions best reflects the content of the passage?
    (A) Indigenous nationalist movements promoted decolonization.
    (B) Algerians were largely interested in assimilating with the French population.
    (C) Native-born professionals in colonial countries sought protection from the poorer classes.
    (D) European countries refused to give up their colonies in the 1950s and 1960s.

11. After World War II, all of the following acted upon the ideas expressed in the passage EXCEPT
    (A) India
    (B) Japan
    (C) Vietnam
    (D) Indonesia

12. All of the following would have supported the ideas expressed in the passage EXCEPT
    (A) Woodrow Wilson
    (B) Mohandas K. Gandhi
    (C) Charles de Gaulle
    (D) Ho Chi Minh

13. Which of the following European countries ended its control over the country from which the writer of the passage lived?
    (A) Britain
    (B) Germany
    (C) Italy
    (D) France

Questions 14–15 refer to the map below.

The Former Yugoslavia after 1991

Source: Pearson Education

14. Which of the following was an underlying cause of the political divisions on the map?
    (A) A worldwide economic recession in 1991
    (B) The fall of the Ottoman Empire
    (C) The development of new communications technologies
    (D) The end of the Cold War

15. Which of the following trends occurred as a result of the political divisions on the map?
    (A) Ethnic cleansing
    (B) Pan-Slavism
    (C) Decolonization
    (D) The welfare state

Short-Answer Question

Answer (a), (b), and (c):
1. a) Explain one cause for the emergence of the Cold War in the 1940s.
   b) Explain one result of the emergence of the Cold War in the 1940s.
   c) Explain one way in which the Cold War affected relations between the United States and the Soviet Union between 1955 and 1975.

Long-Essay Question

Evaluate the extent to which the reform and Cold War policies of Soviet leader Nikita Khrushchev (1956–1964) were different from the reform and Cold War policies of Soviet leader Mikhail Gorbachev (1985–1991).

ANSWERS AND EXPLANATIONS: AP® PRACTICE TEST

Multiple-Choice Questions

1. C (KC: 4.1.IV.A; LO: Unit 9 C) At the Yalta Conference in early 1945, the Allies agreed that free democratic elections would be held in Eastern Europe following the defeat of Nazi Germany. Stalin reneged on this agreement and instituted one-party communist governments throughout most of Eastern Europe. This became a major cause of the hostilities between the U.S. and Soviet Union that led to the Cold War.

2. D (KC: 4.1.IV.C; LO: Unit 9 D) By 1948–49 tensions between the U.S. and USSR reached dangerous levels during the Berlin Blockade initiated by Stalin as a means of forcing the U.S., Britain, and France out of West Berlin. Stalin's plan backfired, and he grudgingly lifted the blockade in 1949. In response to Stalin's bold move against West Berlin, the U.S. and its allies formed NATO—a collective security organization to protect Western Europe from a potential Soviet invasion.

3. A (KC: 4.1.IV.D; LO: Unit 9 D) In response to several U.S.-Western European actions such as the creation of NATO and the Marshall Plan, Stalin created the Warsaw Pact as the Eastern Bloc's answer to NATO. He created COMECON as an answer to the Marshall Plan. All countries in Eastern Europe who were dominated by the Soviets were referred to collectively as the Soviet Bloc, Eastern Bloc, or Communist Bloc. SEATO (A) was a collective security organization organized by the United States to contain communism in Asia.

4. B (KC: 4.2.IV.A; LO: Unit 9 B) The U.S. successfully helped Greece and Turkey defeat communist insurgencies by providing both countries with significant monetary aid—a policy that came to be known as the Truman Doctrine. The success of the Truman Doctrine led to the creation of the far more ambitious Marshall Plan to provide billions of dollars to European nations to help rebuild after the war.

5. A (KC: 4.1.IV.B; LO: Unit 9 C) After the U.S. detonated two atomic bombs over Japanese cities at the end of World War II, the Soviets worked on developing their own nuclear program. In 1949, the Soviets successfully tested their first atomic bomb, leading to a nuclear arms race. By the 1950s both countries possessed thermonuclear weapons that were far more destructive than the atomic bombs dropped in 1945.

6. C (KC: 4.2.V.B; LO: Unit 9 D) Khrushchev sought to make the Soviet Union a shining example of a successful communist state by reducing the oppression that had occurred during Stalin's reign of terror. Relaxing censorship was one welcome reform. He especially sought to increase the standard of living of the average Soviet citizen through increased production of consumer goods while reducing military spending to achieve that goal. A reduction of Cold War tensions with the West would be necessary to achieve decreases in military spending. Although Khrushchev's economic goals were appealing to many, he ultimately failed to achieve these goals thus contributing to his ouster from power in 1964.

7. D   (KC: 4.2.V.C; LO: Unit 9 G) After two decades of economic stagnation and limited re-Stalinization under the Brezhnev regime, in the mid-to-late 1980s Mikhail Gorbachev sought to reform the Soviet system in order to save it. *Glasnost* provided a significant degree of freedom of the press. *Perestroika* introduced some market reforms to address the ailing Soviet economy. Ultimately, *perestroika*'s impact on the economy was a disaster that contributed to the disintegration of the Soviet Union in 1991.

8. B   (KC: 4.2.I.E; LO: Unit 8 I) All of the other answer choices were repressive policies under Stalin.

9. B   (KC: 4.2.V.B; LO: Unit 9 D) See the explanation to question 6.

10. A   (KC: 4.1.IV.C; LO: Unit 9 D) Organized independence movements first began in India in the early twentieth century. During the World War I era, several colonial countries began demanding self-determination based on European ideas of nationalism. After World War II, decolonization of Africa and Asia occurred in the 1950s and 1960s. These independence movements were led by leaders such as Gandhi in India and Ho Chi Minh in northern Vietnam.

11. B   (KC: 4.1.IV.C; LO: Unit 9 D) Japan was the lone Asian nation that became an imperialist power during the New Imperialism. After its defeat in World War II, Japan lost all its colonies. The other answer choices are countries who were colonized by Europeans.

12. C   (KC: 4.1.IV.C; LO: Unit 9 D) French president Charles de Gaulle reluctantly gave Algeria its independence after suffering military setbacks in the Algerian war for independence. U.S. President Woodrow Wilson had earlier called for the end of colonialism as part of his Fourteen Points during World War I. As mentioned above, Gandhi and Ho Chi Minh led independence movements in their countries.

13. D   (KC: 4.1.IV.C; LO: Unit 9 D) The passage's source, Frantz Fanon, was an Algerian who resented French control of his country. Algeria had been a French colony since the nineteenth century.

14. D   (KC: 4.1.IV.E; LO: Unit 9G) Yugoslavia was the only communist country in Eastern Europe that was independent of Soviet control. Its proximity to Soviet influence was a factor that kept Yugoslavia's various states working together for the country's protection. When the USSR fell in 1991, the Soviet threat no longer loomed over Yugoslavia. Several states—including Slovenia and Croatia—broke away from Yugoslavia, resulting in several civil wars during the 1990s.

15. A   (KC: 4.1.V; LO: Unit 9 E) In the wake of successful Slovenian and Croatian struggles for independence, Bosnia-Herzegovina tried to break away from Yugoslavia. Serbian forces inside Bosnia, supported by the Serbian government that remained in control of Yugoslavia, conducted a brutal ethnic-cleansing campaign that killed hundreds of thousands of Bosnian Muslims. Serbia attempted to ethnically cleanse the Serbian province of Kosovo in the late-1990s but NATO forces led by the U.S. bombed Serbia, forcing it to end its attack on Kosovars who were fleeing their province in massive numbers. Kosovo eventually declared its independence after the crisis, although not all European countries have recognized Kosovo as an independent country.

Short Answer Question
(KC: 4.1.IV; LO: Unit 9 A, B, C, D)

Possible responses to part a) include:
- Stalin's refusal to allow free elections in Eastern Europe after the war and Soviet domination of the region
- The temporary monopoly by the U.S. on atomic weapons
- Allied refusal to open a second front in Western Europe until 1944, causing Russia to suspect that the British and the Americans were delaying the much needed second front while fighting the Germans alone for an additional year
- U.S.-Britain collaboration on the atomic bomb project without consulting the Soviet Union.
- Soviet support for communist insurgencies in Turkey, Greece, and later, support for communists in the civil war in China

Possible responses to part b) include:
- U.S. development of the Truman Doctrine and the Marshall Plan
- Stalin's blockade of West Berlin and Truman's Berlin airlift
- The creation of NATO
- The creation of two Germanys
- The emergence of a nuclear arms race
- U.S.-led military intervention on the Korean Peninsula

Possible responses to part c) include:
- "Peaceful coexistence" initiated by Khrushchev
- The development of thermonuclear weapons
- The emergence of a "space race" after the Soviet launching of *Sputnik*
- The building of the Berlin Wall
- The Cuban Missile Crisis
- The Vietnam War
- The Brezhnev Doctrine
- The emergence of *détente*

Long-Essay Question
(KC: 4.2.V.B, 4.2.V.C, 4.2.V.D.i; LO: Unit 9 D, G)

Evaluate the extent to which the reform and Cold War policies of Soviet leader Nikita Khrushchev (1956–1964) were different from the reform and Cold War policies of Soviet leader Mikhail Gorbachev (1985–1991).

Differences might include:
- Khrushchev was responding directly to Stalin's abusive regime (e.g. 1956 secret speech) while Gorbachev was responding largely to stagnation in the Soviet system.
- Khrushchev in reality did little to reduce the nuclear and military arms race, while Gorbachev signed the INF Treaty with the U.S. to eliminate intermediate range missiles in much of Europe.
- Khrushchev crushed the Hungarian Uprising in 1956, while Gorbachev allowed Eastern Europe to leave the Soviet empire in 1989.
- Soviet military capabilities increased under Khrushchev's regime, while Gorbachev's policies, in part, led to the dissolution of the Soviet Union in 1991.
- Khrushchev sought to increase Soviet and communist influence in the Third World while Gorbachev reduced Soviet commitments abroad.

Similarities might include:
- Both leaders sought to improve relations with the United States and its allies.
- Both leaders sought to improve the standard of living of Soviet citizens.
- Both leaders allowed an increase in freedom of speech (although Gorbachev's reforms were more far-reaching).
- Both leaders believed in communist ideology but felt that the system had been destroyed prior to their rule.
- Khrushchev pulled Soviet forces out of Austria in 1955 while Gorbachev pulled Soviet forces out of Afghanistan in the late 1980s.

CHAPTER 22

Social, Cultural, and Economic Challenges in the West through the Present

THE TWENTIETH-CENTURY MOVEMENT OF PEOPLES

- World War II created a terrible refugee problem as millions of people were displaced from their homes. Between 1945 and 1960, half a million Europeans left Europe each year.

AP® FRAMEWORK
TOPIC # 8.9; LO: UNIT 8 L
KC:
4.4.I.B World War II decimated a generation of Russian and German men; virtually destroyed European Jewry; resulted in the murder of millions in other groups targeted by the Nazis including Roma, homosexuals, people with disabilities, and others; forced large-scale migrations; and undermined prewar class hierarchies.

TOWARD A WELFARE STATE

- The emergence of a modern European welfare state evolved after the economic dislocation, unemployment, rise of authoritarian states, and the devastating effects of World War II. After World War II, the concept that social insurance against risks should be available to all citizens came into being. Britain created the first welfare state with universal health coverage for all citizens.
- Western European attitudes toward providing social security and coverage to their citizens grew in response to communist promises (largely unfounded) of the same.

AP® FRAMEWORK
TOPIC # 9.6; LO: UNIT 9 F
KC:
4.2.IV Postwar economic growth supported an increase in welfare benefits; however, subsequent economic stagnation led to criticism and limitation of the welfare state.
4.2.IV.B The expansion of cradle-to-grave social welfare programs in the aftermath of World War II, accompanied by high taxes, became a contentious domestic political issue as the budgets of European nations came under pressure in the late 20th century.

NEW PATTERNS IN WORK AND EXPECTATIONS OF WOMEN

- Women in the years since World War II have made important gains in the workplace. More women are in managerial positions and have better opportunities, but gender inequality remains a problem.

AP® FRAMEWORK
TOPIC # 9.8; LO: UNIT 9 H
KC:

4.4.II The lives of women were defined by family and work responsibilities, economic changes, and feminism.

4.4.II.B In Western Europe through the efforts of feminists, and in Eastern Europe and the Soviet Union through government policy, women finally gained the vote, greater educational opportunities, and access to professional careers, even while continuing to face social inequalities.

4.4.II.D New modes of marriage, partnership, motherhood, divorce, and reproduction gave women more options in their personal lives.

4.4.II.E Women attained high political office and increased their representation in legislative bodies in many nations.

TRANSFORMATIONS IN KNOWLEDGE AND CULTURE

- Many intellectuals in the 1930s viewed communism as a vehicle for protecting humane values. Some did not know of Stalin's terror; others simply ignored it or defended it. Four events that were crucial to the transformation of intellectual thought with regard to communism: the Spanish Civil War, the great public purge trials of the 1930s, the Nazi-Soviet pact, and the Soviet invasion of Hungary in 1956.
- Many intellectuals remained fans of Marxism, which they distinguished from the agenda of the Communist Party. Another powerful intellectual trend during this time was **existentialism**, which had its roots in the thinking of Søren Kierkegaard and Frederick Nietzsche.
- The university populations in Europe expanded in the postwar years, with higher education available to women throughout Europe.
- In the postwar years, the American military presence in Europe, tourism, and student exchanges have all led to the Americanization of Europe.

AP® FRAMEWORK
TOPIC #9.8, 9.13, 9.14; LO: UNIT 9 H, N, O
KC:

4.3.I.B The effects of world war and economic depression undermined this confidence in science and human reason, giving impetus to existentialism and producing postmodernism in the post-1945 period.

4.3.IV During the 20th century, the arts were defined by experimentation, self-expression, subjectivity, and the increasing influence of the United States in both elite and popular culture.

4.3.IV.A New movements in the visual arts, architecture, and music radically shifted existing aesthetic standards, explored subconscious and subjective states, and satirized Western society and its values.

4.3.IV.B Throughout the century, a number of writers challenged traditional literary conventions, questioned Western values, and addressed controversial social and political issues.

4.3.IV.C Increased imports of U.S. technology and popular culture after World War II generated both enthusiasm and criticism.

4.4.II.B In Western Europe through the efforts of feminists, and in Eastern Europe and the Soviet Union through government policy, women finally gained the vote, greater educational opportunities, and access to professional careers, even while continuing to face social inequalities.

4.4.III.C Intellectuals and youth reacted against perceived bourgeois materialism and decadence, most significantly with the revolts of 1968.

ART SINCE WORLD WAR II

- Broadly speaking, the influence of the Cold War was mirrored in artistic developments.
- **Socialist realism** dominated in the Soviet Union, focusing on the heroic.
- In Western Europe and the United States, abstract styles continued to dominate.

AP® FRAMEWORK
TOPIC #9.14; LO: UNIT 9 O
KC:
4.3.I.B The effects of world war and economic depression undermined this confidence in science and human reason, giving impetus to existentialism and producing postmodernism in the post-1945 period.

4.3.IV During the 20th century, the arts were defined by experimentation, self-expression, subjectivity, and the increasing influence of the United States in both elite and popular culture.

4.3.IV.A New movements in the visual arts, architecture, and music radically shifted existing aesthetic standards, explored subconscious and subjective states, and satirized Western society and its values.

THE CHRISTIAN HERITAGE

- Christianity continued to struggle against the **forces of secularization** in contemporary society. Strands of neo-orthodoxy and liberalism are evident in contemporary Christianity.
- The Roman Catholic Church remained generally traditionalist, but some popes, such as John XXIII, attempted sweeping reforms.

AP® FRAMEWORK
TOPIC #9.14; LO: UNIT 9 O
KC:
4.3.III Organized religion continued to play a role in European social and cultural life despite the challenges of military and ideological conflict, modern secularism, and rapid social changes.

344

4.3.III.A The challenges of totalitarianism and communism in Central and Eastern Europe brought mixed responses from the Christian churches.

4.3.III.B Reform in the Catholic Church found expression in the Second Vatican Council, which redefined the church's doctrine and practices and started to redefine its relations with other religious communities.

LATE TWENTIETH-CENTURY TECHNOLOGY: THE ARRIVAL OF THE COMPUTER

- The importance of the computer in the twentieth century cannot be underestimated. It altered forever the way business was done, and it effectively brought the world closer together, with new means of technological communication like email and the Internet.

AP® FRAMEWORK
TOPIC #9.13; LO: UNIT 9 N
KC:
4.4.I.D New communication and transportation technologies multiplied the connections across space and time, transforming daily life and contributing to the proliferation of ideas and to globalization.

THE CHALLENGES OF EUROPEAN UNIFICATION

- Much of Western Europe's political power came from its postwar cooperation.
- In 1957, the members of this group agreed to form a new organization, called the European Economic Community (EEC), or Common Market. This group hoped to achieve the elimination of tariffs, a free flow of capital and labor, and similar benefits in their countries.
- In 1988, the leaders of the EEC decided that by 1992 the EEC was to be a free-trade zone with no trade barriers or restrictive trade policies. In 1991, the Treaty of Maastricht proposed a series of steps leading to a unified European currency (the Euro) and a strong central bank. In 1993, the EEC was renamed the **European Union**. The **euro** was launched in 1999.
- In 2004, the proposed European Constitution triggered controversy. Opposition to the constitution represented the first major challenge to the steady trend of unification.

AP® FRAMEWORK
TOPIC #9.7, 9.10; LO: UNIT 9 G, J, K
KC:
4.1.IV.E The collapse of the USSR in 1991 ended the Cold War and led to the establishment of capitalist economies throughout Eastern Europe. Germany was reunited, the Czechs and the Slovaks parted, Yugoslavia dissolved, and the European Union was enlarged through the admission of former Eastern bloc countries.

4.4.IV European states began to set aside nationalist rivalries in favor of economic and political integration, forming a series of transnational unions that grew in size and scope over the second half of the 20th century.

4.4.IV.A As the economic alliance known as the European Coal and Steel Community, envisioned as a means to spur postwar economic recovery, developed into the European Economic Community (EEC or Common Market) and the European Union (EU), Europe experienced increasing economic and political integration and efforts to establish a shared European identity.

4.4.IV.B EU member nations continue to balance questions of national sovereignty with the responsibilities of membership in an economic and political union.

NEW AMERICAN LEADERSHIP AND FINANCIAL CRISIS

- Europeans reacted sympathetically to the United States regarding the September 11, 2001 terrorist attacks on U.S. soil.
- However, the U.S. invasion of Iraq in 2003 caused considerable strain between the U.S. and Europe.
- Strains between the U.S. and Europe declined in 2008 as a result of unity between the EU and U.S. regarding Russia's invasion of Georgia, and the election of Barack Obama to the U.S. presidency. President Obama was critical of the U.S. invasion of Iraq, and both the EU and the U.S. understood the interconnectness of the international economy in light of the international financial crisis.
- U.S. foreign relations with Russia became more strained in 2014 due to the Russian seizure of the Crimea and military intervention in Syria in 2015.

AP® FRAMEWORK
TOPIC: N/A (THE CED DOES NOT GO BEYOND 2000.)
KC: N/A (THE CED DOES NOT GO BEYOND 2000.)

Multiple-Choice Questions

Questions 1–4 refer to the passage below.

"Europe's ascendant political right is unapologetically xenophobic. It caricatures the religion that I practice and uses those distortions to fan Islamophobia. But ultra-conservative strains of Islam, such as Salafism and Wahhabism, also caricature our religion and use that Islamophobia to silence opposition....

The strains of Islam that promote face veils do not believe in the concept of a woman's right to choose and describe women as needing to be hidden to prove their "worth."... There is no choice in such conditioning. That is not a message Muslims learn in our holy book, the Koran, nor is the face veil prescribed by the majority of Muslim scholars.

The French ban [on veils] has been condemned as anti-liberal and anti-feminist. Where were those howls when niqabs [veils that cover all of the face but the eyes] began appearing in European countries, where for years women fought for rights? A bizarre political correctness tied the tongues of those who would normally rally to defend women's rights.

There are several ideological conflicts here: Within Islam, liberal and feminist Muslims refuse to believe that full-length veils are mandatory.... Feminist groups run by Muslim women in various Western countries fight misogynistic practices justified in the name of culture and religion. Cultural relativists, they say, don't want to "offend" anyone by protesting the disappearance of women behind the veil—or worse."

Mona Eltahawy, "Liberals and Feminists, Unsettling Silence on Rending the Muslim Veil," *Washington Post*, Saturday, July 16, 2010

Source: Washington Post, Saturday July 16, 2010. Available at http://www.washingtonpost.com/sp-dyn/content/article/2010/07/16/AR2010071604356.html2010

1. Which of the following was an underlying cause of the "xenophobia" mentioned in the passage?
   (A) Conservative hatred of liberal policies aimed at helping the middle class
   (B) Changing economic systems in the many Western European countries
   (C) The influx of migrant workers after World War II
   (D) The rise of the women's rights movement

2. Which of the following intensified anti-immigrant sentiment in Europe?
   (A) The economic downturn of the 1970s
   (B) Fears of an economic depression in the 1950s and 1960s
   (C) Decolonization in African and Asian countries
   (D) The rising practice of Christianity in Eastern Europe after World War II

3. Which of the following conclusions best reflects the content of the passage?
   (A) Religion played an increasing role across Europe in the years following World War II.
   (B) Conflict over the role of religion in Europe intensified in the late-twentieth century.
   (C) Women received the right to vote in most European countries.
   (D) Liberals supported laws banning veils.

4. The ethno-religious group to which the writer of the passage belongs eventually became a target of
   (A) Catholic Center parties
   (B) Christian democratic parties
   (C) communist and socialist parties
   (D) extreme nationalist political parties

Questions 5–7 refer to the passage below.

"According to French law, obedience is no longer included among the duties of a wife, and each woman citizen has the right to vote; but these civil liberties remain theoretical as long as they are unaccompanied by economic freedom…. It is through gainful employment that woman has traversed most of the distance that separated her from the male; and nothing else can guarantee her liberty in practice. Once she ceases to be a parasite, the system based on her dependence crumbles; between her and the universe there is no longer any need for a masculine mediator….

When she is productive, active, she regains her transcendence…

There are… a fairly large number of privileged women who find in their professions a means of economic and social autonomy. These come to mind when one considers woman's possibilities and her future…. [E]ven though they constitute as yet only a minority; they continue to be the subject of debate between feminists and antifeminists. The latter assert that the emancipated women of today succeed in doing nothing of importance in the world and that furthermore they have difficulty in achieving their own inner equilibrium. The former exaggerate the results obtained by professional women and are blind to their inner confusion."

Simone de Beauvoir, *The Second Sex*, 1949

Source: *The Second Sex*, Trans. by H. M. Parshley, copyright 1952 and renewed 1980 by Alfred A. Knopf, a division of Random House, Inc.

5. The ideas in the passage best reflect which of the following?
   (A) The end of gender equality
   (B) Rising misogyny
   (C) Second-wave feminism
   (D) The goals of the suffragist movement

6. Which of the following trends seems to justify the author's views regarding women?
   (A) Women achieved high positions of political power by the late-twentieth century.
   (B) Women achieved equal pay for equal work with men by the 1960s.
   (C) Women remained legally subordinated to men throughout the rest of the twentieth century.
   (D) Women gained access to certain professions but were denied participation in others.

7. Which of the following led to the voting rights that are mentioned in the passage?
   (A) The emergence of the welfare state in the mid-twentieth century
   (B) Social levelling as a result of the Great Depression
   (C) The impact of classical liberalism in the twentieth century
   (D) Social changes due to the two world wars

Questions 8–11 refer to the passage below.

"The existentialist frankly states that man is in anguish. His meaning is as follows—When a man commits himself to anything, fully realizing that he is not only choosing what he will be, but is thereby at the same time a legislator deciding for the whole of mankind—in such a moment a man cannot escape from the sense of complete and profound responsibility. There are many, indeed, who show no such anxiety. But we affirm that they are merely disguising their anguish or are in flight from it. Certainly, many people think that in what they are doing they commit no one but themselves to anything: and if you ask them, "What would happen if everyone did so?," they shrug their shoulders and reply, "Everyone does not do so...." Existentialism is nothing else but an attempt to draw the full conclusions from a consistently atheistic position. Its intention is not in the least that of plunging men into despair. And if by despair one means—as the Christians do—any attitude of unbelief, the despair of the existentialist is something different....In this sense existentialism is optimistic. It is a doctrine of action, and it is only by self-deception, by confusing their own despair with ours, that Christians can describe us as without hope."

Jean-Paul Sartre, *Existentialism and Humanism*, 1946

Source: Trans. by Philip Mairet (London: Methuen), in Walter Kaufman, ed., *Existentialism from Dostoyevsky to Sartre* (New York: Meridian Books, 1956), pp. 292, 310–311.

8. Which of the following conclusions best reflects the contents of the passage?
   (A) Sartre questions traditional Western values.
   (B) Sartre's outlook is driven by inaction.
   (C) Sartre's views are based on Freudian psychology.
   (D) Sartre's philosophy is driven by positivism.

9. The ideas in the passage were influenced by the earlier ideas of which of the following?
   (A) August Comte
   (B) Emile Zola
   (C) Friedrich Nietzsche
   (D) Charles Darwin

10. The philosophy expressed in the passage was influenced by which of the following?
   (A) The economic dislocation caused by the Great Depression in France
   (B) The horrors of World War II
   (C) The emergence of the Cold War
   (D) The political changes caused by decolonization

11. Existentialism came to be most closely associated with which of the following?
   (A) Dadaism
   (B) Surrealism
   (C) Realism
   (D) Post-modernism

Questions 12–15 refer to the map below.

Growth of the European Union

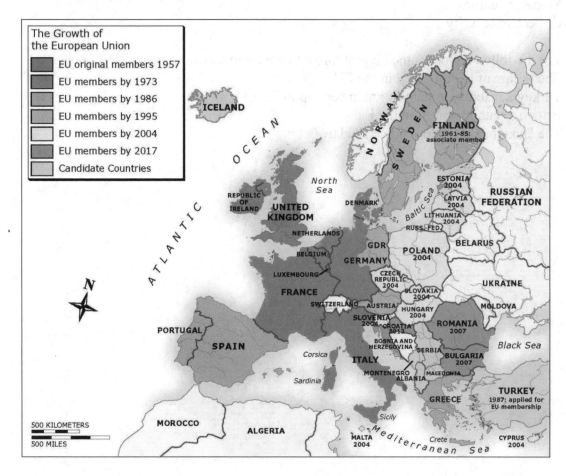

12. Which of the following was the earliest forerunner of the situation shown in the map?
    (A) The Council of Europe
    (B) European Coal and Steel Community
    (C) North Atlantic Treaty Organization
    (D) The United Nations

13. Which of the following has reacted most negatively to the trends shown in the map?
    (A) United States
    (B) North Africa
    (C) Balkans
    (D) Russia

351

14. The trend shown in the map illustrated the decline of which of the following?
    (A) Nationalistic rivalries
    (B) Capitalism
    (C) Monetary union
    (D) Collective security

15. Which of the following poses the biggest threat to the trend shown in the map?
    (A) The failure of Ukraine to join the EU
    (B) Turkey's inability to gain full membership in the EU
    (C) Britain's withdrawal from the EU
    (D) The lack of an army to enforce EU laws

Short-Answer Question

Answer a, b, and c:
1. a) Describe one political motivation for Western European economic integration after World War II.
   b) Describe one economic motivation for Western European economic integration after World War II.
   c) Explain one result of European economic integration between 1950 and 2000.

Long-Essay Question

Evaluate the extent to which immigration in Europe changed European society.

ANSWERS AND EXPLANATIONS: AP® PRACTICE TEST

Multiple-Choice Questions

1. C (KC: 4.4.III.D; LO: Unit 9 L) Enormous human losses during World War II caused labor shortages as European nations in Western Europe worked to rebuild after the war. Immigration from Africa, Asia, and Turkey became a solution. These immigrants legally migrated to European countries as "guest workers." They provided valuable low-wage labor during Europe's recovery from the war. Immigrants were often Muslim, and cultural differences between immigrants and Europeans led to the rise of xenophobia among certain nationalistic groups due to the economic downturn of the 1970s.

2. A (KC: 4.4.III.D; LO: Unit 9 L) See explanation to question 1.

3. B (KC: 4.4.III.D; LO: Unit 9 L) As Muslim immigrant populations grew in Western Europe in countries such as France, cultural issues became divisive. Some Muslim communities sought to practice traditions that were at odds with the European legal system. The passage makes reference to a French law that bans the wearing of overt religious symbols in public schools; however, many French Muslims see this as a law aimed at Muslim headwear.

4. D (KC: 4.4.III.D; LO: Unit 9 L) Europe saw the rise of far-right groups in the 1970s who saw immigration as damaging to the national culture. For example, Jean-Marie Le Pen led the National Front in France, which sought new laws to reduce immigration.

5. C (KC: 4.4.II.B; LO: Unit 9 H) By mid-century, most European adult women had gained the right to vote. The next step was to gain equality of economic opportunity for women. Simone de Beauvoir influenced the women's rights movement of the 1960s with her seminal feminist work, *The Second Sex* (1949).

6. A (KC: 4.4.II.E; LO: Unit 9 H) The success of the women's rights movement in the 1960s and 1970s bore fruit in the ascension of women to power in several European countries. Margaret Thatcher became Prime Minister of Britain in 1979, for example.

7. D (KC: 4.4.II.A/B; LO: Unit 8 M, Unit 9 H) Women played an indispensable role on the home front in many countries during World War I and World War II. Their contributions led governments to give women the right to vote.

8. A (KC: 4.3.IV.B; LO: Unit 9 O) Sartre's atheistic existentialism ran counter to Europe's Christian heritage.

9. C (KC: 3.6.III.A; LO: Unit 7 F) Friedrich Nietzsche's emphasis on the irrational and his criticism of what he saw as a Christian slave morality significantly influenced twentieth-century philosophers such as Jean-Paul Sartre.

10. B (KC: 4.3.I.B; LO: Unit 9 O) The dual horrors of World War I and World War II created an "age of anxiety" in the European psyche. Traditional philosophies and religious views no longer seemed relevant in a world that was disturbing and unpredictable. Existentialism was a response during the "age of anxiety" that dealt with an individual's need to create his or her own meaning to life.

11. D (KC: 4.3.I.B; LO: Unit 9 O) Existentialist writers influenced the emergence of postmodernism in the years following World War II. Postmodernism was characterized by a general skepticism and distrust of language as a reliable vehicle to express meaning as well as a rejection of Enlightenment rationality.

12. B (KC: 4.4.IV.A; LO: Unit 9 J) France and Germany spearheaded the creation of the European Coal and Steel Community in 1950 to integrate the coal and steel industries of six Western European nations including Belgium, Italy, the Netherlands, and Luxembourg. The arrangement was so successful that the same countries created the European Economic Community in 1957 to further integrate their economies.

13. D (KC: 4.1.IV.E; LO: Unit 9 G) Several countries that had been part of the Soviet empire joined the European Union in the 1990s and 2000s. This was a troubling trend for Russia, which saw the liberalism of the West dominating Eastern Europe, a region the Soviet Union had dominated just two decades earlier. Most European Union countries are also in NATO, which has further alienated Russia from the West.

14. A (KC: 4.4.IV.B; LO: Unit 9 K) Countries that joined the European Economic Community and later, the European Union, have subordinated nationalism to some degree in order to integrate their economies with those of other countries. This decline of nationalism after World War II is a major factor in why political tension between countries has been reduced so dramatically.

15. C (KC: 4.4.IV.B; LO: Unit 9K) In 2016, the British people voted to leave the European Union—a movement known as "Brexit." This action is emblematic of the rising Euroskepticism that has emerged in various parts of Europe and questions the efficacy of the EU in benefitting all of its members.

Short Answer Question
(KC: 4.1.IV.E, 4.4.IV.A, 4.4.IV.B; LO: Unit 9 G, J)

Possible responses to part a) include:
- Desire to prevent a future war between France and Germany
- Political stability to facilitate recovery and reorganization after World War II
- Political cooperation in the face of Cold War threats

Possible responses to part b) include:
- Economic recovery from World War II
- Increased economic cooperation among member nations
- Necessity for workers who would now be free to move across national borders for work

Possible responses to part c) include:
- European Coal and Steel Community
- European Economic Community (Treaty of Rome)
- European Union and the creation of a single currency (the *euro*)
- Integration of countries in Eastern Europe that were earlier a part of the Soviet empire
- Peace among member nations
- Creation of the largest and most powerful economic zone in the world

Long-Essay Question
(KC: 4.3.III.C, 4.4.III.D; LO: Unit 9 L)

Evaluate the extent to which immigration in Europe changed European society.

Changes might include:
- The importation of a large immigrant labor force facilitated continued economic growth.
- "Guest workers" were generally not allowed to integrate into mainstream society; many countries denied them citizenship.
- Cultural conflicts emerged, especially among large Muslim populations who at times sought to practice traditions that were at odds with European laws.
- The rise of xenophobia in the 1970s and right-wing political parties sought to limit immigration.
- Terrorist attacks have at times exacerbated relations between many Europeans and their immigrant communities.

Continuities might include:
- Certain immigrant communities today continue to feel alienated from mainstream society as they did back in the 1950s and 1960s.
- Low-wage immigrant labor remains an important labor source in the growing economy.
- Xenophobia remains in effect today.

PART III

Practice Document-Based Questions with Sample Essays

On the following pages are six practice Document-based Questions. They mirror the actual section in the AP exam in format and question types. Set aside a time to write essay responses to these questions, timing yourself as you will be timed when you take the actual exam. This will help you prepare for your test-taking experience.

DOCUMENT-BASED QUESTION 1

Evaluate the extent to which the Protestant Reformation was primarily caused by Church abuses.

Document 1

Source: Anonymous, woodcut shows indulgence preacher Johann Tetzel on his mule selling indulgences distributed by Luther's followers, early 16ᵗʰ century.

Source: De Agostini Picture Library/Getty Images

Document 2

Source: Martin Luther, "*An Open Letter to the Christian Nobility of the German Nation*," 1520

4. It should be decreed that no temporal matter shall be taken to Rome, but that all such cases shall be left to the temporal authorities, as the Romans themselves decree in that canon law of theirs, which they do not keep...So St. Paul teaches in Corinthians 6:7 and takes the Corinthians severely to task for their concern with worldly things...

Moreover, the outrageous extortion practiced by the officials must be forbidden in all the dioceses, so that they may attend to nothing else than matters of faith and good morals, and leave to the temporal judges the things that concern money, property, life and honor...

9. The pope should have no authority over the emperor, except that he anoints and crowns him at the altar, just as a bishop anoints and crowns a king; and we should not henceforth yield to that devilish pride which compels the emperor to kiss the pope's feet or sit at his feet, or, as they claim, hold his stirrup or the bridle of his mule when he mounts for a ride; still less should he do homage and swear faithful allegiance to the pope, as the popes have shamelessly ventured to demand as if they possessed that right. The chapter...in which the papal authority is raised above the imperial authority, is not worth a heller, nor are any of those who rest upon it or fear it; for it does nothing...

Source: Luther, Martin, *An Open Letter to the Christian Nobility of the German Nation Concerning the Reform of the Christian Estate, 1520*, trans. by C.M. Jacobs, Philadelphia: A.J. Holman Company, 1915

Document 3

Source: Anonymous, *Parody of the Apostles Creed*, c. 1520

I believe in the Pope, binder and looser in heaven, earth, and hell,
and in Simony, his only son our lord,
Who was conceived by the canon law
and born of the Romish church.
Under his power truth suffered,
was crucified, dead and buried,
and through the ban descended to hell,
rose again through the gospel and Paul
and was brought to Charles,
sitting at his right hand,
who in future is to rule over spiritual and worldly things.
I believe in canon law,
in the Romish church,
in the destruction of faith and of the communion of saints,
in indulgences both for the remission of guilt and penalty in purgatory,
in the resurrection of the flesh in an Epicurean life,
because given to us by the Holy Father, the Pope. Amen.

Source: Bainton, *Here I Stand: A Life of Martin Luther*, Peabody, MA, Hendrickson Pub, 2009, p. 54

Document 4

Source: Martin Luther, letter to his wife Katharine von Bora, October 4, 1529

Grace and peace in Christ, dear…Käth! Know that our friendly colloquy in Marburg has ended, and we have agreed on nearly all points, except that our opponents vainly insist that only bread is present in the Lord's Supper, though they acknowledge the spiritual presence of Christ therein. Today, the landgrave [Philip I of Hesse] is endeavoring [to determine] whether we could become united, or, if we remained divided, whether we could at least consider each other brethren and members of Christ. The landgrave is working very hard at this. But while we do not wish to be brethren and members, we do want peace and good will. I reckon that tomorrow, or the day after, we shall set out and journey…

Source: Luther, Martin. *The Letters of Martin Luther*, edited and translated by Margaret A. Currie, Macmillan and Co., Limited, 1908.

Document 5

Source: John Calvin, Protestant reformer, *Institutes of the Christian Religion,* 1536

The covenant of life not being equally preached to all, and among those to whom it is preached not always finding the same reception, this diversity discovers the wonderful depth of the Divine judgment. Nor is it to be doubted that this variety also follows, subject to the decision of God's eternal election. If it be evidently the result of the Divine will, that salvation is freely offered to some, and others are prevented from attaining it—this immediately gives rise to important and difficult questions, which are incapable of any other explication, than by the establishment of pious minds in what ought to be received concerning election and predestination—a question, in the opinion of many, full of perplexity; for they consider nothing more unreasonable, than that, of the common mass of mankind, some should be predestinated to salvation, and others to destruction.

Source: Oliver J. Thatcher, ed., The Library of Original Sources (Milwaukee: University Research Extension Co., 1907), Vol. V: 9th to 16th Centuries, pp. 141–150.

Document 6

Source: Philip Melanchthon, German humanist and religious scholar, Treatise compiled at Assembly of Smalcald, *Of the Power and Primacy of the Pope,* 1537.

On this account our consciences are sufficiently excused; for the errors of the kingdom of the Pope are manifest. And Scripture with its entire voice exclaims that these errors are a teaching of demons and of Antichrist. The idolatry in the profanation of the masses is manifest, which, besides other faults are shamelessly applied to most shameful gain. The doctrine of repentance has been utterly corrupted by the Pope and his adherents. For they teach that sins are remitted because of the worth of our works. Then they bid us doubt whether the remission takes place. They nowhere teach that sins are remitted freely for Christ's sake, and that by this faith we obtain remission of sins.

Thus they obscure the glory of Christ, and deprive consciences of firm consolation, and abolish true divine services, namely, the exercises of faith struggling with despair concerning the promise of the Gospel.

They have obscured the doctrine concerning sin, and have invented a tradition concerning the enumeration of offenses, producing many errors and despair.

They have devised, in addition, satisfactions, whereby they have also obscured the benefit of Christ.

From these, indulgences have been born, which are pure lies, fabricated for the sake of gain.

Then, how many abuses and what horrible idolatry the invocation of saints has produced!

What shameful acts have arisen from the tradition concerning celibacy!

Source: Melanchthon, Philip (or theologians assembled at Smalcald), *Of the Power and Primacy of the Pope, 1530,* published in *Triglot Concordia: the Symbolical Books of the Ev. Lutheran Church*, St. Louis: Concordia Publishing House, 1921, p. 503–529 http://www.iclnet.org/pub/resources/text/wittenberg/concord/web/smc-pope.html

Document 7

Source: Mary Tudor, daughter of Henry VIII and Catherine of Aragon, letter to her father, 1536.

First I confess and acknowledge the king's majesty to be my sovereign lord and king, in the imperial crown of this realm of England; and do submit myself to his highness and to each and every law and statute of this realm…

I do recognize, accept, take, repute and acknowledge the king's highness to be supreme head on earth, under Christ, of the church of England; and do utterly refuse the bishop of Rome's pretended authority, power and jurisdiction within this realm, formerly usurped, according to the laws and statutes made on that behalf, and by all the king's true subjects humbly received, admitted, obeyed, kept and observed.

And I do also utterly renounce and forsake all manner of remedy, interest and advantage which I may by any means claim by the bishop of Rome's laws, processes, jurisdiction or sentence, at this time or in any way hereafter, by any manner of title, colour, means or cause that is, shall or can be devised for that purpose.

I do freely, frankly and for the discharge of my duty towards God, the king's highness and his laws, without other respect, recognize and acknowledge that the marriage formerly had between his majesty and my mother, the late princess dowager, was by God's law and man's law incestuous and unlawful.'

Source: Henry Colburn (1844) "Lives of the Queens of England, from the Norman Conquest: With Anecdotes of Their Courts, Now First Published from Official Records and Other Authentic Documents, Private as Well as Public, Volume 5" [Henry Colburn, Publisher] pp 188–189

DOCUMENT-BASED QUESTIONS SAMPLE RATIONALES

Document-Based Question 1

Evaluate the extent to which the Protestant Reformation was primarily caused by Church abuses.

(KC: 1.1.II.B, 1.2.I.B, 1.2.I.C, 1.2.II.C; LO: Unit 2 B)

Part A Thesis (0–1 point): The thesis should briefly explain whether the Protestant Reformation was mainly caused by Church abuses and/or other factors.

Acceptable Thesis: To a great extent, the Protestant Reformation was primarily caused by church abuses including nepotism, simony, clerical immorality and the sale of indulgences. However, other factors such as doctrinal and political differences were also important causes.

Part B Contextualization (0–1 point): Students should give a broad overview of events prior to, during, and/or after the time of the Protestant Reformation. Acceptable responses should explain (not just mention) developments such as:

- Renaissance curiosity and questioning of the world
- Christian Humanism
- Works of Erasmus criticizing the Catholic Church
- Earlier movements such as John Wycliffe in England and Jan Hus in Bohemia
- Babylonian Captivity and the Great Schism
- Religious Wars and degrees of religious tolerance
- The Scientific Revolution's challenge to both antiquity and Church teachings
- Habsburg-Valois Wars

The above list is not exhaustive.

Part C Evidence (0–3 points): Evidence from the documents (up to 2 points) and Evidence beyond the documents (1 point):

<u>Evidence from the documents</u>
1 point--Student correctly uses the content of at least THREE documents
Acceptable:

- Luther's supporters criticize Johann Tetzel for selling indulgences in the German states. (Doc. 1)
- Luther appeals to German nobles to support his ideas critical of the pope. (Doc. 2)
- The parody of the Apostle's Creed criticizes papal abuses such as simony and the sale of indulgences. (Doc. 3)
- In a letter to his wife, Martin Luther discusses doctrinal differences over whether Christ is present in the Lord's Supper. (Doc. 4)

365

- John Calvin discusses his reformist ideas about religious doctrine, notably predestination. (Doc. 5)
- In a treatise at the Assembly of Smalcald, Philip Melancthon criticizes the corruption of the pope regarding religious doctrine. (Doc. 6)
- Mary Tudor expresses support for her father's break from the Catholic Church and the formation of the Church of England. (Doc. 7)

OR

2 points--Student correctly uses the content of at least SIX documents to support an argument/thesis

Acceptable:
- Church abuses as a primary cause of the Reformation are suggested by the cartoon by Luther's followers, implying that Tetzel is only concerned with money and is hawking indulgences to the German people. (Doc.1)
- Luther's letter to the German nobility highlights both the political and economic benefits to the German princes if they were to support Luther and break away from the Catholic Church. (Doc. 2)
- The parody of the Apostle's Creed and the emphasis that Catholic leaders were far more concerned about worldly ideas is supportive of the idea that the Reformation was primarily caused by church abuses. (Doc. 3)
- Luther's discussion of the differences in Marburg is indicative of factors other than church abuses contributing to the Protestant Reformation. (Doc. 4)
- Doctrinal differences, even among the reformers as expressed by John Calvin's theology regarding pre-destination, contributed to both the Reformation itself and the continued spread of Protestantism in Europe. (Doc. 5)
- Melanchthon's emphasis on both church abuses as well as doctrinal differences with the pope and the Catholic Church suggest that both of these issues were factors leading to the Reformation. (Doc. 6)
- Mary Tudor's deference to her father as her sovereign lord and king and her repudiation of the pope (bishop of Rome) support the idea that kings should be more powerful than Catholic Church officials and advocate a political reason for the Reformation. (Doc. 7)

Evidence beyond the documents
1 point--Student uses evidence not included in the document. Common examples could include the following if explained:

- Erasmus's condemnation of church practices
- Simony
- Nepotism
- Pluralism
- Absenteeism
- Clerical ignorance
- Specific popes who were corrupted such as Alexander VI or Julius II
- 95 Theses
- Salvation by faith alone

- Consubstantiation v. Transubstantiation
- Protestant emphasis on only two sacraments
- Peasant Revolts
- Mary Tudor later restored Catholicism to England when she became queen

The above list is not exhaustive.

Part D Analysis and Reasoning (0–2 points):
1 point—Sourcing: Student explains the relevance of the document's audience, purpose, point of view, or historical situation in relation to the argument.

Acceptable example of audience:
The audience of Mary Tudor's letter was her father, Henry VIII, and she expresses to him her renunciation of the Catholic Church as well as her support for his creation of the Church of England and his decision to annul his marriage to her mother, Catherine of Aragon. (Doc. 7)

Acceptable example of purpose:
The purpose of the woodcut by Luther's followers was to show the abuses of the Catholic Church through Tetzel's sale of indulgences and more importantly, to gain support for Luther's actions against the church. (Doc. 1)

Acceptable example of point of view:
Martin Luther's letter to the German nobles was an attempt to gain their support for his actions against the Catholic Church. Luther knew that he might be condemned for heresy by church officials and most likely believed that the support of the princes would keep his movement growing and might even save his life. (Doc. 2)

Acceptable example of historical situation:
Luther's success during the early stages of the Reformation led to a second generation of Protestant reformers whose ideas did not always agree with Lutheranism. John Calvin, in his Institutes of Christian Religion, expressed his idea of predestination as an alternative to Lutheranism. Calvinism grew rapidly becoming the most international of the new Protestant religions. (Doc. 5)

1 point—Complexity: Student demonstrates a complex understanding of both the prompt and the documents. Examples demonstrating complexity might include:

- Explaining a nuance by exploring the many different factors that contributed to the Protestant Reformation (e.g., German princes wanted independence from Church laws and taxation OR new doctrinal ideas emerged such as individual interpretation of the vernacular Bible and the belief in salvation by faith alone).
- Explaining connections to other time periods such as the origins of the Renaissance and the New Monarchies and their relationship to the Reformation.

- Comparing and contrasting documents as evidence to support a main point. (e.g., although both Documents 1 and 2 condemn the pope, Document 2 emphasizes political independence from the pope whereas Document 3 parodies papal corruption).
- Proving the relative importance of the different causes throughout the entire paper with detailed evidence and excellent explanations.
- Qualifying or modifying an argument by considering diverse or alternative views or evidence, such as the idea that political and economic factors were important causes of the Protestant Reformation.

DOCUMENT-BASED QUESTION 2

Evaluate whether the ideas of the Enlightenment were primarily political or social.

Document 1

Source: Baron de Montesquieu, French political philosopher, *The Spirit of Laws,* 1748.

In every government there are three sorts of power; the legislative; the executive, in respect to things dependent on the law of nations; and the executive, in regard to things that depend on the civil law.

By virtue of the first, the prince or magistrate enacts temporary or perpetual laws, and amends or abrogates those that have been already enacted. By the second, he makes peace or war, sends or receives embassies; establishes the public security, and provides against invasions. By the third, he punishes criminals, or determines the disputes that arise between individuals. The latter we shall call the judiciary power, and the other simply the executive power of the state.

When the legislative and executive powers are united in the same person, or in the same body of magistrates, there can be no liberty; because apprehensions may anse, lest the same monarch or senate should enact tyrannical laws, to execute them in a tyrannical manner.

Again, there is no liberty, if the power of judging be not separated from the legislative and executive powers. Were it joined with the legislative, the life and liberty of the subject would be exposed to arbitrary control, for the judge would then be the legislator. Were it joined to the executive power, the judge might behave with all the violence of an oppressor.

Source: Montesquieu, *The Spirit of the Laws, vol. 1,* trans. Thomas Nugent (London: J. Nourse, 1777), pp. 221–237, passim.

Document 2

Source: Jean-Jacques Rousseau, French philosopher, excerpt from the novel *Émile* or *On Education,* 1762.

Once it is demonstrated that man and woman are not and ought not be constituted in the same way in either character or temperament, it follows that they ought not to have the same education. In following nature's directions, man and woman ought to act in concert, but they ought not to do the same things. The goal of their labors is common, but their labors themselves are different, and consequently so are the tastes directing them.…

The good constitution of children initially depends on that of their mothers. The first education of men depends on the care of women. Men's morals, their passions, their tastes, their pleasures, their very happiness also depend on women. Thus the whole education of women ought to relate to men. To please men, to be useful to them, to make herself loved and honored by them, to raise them when young, to care for them when grown, to counsel them, to console them, to make their lives agreeable and sweet—these are the duties of women at all times, and they ought to be taught from childhood. So long as one does not return to this principle, one will deviate from the goal, and all the precepts taught to women will be of no use for their happiness or for ours.

Source: From *Émile* or *On Education* by Jean-Jacques Rousseau by Allan Bloom, trans. Copyright © 1979 by Basic Books, Inc. Reprinted by permission of Basic Books, member of Perseus Books, LLC

Document 3

Source: François Marie Arouet de Voltaire, French author, *Philosophical Dictionary,* 1764

Fanaticism is to superstition what delirium is to fever and rage to anger. The man visited by ecstasies and visions, who takes dreams for realities and his fancies for prophecies, is an enthusiast; the man who supports his madness with murder is a fanatic …

The most detestable example of fanaticism was that of the burghers of Paris who on St. Bartholomew's Night [1572] went about assassinating and butchering all their fellow citizens who did not go to mass, throwing them out of windows, cutting them in pieces…

The only remedy for this epidemic malady is the philosophical spirit which, spread gradually, at last tames men's habits and prevents the disease from starting; for once the disease has made any progress, one must flee and wait for the air to clear itself. Laws and religion are not strong enough against the spiritual pest; religion, far from being healthy food for infected brains, turns to poison in them …

Even the law is impotent against these attacks of rage; it is like reading a court decree to a raving maniac. These fellows are certain that the Holy Spirit with which they are filled is above the law, that their enthusiasm is the only law they must obey.

What can we say to a man who tells you that he would rather obey God than men, and that therefore he is sure to go to heaven for butchering you?

Source: Voltaire, *Philosophical Dictionary*, ed. Peter Gay, 2 vols. (New York: Basic Books, 1962), pp. 267–269.
See also: http://chnm.gmu.edu/revolution/d/273/

Document 4

Source: Immanuel Kant, German philosopher, *What is Enlightenment,* 1784.

A prince who does not find it unworthy to say that he considers it his duty not to prescribe anything to men in matters of religion, but to allow them complete freedom ...is himself enlightened and deserves to be esteemed by the grateful world and posterity as the one who first praised the human race of immaturity, at least on the part of the government ...Below him, venerable clerics, without prejudice to their official duty, may freely and publicly present to the world, for their consideration, their judgments and insights in the quality of the scholars, deviating from the accepted symbol here and there; but even more so anyone else who is not restricted by any official duty...

I have [placed] the main point of the Enlightenment, the outcome of the people out of their self-inflicted immaturity...in matters of religion, because in view of the arts and sciences our rulers have no interest in playing the guardian over their subjects...But the mindset of a head of state who favors the former [religious enlightenment] goes even further, and sees that even in the light of his legislation there is no danger of allowing his subjects to be public by [use] their own reason, to make use of them and publicly present their thoughts on a better formulation of them, even with an outspoken criticism of those already given, to the world; of which we have a glorious example, whereby no monarch yet went before the one whom we worship.

Source: *Immanuel Kant's works. Volume IV.* Writings from 1783–1788. Edited by dr. Artur Buchenau and Dr. med. Ernst Cassirer. Berlin: Bruno Cassirer 1913. Pp. 167–176 and 538–539. Also: http://www.gutenberg.org/files/30821/30821-h/30821-h.htm

Document 5

Source: List of grievances from the nobility of the bailliage of Blois to the…deputies of the order to the States General, 1789.

The object of every social institution is to confer the greatest possible happiness upon those who live under its laws…

Art. I. In order to assure the exercise of this first and most sacred of the rights of man, we ask that no citizen may be exiled, arrested or held prisoner except in cases contemplated by the law and in accordance with a decree originating in the regular courts of justice…

We indicate…a number of instances in which natural liberty is abridged:

1. The abuse of police regulations, which every year, in an arbitrary manner and without regular process, thrusts a number of artisans and useful citizens into prisons, work-houses and places of detention, often for trivial faults and even upon simple suspicion;

2. The abuse of exclusive privileges which fetter industry;

3. The guilds and corporations which deprive citizens of the right of using their faculties;

4. The regulations governing manufactures, the rights of inspection and marque, which impose restrictions that have lost their usefulness, and which burden industry with a tax that yields no profit to the public treasury.

Source: From John Hall Stewart, *A Documentary Sruvery of the French Revoultion*, 1st ed. (New York: Macmillan, 1951).

Document 6

Document 7

Source: Mary Wollstonecraft, British author, excerpt from *A Vindication of the Rights of Women*, 1792.

… Rousseau declares that a woman should never, for a moment, feel herself independent, that she should be governed by fear to exercise her natural cunning, and made a coquettish slave in order to render her a more alluring object of desire, a sweeter companion to man, whenever he chooses to relax himself. He carries the arguments, which he pretends to draw from the indications of nature, still further, and insinuates that truth and fortitude, the cornerstones of all human virtue, should be cultivated with certain restrictions, because, with respect to the female character, obedience is the grand lesson which ought to be impressed with unrelenting rigour.

What nonsense! When will a great man arise with sufficient strength of mind to put away the fumes which pride and sensuality have thus spread over the subject! If women are by nature inferior to men, their virtues must be the same in quality, if not in degree, or virtue is a relative idea; consequently, their conduct should be founded on the same principles, and have the same aim.

Connected with man as daughters, wives, and mothers, their moral character may be estimated by their manner of fulfilling those simple duties; but the end, the grand end of their exertions should be to unfold their own faculties and acquire the dignity of conscious virtue.…

… I … will venture to assert, that till women are more rationally educated, the progress of human virtue and improvement in knowledge must receive continual checks.…

Source: Mary Wollstonecraft, *A Vindication of the Rights of Woman* (1792).

DOCUMENT-BASED QEUSTIONS SAMPLE RATIONALES

Document-Based Question 2

> *Evaluate whether the ideas of the Enlightenment were primarily political or social.*

(KC: 2.3.I, 2.3.III, 2.3.IV; LO: Unit 4 C, D)

Part A Thesis (0–1 point): The thesis should take a position and explain whether Enlightenment ideas were primarily political or social.

Acceptable Thesis: The ideas of the Enlightenment were primarily political as most Enlightened thinkers advocated natural law and liberties through benevolent governments.

Part B Contextualization (0–1 point): Students should give a broad overview of events prior to, during, and/or after the time of the ideas of the Enlightenment. Acceptable responses should explain (not just mention) developments such as:

- The Scientific Revolution and emphasis on reason
- Influence of Locke and Newton on the Enlightenment
- Ideas of John Locke
- The Glorious Revolution and English Bill of Rights
- The growth of salons in France
- The rising middle class
- Increasing literacy rates and the growth of publishing
- Debates about women's roles
- Enlightened Despotism
- The weaknesses of absolute monarchy
- Louis XVI's France
- Early stages of the French Revolution

The above list is not exhaustive.

Part C Evidence (0–3 points): Evidence from the documents (up to 2 points) and Evidence beyond the documents (1 point):

Evidence from the documents
1 point—Student correctly uses the content of at least THREE documents
Acceptable:

- Montesquieu explains that branches of government must be separate from each other to ensure the liberty of the people. (Doc. 1)
- The excerpt from Rousseau's novel *Émile* explains that the proper gender roles are patriarchal, and women must be valuable to men. (Doc. 2)

- Voltaire expresses that religious beliefs are detrimental to human beings and leads to fanaticism. (Doc. 3)
- German philosopher Immanuel Kant champions religiously tolerant rulers. (Doc. 4)
- The list of grievances from the French nobility express their dissatisfaction with French laws that hinder liberty. (Doc. 5)
- The political cartoon highlights the rise of the Third Estate in France during the early stages of the French Revolution. (Doc. 6)
- Mary Wollstonecraft argues that women should be better educated and are not naturally inferior to men. (Doc. 7)

OR

2 points—Student correctly uses the content of at least SIX documents to support an argument/thesis

Acceptable:
- Montesquieu suggests that that the ideal form of government would have three branches—the legislative, the executive and the judicial—and that liberty is not possible without these three branches. (Doc.1)
- In the novel *Émile*, Rousseau advocates that proper gender roles are necessary for happiness. Women must be educated to attend to the needs of men throughout their lives and there should be no deviations. (Doc. 2)
- Voltaire discusses the St. Bartholomew's Night Massacre and argues that religious fanaticism has no place in society and the only way to overcome it is through a new philosophical spirit reminiscent of the Enlightenment. (Doc. 3)
- According to Emmanuel Kant, rulers who allow their subjects to make their own religious choices are ruling according to Enlightenment ideals and in the best interest of their subjects. (Doc. 4)
- French nobles wishing to reform the French government on the eve of the revolution are demanding natural liberties including justice before the law as well as an end to restrictions that hinder economic development. (Doc. 5)
- The political cartoon representing the Three Estates in revolutionary France expresses hope that the Third Estate will reform French government and end the rights and privileges of the First and Second Estates after the storming of the Bastille. (Doc. 6)
- Mary Wollstonecraft refutes Rousseau's argument regarding the inferiority of women and suggests vast social changes as she advocates increased educational opportunities for women. (Doc. 7)

Evidence beyond the documents
1 point—Student uses evidence not included in the document. Common examples could include the following if explained:

- British government after the Glorious Revolution
- Rousseau's idea of 'separate spheres' for men and women
- Enlightenment debates regarding the role of women

- Enlightened despotism (Frederick the Great, Catherine the Great, Joseph II, and Napoleon)
- The growth of salons and coffeehouses
- Enlightened thinkers not mentioned in the documents
- Adam Smith and/or the physiocrats
- French governmental policies prior to the revolution
- The growth of the bourgeoisie
- The influence of the American Revolution in France
- American Revolution and republican government in the United States
- *The Declaration of Rights of Man and Citizen*
- The August Decrees
- Olympe de Gouge and the *Declaration of Rights of Women and Citizen*

The above list is not exhaustive.

Part D Analysis and Reasoning (0–2 pt.):
1 point—Sourcing: Student explains the relevance of the document's audience, purpose, point of view, or historical situation in relation to the argument.

Acceptable example of audience:
The Baron de Montesquieu is writing to a middle- and upper-class audience whose members are educated and may find his ideas appealing because it would create for them a legislative body similar to Great Britain's Parliament. (Doc. 1)

Acceptable example of purpose:
Wollstonecraft most likely wrote *A Vindication of the Rights of Women* as an appeal to apply Enlightenment ideals, including increased educational and political opportunities, for women. (Doc. 7)

Acceptable example of point of view:
The list of grievances expressed by the nobility to the States General in 1789 emphasizes Enlightenment ideals of natural rights and liberty. This is not surprising considering that the nobility often frequented the salons and corresponded with the philosophes that espoused these ideas. (Doc. 5)

Acceptable example of historical situation:
Voltaire's negative sentiments towards organized religion are not surprising. Many philosophers condemned organized religion as superstitious and opposed to reason, an important ideal often stated during the Enlightenment. (Doc. 3)

1 point—Complexity: Student demonstrates a complex understanding of both the prompt and the documents. Examples demonstrating complexity might include:

- Explaining a nuance by exploring the many different ideals that were a part of the Enlightenment (e.g., although Enlightenment thinkers valued the idea of representative government, they did not support the idea of mass democracy because they believed that the masses were not capable of making such decisions. Most supported the idea of benevolent absolutism).
- Explaining connections to other time periods such as the Scientific Revolution and the spread of liberalism during and after the Napoleonic period.
- Comparing and contrasting documents as evidence to support a main point. (e.g., Wollstonecraft's response to Rousseau's ideas concerning women).
- Proving the relative importance of both political and social ideas throughout the entire paper with detailed evidence and excellent explanations.
- Qualifying or modifying an argument by considering diverse or alternative views or evidence, such as the idea that the religious ideals of the Enlightenment were of equal importance to political ideals.

Evaluate the relative importance of the different factors that led to the outbreak and spread of the French Revolution and its ideals during the period 1750–1800.

Document 1

Source: David Hume, Scottish Philosopher, *An Enquiry Concerning Human Understanding,* 1748

A miracle is a violation of the laws of nature; and as a firm and unalterable experience has established these laws, the proof against a miracle, from the very nature of the fact, is as entire as any argument from experience can possibly be imagined. Why is it more than probable, that all men must die; that lead cannot, of itself, remain suspended in the air; that fire consumes wood, and is extinguished by water; unless it be, that these events are found agreeable to the laws of nature, and there is required a violation of these laws, or in other words, a miracle to prevent them? Nothing is esteemed a miracle, if it ever happen in the common course of nature. It is no miracle that a man, seemingly in good health, should die on a sudden: because such a kind of death, though more unusual than any other, has yet been frequently observed to happen. But it is a miracle, that a dead man should come to life; because that has never been observed in any age or country....

Source: David Hume, *An Enquiry Concerning Human Understanding*, L. A. Selby Bigge, ed. (Oxford: Clarendon Press, 1902), pp. 114–16.

Document 2

Source: Voltaire, French *philosophe*, *Letters on the English*, 1778

No one is exempted in this country from paying certain taxes because he is a nobleman or a priest. All duties and taxes are settled by the House of Commons, whose power is greater than that of the Peers, though inferior to it in dignity. The spiritual as well as temporal Lords have the liberty to reject a Money Bill brought in by the Commons; but they are not allowed to alter anything in it, and must either pass or throw it out without restriction. When the Bill has passed the Lords and is signed by the king, then the whole nation pays, every man in proportion to his revenue or estate, not according to his title, which would be absurd.

The land-tax continues still upon the same foot, though the revenue of the lands is increased. Thus no one is tyrannised over, and every one is easy. The feet of the peasants are not bruised by wooden shoes; they eat white bread, are well clothed, and are not afraid of increasing their stock of cattle, nor of tiling their houses from any apprehension that their taxes will be raised the year following. The annual income of the estates of a great many commoners in England amounts to two hundred thousand livres, and yet these do not think it beneath them to plough the lands which enrich them, and on which they enjoy their liberty.

Source: *French and English philosophers: Descartes, Rousseau, Voltaire, Hobbes*: with introductions and notes. New York: P.F. Collier, c1910. Series: The Harvard classics v. 34.

Document 3

Source: Petition of the Women of the Third Estate to the King, January, 1789

Sire,

At a time when the different orders of the state are occupied with their interests; when everyone seeks to make the most of his titles and rights; when some anxiously recall the centuries of servitude and anarchy, while others make every effort to shake off the last links that still bind them to the imperious remains of feudalism; women—continual objects of the admiration and scorn of men—could they not also make their voices heard midst this general agitation?

Excluded from the national assemblies by laws so well consolidated that they allow no hope of infringement, they do not ask, Sire, for your permission to send their deputies to the Estates General; they know too well how much favor will play a part in the election, and how easy it would be for those elected to impede the freedom of voting.

We prefer, Sire, to place our cause at your feet; not wishing to obtain anything except from your heart, it is to it that we address our complaints and confide our miseries.

The women of the Third Estate are almost all born without wealth; their education is very neglected or very defective.

Source: *The French Revolution and Human Rights: A Brief Documentary History*, translated, edited, and with an introduction by Lynn Hunt (Bedford/St. Martin's: Boston/New York), 1996, 60–63.

Document 4

Source: Abbé Emmanuel Joseph Sieyès, *What is the Third Estate?*, January 1789

The plan of this book is fairly simple. We must ask ourselves three questions.

-What is the Third Estate? Everything.
-What has it been until now in the political order? Nothing.
-What does it want to be? Something…

Who then shall dare to say that the Third Estate has not within itself all that is necessary for the formation of a complete nation? It is the strong and robust man who has one arm still shackled. If the privileged order should be abolished, the nation would be nothing less, but something more. Therefore, what is the Third Estate? Everything; but an everything shackled and oppressed. What would it be without the privileged order? Everything, but an everything free and flourishing. Nothing can succeed without it, everything would be infinitely better without the others…

The Third Estate embraces then all that which belongs to the nation; and all that which is not the Third Estate, cannot be regarded as being of the nation.

What is the Third Estate?

It is the whole.

Source: Translations and Reprints from the Original Sources of European History. Published by The Departments of History of the University of Pennsylvania, 1900. https://archive.org/details/translationrepr1899univ

Document 5

Source: The Declaration of Rights of Man and Citizen, August 1789

…[T]he National Assembly recognizes and declares, in the presence and under the auspices of the Supreme Being, the following rights of man and citizen:

Articles:

1. Men are born free and remain free and equal in rights. Social distinctions can be based only on public utility.

2. The aim of every political association is the preservation of the natural and imprescriptible rights of man. These rights are liberty, property, security, and resistance to oppression.

3. The sources of all sovereignty resides essentially in the nation; no body, no individual can exercise authority that does not proceed from it in plain terms.

4. Liberty consists in the power to do anything that does not injure others; accordingly, the exercise of the rights of each man has no limits except those that secure the enjoyment of these same rights to the other members of society. These limits can be determined only by law.

Source: Frank Maloy Anderson, ed., *The Constitution and Other Select Documents Illustrative of the History of France, 1789–1907* (New York: Russell and Russell, 1908), pp. 59–61.

Source: Louis XVI guillotined, January 1793

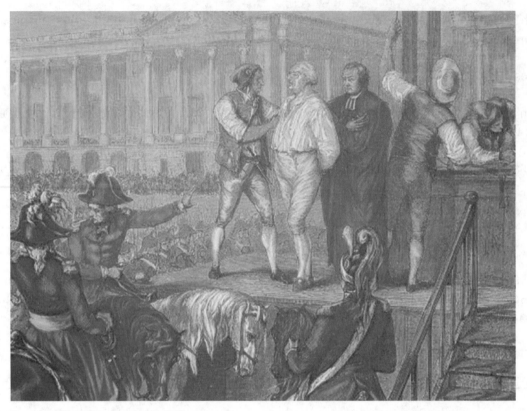

Source: Album/Art Resource, NY

Document 7

Source: The National Convention, legislation establishing the worship of a Supreme Being, May 1794

1. The French people recognize the existence of the Supreme Being and the immortality of the soul.

2. They recognize that the worship worthy of the Supreme Being is the observance of the duties of man.

3. They place in the forefront of such duties detestation of bad faith and tyranny, punishment of tyrants and traiters, succoring of unfortunates, respect of weak persons, defence of the oppressed, doing to others all the good that one can, and being just towards everyone.

4. Festivals shall be instituted to remind man of the concept of the Divinity and of the dignity of his being.

5. They shall take their names from the glorious events of our Revolution, or from the virtues most dear and most useful to man, or from the greatest benefits of nature....

6. On the days of *décade*, the name given to a particular day in each month of the revolutionary calendar, it shall celebrate the following festivals:

Source: From John Hall Stewart, *A Documentary Survey of the French Revolution*, 1st ed. (New York: Macmillan, 1951).

Document-Based Question 3

> *Evaluate the relative importance of the different factors that led to the outbreak and spread of the French Revolution and its ideals during the period 1750–1800.*

(KC: 2.1.IV; LO: Unit 5 D, E)

Part A Thesis (0–1 point): The thesis should briefly explain the causes of the French Revolution and evaluate the relative significance of the causes.

Acceptable Thesis: There were multiple factors that led to the French Revolution, including government debt and the food crisis that affected the lower classes; however, the privileges of the First and Second Estates and their refusal to accept any type of reform led to great resentment from the Third Estate. As a result, the Third Estate, particularly the bourgeoisie, initiated the revolution by forming the National Assembly and transformed France into a constitutional monarchy.

Part B Contextualization (0–1 point): Students should give a broad overview of events prior to, during, and/or after the time of the French Revolution. Acceptable responses should explain (not just mention) developments such as:
- Debt due to warfare
- Enlightenment began in France
- Enlightened thinkers admired British government forms
- New ideas regarding religious tolerance
- New ideas advocating a republic
- Impact of the American Revolution
- French revolutionary ideals inspired the Haitian Revolution

The above list is not exhaustive.

Part C Evidence (0–3 points): Evidence from the documents (up to 2 points) and Evidence beyond the documents (1 point):

<u>**Evidence from the documents**</u>
1 point—Student correctly uses the content of at least THREE documents

Acceptable:
- Hume believes that miracles go against the ideas of the laws of nature. (Doc. 1)
- Voltaire suggests that the system of taxation in Britain is exemplary because the House of Commons wields more power than the hereditary House of Lords. (Doc. 2)
- The petition of the women of the Third Estate appeals directly to the king to improve their condition. (Doc. 3)

- Sieyès believes that the Third Estate is the most important caste in France and should have a say in politics. (Doc. 4)
- The Declaration of Rights of Man and Citizen expresses the idea that men have natural rights. (Doc. 5)
- The image shows supporters of the revolution holding Louis XVI's severed head after his execution by guillotine. (Doc. 6)
- The National Convention authorized the worship of a Supreme Being and created festivals and rituals for French citizens to celebrate. (Doc. 7)

OR

2 points—Student correctly uses the content of at least SIX documents to support an argument/thesis

Acceptable:
- Hume's belief that a "dead man coming to life has never been observed in any age or country" emphasizes the idea of scientific reason and would later influence revolutionary leaders such as Robespierre and Danton. (Doc.1)
- Voltaire's suggests that taxation is fairer in Britain because it is determined by commoners rather than by the nobility. Prior to the French Revolution, the Third Estate was burdened with taxation in France, and this unfair tax system was a major cause of the revolution. (Doc. 2)
- The Petition of the Women of the Third Estate appeals directly to the king for improved conditions and was most likely inspired by the Enlightenment's idea of legal equality. (Doc. 3)
- The Third Estate's desire for political and legal equality is best summed up by Sieyès and contributed to the Tennis Court Oath. (Doc. 4)
- The Declaration of Rights of Man and Citizen exemplifies Enlightenment ideas regarding liberty, property, and the law. (Doc. 5)
- Revolutionary fervor and the desire to end the French monarchy and begin a republic led radical revolutionaries to execute Louis XVI and Marie Antoinette. (Doc. 6)
- The emphasis on the Enlightenment ideal of reason led to the de-Christianization of France and the National Convention's legislation that mandated the worship of a Supreme Being. Notre Dame was even renamed the Temple of Reason. (Doc. 7)

Evidence beyond the documents

1 point—Student uses evidence not included in the document. Common examples could include the following if explained:
- Louis XVI as a weak king who is unfit to rule
- The financial crisis of the French treasury
- Bourgeois economic successes during the 18th century
- 1788–89 Agricultural Crisis
- Feudal restrictions on the peasantry
- An emphasis on reason
- De-Christianization of Europe

The above list is not exhaustive.

Part D Analysis and Reasoning (0–2 points):
1 point—Sourcing: Student explains the relevance of the document's audience, purpose, point of view, or historical situation in relation to the argument.

Acceptable example of audience:
The intended audience of Emmanuel Sieyes's pamphlet, *What is the Third Estate?*, included the literate bourgeoisie who would benefit politically and economically from the changes suggested. (Doc. 4)

Acceptable example of purpose:
The purpose of the women's petition to the Third Estate is to convince the Third Estate to consider women's concerns and complaints. (Doc. 3)

Acceptable example of point of view:
The Jacobins and the Committee of Public Safety would prefer that the entire nation support their agenda while legislating laws through the National Convention could be seen as part of a democratic process. (Doc. 7)

Acceptable example of historical situation:
Louis XVI and his wife, Marie Antoinette, had tried to leave France and join counter-revolutionaries in Austria. They were captured a few miles from the border at Varennes proving to many revolutionary leaders that they were traitors against the Revolution. Louis was then tried and sentenced to death by guillotine. (Doc. 6)

1 point—Complexity: Student demonstrates a complex understanding of both the prompt and the documents. Examples demonstrating complexity might include:
- Explaining a nuance by exploring the many different factors that contributed to the outbreak and spread of the revolution (e.g., nobility originally wanted to gain political power; however, after the bourgeoisie began to dominate the revolution the nobility lost its recognized status and privileges).
- Explaining connections to other time periods such as the Glorious Revolution in England or the American Revolution.
- Comparing and contrasting documents as evidence to support a main point.
  (e.g., explaining the contrast of the emphasis on liberty in Document 5 with the establishment of the worship of a Supreme Being in Document 7)
- Proving the relative importance of the different causes throughout the entire paper with detailed evidence and developed explanations.
- Qualifying or modifying an argument by considering diverse or alternative views or evidence, such as the idea that the revolutions should spread throughout all of Europe.

388

DOCUMENT-BASED QUESTION 4

Evaluate the extent to which urbanization transformed the experiences of everyday life prior to the First World War.

Document 1

Source: Elizabeth Poole Sandford, British author, *Woman in Her Social and Domestic Character*, 1842

The changes wrought by Time are many. It influences the opinions of men as familiarity does their feelings; it has a tendency to do away with superstition, and to reduce every thing to its real worth. It is thus that the sentiment for woman has undergone a change. The romantic passion which once almost deified her is on the decline; and it is by intrinsic qualities that she must now inspire respect. She is no longer the queen of song and the star of chivalry. But if there is less of enthusiasm entertained for her, the sentiment is more rational, and, perhaps, equally sincere; for it is in relation to happiness that she is chiefly appreciated. And in this respect it is, we must confess, that she is most useful and most important. Domestic life is the chief source of her influence; and the greatest debt society can owe to her is domestic comfort; for happiness is almost an element of virtue; and nothing conduces more to improve the character of men than domestic peace. A woman may make a man's home delightful, and may thus increase his motives for virtuous exertion. She may refine and tranquilize his mind, -- may turn away his anger or allay his grief. Her smile may be the happy influence to gladden his heart, and to disperse the cloud that gathers on his brow. And in proportion to her endeavors to make those around her happy, she will be esteemed and loved.

Source: Mrs. John Sandford (Elizabeth Poole Sandford), *Woman in her Social and Domestic Character* (Boston: Otis, Broaders and Co, 1842), pp. 5–7, 15–16

Document 2

Source: Heinrich Heine, German poet, reflection on the opening of the railway lines from Paris to Rouen and Orleans, 1843

What changes must now occur, in our way of looking at things, in our notions! Even the elementary concepts of time and space have begun to vacillate. Space is killed by the railways, and we are left with time alone…. Now you can travel to Orléans in four and a half hours, and it takes no longer to get to Rouen. Just imagine what will happen when the lines to Belgium and Germany are completed and connected with their railways! I feel as if the mountains and forests of all countries were advancing on Paris. Even now, I can smell the German linden trees; the North Sea's breakers are rolling against my door.

Source: Wolfgang Schivelbusch, *The Railway Journey: The Industrialization of Space and Time in the 19th Century* (Berkeley: University of California Press, 1986), pp. 37, 118.

Document 3

Source: Edwin Chadwick, British Social Reformer, report on sanitary conditions, 1842

That the various forms of epidemic, endemic, and other disease caused, or aggravated, or propagated chiefly amongst the labouring classes by atmospheric impurities produced by decomposing animal and vegetable substances, by damp and filth, and close and overcrowded dwellings prevail amongst the population in every part of the kingdom, whether dwelling in separate houses, in rural villages, in small towns, in the larger towns--as they have been found to prevail in the lowest districts of the metropolis.

That such disease, wherever its attacks are frequent, is always found in connexion with the physical circumstances above specified, and that where those circumstances are removed by drainage, proper cleansing, better ventilation, and other means of diminishing atmospheric impurity, the frequency and intensity of such disease is abated; and where the removal of the noxious agencies appears to be complete, such disease almost entirely disappears. That high prosperity in respect to employment and wages, and various and abundant food, have afforded to the labouring classes no exemptions from attacks of epidemic disease, which have been as frequent and as fatal in periods of commercial and manufacturing prosperity as in any others.

That the formation of all habits of cleanliness is obstructed by defective supplies of water.

That the annual loss of life from filth and bad ventilation are greater than the loss from death or wounds in any wars in which the country has been engaged in modern times.

Source: Chadwick, Edwin. 1842. Report…from the Poor Law Commissioners on an Inquiry into the Sanitary Conditions of the Labouring Population of Great Britain, London

Document 4

Source: Henry Mayhew, British Journalist and Activist, *London Labour and the London Poor,* 1862

The narrative which follows – that of a prostitute, sleeping in the low-lodging houses, where boys and girls are huddled promiscuously together, discloses a system of depravity, atrocity, and enormity, which certainly cannot be paralleled in any nation, however, barbarous, nor in any age, however "dark"…

A good-looking girl of sixteen gave me the following awful statement: "I am an orphan. When I was ten I was sent to service as maid of all-work, in a small tradesman's family. It was a hard place, and my mistress used me very cruelly, beating me often. She beat me with sticks as well as her hands. I was black and blue, and at last I ran away. I got to Mrs. -----, a low lodging-house…"During this time I used to see boys and girls from ten and twelve years old sleeping together, but understood nothing wrong. "At the month's end, when I was beat out, I met with a young man of fifteen – I myself was going on twelve years old – and he persuaded me to take up with him. I stayed with him three months in the same lodging house, living with him as his wife, At the three months' end he was taken up for picking pockets, and got six months…[I] was forced to go into the streets for a living. I continued walking the streets for three years, sometimes making a good deal of money, sometimes none, feasting one day and starving the next…"

Source: Henry Mayhew, *London Labour and the London Poor: Cyclopedia of the Conditions and Earnings of Those that Will Work, Those that Cannot Work, and Those that Will Not Work* (London: Charles Griffin & Co., 1862) Vol. 1, pp. 458–460

Document 5

Source: Gustave Caillebotte, French artist, *Paris Street; Rainy Day,* 1877

Source: Archivart/Alamy Stock Photo

Document 6

Source: Fred Barnard, *The Ardor and the Joy of a Game at Foot-Ball"*, Harper's Weekly, 1888

Source: Courtesy of victorianweb.org

Document 7

Source: Émile Levasseur, French Economist, description of the growth of department stores in Paris, 1907

It was in the reign of Louis Philippe [1830–1848] that department stores for fashion goods and dresses… began to be distinguished. These stores have increased in number and several of them have become extremely large. Combining in their different departments all articles of clothing, toilet articles, furniture and many other ranges of goods, it is their special object so to combine all commodities as to attract and satisfy customers who will find conveniently together an assortment of a mass of articles corresponding to all their various needs. They attract customers by permanent display, by free entry into the shops, by periodic exhibitions, by special sales, by fixed prices, and by their ability to deliver the goods purchased to customers' homes, in Paris and to the provinces. Turning themselves into direct intermediaries between the producer and the consumer, even producing sometimes some of their articles in their own workshops, buying at lowest prices because of their large orders and because they are in a position to profit from bargains, working with large sums, and selling to most of their customers for cash only, they can transmit these benefits in lowered selling prices. They can even decide to sell at a loss, as an advertisement or to get rid of out-of-date fashions.

The success of these department stores is only possible thanks to the volume of their business, and this volume needs considerable capital and a very large turnover.

Source: From Sidney Pollard and Colin Holmes, *Documents of European Economic History*, Vol. 3. (London: Edward Arnold, 1972), pp. 95–96

DOCUMENT-BASED QUESTIONS SAMPLE RATIONALES

Document-Based Question 4

Evaluate the extent to which urbanization transformed the experiences of everyday life prior to the First World War.

(KC: 3.2.I, 3.2.II, 3.2.III; LO: Unit 6 A, E)

Part A Thesis (0–1 point): The thesis should take a position and explain the extent to which urbanization transformed everyday life experiences prior to the First World War.

Acceptable Thesis: Increased urbanization greatly changed the lives of the people who lived in cities prior to World War I. In many ways the changes were negative because of overcrowding and disease; however, by the beginning of World War I, city dwellers had increased leisure time that allowed them to travel more frequently, attend sporting events, and shop at large department stores.

Part B Contextualization (0–1 point): Students should give a broad overview of events prior to, during, and/or after the urbanization of much of Western Europe. Acceptable responses should explain (not just mention) developments such as:

- The Industrial Revolution
- The growth of the factory system
- Enclosure movements that forced people to move from rural areas
- The growth of industrial cities such as Manchester and Leeds in Britain
- Overcrowding and the growth of tenement houses
- Increased pollution
- The growth of reform movements
- Economic opportunities in cities
- Growth of nationalism
- Urban planning
- Increased standard of living
- The growth of unions
- Increased leisure time

The above list is not exhaustive.

Part C Evidence (0–3 points): Evidence from the documents (up to 2 points) and Evidence beyond the documents (1 point):

Evidence from the documents
1 point—Student correctly uses the content of at least THREE documents
Acceptable:

- Elizabeth Poole Sandford explains the role of women in relation to the "cult of domesticity." (Doc. 1)
- Heinrich Heine's reflection in reference to the opening of the railway lines connecting major cities in France discusses how technology is making the world a smaller place. (Doc. 2)
- Edwin Chadwick highlights the increase of epidemics and disease in urban areas during the early 19th century. (Doc. 3)
- An article by Henry Mayhew in *London Labour and the London Poor in 1862* gives a first-hand account of the horrid conditions of the poor. (Doc. 4)
- The painting *Paris Street; Rainy Day* highlights urban life in Paris during the second half of the 19th century. (Doc. 5)
- The 1888 image from *Harper's Weekly* shows spectators rooting for their football team. (Doc. 6)
- Levasseur discusses the growth and impact of department stores in France during the 19th century. (Doc. 7)

OR

2 points—Student correctly uses the content of at least SIX documents to support an argument/thesis

Acceptable:

- Poole's characterization of women's role is reflective of the 19th century notion of the "cult of domesticity." which became the standard for middle class urban women during the period prior to World War I. (Doc.1)
- Heinrich Heine, in his reflection of the opening of the railway lines, implies that decreased travel time because of the growth of railroads will make it easier for urban residents to travel to other places. (Doc. 2)
- Edwin Chadwick, a social reformer, explains how the rapid growth of cities did not take into account sanitation, resulting in the spread of disease and death as a result of urbanization. (Doc. 3)
- Henry Mayhew, a British journalist and activist, gives an example of how urban life affected the poor and destitute in London. (Doc. 4)
- The painting, *Paris Street: Rainy Day*, by Gustave Caillebotte, displays the positive effects of urbanization on the middle classes. (Doc. 5)
- The image from the 1888 *Harper's Weekly* shows spectators watching a football game. Sports entertainment was affordable and something urbanites of all classes were able to participate in. (Doc. 6)
- Levasseur suggests that the success of department stores was due to the volume of business that they were able to generate. Although department stores could deliver goods to those in the countryside, they appealed to a large urban population that had more money to spend by the end of the century. (Doc. 7)

Evidence beyond the documents

1 point—Student uses evidence not included in the document. Common examples could include the following if explained:

- Tenement houses
- Cholera outbreak in London during the 1850s
- Robert Owen and other reformers
- Model industrial cities such as New Lanark
- The rebuilding of Paris and Vienna
- The development of better transportation within cities such as subways and trolley cars
- Electrical lighting
- The development of the film industry
- Compulsory elementary education
- Universal male suffrage

The above list is not exhaustive

Part D Analysis and Reasoning (0–2 points):

1 point—Sourcing: Student explains the relevance of the document's audience, purpose, point of view, or historical situation in relation to the argument.

Acceptable example of audience:
Mayhew, a journalist and activist, is writing this to make the public aware of the horrid conditions of the poor in urban areas with the hope that public demand would lead to improved conditions. (Doc. 4)

Acceptable example of purpose:
The purpose of Chadwick's report is to bring attention to the filthy conditions in the industrial cities that have led to epidemics. Most likely, he hopes that the British government would begin legislation to improve urban sanitation. (Doc. 3)

Acceptable example of point of view:
An economist, Levasseur is obviously impressed with the growth of department stores. Naturally, he would be looking at this growth as an indicator of French economic success during the period prior to World War I. (Doc. 7)

Acceptable example of historical situation:
Caillebotte's painting shows a beautiful Paris, even if it is raining, with wide boulevards and middle-class people strolling through the city. Napoleon III had Paris rebuilt a decade before and dislocated much of the working-class housing from the city center. (Doc. 5)

1 point—Complexity: Student demonstrates a complex understanding of both the prompt and the documents. Examples demonstrating complexity might include:

- Explaining a nuance by exploring the many contradictions of urban life (e.g., Sandford advocates the idea of the cult of domesticity, while many middle-class women joined suffrage movements at the same time).
- Explaining connections to other time periods such as the Industrial Revolution or the growth of suburbia after World War II.
- Comparing and contrasting documents as evidence to support a main point.
  (e.g., middle-class experiences in cities such as in Document 3 versus the experiences of the poor such as in Document 4).
- Analyzing how urban experiences changed over time using detailed evidence and excellent explanations.
- qualifying or modifying an argument by considering diverse or alternative views or evidence, such as the idea that those in Eastern Europe did not have the same experiences as those in Western Europe.

DOCUMENT-BASED QUESTION 5

Evaluate the relative importance of the different factors that led to European Imperialism during the period 1850–1914.

Document 1

Source: John Ruskin, British lecturer, *Imperial* Duty, inaugural lecture, Oxford University, 1870.

There is a destiny now possible to us—the highest ever set before a nation to be accepted or refused. We are still undegenerate in race; a race mingled of the best northern blood. We are not yet dissolute in temper, but still have the firmness to govern, and the grace to obey. We have been taught a religion of pure mercy, which we must either now betray, or learn to defend by fulfilling. And we are rich in an inheritance of honour, bequeathed to us through a thousand years of noble history, which it should be our daily thirst to increase with splendid avarice, so that Englishmen, if it be a sin to covet honour, should be the most offending souls alive. Within the last few years we have had the laws of natural science opened to us with a rapidity which has been blinding by its brightness; and means of transit and communication given to us, which have made but one kingdom of the habitable globe…youths of England, make your country again a royal throne of kings; a sceptred isle, for all the world a source of light, a centre for peace; mistress of Learning and of the Arts; faithful guardian of great memories in the midst of irreverent and ephemeral visions; faithful servant of time-tried principles, under temptation from fond experiments and licentious desires; and amidst the cruel and clamorous jealousies of the nations, worshipped in her strange valour of goodwill towards men?

Source: *The Complete Works of John Ruskin*, (London: George Allen, 156 Charing Cross Road, New York: Longmans, Green, and Co. 1908) ALSO:
https://www.wwnorton.com/college/english/nael/20century/topic_1/jnruskin.htm

Document 2

Source: Letter Published by John G. Paton, New Hebrides, Mission, 1883

For the following reasons we think the British government ought now to take possession of the New Hebrides group of the South Sea islands, of the Solomon group, and of all the intervening chain of islands from Fiji to New Guinea:

2. The sympathy of the New Hebrides natives are all with Great Britain, hence they long for British protection, while they fear and hate the French, who appear eager to annex the group...

4. All the men and all the money used in civilizing and Christianizing the New Hebrides have been British. Now fourteen missionaries and the Dayspring mission ship, and about 150 native evangelists and teachers are employed in the above work on this group...

6. The islands on this group are generally very rich in soil and in tropical...they would soon, and for ages to come, become rich sources of tropical wealth to these colonies, as sugar cane is extensively cultivated on them by every native of the group, even in his heathen state. . .The islands also grow corn, cotton, coffee, arrowroot, and spices, etc., and all tropical products could be largely produced on them.

7. Because if any other nation takes possession of them, their excellent and spacious harbors...would in time of war make them dangerous to British interests and commerce in the South Seas and her colonies.

Source: Accounts and Papers 1883, (London: HMSO, 1883), Vol. XLVII, pp. 29–30

Document 3

Source: Carl Peters, *Manifesto of the Society for German Colonization*, April 1884

In the partition of the earth, as it has proceeded from the beginning of the fifteenth century up to our times, the German nation received nothing. All the remaining European culture-bearing peoples possess areas outside our continent where their languages and customs can take firm root and flourish. The moment that the German emigrant leaves the borders of the Reich behind him, he is a stranger sojourning on foreign soil. The German Reich, great in size and strength through its bloodily achieved unity, stands in the leading position among the continental European powers: her sons abroad must adapt themselves to nations which look upon us with either indifference or even hostility. For centuries the great stream of German emigration has been plunging down into foreign races where it is lost sight of. Germandom outside Europe has been undergoing a perpetual national decline.…

The Society for German Colonization aims to undertake on its own, in a resolute and sweeping manner, carefully chosen colonization projects and thereby supplement the ranks of organizations with similar tendencies.

Its particular tasks will be:

     1. to provide necessary sums of capital for colonization;

     2. to seek out and lay claim to suitable districts for colonization;

     3. to direct German emigrants to these regions

Source: Society for German Colonization, founding manifesto by Carl Peters (March 28, 1885), in E.A. Jacob, Deutsche Kolonialpolitik in Dokumenten, Gedanken, und Gestalten der letzten fünfzig Jahre [German Colonial Politics in Documents, Reflections, and Figures From the Last Fifty Years]. Leipzig, 1938, pp. 85–87.

Document 4

Source: Rudyard Kipling, English writer, *The White Man's Burden,* poem, 1899.

Take up the White Man's Burden—
Send forth the best ye breed—
Go bind your sons to exile
To serve your captives' need;
To wait in heavy harness
On fluttered folk and wild—
Your new-caught, sullen peoples,
Half devil and half child.

Take up the White Man's burden
In patience to abide
To veil the threat of terror
And check the show of pride;
By open speech and simple
An hundred times made plain
To seek another's profit
And work another's gain…

Source: Kipling, Rudyard, *The White Man's Burden*, McClure's Magazine, 1899

Document 5

Source: Photo of Diamond Mines in South Africa, c. 1900.

Source: Howes/Chris Wild Places Photography/Alamy Stock Photo

Document 6

Source: Winston Churchill, British journalist and politician, *The River War: An Historical Account of the Reconquest of the Soudan [Sudan],* 1902

Great clouds of smoke appeared all along the front of the British and Soudanese brigades. One after another four batteries opened on the enemy at a range of about 3,000 yards. The sound of the cannonade rolled up to us on the ridge, and was re-echoed by the hills. Above the heads of the moving masses shells began to burst, dotting the air with smoke-balls and the ground with bodies. But a nearer tragedy impended. The 'White Flags' were nearly over the crest. In another minute they would become visible to the batteries. Did they realise what would come to meet them?…It was a matter of machinery…. In a few seconds swift destruction would rush on these brave men…. Forthwith the gunboats… and other guns… opened on them…

… at the critical moment the gunboat arrived on the scene and began suddenly to blaze and flame from Maxim guns, quick-firing guns, and rifles. The range was short; the effect tremendous. The terrible machine, floating gracefully on the waters—a beautiful white devil— wreathed itself in smoke….

… the great Dervish army, who had advanced at sunrise in hope and courage, fled in utter rout, pursued by the Egyptian cavalry, harried by the 21st Lancers, and leaving more than 9,000 warriors dead and even greater numbers wounded behind them.

Thus ended the battle of Omdurman—the most signal triumph ever gained by the arms of science over barbarians.

Source: Winston Spencer Churchill, *The River War: An Historical Account of the Reconquest of the Soudan,* ed. F. Rhodes, new rev. ed. (London: Longmans, Green, and Co., 1902), pp. 272–273, 274, 279, 300.

Document 7

Source: Karl Pearson, English author, *National Life from the Standpoint of Science,* 1907.

History shows me one way, and one way only, in which a state of civilization has been produced, namely, the struggle of race with race, and the survival of the physically and mentally fitter race.

This dependence of progress on the survival of the fitter race, terribly black as it may seem to some of you, gives the struggle for existence its redeeming features; it is the fiery crucible out of which comes the finer metal. You may hope for a time when the sword shall be turned into the ploughshare, when American and German and English traders shall no longer compete in the markets of the world for raw materials, for their food supply, when the white man and the dark shall share the soil between them, and each till it as he lists .... The path of progress is strewn with the wreck of nations; traces are everywhere to be seen of the hecatombs of inferior races, and of victims who found not the narrow way to the greater perfection. Yet these dead peoples are, in very truth, the stepping stones on which mankind has arisen to the higher intellectual and deeper emotional life of today.

Source: Pearson, Karl, *National Life from the Standpoint of Science,* 2nd ed. (Cambridge, UK: Cambridge University Press, 1907)

Document-Based Question 5

> *Evaluate the relative importance of the different factors that led to European Imperialism during the period 1850–1914.*

KC 3.5.I, 3.5.II; LO: Unit 7 G, H

Part A Thesis (0–1 point): The thesis should briefly explain at least two factors that led to European Imperialism and evaluate the relative significance of these factors.

Acceptable Thesis: While Social Darwinism and the desire for enhanced international prestige were factors for European imperialism, the most important factor was the desire to tap natural resources in Africa and Asia for the benefit of European businesses and consumers.

Part B Contextualization (0–1 point): Students should give a broad overview of events prior to, during, and/or after the time of European imperialism between 1850 and 1914. Acceptable responses should explain (not just mention) developments such as:

- Europeans had earlier been unable to penetrate the interior of Africa due to tropical diseases and lack of viable transportation.
- Prior to the New Imperialism, Europeans had been interested in trade with indigenous peoples rather than outright conquest of territory. This pattern is similar to the "Old Imperialism" of the sixteenth and seventeenth centuries.
- Conflicts among European nations regarding imperialistic activities was a factor leading to the First World War.
- Rising consumerism in Europe (and America) stimulated the desire of businesses to profit from the sale of goods acquired from colonial regions.
- After the Second World War, virtually all European colonies in Africa and Asia had become independent by 1970.

The above list is not exhaustive.

Part C Evidence (0–3 points): Evidence from the documents (up to 2 points) and Evidence beyond the documents (1 point):

Evidence from the documents
1 point--Student correctly uses the content of at least THREE documents
Acceptable:

- John Ruskin believes that the British people and British civilization is superior. (Doc. 1)
- Document 2 highlights several factors for British imperialism including civilizing and Christianizing indigenous peoples, the economic benefit of natural resources, and protecting British interests from other European competitors. (Doc. 2)

- Carl Peters claims that Germany should acquire colonies and increase its influence outside of Germany. (Doc. 3)
- Rudyard Kipling's poem shows how he believes British civilization is superior to those of Africa. (Doc. 4)
- The photo in Document 5 shows how Europeans were interested in extracting valuable raw materials in South Africa.
- Winston Churchill illustrates the military superiority British forces had against the Sudanese warriors. (Doc. 6)
- Karl Pearson claims that white civilization is superior to non-white civilization. (Doc. 7)

OR

2 points--Student correctly uses the content of at least SIX documents to support an argument/thesis

Acceptable:
- John Ruskin believes that the British people and British civilization are superior, illustrating how racism and nationalism were important factors in justifying the conquest of "inferior" peoples in Africa and Asia. (Doc. 1)
- Document 2 highlights several factors for British imperialism including civilizing and Christianizing indigenous peoples, the economic benefit of natural resources, and protecting British interests from other European competitors. Of these factors, the protection of the British Empire is the most important as the French and rising German empires were seen as major threats to British security around the world. (Doc. 2)
- Carl Peters claims that Germany should acquire colonies and increase its influence outside of Germany thus illustrating how nationalism was a primary driving force behind Germany's imperialistic activities as well as the imperialistic activities of the other European nations. (Doc. 3)
- Rudyard Kipling's poem shows how bringing Britain's "superior" civilization to indigenous people became a major justification for Britain's conquest of African and Asian peoples. (Doc. 4)
- The photo in Document 5 shows how Europeans were interested in extracting valuable raw materials in South Africa. Raw materials enriched wealthy industrialists and provided coveted goods that Europeans wished to purchase.
- Winston Churchill's account of Britain's victory over Sudanese warriors illustrates the significance of military technology and industrialism in giving Europeans a decided advantage over African and Asian forces. Military and technological superiority was the most important factor in the development of the New Imperialism after 1880. (Doc. 6)
- The views of Karl Pearson illustrate Social Darwinism—the belief that white civilization is superior to non-white civilization. This "superiority" justifies the conquest of African and Asian peoples in the eyes of people like Pearson. (Doc. 7)

Evidence beyond the documents

1 point--Student uses evidence not included in the document. Common examples could include the following if explained:

- The Opium Wars between Britain and China
- Belgium's conquest of the Congo
- The "scramble for Africa" after the Berlin Conference in 1886
- The role of quinine, machine guns, and iron steamboats that enabled Europeans to penetrate the interior of Africa
- The Fashoda Crisis, Kruger Telegram, and Moroccan Crises as examples of how imperialistic competition heightened tensions among the Great Powers.
- Missionary activities such as those of Dr. David Livingstone
- The "empire upon which the sun never sets" (British Empire)
- English conquest of India
- Spheres of influence in China
- Social Darwinism

The above list is not exhaustive.

Part D Analysis and Reasoning (0–2 points):

1 point—Sourcing: Student explains the relevance of the document's audience, purpose, point of view, or historical situation in relation to the argument.

Acceptable example of audience:
Carl Peters's intended audience is most likely German policy makers and supporters of imperialism who he wishes to support in expanding German influence overseas. (Doc. 3)

Acceptable example of purpose:
Karl Pearson seeks to justify the unbridled conquest of "lesser peoples" in Africa and Asia by promoting the racial superiority of white (especially European) civilization. (Doc. 7)

Acceptable example of point of view:
It is not surprising that Winston Churchill, as an Englishman, would see the British victory as triumphant as he views his people as superior while the Sudanese are characterized as "barbarians." (Doc. 6)

Acceptable example of historical situation:
Kipling's poem was actually intended for the United States as Kipling encourages Americans to embrace the civilizing mission of the white race even though indigenous peoples will likely resist. (Doc. 4)

1 point—Complexity: Student demonstrates a complex understanding of both the prompt and the documents. Examples demonstrating complexity might include:

- Explaining a nuance by exploring the many different factors that contributed to the European imperialism (e.g., nationalism, racism, economic motives, missionary activity, and military protection from competitors).
- Explaining connections to other time periods such as the "Old Imperialism" in the sixteenth and seventeenth centuries or decolonization after World War II.
- comparing and contrasting documents as evidence to support a main point. (e.g., explaining the contrast of the emphasis on civilization in Document 4 with the horrific violence in Document 6)
- Proving the relative importance of the different factors throughout the entire paper with detailed evidence and developed explanations.
- Qualifying or modifying an argument by considering diverse or alternative views or evidence, such as anti-imperialistic views by Hobson or Lenin.

Evaluate the extent to which the failure of the Treaty of Versailles contributed to the outbreak of World War II.

Document 1

Source: Count von Brockdorff-Rantzau (leader of the German peace delegation at Versailles), letter to Paris Peace Conference President Georges Clemenceau on the Subject of Peace Terms, May 1919

Mr. President:

…We came to Versailles in the expectation of receiving a peace proposal based on the agreed principles. We were firmly resolved to do everything in our power with a view of fulfilling the grave obligations which we had undertaken. We hoped for the peace of justice which had been promised to us.

We were aghast when we read in documents the demands made upon us, the victorious violence of our enemies… The exactions of this treaty are more than the German people can bear.

With a view to the re-establishment of the Polish State we must renounce indisputably German territory - nearly the whole of the Province of West Prussia, which is preponderantly German; of Pomerania; Danzig, which is German to the core…
We must agree that East Prussia shall be amputated from the body of the State, condemned to a lingering death, and robbed of its northern portion…which is purely German.

We must renounce Upper Silesia for the benefit of Poland and Czecho-Slovakia, although it has been in close political connection with Germany for more than 750 years, is instinct with German life, and forms the very foundation of industrial life throughout East Germany…

Thus must a whole people sign the decree for its proscription, nay, its own death sentence.

Source: *Source Records of the Great War, Vol. VII,* ed. Charles F. Horne, *National Alumni 1923* ALSO
http://www.firstworldwar.com/source/parispeaceconf_dutcheditorial.htm

Document 2

Source: Algemeen Handelsblad, Dutch citizen, Editorial on the Treaty of Versailles, June 1919

The peace conditions imposed upon Germany are so hard, so humiliating, that even those who have the smallest expectation of a "peace of justice" are bound to be deeply disappointed...

Our opinion on the lust of power and conquest of Germany is well known. But a condemnation of wartime actions must not amount to a lasting condemnation of a people. In spite of all they have done, the German people is a great and noble nation…
The Entente evidently desires the complete annihilation of Germany. Not only will the whole commercial fleet be confiscated, but the shipbuilding yards will be obliged to work for the foreigner for some time to come.

…This peace is a mockery of President Wilson's principles. Trusting to these, Germany accepted peace. That confidence has been betrayed in such a manner that we regard the present happenings as a deep humiliation, not only to all governments and nations concerned in this peace offer, but to all humanity.

These conditions will never give peace. All Germans must feel that they wish to shake off the heavy yoke imposed by the cajoling Entente, and we fear very much that that opportunity will soon present itself. For has not the Entente recognized in the proposed so-called "League of Nations" the evident right to conquer and possess countries for economic and imperialistic purposes? Fettered and enslaved, Germany will always remain a menace to Europe…

Source: *Source Records of the Great War, Vol. VII,* ed. Charles F. Horne, *National Alumni 1923* ALSO: http://www.firstworldwar.com/source/parispeaceconf_dutcheditorial.htm

Document 3

Source: Adolf Hitler, speech delivered in Munich, April 1923

With the armistice begins the humiliation of Germany. If the Republic on the day of its foundation had appealed to the country: "Germans, stand together! Up and resist the foe! The Fatherland, the Republic expects of you that you fight to your last breath," then millions who are now the enemies of the Republic would be fanatical Republicans. Today they are the foes of the Republic not because it is a Republic but because this Republic was founded at the moment when Germany was humiliated, because it so discredited the new flag that men's eyes must turn regretfully towards the old flag…

So long as this Treaty stands there can be no resurrection of the German people: no social reform of any kind is possible! The Treaty was made in order to bring 20 million Germans to their deaths and to ruin the German nation. But those who made the Treaty cannot set it aside…

There is thus one thing which is the first task of this Movement: it desires to make the German once more National, that his Fatherland shall stand for him above everything else. It desires to teach our people to understand afresh the truth of the old saying: He who would not be a hammer must be an anvil. An anvil are we today, and that anvil will be beaten until out of the anvil we fashion once more a hammer, a German sword!

Source: From a speech delivered in Munich on April 17, 1923, by Adolf Hitler, from *The Speeches of Adolf Hitler, April 1922–August 1939*, trans. by Norman H. Baynes (London and New York: Oxford University Press, 1942), pp. 56–57

Document 4

Source: Horace Rumbold, Britain's Ambassador to Germany, dispatch to London, April 1933

The outlook for Europe is far from peaceful if the speeches of Nazi leaders, especially of the Chancellor [Adolph Hitler], are borne in mind. The Chancellor's account of his political career in *Mein Kampf* contains not only the principles which have guided him during the last fourteen years, but explains how he arrived at these fundamental principles. Stripped of the verbiage in which he has clothed it, Hitler's thesis is extremely simple. He starts with the assertions that man is a fighting animal; therefore the nation is, he concludes, a fighting unit, being a community of fighters. Any living organism which ceases to fight for its existence is, he asserts, doomed to extinction. A country or a race which ceases to fight is equally doomed. The fighting capacity of a race depends on its purity. Hence the necessity for ridding it of foreign impurities. The Jewish race, owing to its universality, is of necessity pacifist and internationalist. Pacifism is the deadliest sin, for pacifism means the surrender of the race in the fight for existence. The first duty of every country is, therefore, to nationalise the masses: intelligence is of secondary importance in the case of the individual; will and determination are of higher importance. The individual who is born to command is more valuable than countless thousands of subordinate natures. Only brute force can ensure the survival of the race.

Source: https://www.jewishvirtuallibrary.org/jsource/History/UK/cab24_259_13_Germandanger.pdf ALSO: The National Archives

Document 5

Source: Haile Selassie, emperor of Ethiopia, speech to League of Nations, June 30, 1936.

The Wal-Wal incident, in December, 1934, came as a thunderbolt to me. The Italian provocation was obvious and I did not hesitate to appeal to the League of Nations. I invoked the provisions of the treaty of 1928, the principles of the Covenant; I urged the procedure of conciliation and arbitration. Unhappily for Ethiopia this was the time when a certain Government considered that the European situation made it imperative at all costs to obtain the friendship of Italy. The price paid was the abandonment of Ethiopian independence to the greed of the Italian Government. This secret agreement, contrary to the obligations of the Covenant, has exerted a great influence over the course of events. Ethiopia and the whole world have suffered and are still suffering today its disastrous consequences. This first violation of the Covenant was followed by many others. Feeling itself encouraged in its policy against Ethiopia, the Rome Government feverishly made war preparations, thinking that the concerted pressure which was beginning to be exerted on the Ethiopian Government, might perhaps not overcome the resistance of my people to Italian domination …

Source: *Selected speeches of His Imperial Majesty Haile Selassie, 1918 to 1967* (Addis Ababa: The Imperial Ethiopian Ministry of Information, 1967).

Document 6

Source: David Low, British political cartoonist, *Europe Can Look Forward to a Christmas of Peace,* The Evening Standard, Oct. 1938

The label on the bag reads, "Germany over all others."

Source: David Low/Solo Syndication

Document 7

Source: Winston Churchill, Conservative member of the British House of Commons, speech to Parliament, Oct. 1938

I will begin by saying what everybody would like to ignore or forget but which must nevertheless be stated, namely, that we have sustained a total and unmitigated defeat [at the Munich Conference], and that France has suffered even more than we have....

All is over. Silent, mournful, abandoned, broken, Czechoslovakia recedes into the darkness. She has suffered in every respect by her association with the Western democracies and with the League of Nations, of which she has always been an obedient servant....

We have been reduced in these five years from a position of security so overwhelming and so unchallengeable that we never cared to think about it. We have been reduced from a position where the very word "war" was considered one which could be used only by persons qualifying for a lunatic asylum. We have been reduced from a position of safety and power—power to do good, power to be generous to a beaten foe, power to make terms with Germany, power to give her proper redress for her grievances, power to stop her arming if we chose, power to take any step in strength or mercy or justice which we thought right—reduced in five years from a position safe and unchallenged to where we stand now....

Source: *Parliamentary Debates*, 5th series, vol. 339 (1938).

DOCUMENT-BASED QUESTIONS SAMPLE RATIONALES

Document-Based Question 6

Evaluate the extent to which the failure of the Treaty of Versialles contributed to the outbreak of World War II.

KC: 4.1.II.C, 4.1.III; LO: Unit 8 F, J

Part A Thesis (0–1 point): The thesis should briefly explain whether the Treaty of Versailles contributed to World War II or if there were other factors that were also important.

Acceptable Thesis: To a great extent, the Treaty of Versailles led to World War II as its severe punishment of Germany led to the rise of Hitler and Nazism.

Part B Contextualization (0–1 point): Students should give a broad overview of events prior to, during, and/or after the interwar period. Acceptable responses should explain (not just mention) developments such as:

- The military outcome of World War I
- Hyperinflation in the early-mid 1920s
- German economic recovery after the Ruhr Crisis
- The Great Depression
- The rise of fascism in Italy and Germany
- Militarism in Japan
- The results of World War II

The above list is not exhaustive.

Part C Evidence (0–3 points): Evidence from the documents (up to 2 points) and Evidence beyond the documents (1 point):

<u>Evidence from the documents</u>
1 point--Student correctly uses the content of at least THREE documents
Acceptable:
- Count von Brockdorff-Rantzau claims that Germany is being destroyed unfairly by the Versailles Treaty. (Doc. 1)
- Algemeen Handelsblad, a Dutch editorialist, believes that Germany is being grossly mistreated by the Versailles Treaty and that Wilson's principles have largely been ignored. (Doc. 2)
- Hitler states that the Weimar Republic has no credibility among the German people because it sold out Germany when it signed the Versailles Treaty. (Doc. 3)
- Horace Rumbold, Britain's Ambassador to Germany, argues that Hitler is not interested in peace but rather the use of military force to achieve Germany's interests. (Doc. 4)

- In Document 5, the Ethiopian emperor complains that the League of Nations did nothing to support Ethiopia's independence from Italian aggression. (Doc. 5)
- David Low's political cartoon criticizes Hitler's aggression in taking control of Austria and Czechoslovakia and implies that Hitler is keen on taking over other European countries in the future. (Doc. 6)
- Winston Churchill laments that the loss of part of Czechoslovakia due to the Munich Conference is largely due to the ineffectiveness of the League of Nations. (Doc. 7)

OR

2 points--Student correctly uses the content of at least SIX documents to support an argument/thesis

Acceptable:
- Count von Brockdorff-Rantzau claims that Germany is being destroyed unfairly by the Versailles Treaty due to the loss of Germany territory. The loss of territory was a major cause of German resentment over the treaty that fed the rise of Hitler. (Doc. 1)
- Algemeen Handelsblad, a Dutch editorialist, believes that Germany is being grossly mistreated by the Versailles Treaty and that Wilson's principles have largely been ignored. This demonstrates that the Germans are not the only ones who believe they have been victimized by a treaty that was meant to punish and humiliate Germany. (Doc. 2)
- Hitler states that the Weimar Republic has no credibility among the German people because it sold out Germany when it signed the Versailles Treaty. The resentment of the German people over the treaty eventually gave rise to their support of Hitler's militarism that started World War II. (Doc. 3)
- Horace Rumbold, Britain's Ambassador to Germany, argues that Hitler is not interested in peace but rather the use of military force to achieve Germany's interests. Hitler's fascist, militaristic goals clearly became the foundation of Germany's aggressive actions leading to World War II. (Doc. 4)
- In Document 5, the Ethiopian emperor complains that the League of Nations did nothing to support Ethiopia's independence from Italian aggression. This illustrates that Germany was not the only country that turned to militarism in the 1930s. In fact, Italy's attack on Ethiopia predated any of Hitler's aggressive actions. Therefore, the Versailles Treaty was not responsible for Italy's militarism. (Doc. 5)
- David Low's political cartoon criticizes Hitler's aggression in taking control of Austria and Czechoslovakia and implies that Hitler is keen on taking over other European countries in the future. Considering that Hitler's rise to power in Germany was largely due to German resentment concerning the Versailles Treaty, the treaty can be seen as a cause of Germany's rising militarism and World War II. (Doc. 6)
- Winston Churchill laments that the loss of part of Czechoslovakia due to the Munich Conference is largely due to the ineffectiveness of the League of Nations. This demonstrates that the Versailles Treaty was not the only factor contributing to World War II. The democracies' inability through the League of Nations to check German expansion was a huge factor as well. (Doc. 7)

417

Evidence beyond the documents
1 point--Student uses evidence not included in the document. Common examples could include the following if explained:

- Article 231 and reparations
- Treaty provisions limiting the size of Germany's military
- Demilitarization of the Rhineland and French takeover of the Saar
- The Weimar Republic's acquiescence to the treaty's provisions
- The Ruhr crisis and hyperinflation
- Hitler's main ideas in *Mein Kampf*
- The Great Depression as a cause for the rise of Hitler
- The Spanish Civil War
- German remilitarization of the Rhineland
- Germany's takeover of Austria
- Sudetenland
- Appeasement and pacifism
- American isolationism
- Germany's invasion of Czechoslovakia
- Nazi-Soviet Non-aggression pact
- Germany's invasion of Poland

The above list is not exhaustive.

Part D Analysis and Reasoning (0–2 points):
1 point—Sourcing: Student explains the relevance of the document's audience, purpose, point of view, or historical situation in relation to the argument.

Acceptable example of audience:
Haile Selassie, the emperor of Ethiopia, appeals directly to the League of Nations concerning the plight of his people. He likely wants the European democratic nations who have representatives at the League to support his country against Italian aggression. (Doc. 5)

Acceptable example of purpose:
Hitler's speech is most likely intended to rally his Nazi followers in working toward undermining the Weimar Republic since Hitler sees the Republic as having stabbed Germany in the back by signing the Versailles Treaty. (Doc. 3)

Acceptable example of point of view:
David Low was a British cartoonist, so it is not surprising that a negative view of Germany's expansion in Europe would be published by a British source. The British felt threatened by Germany's aggression. (Doc. 6)

Acceptable example of historical situation:
Churchill's speech is a reaction to the outcome of the Munich Conference where British Prime Minister Neville Chamberlain, along with his French allies, agreed to allow Germany to take the Sudetenland region of Czechoslovakia in return for Hitler's guarantee of no further territorial demands. This became the most notorious example of appeasement prior to World War II. (Doc. 7)

1 point—Complexity: Student demonstrates a complex understanding of both the prompt and the documents. Examples demonstrating complexity might include:
- Explaining a nuance by exploring various factors that contributed to the Second World War (e.g., the Great Depression, appeasement and pacifism, Italian aggression, American isolationism).
- Explaining connections to other time periods such as the causes of World War I, the results of World War II and the Cold War.
- Comparing and contrasting documents as evidence to support a main point. (e.g., although both Documents 1 and 2 condemn the Versailles Treaty, Document 2 is a Dutch document that is arguably more objective than Document 1 which is a German document that blasts the treaty).
- Proving the relative importance of the different causes throughout the entire paper with detailed evidence and excellent explanations.
- Qualifying or modifying an argument by considering diverse or alternative views or evidence, such as the idea that American isolationism along with British and French appeasement and pacifism were bigger factors contributing to the onset of World War II than resentment over the Versailles Treaty.

PART IV

SAMPLE PRACTICE TESTS

On the following pages are two sample exams. They mirror the
AP exam in format and question types. Set aside a time to take these
exams, timing yourself as you will be timed when you take the real test,
to prepare you for the actual test-taking experience.

SAMPLE PRACTICE TEST 1

SECTION I

PART A: MULTIPLE-CHOICE QUESTIONS

Questions 1–3 refer to the image below.

Sandro Botticelli, La Primavera *(The Allegory of Spring), 1482*

Source: Scala/Art Resource, NY

1. The image is most representative of which of the following eras?
   (A) The Lutheran Reformation
   (B) The Middle Ages
   (C) The Catholic Reformation
   (D) The Italian Renaissance

2. The artist was most likely influenced by
    (A) secularism and individualism advanced by humanists
    (B) the preoccupation with death shared by many artists of the Northern Renaissance
    (C) Christian imagery advanced by members of the Jesuit order
    (D) aesthetic ideals promoted by the French salon

3. The artistic style of the image is most similar to which of the following?
    (A) Rococo
    (B) Baroque
    (C) Neoclassical
    (D) Realism

Questions 4–7 refer to the passage below.

"All who consider other teachings equal to or higher than the Gospel err, and they do not know what the Gospel is.

In the faith rests our salvation, and in unbelief our damnation; for all truth is clear in Christ.

In the Gospel one learns that human doctrines and decrees do not aid in salvation."

Ulrich Zwingli, Sixty-Seven Articles, 1523

Source: Ulrich Zwingli, *Selected Works,* ed. by Samuel M. Jackson (Philadelphia University of Pennsylvania Press, 1972), pp. 111–117.

4. Which of the following was a major influence on the ideas contained in the passage?
   (A) Italian Renaissance
   (B) Christian humanism
   (C) Council of Trent
   (D) Scholasticism

5. The ideas expressed in the passage are most similar to those of
   (A) Charles V
   (B) Martin Luther
   (C) Pope Paul III
   (D) Ignatius Loyola

6. The views expressed in the passage eventually led to
   (A) the rise of the Holy Roman Empire in western Europe
   (B) French support for the Habsburg Empire
   (C) the development of the heliocentric theory
   (D) decline of Catholic unity across Europe

7. Which of the following groups was inspired to action by ideas similar to the ones expressed in the passage?
   (A) Anabaptists
   (B) Jesuits
   (C) Ursuline Order
   (D) Hanseatic League

Questions 8–10 refer to the image below.

Martin Behaim, spherical globe of the world, 1492

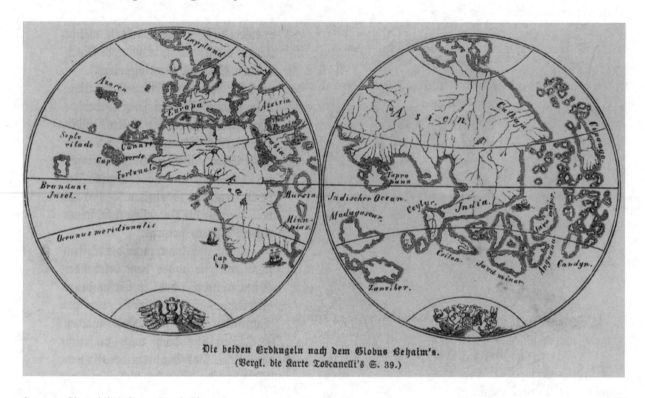

Die beiden Erdkugeln nach dem Globus Behaim's.
(Vergl. die Karte Toscanelli's S. 39.)

Source: Chronicle/Alamy Stock Photo

8. Which of the following conclusions can be drawn from the map?
    (A) Cartographers had developed techniques to measure longitude accurately.
    (B) Cartographers had successfully charted the African continent.
    (C) Cartographers had not yet charted all the world's major continents.
    (D) Cartographers had little knowledge of measuring latitude.

9. The map most likely encouraged which of the following actions in the fifteenth century?
    (A) Explorers on behalf of Spain sailed westward hoping to reach India.
    (B) Explorers on behalf of Portugal sailed westward to reach China.
    (C) Explorers on behalf of England sailed eastward to reach Indonesia.
    (D) Explorers on behalf of France sailed southward to round the southern tip of Africa.

10. The use of images such as the one shown above by European explorers led to all of the following developments in the sixteenth and seventeenth centuries EXCEPT
    (A) the emergence of the Columbian Exchange
    (B) the rise of the New Imperialism in Africa
    (C) conflicts and rivalries among European powers
    (D) the shift in economic power from the Mediterranean to the Atlantic

Questions 11–14 refer to the passage below.

"I can readily imagine, Holy Father, that as soon as some people hear that in this volume, which I have written about the revolutions of the spheres of the universe, I ascribe certain motions to the terrestrial globe, they will shout that I must be immediately repudiated together with this belief. For I am not so enamored of my own opinions that I disregard what others may think of them. I am aware that a philosopher's ideas are not subjected to the judgement of ordinary persons, because it is his endeavor to seek the truth in all things, to the extent permitted to human reason by God. Yet I hold that completely erroneous views should be shunned. Those who know that the consensus of many centuries has sanctioned the conception that the earth remains at rest in the middle of the heaven as its center would, I reflected, regard it as an insane pronouncement if I made the opposite assertion that the earth moves. Therefore I debated with myself for a long time whether to publish the volume which I wrote to prove the earth's motion…"

Nicolas Copernicus, *On the Revolutions of Heavenly Spheres*, 1543

Source: Copernicus, Nicholas. *On the Revolutions*: *Nicholas Copernicus Complete Works*. Edited by Jerzy Dobrzycky and translated by Edward Rosen (Baltimore: The Johns Hopkins University Press, 1978).

11. Which of the following conclusions best reflects the ideas in the passage?
    (A) Copernicus supported creationism in the Bible.
    (B) The pope supported new scientific ideas.
    (C) Medieval notions of the heavens were no longer accepted by European elites.
    (D) New ideas in science challenged classical views of the cosmos.

12. The views expressed in the passage BEST reflect which of the following views?
    (A) Geocentric view of the universe
    (B) Heliocentric view of the universe
    (C) Laws of universal gravitation
    (D) Deism and its rejection of orthodox Christianity

13. Which of the following would most likely have been supportive of the views expressed in the passage?
    (A) Cardinal Bellarmine
    (B) Pythagoras
    (C) William Harvey
    (D) Tomás de Torquemada

14. New ideas in science, such as those in the passage, eventually led to the
    (A) Enlightenment
    (B) Catholic Reformation
    (C) Baroque era
    (D) Commercial Revolution

425

Questions 15–18 refer to the passage below.

"We ordain that the Catholic, Apostolic and Roman religion shall be restored and re-established in all places and districts of this our kingdom and the countries under our rule, where its practice has been interrupted, so that it can be peacefully and freely practiced there, without any disturbance or hindrance…We also forbid very expressly those of the so-called Reformed religion to hold prayer meetings or any devotions of the aforesaid religion in churches, houses and dwellings of the above-said clerics....

And in order not to leave any cause for discords and disputes between our subjects, we have permitted and we permit those of the so-called Reformed religion to live and dwell in all the towns and districts of this our kingdom and the countries under one rule, without being annoyed, disturbed, molested or constrained to do anything against their conscience, or for this cause to be sought out in their houses and districts where they wish to live, provided that they conduct themselves in other respects according to the provisions of our present Edict...

Henry IV, "The Edict of Nantes," 1598

Source: Sidney Z. Ehler and John B. Morrall, eds. and trans., *Church and State Through the Centuries: A Collection of Historic Documents* (London: Burns and Gates, 1954), pp. 185–188.

15. The "Reformed religion" to which the passage refers includes
    (A) Anglicans
    (B) Calvinists
    (C) Methodists
    (D) Lutherans

16. As a result of the provisions in the passage
    (A) France supported the Holy Roman Empire in the Thirty Years' War
    (B) England ended its association with the Catholic Church
    (C) England reinstituted Catholicism
    (D) France saw an end to civil war

17. Based on the ideas expressed in the passage, Henry IV is most similar to which of the following reformers?
    (A) Elizabeth I of England
    (B) Catherine the Great of Russia
    (C) Catherine de Médicis of France
    (D) Isabella of Spain

18. Which of the following rulers would have most disagreed with the purpose of the passage?
    (A) Peter the Great of Russia
    (B) Charles II of England
    (C) Louis XIV of France
    (D) Frederick the Great of Prussia

Questions 19–21 refer to the passage below.

"From this equality of ability, ariseth equality of hope in the attaining of our Ends. And therefore if any two men desire the same thing, which neverthelesse they cannot both enjoy, they become enemies; and in the way to their End, (which is principally their owne conservation, and sometimes their delectation only,) endeavour to destroy, or subdue one an other. And from hence it comes to passe, that where an Invader hath no more to feare, than an other mans single power; if one plant, sow, build, or possesse a convenient Seat, others may probably be expected to come prepared with forces united, to dispossesse, and deprive him, not only of the fruit of his labour, but also of his life, or liberty. And the Invader again is in the like danger of another…

Hereby it is manifest, that during the time men live without a common Power to keep them all in awe, they are in that condition which is called Warre; and such a warre, as is of every man, against every man."

Thomas Hobbes, English philosopher, *Leviathan*, 1651

Source: Thomas Hobbes, *The Leviathan*, in *Cambridge Texts in the History of Political Thought*, ed. by Richard Tuck (New York: Cambridge University Press, 1996), pp. 86–90.

19. The passage could best be used to illustrate which of the following conclusions?
    (A) Men are unable to secure their safety without the protection of a powerful ruler.
    (B) Men should be free from any excessive interference by a powerful government.
    (C) Men are essentially good in nature and are capable of governing themselves.
    (D) Men are inherently evil, and the creation of an orderly society is impossible.

20. Which form of government in the eighteenth century was most likely developed based on the ideas expressed in the passage?
    (A) Democracy
    (B) Enlightened despotism
    (C) Representative government
    (D) Theocracy

21. The ideas in the passage would likely have been least attractive to which of the following?
    (A) Jean Bodin
    (B) Bishop Bossuet
    (C) John Locke
    (D) Otto von Bismarck

427

Questions 22–23 refer to the map below.

Rise of Prussia 1440–1795

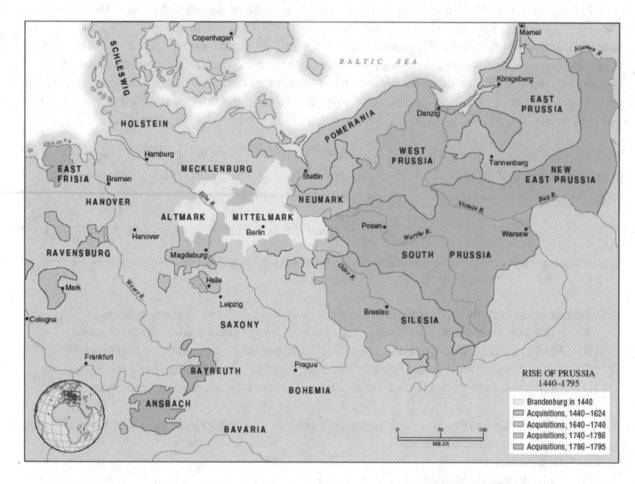

22. Based on the map, it can be inferred that Prussia gained territory at the expense of
    (A) France
    (B) Russia
    (C) Saxony
    (D) Holy Roman Empire

23. Prussia's territorial expansion between 1740 and 1795 was largely due to which of the following?
    (A) Russia declined in military power after the death of Peter the Great and the Pugachev Rebellion.
    (B) Prussia dominated the Atlantic trade and gained valuable resources for waging war in eastern Europe.
    (C) Poland was partitioned as its monarchy was unable to consolidate its authority over the nobility.
    (D) The continued growth of Catholicism in northern Germany provided an impulse for religious unity.

Questions 24–26 refer to the images below.

Source 1

Gian Bernini, Baldacchino, 1623–1634

Source: Scala/Art Resource, NY

Source 2

Versailles Palace, c. 1668

Source: Pierre Patel, Perspective View of Versailles. Musée du Chateau de Versailles/ DEA/G. DAGLI ORTI/Getty Images

24. Based on the image in Source 1, the purpose of the work is most likely to
   (A) promote religious feeling in the Catholic Church
   (B) further the influence of the Calvinist faith
   (C) promote the economic interest of Dutch burghers
   (D) convey the power of the Spanish empire in the New World

25. Based on the image in Source 2, the purpose of the palace is to
   (A) promote republican principles
   (B) promote Enlightened despotism
   (C) promote absolutism
   (D) promote the power of New Monarchies

26. Both Source 1 and Source 2 are representative of which of the following styles?
   (A) Neoclassicism
   (B) Rococo
   (C) Romanticism
   (D) Baroque

Questions 27–28 refer to the passage below.

"The plan of this book is fairly simple. We must ask ourselves three questions.

What is the Third Estate? Everything.

What has it been until now in the political order? Nothing.

What does it want to be? Something…

Public services can also, at present, be divided into four known categories, the army, the law, the Church, and the bureaucracy. It needs no detailed analysis to show that the Third Estate everywhere constitutes nineteen-twentieths of them, except that it is loaded with all the really arduous work, all the tasks which the privileged order refuses to perform. Only the well-paid and honorific posts are filled by members of the privileged order. Are we to give them credit for this? We could do so only if the Third Estate was unable or unwilling to fill these posts. We know the answer. Nevertheless, the privileged have dared to preclude the Third Estate. "No matter how useful you are," they said, "no matter how able you are, you can go so far and no further. Honours are not for the like of you." The rare exceptions, noticeable as they are bound to be, are mere mockery, and the sort of language allowed on such occasions is an additional insult."

Emmanuel Joseph Sieyès, clergy member, *What is the Third Estate?*, 1789

Source: Translations and Reprints from the Original Sources of European History. Published by The Department of History of the University of Pennsylvania, 1900.

27. Views such as the ones in the passage contributed most directly to which of the following?
   (A) The *Fronde*, consisting of French nobles, attempted to overthrow the child-king Louis XIV.
   (B) Cardinal Richelieu, the chief counselor to Louis XV, suppressed the rebellious Huguenot nobility.
   (C) The French Revolution overturned the existing political and social order.
   (D) Napoleon Bonaparte instituted a dictatorship based on Enlightened despotism.

28. Which of the following most likely would have supported the views in the passage?
   (A) Jean-Jacques Rousseau
   (B) Edmund Burke
   (C) Empress Maria Theresa
   (D) Joseph de Maistre

Questions 29–30 refer to the map below.

The Austrian Empire, c. 1866

29. Which of the following conclusions best reflects the map?
    (A) The Austrian Empire was the largest political entity in eastern Europe.
    (B) The multiethnic composition of the Austrian Empire posed challenges related to nationalism.
    (C) The Austrian Empire was the most powerful political entity in eastern Europe.
    (D) Russia posed the biggest threat to the security of the Habsburg Empire.

30. The relationships among various political entities in the map led to which of the following?
    (A) Austria formed the Triple Entente prior to the onset of the First World War.
    (B) Germany absorbed the Austrian Empire after the Austro-Prussian War.
    (C) Russia reinforced its borders fearing its culture would be affected by immigration.
    (D) The dual monarchy recognized the power of the largest ethnic minority within the empire.

Questions 31–33 refer to the passage below.

English Parliamentary investigation into child labor, 1831

"Mr. Abraham Whitehead…

436. Are the children and young persons of both sexes employed in these mills?—Yes.

437. At how early an age are children employed?—The youngest age at which children are employed is never under five, but some are employed between five and six in woollen mills at piecing.

438. How early have you observed these young children going to their work, speaking for the present in the summer time?—In the summer time I have frequently seen them going to work between five and six in the morning, and I know the general practice is for them to go as early to all the mills…

439. How late in the evening have you seen them at work, or remarked them returning to their homes?—I have seen them at work in the summer season between nine and ten in the evening; they continue to work as long as they can see…"

English Parliamentary investigation into child labor, 1831

Source: Stearns, Peter N., ed., et al. British Sessional Papers 1831–1832, House of Commons, vol. XV, pp. 17–19; reprinted in *Documents in World History, vol. 2: The Modern Centuries: From 1500 to the Present* (New York: Harper Collins Publishers, 1988), pp. 26–27.

31. The passage can best be understood within the context of
    (A) the Agricultural Revolution
    (B) the Cottage Industry
    (C) the Commercial Revolution
    (D) the Industrial Revolution

32. The influence of the investigation in the passage eventually led to
    (A) increased influence of conservatives leading to the public health movement
    (B) increased influence of factory owners leading to the passage of the Corn Laws
    (C) greater Parliamentary regulation of factories
    (D) greater Parliamentary regulation of large landowners

33. The conditions expressed in the passage led to the development of
    (A) positivism
    (B) scientific socialism
    (C) classical liberalism
    (D) nihilism

Questions 34–36 refer to the passage below.

"At the Congress of Vienna, the major powers—Russia, Austria, Prussia, and Great Britain—had agreed to consult with each other from time to time on matters affecting Europe. Such consultation was one of the new departures in international relations the Congress achieved. The vehicle for this consultation was a series of postwar congresses, or conferences. Later, as differences arose among the powers, the consultations became more informal. This new arrangement for resolving mutual foreign policy issues was known as the Concert of Europe. It prevented one nation from taking a major action in international affairs without working in concert with and obtaining the assent of the others. Its goal—a novel one in

European affairs—was to maintain the peace. Initially, this meant maintaining the balance of power against new French aggression and against the military might of Russia. The Concert of Europe continued to function, however, on large and small issues until the third quarter of the [nineteenth] century."

Donald Kagan, *The Western Heritage, 11th edition* (Boston: Pearson Learning, 2016)

34. The events described in the passage were most likely a response to which of the following?
 (A) The Napoleonic Wars
 (B) Italian unification
 (C) The Russian Revolution
 (D) The American Revolution

35. The passage best exemplifies the views of which of the following?
 (A) Pierre Proudhon
 (B) Klemens von Metternich
 (C) John Stuart Mill
 (D) Voltaire

36. The events described in the passage best reflect which of the following?
 (A) Liberalism
 (B) Fascism
 (C) Conservatism
 (D) Nationalism

Questions 37–39 refer to the passage below.

Emmeline Pankhurst, speech, "Freedom or Death," 1913

"'Put them in prison,' they said, 'that will stop it.' But it didn't stop it. They put women in prison for long terms of imprisonment, for making a nuisance of themselves—that was the expression when they took petitions in their hands to the door of the House of Commons; and they thought that by sending them to prison, giving them a day's imprisonment would cause them to all settle down again and there would be no further trouble. But it didn't happen so at all: instead of the women giving it up, more women did it, and more and more and more women did it until there were three hundred women at a time, who had not broken a single law, only 'made a nuisance of themselves' as the politicians say…

They have said to us government rests upon force, the women haven't force so they must submit. Well, we are showing them that government does not rest upon force at all: it rests upon consent. As women consent to be unjustly governed, they can be, but directly women say: 'We withhold our consent, we will not be governed any longer so long as that government is unjust.'

…Human life for us is sacred, but we say if any life is to be sacrificed it shall be ours; we won't do it ourselves, but we will put the enemy in the position where they will have to choose between giving us freedom and giving us death."

Emmeline Pankhurst, speech, "Freedom or Death," 1913

Source: Pankhurst, Emmeline. "Freedom or Death" 13 November 1913.
www.theguardian.com/theguardian/2007/apr/27/greatspeeches

37. Which of the following is most likely the purpose of the passage?
    (A) Women should have equal opportunities in the workplace.
    (B) Women should have full access to birth control.
    (C) Women should have primary custody of children in case of divorce.
    (D) Women should have suffrage rights.

38. The ideas upon which the speaker is arguing are based on which of the following?
    (A) Romanticism
    (B) Enlightenment
    (C) Socialism
    (D) Capitalism

39. The views in the passage likely influenced which of the following movements later in the twentieth century?
    (A) Feminism
    (B) Right-wing nationalists
    (C) Student revolts
    (D) The New Left

Questions 40–43 refer to the image below.

Scene—The Congo 'Free' State

CAPTION: IN THE RUBBER COILS

Source: Punch Magazine, Edward Linley Sambourne, cartoon, November 28, 1906, Chronicle/Alamy Stock Photo

40. The purpose of the cartoon was most likely to
    (A) glorify the power of the Belgian empire
    (B) criticize the policies of the Belgian king
    (C) justify the conquest of African nations
    (D) promote increased trade among European nations

436

41. Which of the following statements best explains Leopold II's primary motives in colonizing the Congo?
    (A) The desire to civilize African peoples
    (B) The desire to increase Belgium's strategic power in European affairs
    (C) The desire to benefit economically from raw materials
    (D) The desire to increase trade in the Indian Ocean

42. Which of the following was most responsible for Belgium's dominant position in the cartoon?
    (A) The Second Industrial Revolution
    (B) The development of trench warfare
    (C) The smallpox vaccine
    (D) The Congress of Vienna

43. The event portrayed in the cartoon is most similar to which of the following situations?
    (A) The Portuguese establishing a commercial network along the African coast in the fifteenth century
    (B) The French tapping into the Native American fur trade in North America in the seventeenth century
    (C) The British Empire's creation of the British Commonwealth of nations in the mid-twentieth century
    (D) The Spanish Empire's relationship with American Indians in the sixteenth century

Questions 44–46 refer to the passage below.

"Article 8

The members of the League recognize that the maintenance of peace requires the reduction of national armaments to the lowest point consistent with national safety and the enforcement by common action of international obligations…

Article 10

The members of the League undertake to respect and preserve as against external aggression the territorial integrity and existing political independence of all Members of the League. In case of any such aggression or in case of any threat or danger of such aggression the Council shall advise upon the means by which this obligation shall be fulfilled…

Article 11

Any war or threat of war, whether immediately affecting any of the members of the League or not, is hereby declared a matter of concern to the whole League, and the League shall take any action that may be deemed wise and effectual to safeguard the peace of nations…"

The Covenant of the League of Nations, 1924

Source: Covenant of the League of Nations 1924. http://avalon.law.yale.edu/20th_century/leagcov.asp

44. The passage best reflects which of the following?
    (A) French vengeance for World War I losses
    (B) Wilsonian idealism
    (C) The doctrine of preemption
    (D) Neutrality and isolationism

45. The goals articulated in the passage ultimately failed due in part to which of the following?
    (A) The non-participation of certain major powers
    (B) The destabilizing impact of the Bolshevik Revolution
    (C) The refusal of the Weimar Republic to adhere to the Versailles Treaty in the 1920s
    (D) International conflicts related to African colonialism

46. Which of the following undermined the goals stated in the passage?
    (A) The crisis in the Balkans
    (B) The Ruhr Crisis
    (C) The Locarno Pact
    (D) British and French policies of appeasement

Questions 47–49 refer to the passage below.

"What was the task of the five-year plan?

The fundamental task of the five-year plan was to transfer our country, with its backward, and in part medieval, technology, on to the lines of new, modern technology.

The fundamental task of the five-year plan was to convert the U.S.S.R. from an agrarian and weak country, dependent upon the caprices of the capitalist countries, into an industrial and powerful country, fully self-reliant and independent of the caprices of world capitalism. The fundamental task of the five-year plan was, in converting the U.S.S.R. into an industrial country, to completely oust the capitalist elements, to widen the front of socialist forms of economy, and to create the economic basis for the abolition of classes in the U.S.S.R…, for the building of a socialist society."

Joseph Stalin, speech to the Central Communist Party, 1933

Source: Works, Vol. 13, 1930 - January 1934 Publisher: Foreign Languages Publishing House, Moscow, 1954
Public Domain: Marxists Internet Archive (2008).

47. The plan expressed in the passage resulted in which of the following?
    (A) The onset of the Russian Civil War
    (B) The spread of the Great Depression in Russia
    (C) The end of Lenin's New Economic Policy
    (D) The formation of the Comintern

48. The ideas expressed in the passage are most similar to which of the following?
    (A) Socialist revisionism
    (B) Marxist-Leninist theory
    (C) The welfare state
    (D) The corporate state

49. The policies stated in the passage resulted in which of the following?
    (A) Liquidation of the kulaks
    (B) *Pogroms* against Russian Jews
    (C) Dramatic increases in agricultural production
    (D) The development of *perestroika*

Questions 50–53 refer to the passage below.

Pope John Paul II, Centesimus Annus, *Encyclical Letter, 1991*

"Among the many factors involved in the fall of oppressive regimes, some deserve special mention. Certainly, the decisive factor which gave rise to the changes was the violation of the rights of workers. It cannot be forgotten that the fundamental crisis of systems claiming to express the rule and indeed the dictatorship of the working class began with the great upheavals which took place in Poland in the name of solidarity. It was the throngs of working people which foreswore the ideology which presumed to speak in their name. On the basis of a hard, lived experience of work and of oppression, it was they who recovered and, in a sense, rediscovered the content and principles of the Church's social doctrine.

Also worthy of emphasis is the fact that the fall of this kind of "bloc" or empire was accomplished almost everywhere by means of peaceful protest, using only the weapons of truth and justice. While Marxism held that only by exacerbating social conflicts was it possible to resolve them through violent confrontation, the protests which led to the collapse of Marxism tenaciously insisted on trying every avenue of negotiation, dialogue, and witness to the truth, appealing to the conscience of the adversary and seeking to reawaken in him a sense of shared human dignity."

Pope John Paul II, *Centesimus Annus*, Encyclical Letter, 1991

Source: Pope John Paul II, On the Hundredth Anniversary of Rerum Novarum: Centesimus Annus. Encyclical Letter of May 1, 1991 (Washington, DC: Office for Publishing and Promotion Services, United States Catholic Conference, 1991), pp. 66–97.

50. Which of the following *best* explains the purpose underlying the passage above?
    (A) The pope seeks to promote Catholic control over eastern Europe.
    (B) The pope seeks to promote peaceful resolution of conflict throughout the world.
    (C) The pope seeks to undermine the Soviet Union.
    (D) The pope seeks to promote conservative authoritarianism throughout Europe.

51. The passage above reflects which of the following trends in the late-twentieth century?
    (A) A movement among many western nations away from a free-market economy
    (B) The independence of several African countries from control by the Soviet Union
    (C) The opposition to totalitarian regimes by Christian churches
    (D) The embrace of socialism by the Catholic Church

52. The passage reflects which of the following historical events?
    (A) The collapse of the Soviet Union
    (B) The rise of China as a dominant economic power
    (C) The emergence of détente as an American foreign policy
    (D) The failure of containment

53. Which of the following was a result of the situation described in the passage?
    (A) The rise of Vladimir Putin as dictator of Russia in the 1990s
    (B) The dismantling of NATO
    (C) The inclusion of Russia in the European Union
    (D) The establishment of capitalist economies in Eastern Europe

Questions 54–55 refer to the passage below.

"I will be going about my business in my full veil as I have for the last 12 years and nothing and nobody is going to stop me…. This whole law [to ban women from wearing a full veil] makes France look ridiculous…. I never thought I'd see the day when France, my France, the country I was born in and I love, the country of *liberté*, *égalité*, *fraternité*, would do something that so obviously violates people's freedom.

I'll be getting on with my life and if they want to send me to prison for wearing the niqab then so be it. One thing's for sure: I'm not taking it off.

[Wearing a veil] is not a religious constraint since it is not laid down in Islam or the *Qur'an* that I have to wear a full veil. It is my personal choice….

I would never encourage others to do it just because I do. That is their choice. My daughters can do what they like. As I tell them, this is my choice, not theirs…."

Kenza Drider, French citizen and Muslim woman France: "housewife vows to face jail rather than submit" in From Kim Willsher, 'Burqa ban' *The Observer*, April 9, 2011.

Source: Kenza Drider, French citizen and Muslim woman quoted in *The Observer*, April 9, 2011

54. The passage highlights which of the following trends in twenty-first century European society?
   (A) Conflict over the role of religion in social life
   (B) Conflict among Muslim leaders trying to impose Sharia law
   (C) Activity of women's rights advocates seeking to help Muslim women
   (D) Activity of xenophobic groups seeking to restrict immigration

55. An underlying cause of the situation described in the document is
   (A) the rise of far-right political parties during the last half of the twentieth century
   (B) increased terrorist activity after 2001
   (C) increased immigration into Europe after the Second World War
   (D) the decline in the average standard of living in Western Europe in the early twenty-first century

SECTION I

PART B: SHORT-ANSWER QUESTIONS

Directions: Answer Question 1 **and** Question 2. Answer **either** Question 3 **or** Question 4.

Read the passage below and answer all parts of the question that follows.

"**Romanticism**, which became a dominant intellectual trend in many European countries in the second quarter of the nineteenth century, is seen by some historians essentially as a reaction to the Enlightenment. By others it is seen as an emanation of attitudes generated by the Industrial Revolution and the Napoleonic Wars. Actually it was all these things. The circumstances of its origins in the 1770s were closely connected indeed to the fading appeal of the Enlightenment. At the same time, the reasons for its mass appeal in the 1820s and 1830s were closely bound up with the experiences of a generation which lived through the revolutionary ordeal, which felt the impact of machines and factories, and which fumed after 1815 under the dead weight of the reactionary regimes."

Norman Davies, *Europe: A History*, 1996

Source: Norman Davies, *Europe: A History,* 1996, Oxford: Oxford University Press, p. 782.

Answer a, b, and c:
1. a) Explain how one piece of evidence supports Davies's argument regarding the effects of the Enlightenment on European society.
   b) Explain how one piece of evidence supports Davies's argument regarding the attitudes generated by the Industrial Revolution in European society.
   c) Explain one example of how Romanticism affected European society in the nineteenth century.

Use the image below to answer all parts of the question that follows.

December 1892 cartoon from a British magazine showing British businessman Cecil John Rhodes after he announced plans for a telegraph line and railroad from Cape Town to Cairo.

"The Rhodes Colossus"

266   PUNCH, OR THE LONDON CHARIVARI.   [DECEMBER 10, 1892.

THE RHODES COLOSSUS
STRIDING FROM CAPE TOWN TO CAIRO.

Source: World History Archive/Alamy Stock Photo

Answer a, b, and c:

2. a) Describe one <u>cause</u> of the international situation depicted in the cartoon.
    b) Describe one <u>effect</u> of the international situation depicted in the cartoon.
    c) Explain one philosophical justification for the situation depicted in the cartoon.

Directions: Answer **either** Question 3 **or** Question 4.

Answer a, b, and c:

3. a) Describe one significant continuity in the role of women during the period 1450 to 1600.
    b) Describe one significant <u>change</u> in the role of women during the period 1450 to 1600.
    c) Explain one reason for the change in the role of women during the period 1450 to 1600.

Answer a, b, and c:

4. a) Describe a continuity in the development of Western European unity during the period from 1949 to 2001.
    b) Describe a <u>change</u> in the development of Western European unity during the period 1949 to 2001.
    c) Explain how one political or economic development affected the development of Western European unity during the twentieth century.

SECTION II

PART A: DOCUMENT-BASED QUESTION

Question 1. Evaluate whether the policies of the Enlightened Despots were designed primarily for reform or primarily for increased political power in the years between 1740 and 1815.

Document 1

Source: Frederick the Great, "Essay on the Form of Government," 18th century.

A sovereign must possess an exact and detailed knowledge of the strong and of the weak points of his country. He must be thoroughly acquainted with its resources, the character of the people. and the national commerce.... Rulers should always remind themselves that they are men like the least of their subjects…Therefore, he should perform with care the duties connected with these offices. He is merely the principal servant of the State. Hence, he must act with honesty, wisdom, and complete disinterestedness in such a way that he can render an account of his stewardship to the citizens at any moment. Consequently, he is guilty if he wastes the money of the people, the taxes which they have paid, in luxury, pomp and debauchery. He who should improve the morals of the people, be the guardian of the law, and improve their education should not pervert them by his bad example…The sovereign is the representative of his State. He and his people form a single body. Ruler and ruled can be happy only if they are firmly united. The sovereign stands to his people in the same relation in which the head stands to the body. He must use his eyes and his brain for the whole community, and act on its behalf to the common advantage. If we wish to elevate monarchical above republican government, the duty of sovereigns is clear. They must be active, hard-working, upright and honest, and concentrate all their strength upon filling their office worthily. That is my idea of the duties of sovereigns.

Source: *The Foundations of Germany,* J. Ellis Barker, trans. (New York: E. P. Dutton, 1916), pp. 22–23.

Document 2

Source: Catherine the Great, *The Grand Instructions to the Commissioners Appointed to Frame a New Code of Laws for the Russian Empire*, 1768.

1. The Christian Law teaches us to do mutual Good to one another, as much as possibly we can.
2. Laying this down as a fundamental Rule prescribed by that Religion, which has taken, or ought to take Root in the Hearts of the whole People; we cannot but suppose, that every honest Man in the Community is, or will be, desirous of seeing his native Country at the very Summit of Happiness, Glory, Safety, and Tranquillity.
3. And that every Individual Citizen in particular must wish to see himself protected by Laws, which should not distress him in his Circumstances, but, on the Contrary, should defend him from all Attempts of others that are repugnant to this fundamental rule....
9. The Sovereign is absolute; for there is no other Authority but that which centers in his single Person, that can act with a Vigour proportionate to the Extent of such a vast Dominion.

Source: Catherine the Great, *The Grand Instructions to the Commissioners Appointed to Frame a New Code of Laws for the Russian Empire*, 1768, Translated by Michael Tatischeff. London.

Document 3

Source: Le Mire, Engraving, "The Cake of Kings: First Partition of Poland, 1773." Catherine the Great, Maria Theresa, and Frederick the Great join in carving up Poland while the Polish king clutches his tottering crown.

Source: Photo12/UIG/Getty Images

Document 4

Source: Emperor Joseph II of Austria Issues Edict of Tolerance, 1782.

As it is Our goal to make the Jewish nation useful and serviceable to the State, mainly through better education and enlightenment of its youth as well as by directing them to the sciences, the arts and the crafts, We hereby grant and order- . . .

8. Graciously, that the tolerated Jews may send their children in such places where they have no German schools of their own, to the Christian primary and secondary schools so that they have at least the opportunity to learn reading, writing and counting. And although they do not have a proper synagogue in Our residence, still We hereby permit them to establish for their children at their own expense their own school organized in the standard way with teachers appointed from amongst their co-religionists....

10. In order to facilitate their future means of support and to prepare the necessary ways of gaining a livelihood, We hereby most graciously permit them from now to learn all kinds of crafts or trades here as well as elsewhere from Christian masters, certainly also amongst themselves, and to this end to apprentice themselves to Christian masters or to work as their journeymen, and the latter (the Christian craftsmen) may accept them without hesitation...

12. Grant to the Jewish co-religionists the completely free choice of all non-civic branches of commerce and authorize them to apply for the right of wholesale trade under the same conditions and with the same liberties as are obtained and carried on by Our Christian subjects...

Source: Paul Mendes-Flohr and Jehuda Reinharz, The Jew in the Modern World: A Documentary History (New York: Oxford University Press, 1995), pp. 36–37.

Document 5

Source: Joseph II, letter to his mother, Empress Maria Theresa, July 20, 1777

"Dear Mother,

…the definition of the word "toleration" is to blame for our entire misunderstanding. You have taken it in an entirely different sense. God preserve me from thinking it is a matter of no consequence of your subjects become Protestant or remain Catholic, still less, if they do not believe in or at least observe the religion which they have been given by their fathers. I would give all I possess if all the Protestants of your lands would become Catholics!

As I use it, "tolerance" means only that, when it comes to purely temporal affairs, I would employ, allow to own property, pursue trades, be citizens, without regard to religion, all those who are capable ad can bring advantage or industry to our lands. those who unfortunately hold a false faith are even further from conversion if they remain in their own country than if they move to one in which they will see and hear the striking truths of the Catholic faith. At the same time, the undisturbed practice of their religion makes them far better subjects and causes them to avoid atheism, which is much more dangerous to our Catholics than the observation of other religions."

Source: Alfred Arneth, ed., *Maria Theresa und Joseph II, Ihre Correspondenz* vol. II [Vienna: Carl Gerold's Sohn, 1867), pp. 151–152 [Translation by Alison Frank].

Document 6

Source: Immanuel Kant, *Foundations of the Metaphysics of Morals,* 1784

"For this enlightenment, however, nothing is required but freedom, and indeed the most harmless among all the things to which this term can properly be applied. It is the freedom to make public use of one's reason at every point. But I hear on all sides, "Do not argue! The officer says: "Do not argue but drill!" The tax collector: "Do not argue but pay! the cleric: "Do not argue but believe!" Only one prince in the world [Frederick the Great of Prussia] says, "Argue as much as you will, and about what you will, but obey!" Everywhere there is a restriction of freedom…"

Source: Beck, L.W, trans. Immanuel Kant, Foundations of the Metaphysics of Morals 2/e © 1990 pp. 83–85, 88. Pearson Education Inc., Upper Saddle River NJ.

Document 7

Source: Jean-Dominique Ingres, *Napoleon I on His Imperial Throne*, 1806

Source: Oil on Canvas, Musée d 'l'Armée, Les Invalides, Paris Erich Lessing/Art Resource

SECTION II

PART B: LONG-ESSAY QUESTIONS

Directions: Answer Question 1 **or** Question 2 **or** Question 3.

Question 1.   Evaluate the extent to which Protestant views of government in Europe differed from Catholic views of government in Europe in the period 1500 to 1648.

Question 2.   Evaluate the extent to which absolute monarchies in western Europe differed in their views of government with absolute monarchies in eastern Europe in the period 1648 to 1750.

Question 3.   Evaluate the extent to which fascist dictatorships in Europe differed in their views of government with communist dictatorships in Europe in the period 1919 to 1989.

ANSWERS AND EXPLANATIONS: AP® PRACTICE TEST

SECTION I

PART A: MULTIPLE-CHOICE QUESTIONS

1. D (KC: 1.1.III.A; LO: Unit 1 C) Botticelli was a major Florentine artist during the fifteenth century who exemplified the new painting techniques of geometric perspective, chiaroscuro, and naturalism. The painting also exemplifies secularism as the scene in *La Primavera* is not a religious one.

2. A (KC: 1.1.I.A; LO: Unit 1 B) The Italian Renaissance embodied the ideals of ancient Greek and Roman writers and artists—the foundation of Italian humanism. Botticelli's choice of a secular scene with the portrayal of individuals with clear and unique facial features is emblematic of the humanistic approach many artists took during this period.

3. C (KC: 2.3.V.B; LO: Unit 4 F) In the late eighteenth century, artists such as Jacques-Louis David revisited the approach of the Italian humanists in highlighting ancient Greek and Roman virtues. Their approach became known as Neo-Classicism and corresponded with the philosophy of the Enlightenment.

4. B (KC: 1.2.I.A; LO: Unit 1 D) Christian humanism of the Northern Renaissance profoundly influenced religious reformers such as Martin Luther, John Calvin, and Ulrich Zwingli. The most influential of the Northern humanists was Erasmus of Rotterdam, whose *In Praise of Folly* lambasted the corruption of the Catholic Church. One contemporary remarked that "Erasmus laid the egg that Luther hatched."

5. B (KC: 1.2.I.B; LO: Unit 2 B) One of Luther's central ideas was that faith in God alone was enough to earn one's eternal salvation. He rejected the Catholic position that salvation was only possible through following the Catholic Church's sacraments and practices. Luther emphasized the primacy of scripture.

6. D (KC: 1.2.III.C; LO: Unit 2 C) Reformers such as Luther and Zwingli inspired state leaders within the Holy Roman Empire to break away from Catholic Church control. Zwingli's influence in the Swiss city of Zurich is one such example. Many northern German princes adopted Lutheranism and removed Catholic authorities from their realms.

7. A (KC: 1.2.I.B; LO: Unit 2 B) Anabaptists likewise no longer accepted the authority of the Catholic Church and formed their own communities within the Holy Roman Empire. Unlike Luther, the Anabaptists rejected secular political authority and believed their only allegiance was to God.

8. C (KC: 1.3.II; LO: Unit 1 G) The map with which Columbus set out westward from Spain in 1492 did not include the Americas. The prevailing view of mapmakers at the time was the Atlantic Ocean as a vast body that separated Europe from Asia. When Columbus first landed in the Caribbean, he believed he had reached Indonesia.

9. A (KC: 1.3.III.B; LO: Unit 1 I) The Portuguese were ahead of Spain in navigating a course around the southern cape of Africa. Rather than trying to outdo Portugal at its own game in Africa, Columbus proposed an alternate route westward in hopes of reaching India more quickly.

10. B (KC: 1.3.III.D; 1.3.IV.A; 1.3.IV.B; LO: Unit 1 I, J) The New Imperialism of the late nineteenth century resulted in the carving up of Africa and domination of much of Asia by European powers. This was similar to Spain's exploits in the New World during the sixteenth and seventeenth centuries, but it was not similar to the trade-driven relationship Europeans developed with Africans and Asians in the early modern period.

11. D (KC: 1.1.IV.A; LO: Unit 4 B) From antiquity through the Middle Ages, European elites held the geocentric view of the universe. Both the Bible and scientific views—such as those of Aristotle—held that the earth was the center of the universe. Copernicus's hypothesis based on his observations turned these earlier views upside down.

12. B (KC: 1.1.IV.A; LO: Unit 4 B) Copernicus's heliocentric view placed the sun at the center of the universe with the earth and other planets orbiting around it. The Church considered this theory as blasphemous.

13. C (KC: 1.I.IV.B; LO: Unit 4 B) William Harvey developed the hitherto most accurate and detailed description of the circulatory system in the human body. As a scientist during the Scientific Revolution, he would have most likely agreed with Copernicus's scientific and mathematical methods of reaching conclusions based on observation.

14. A (KC: 2.3.I.A; LO: Unit 4 C) The rationalism of the Scientific Revolution in the sixteenth and seventeenth centuries profoundly influenced European Enlightenment philosophers in the eighteenth century. In particular, Isaac Newton's theory of universal gravitation inspired thinkers to develop the notion of deism—a naturalistic view of God.

15. B (KC: 1.2.II.B; LO: Unit 2 B) The "Reformed" religion to which the Edict of Nantes refers is Calvinism. A student with knowledge of Henry IV—a Huguenot much of his life—and his religiously tolerant views toward those who shared his faith, would be expected to connect these contextual clues with the reference to those of the "Reformed" faith.

16. D (KC: 1.2.III.D; LO: Unit 2 C) The Edict of Nantes finally ended several decades of brutal civil warfare between various noble factions in France. Although Henry IV was a Calvinist, he publicly converted to Catholicism in order to gain the loyalty of Paris.

17. A (KC: 1.2.II.A; LO: Unit 1 F) Due to his willingness to compromise on important issues to increase the stability of his rule, such as his converting to Catholicism, Henry has been labeled a "politique" by historians. Another "politique" ruler of the era was Elizabeth I of England, who publicly adopted certain tenets of the Anglican Church to gain the loyalty of her people. Privately, Elizabeth's beliefs were based on Lutheran and Calvinist principles.

18. C (KC: 2.1.I.B; LO: Unit 3 G) Peter the Great, Charles the II, and Frederick the Great were rulers who either sought to reform and westernize their realms, or in the case of Charles, compromise absolutist tendencies to gain power. Louis XIV, however, was the quintessential absolute monarch of the age who sought to impose his will on his country along traditional lines. He refused, for example, to allow religious toleration by revoking the earlier Edict of Nantes.

19. A (KC: 2.1.I; LO: Unit 3 H) Hobbes believed that in a state of nature men were "nasty, brutish, and short" thus leading to chaos and violence. Although he believed that the people were sovereign, he also believed that people transfer their sovereignty to a ruler in order to gain protection and preserve law and order. His views later influenced the notion of Enlightened Despotism in which absolute rulers governed their realms as benevolent dictators who instituted enlightened reforms.

20. B (KC: 2.1.I.C; LO: Unit 4 G) See the explanation to Question 19.

21. C (KC: 2.3.I.B; LO: Unit 4 C) Locke did not believe in absolutism. Rather, he believed in constitutionalism—that the people are sovereign but are willing to obey just governments that protect their life, liberty, and property. Locke termed this arrangement the "social contract."

22. D (KC: 2.1.III; LO: Unit 3 E) At its height, the Habsburg-controlled Holy Roman Empire included most of central Europe and parts of eastern Europe such as territory in modern-day Poland. As Prussia increased its territorial holdings due to the Thirty Years' War and later, the War of Austrian Succession, the Holy Roman Empire disappeared as a viable political entity. Those territories that remained under the effective control of the Austrian Habsburgs comprised the Austrian Empire.

23. C (KC: 2.1.I.D; LO: Unit 3 E) Polish nobles traditionally enjoyed much power and a large degree of independence from the Polish government. The *liberum veto* allowed nobles to veto any proposed laws. Laws in Poland had to pass with the unanimous approval of the noble class. This lack of centralized power in Poland rendered it weak to deal with the aggressive rising powers of Russia, Prussia, and Austria. During the last half of the eighteenth century, Poland was partitioned by these three empires and ceased to exist as a sovereign nation in eastern Europe.

24. A (KC: 2.3.V.A; LO: Unit 4 F) Gian Bernini ranks as one of the great Baroque artists of the seventeenth century. His large works such as the colonnade in front of St. Peter's Basilica and his Baldachin over the tomb of St. Peter inside the basilica were meant to inspire awe among worshippers.

25. C (KC: 2.1.I.B; LO: Unit 1 G) While the Catholic Church employed Baroque artists to convey its power and majesty, absolute rulers likewise utilized Baroque architecture to enhance their power and prestige. Louis XIV's palace at Versailles is the most impressive example of this trend. Other absolute monarchs such as the Habsburgs in Austria, who commissioned the building of Schönbrunn in Vienna, and Peter the Great of Russia who built the Peterhof in his newly-built city of St. Petersburg, utilized the Baroque style to enhance their rule.

26. D (KC: 2.3.V.A; LO: Unit 4 F) See explanations to Questions 24 and 25.

27. C (KC: 2.1.IV; LO: Unit 5 D) The Third Estate declared itself the sovereign power in France in June 1789. Sieyes, along with a few other clergy members of the First Estate, supported the creation of the new National Assembly that established a constitutional monarchy.

28. A (KC: 2.3.I.B; LO: Unit 4 C) A foremost Enlightenment philosopher, Rousseau published the *Social Contract* in 1762 claiming that the "General Will" of the majority of people in a nation should prevail rather than arbitrary rule by absolute monarchs. Rousseau's views were heavily influenced by John Locke.

29. B (KC: 3.4.II.C; LO: Unit 7 B) The Habsburg Empire was a "polyglot" empire that consisted of a multitude of ethnic groups, most of whom did not wish to be ruled by their German Austrian rulers. Most notably, the Hungarians nearly won their independence during the Revolution of 1848.

30. D (KC: 3.4.II.C; LO: Unit 7 B) After Austria's defeat in the Austro-Prussian War of 1866, the weakened empire reluctantly gave Hungary its independence in 1867 through the creation of a "Dual Monarchy" within a new Austro-Hungarian Empire. The Austrians and Hungarians agreed to act as a single entity regarding foreign affairs.

454

31. D (KC: 3.2.III.B; LO: Unit 6 E) In the early decades of the Industrial Revolution, factories utilized child labor as they could pay these children far less than an adult male would accept. English liberal reformers of the early eighteenth century demanded a significant reduction in child labor prompting the passage of several important labor laws in the 1830s and 1840s.

32. C (KC: 3.2.III.B; LO: Unit 6 E) Examples of child labor laws passed by Parliament include the Factory Act of 1833, the Mines Act of 1842 and the Ten Hours Act of 1847.

33. B (KC: 3.3.I.D; LO: Unit 6 G) The often-brutal working conditions laborers endured during the first half of the nineteenth century prompted socialist thinkers Karl Marx and Friedrich Engels to develop scientific socialism in their seminal *Communist Manifesto* (1848). Marx and Engels looked at human history through an economic lens and argued that the "haves" traditionally exploited the "have nots." Both men saw the desperation among the growing proletariat as a force that would result in the violent overthrow of the bourgeoisie and the creation of a "dictatorship of the proletariat" within a classless society.

34. A (KC: 2.1.5.D; LO: Unit 5 H) The victors of the Napoleonic Wars saw the liberalism of the French Revolution and Napoleon's rule as a dangerous force needing to be suppressed at any cost. The Concert of Europe sought to root out liberalism and nationalism throughout Europe.

35. B (KC: 3.4.I.A; LO: Unit 6 F) Metternich was the principal architect of the new conservative order that emerged from the Congress of Vienna in 1815. He sought to preserve the primacy of conservatism throughout Europe through a Congress System consisting of Austria, Prussia, Russia, Britain, and later, France.

36. C (KC: 3.4.I.B; LO: Unit 6 F) See explanation to Question 35.

37. D (KC: 3.3.III.C; LO: Unit 6 I) Militant suffragists such as Emmeline Pankhurst and her daughter, Sylvia, demanded the franchise for women in the late-eighteenth and early-nineteenth centuries. Their tactics included aggressive public demonstrations and the destruction of property.

38. B (KC: 2.3.III.A; LO: Unit 4 D) Suffragists argued that the natural rights of life, liberty, and property should be universal for all human beings, not just men.

39. A (KC: 4.4.II.B; LO: Unit 9 H) While women demanded the vote and other laws that would protect women, such as improved property rights, increased access to divorce, and increased work opportunities, feminists of the 1960s and 1970s fought for equality of economic opportunity and equal pay for equal work.

40. B (KC: 3.5.III.B; LO: Unit 7 I) The head of the snake is King Leopold of Belgium. The atrocities committed by Leopold's agents in the Congo drew the ire of critics. Aghast at the horrors perpetuated at the behest of the king, Belgium's parliament took control of the colony thus stripping the king of his personal colonial possession.

41. C (KC: 3.5.I.B; LO: Unit 7 G) The lure of valuable raw materials in Africa and Asia prompted European empires toward aggressive conquest during the age of the "New Imperialism." Rubber and ivory were among the most valuable raw materials in the Congo.

42. A (KC: 3.5.II; LO: Unit 7 K) The Second Industrial Revolution saw the advent of steel gunboats and machine guns that gave Europeans an overwhelming technological advantage in warfare against Africans and Asians.

43. D (KC: 1.3.III.B; LO: Unit 1 I) Just as European empires carved up Africa during the "New Imperialism," the Spanish conquered much of the Americas in the sixteenth century. Amerindians were subjugated against their will and raw materials such as sugar and silver were extracted with slave labor.

44. B (KC: 4.1.II.A; LO: Unit 8 F) In his Fourteen Points, American President Woodrow Wilson sought to create a new world order after the resolution of hostilities of the First World War. Wilson proposed the creation of a new international organization—a League of Nations—that would provide collective security for all member nations. In this way, war could be avoided in the future.

45. A (KC: 4.1.II.B; LO: Unit 8 F) Ironically, the United States refused to join the organization that Wilson had worked to create. Other major powers, such as Germany and the Soviet Union, were not allowed into the League until 1926 and 1934, respectively, thus rendering it impotent from the outset.

46. D (KC: 4.1.III; LO: Unit 8 J) Rather than creating a united front against fascism in the 1930s through collective security, Britain and France repeatedly appeased Hitler in hopes of avoiding a world war.

47. C (KC: 4.2.I.D; LO: Unit 8 E) War Communism during the Russian Civil War destroyed the country's economy. Seeking to recover economically from the catastrophe, Lenin instituted the New Economic Policy (NEP) that provided some elements of capitalism for peasants and merchants. As a result, the Soviet economy showed some modest improvement in the 1920s, but Stalin brought the NEP to an abrupt halt when he implemented his first Five-Year Plan in 1928.

48. B (KC: 4.2.I; LO: Unit 8 E) Lenin modified Marx's socialist views by arguing that a successful communist revolution in Russia had to occur from above, through a highly organized and professional group of revolutionary leaders that would force the revolution forward even though Russia was not yet a fully industrialized nation with a large proletariat. Lenin's views came to be known as Marxist-Leninist theory. Stalin later adopted this strategy with "Socialism from Above"—the philosophical underpinning of his Five-Year Plans.

49. A (KC: 4.2.I.E; LO: Unit 8 I) The kulaks were peasants who were relatively well-off compared to landless peasants. Kulaks in the Ukraine stubbornly opposed Stalin's program of collectivization of agriculture—a component of his Five-Year Plans. In response, Stalin ordered the kulaks to be liquidated as a class. Between 7 to 10 million kulaks ultimately perished as a result of Stalin's forced starvation of the Ukraine.

50. B (KC: 4.3.III; LO: Unit 9 P) Pope John Paul II argued for the reduction of human rights abuses in Soviet Eastern Europe.

51. C (KC: 4.3.III.A; LO: Unit 9 O) In 1979, Pope John Paul II traveled to his native Poland urging that people be given more freedoms under the communist regime.

52. A (KC: 4.1.IV.E; LO: Unit 9 G) Due to a stagnating economy coupled with increased nationalism among Eastern Bloc nations and even within Soviet states such as Latvia, Lithuania, and Estonia, the Soviet empire in Eastern Europe collapsed in 1989 and the Soviet Union itself disintegrated in 1991.

53. D (KC: 4.1.IV.E; LO: Unit 9 G) Most Eastern European countries after 1989 rejected authoritarian one-party rule in place of a multiparty system. Most also sought to transition to a market economy as the communist economic system in the old Soviet empire had clearly failed. Poland, Czechoslovakia, and Hungary were the most successful among former Eastern Bloc nations to transition to a capitalist economy—although struggles remained. Eventually, most Eastern European countries joined the European Union by the early 2000s.

54. A (KC: 4.3.III.C; LO: Unit 9 L) The large migration of Muslims from North Africa and Turkey into Europe after World War II created social tensions that were partially the result of religious differences. France, for example, has largely rejected the official existence of Sharia Law, citing its limitation of rights for females violates French law.

55. C (KC: 4.3.III.C; LO: Unit 9 L) After World War II, a shortage of workers prompted European countries to import large numbers of immigrants from Africa and certain parts of Asia. These immigrants came as "guest workers." They were to work for a specified time before returning home. In many cases, the immigrants remained in their adopted country but lacked citizenship rights.

SECTION I

PART B: SHORT-ANSWER QUESTIONS

Sample Answers

Question 1
(KC: 2.3.VI; LO: Unit 5 J)

Possible responses to part a) include:
- Rather than Enlightenment reasoning, romanticism was based on emotion and nature.
- Rousseau and Kant had even questioned the overuse of "reason."
- French revolutionaries wanted to spread their ideals throughout the continent, even going to war with much of the rest of Europe.
- The return of the legitimate monarchies after the Congress of Vienna enraged many nationalists who wanted either unification or independence.

Possible responses to part b) include:
- Many people who rejected the impersonal factory system found romantic art and literature appealing.
- Urban- and social reformers might have found romanticism appealing because of their own rejection of Enlightenment economic liberalism.
- The growth of industry correlated with a growing number of landless out-of-work peasantry.

Possible responses to part c) include:
- Romanticism led to many writings that emphasized national pride, such as the literary works of the Grimm Brothers, increasing German nationalism and leading to the Frankfurt Assembly in 1848 and the rise of Bismarck.
- Romantic works such as "Liberty Leading the People" emphasized the ideas of liberalism.

Question 2
(KC: 3.5.I, 3.5.II, 3.5.III; LO: Unit 7 H, I)

Possible responses to part a) include:
- Competition and nationalistic rivalry between the European nations
- Economic motives to acquire raw materials and guaranteed markets
- Geopolitical control of parts of Africa and Asia for strategic reasons such as fueling stations
- Advanced weaponry that allowed the Europeans to easily conquer new areas in Africa and Asia
- The discovery that quinine could be used to prevent malaria
- New communication technologies such as the telegraph
- New transportation technologies such as the steam engine

Possible responses to part b) include:
- Increased tensions among the European powers, particularly the German rivalry with both France and Britain
- Non-European influences on European art movements, including Impressionism and Post-Impressionism
- Literary works were influenced by the new imperialism, including Joseph Conrad's *Heart of Darkness*
- Communists such as V.I. Lenin that believed imperialism was the highest stage of capitalism

Possible responses to part c) include:
- Social Darwinist theories justified European racial superiority.
- Missionaries felt it was their duty to convert the natives.
- The "White Man's Burden" aimed to spread European civilization to non-civilized areas of the world.

Question 3
(KC: 1.4.IV.B; LO: Unit 2 E)

Possible responses to part a) include:
- Patriarchy continued throughout the entire continent.
- In Catholic countries, women who did not have a large enough dowry or for other reasons did not get married had the option of joining the convent.
- Women's work often complemented their husbands' work, particularly in rural areas, where there were gender specific jobs.

Possible responses to part b) include:
- Due to social and economic upheavals, accusations of witchcraft increased during the later sixteenth century.
- Debates about women's societal roles increased.
- Protestant women achieved "spiritual equality" even though part of a patriarchal system.
- Protestant women increased their literacy rates.

Possible responses to part c) include:
- Renaissance humanists encouraged women's education.
- The Protestant Reformation led to the need for a semi-literate body of believers, thus increasing education for women.
- Many historians contend that the role of single woman declined in Protestant countries because they no longer had the option of joining the convent.

Question 4
(KC: 4.4.IV; LO: Unit 9 J, K)

Possible responses to part a) include:
- France and West Germany (Germany) were the two leaders of the movement.
- Although Britain ultimately joined the Common Market, it remained aloof to continental politics, even refusing to use the euro.
- Europe experienced a time of economic prosperity.

Possible responses to part b) include:
- The adoption of a single currency, the euro
- Membership of former Eastern Bloc nations in the European Union increased after the Cold War.
- Countries had to meet certain criteria to be a member of the European Union, such as the abolition of the death penalty.

Possible responses to part c) include:
- The Great Depression increased the need for some type of economic cooperation in order to avoid a similar catastrophe.
- After two world wars, the United States encouraged economic cooperation to avoid another major war.
- The Marshall Plan also encouraged recipient countries to work together, partly in response to the Cold War.
- The prosperity of member nations led nonmember nations to seek inclusion in the Common Market/European Union.
- Open borders by the late 1990s further united Western European countries.

SECTION II

PART A: DOCUMENT-BASED QUESTION

(KC: 2.1.I.C; LO: Unit 4 G)

Question 1. Evaluate whether the policies of the Enlightened Despots were designed primarily for reform or primarily for increased political power in the years between 1740 and 1815.

Part A Thesis (0–1 point): The thesis should briefly explain whether the policies of the Enlightened Despots were designed primarily for reform or for political power in the years between 1740 and 1815. BOTH reform and political power must be addressed to earn the point.

Acceptable Thesis: While the Enlightened Despots were influenced by Enlightenment ideas and sought reforms in society, their primary motive was to increase their political power in their countries and abroad.

Part B Contextualization (0–1 point): Students should give a broad overview of events prior to, during, and/or after the time of Enlightened Despotism. Acceptable responses should explain (not just mention) developments such as:
- The development of absolutism in the seventeenth and eighteenth centuries
- The influence of the Scientific Revolution and Enlightenment on European thought (e.g., natural law, religious toleration, equality before the law)
- The gradual realization in eastern Europe that serfdom was counterproductive to economic growth
- Many of the reforms of Joseph II not lasting beyond his death
- The long-term influence of Napoleon's reforms in France (and Germany)

The above list is not exhaustive.

Part C Evidence (0–3 points): Evidence from the documents (up to 2 points) and Evidence beyond the documents **(1 point):**

<u>Evidence from the documents</u>
1 point—Student correctly uses the content of at least THREE documents.

Acceptable:
- Frederick the Great seeks to reduce serfdom in lands over which he rules. (Doc. 1)
- Catherine the Great believed in just laws. (Doc. 2)
- Frederick the Great and Catherine the Great were eager to increase their territories. (Doc. 3)
- Joseph II extended rights for Jews in Austria. (Doc. 4)
- Joseph II believed that people in Austria should have freedom of religion. (Doc. 5)
- Kant seems to convey the idea that Frederick the Great is an absolute ruler. (Doc. 6)
- The image shows Napoleon as an absolute ruler. (Doc. 7)

OR

2 points—Student correctly uses the content of at least SIX documents to support an argument/thesis.

Acceptable:
- Frederick the Great sought to reduce serfdom in lands he ruled over, primarily because he was interested in improving the lives of the peasantry. (Doc. 1)
- Catherine the Great believed in laws that were just for all citizens, demonstrating that she was inspired by the Enlightenment's call for equality before the law. (Doc. 2)
- Both Frederick and Catherine betrayed their reform impulses by grabbing Polish territory, thus demonstrating that their primary goals were more political and reform-oriented. (Doc. 3)
- Joseph II extended rights for Jews in Austria and tried to improve their condition, thus demonstrating that he was interested in reforming Austrian society. (Doc. 4)
- While Joseph's mother, Maria Theresa did not believe in religious toleration, Joseph's Enlightenment influence drove him to provide religious toleration for his people. (Doc. 5)
- Although Frederick the Great cast himself as an enlightened despot, philosophers like Kant saw Frederick as an absolute ruler who was mostly preoccupied with political power. (Doc. 6)
- The image shows that Napoleon sees himself as a powerful emperor and is obsessed with political power. (Doc. 7)

Evidence beyond the documents

1 point—Student uses evidence not included in the document. Common examples could include the following but must be explained.

Acceptable:

- Frederick II invaded Silesia, violating the Pragmatic Sanction, and plunging Prussia into destructive wars.
- Frederick II saw himself as the "first servant of the state."
- Frederick II promoted the establishment of schools and universities.
- Frederick II streamlined and codified overlapping laws, reduced censorship, and abolished the death penalty.
- Catherine II imported western culture into Russia.
- Catherine II restricted torture and provided a limited degree of religious toleration.
- Catherine II needed the support of the nobility and could not institute sweeping reforms (e.g., ending serfdom).
- Joseph II allowed a degree of freedom of the press, reformed the judicial system, and abolished torture.
- Joseph II established hospitals, insane asylums, poorhouses, and orphanages.
- Napoleon established the Code Napoleon, the *lycée* system, religious toleration, and economic reforms.
- Napoleon during the last half of his reign became more obsessed with the conquest of Europe than reforming France.

Part D Analysis and Reasoning (0–2 points):

1 point—Sourcing: Student explains the relevance of the document's audience, purpose, point of view, or historical situation in relation to the argument.

Acceptable example of audience:
The intended audience of the Edict of Tolerance was most likely community leaders and business people who would be responsible for overseeing the reforms aimed at bringing Jews into the mainstream. (Doc. 4)

Acceptable example of purpose:
The purpose of Ingres's painting was to glorify Napoleon as a powerful emperor as it utilizes imagery from the Roman Empire. (Doc. 7)

Acceptable example of point of view:
It is not surprising that Emmanuel Kant would champion freedom as he is an Enlightenment philosopher who believed in natural rights. (Doc. 6)

Acceptable example of historical situation:
In the letter, Joseph II justifies his views of granting religious toleration to his subjects. Joseph II was inspired by the granting of religious toleration to various degrees in Russia under Catherine the Great and Prussia under Frederick the Great prior to Joseph assuming the throne in Austria. (Doc. 5)

1 point—Complexity: Student demonstrates a complex understanding of both the prompt and the documents. Examples demonstrating complexity might include:

- Explaining a nuance by exploring various actions enlightened despots took to reform their countries and advance their political interests
- Explaining connections to other time periods such as the absolutism of Louis XIV and Peter the Great in the late-seventeenth and early-eighteenth centuries
- Explaining both reform and political motivations that drove Enlightenment despots to establish their policies
- Qualifying or modifying an argument by considering diverse or alternative views or evidence, such as economic issues

SECTION II

PART B: LONG-ESSAY QUESTIONS

Question 1: Evaluate the extent to which Protestant views of government in Europe differed from Catholic views of government in Europe in the period 1500 to 1648.
(KC: 1.2.II, 1.2.III, 1.5.I; LO: Unit 2 A, B, C)

Differences might include:
- National churches in Lutheran countries were often subordinate to political authorities or at least worked together.
- Many Calvinist groups used religious conflict to justify revolts against monarchical rule.
- Calvinists and Anabaptists refused to be subordinate to the state.
- Anabaptists refused to take an oath to the state and to serve in the military.

Similarities might include:
- Both Protestants and Catholics believed the Church to be superior to the state.
- Both Protestants and Catholics needed support from princes and kings.
- The French and Spanish monarchies had great influence over the Catholic Church in their countries similar to Protestant princes and leaders.
- Both Protestants and Catholics exploited religious conflict.

Question 2: Evaluate the extent to which absolute monarchies in western Europe differed in their views of government with absolute monarchies in eastern Europe in the period 1648 to 1750.
(KC: 2.1.I, 2.1.III; LO: Unit 3 A, E, G)

Differences might include:
- Western European absolute monarchies often gave the nobles social prestige in return for their support exemplified by noble obligations at Versailles.
- Eastern European absolute monarchies often gave the nobility some type of standing to the state; for example, Prussian nobility were officers, and Peter the Great created the Table of Ranks.
- Western European absolute monarchies gave a nod toward some form of representation such as the French Estates-General (which did not meet during this time period) whereas eastern European absolute monarchies, such as Peter the Great in Russia, made no such nod.
- Louis XIV and French monarchs considered themselves to be the state (*L'Etat, c'est moi*—I am the state) whereas Frederick the Great considered himself to be First Servant of the State).

Similarities might include:
- Although different methods, both western and eastern absolute monarchies subdued the nobility in return for greater power over the state.
- Both western and eastern absolute monarchies believed in some type of "divine right theory" regarding rule.
- Both western and eastern absolute monarchies tended to dominate religion, such as Louis XIV's control of the French Catholic Church and Peter the Great's Holy Synod.
- Both western and eastern absolute monarchies invited scientists to their countries in order to increase their own prestige.

Question 3: Evaluate the extent to which fascist dictatorships in Europe differed in their views of government with communist dictatorships in Europe in the period 1919 to 1989.
(KC: 4.2.I, 4.2.II, 4.2.V; LO: Unit 8 E, H, I, Unit 9 D)

Differences might include:
- Very ideological—fascist governments believed in extreme nationalism whereas communists believed in internationalism.
- Fascist governments worked more closely with big business such as the corporate state in Italy, whereas communist governments nationalized corporations.
- Fascist governments tended to use religious affiliation to their advantage (e.g., the Lateran Treaty), whereas communist governments often tried to abolish organized religion.

Similarities might include:
- Both used a secret police to maintain order (Gestapo in Nazi Germany and the Cheka/KGB in the Soviet Union).
- Both emphasized a cult of personality (Hitler and Stalin).
- Both used propaganda effectively.
- Both used totalitarian methods and controlled the media.
- Both banned works that criticized the state.
- Both used parades to inspire nationalism (despite the fact that communists were avowed anti-nationalists).
- Both created youth groups to better serve the needs of the state.
- Both had an extensive prison system for "enemies of the state."

SAMPLE PRACTICE TEST 2

SECTION I

PART A: MULTIPLE-CHOICE QUESTIONS

Questions 1–4 refer to the passage below.

JULIUS:
What's the trouble here? Won't the gates open? I believe the lock has been changed.
GENIUS:
Better check to see if you've brought the right key. The one for the treasury won't open this door, you know. Why didn't you bring both keys? This is the key of power, not of knowledge.
JULIUS:
Why, this is the only one I've ever used! I've never seen what good the other one was.
GENIUS:
Meanwhile we're locked out.
JULIUS:
I'm losing my temper. I'm going to beat on the gate. Hey there! Somebody open this door instantly! What's holding up the doorman? Asleep, I suppose, probably drunk.
GENIUS:
(Aside) This fellow judges everyone by himself.

Desiderius Erasmus, Dialogue: *Julius Locked Out of Heaven* (1514)

Source: Desiderius Erasmus, The Praise of Folly and Other Writings, trans. Robert M. Adams (New York and London: Norton Critical Edition, 1989), pp. 142–73.

1. Which of the following most likely reflects the purpose of this passage?
   (A) Religious reform
   (B) State building
   (C) Civic humanism
   (D) Absolutism

2. The author's point of view in the passage reflects which of the following?
   (A) Civic humanism
   (B) Christian humanism
   (C) Scholasticism
   (D) Secularism

3. The influence of the passage above led most directly to which of the following?
   (A) The Catholic Reformation
   (B) Development of National Monarchies
   (C) The Protestant Reformation
   (D) The Thirty Years' War

4. Which of the following would be most likely to *disagree* with the views represented in the document?
   (A) Protestant reformers
   (B) Protestant monarchs
   (C) Anabaptists
   (D) Habsburg rulers

Questions 5–8 refer to the passage below.

"…Bruges [in Flanders] was the principal exchange mart for…trading activity. Then the [Flemish] inhabitants of Antwerp took advantage of their port, facilities and attracted trade there. After the wars between the Spanish and the Dutch, the self-discipline, the moderation and the zeal of the Dutch attracted world trade to Amsterdam and to the other cities of Holland. But they were not satisfied with being the central exchange mart for all Europe and especially for the North. They decided to gain control of foreign trade at its very source. To this end they ruined the Portuguese in the East Indies. They inhibited or disturbed…the business ventures which the English had established there. They employed and are still employing every means, are exerting every effort, are applying their full resources to assume full control of world trade and to keep it out of the hands of all other nations."

Jean-Baptiste Colbert, French Finance Minister, *Dissertation on Alliances*, 1669

Source: Wallace E. Adams, Richard B. Barlow, Gerald R. Kleinfeld, Ronald D. Smith, William W. Wootton, eds., *The Western World, vol. 1,* (New York: Dodd, Mead and Company, 1969), pp. 545–550.

5. The passage highlights which of the following features of early modern European history?
   (A) Market economy
   (B) Capitalism
   (C) Mercantilism
   (D) Nationalism

6. Colbert oversaw France's economy under which of the following rulers?
   (A) Francis I
   (B) Henry IV
   (C) Napoleon
   (D) Louis XIV

7. Which of the following developments can be directly linked to the ideas expressed in the passage?
   (A) State interests influenced the diplomacy of European states and frequently led to war.
   (B) The Netherlands became the dominant military power in Europe between 1600 and 1800.
   (C) France adopted increased trade relations with the Netherlands in order to avoid war and boost its economy.
   (D) Religious conflict increasingly dominated European diplomacy after 1648.

8. Which of the following was a practice common to many European states at that time, which is NOT explicitly mentioned in the passage?
   (A) Discoveries of large deposits of gold in their respective colonies
   (B) Trade in and use of African slaves
   (C) The development of power-driven ships and machines
   (D) A decline in the volume of commerce between Europe and Asia

Questions 9–12 refer to the passage below.

"In my preceding pamphlet I had no occasion to condemn the peasants, because they promised to yield to law and better instruction, as Christ also demands. But before I can turn around, they go out and appeal to force, in spite of their promises, and rob and pillage and act like mad dogs… They practice mere devil's work, and it is the arch-devil himself who reigns at Mühlhausen, Thomas Münzer, indulging in nothing but robbery, murder, and bloodshed. Since those peasants allow themselves to be led astray and act differently from what they declared, I likewise must write differently concerning them; and first bring their sins before their eyes, as God commands."

Martin Luther, *Against the Murderous, Thieving Hordes of Peasants* (1525)

Source: James Harvey Robinson, *Readings in European History,* 2 vols (Boston: Ginn & Company, 1906), 2:106–108.

9. The passage above represents a conflict over which of the following?
   (A) The purpose of the Protestant Reformation
   (B) The purpose of the Renaissance
   (C) The purpose of the Catholic Reformation
   (D) The purpose of absolutism in government

10. Which Protestant leader might well have disagreed with Luther on the main issue in the passage?
   (A) Henry VIII
   (B) John Calvin
   (C) Henry IV
   (D) Elizabeth I

11. All of the following occurred as a result of groups such as the nobility challenging monarchial authority based on religious reform EXCEPT
   (A) the Thirty Years' War
   (B) the Edict of Nantes
   (C) the French Wars of Religion
   (D) the English Reformation

12. Which of the following developments most likely explains the reason for the conflict that led to the production of the above document?
   (A) The refusal of peasants to accept Protestant teachings
   (B) The belief that the Catholic Church was above all secular institutions
   (C) New interpretations of Christian doctrine and practice
   (D) The use of Jesuit teachings

Questions 13–15 refer to the passage below.

"That the various forms of epidemic, endemic, and other disease caused, or aggravated, or propagated chiefly amongst the labouring classes by atmospheric impurities produced by decomposing animal and vegetable substances, by damp and filth, and close and overcrowded dwellings prevail amongst the population in every part of the kingdom, whether dwelling in separate houses, in rural villages, in small towns, in the larger towns— as they have been found to prevail in the lowest districts of the metropolis.

That such disease, wherever its attacks are frequent, is always found in connexion with the physical circumstances above specified, and that where those circumstances are removed by drainage, proper cleansing, better ventilation, and other means of diminishing atmospheric impurity, the frequency and intensity of such disease is abated; and where the removal of the noxious agencies appears to be complete, such disease almost entirely disappears.

Contaminated London drinking water containing various micro-organisms, refuse, and the like…

That the annual loss of life from filth and bad ventilation are greater than the loss from death or wounds in any wars in which the country has been engaged in modern times."

> Edwin Chadwick, Report...from the *Poor Law Commissioners on an Inquiry into the Sanitary Conditions of the Labouring Population of Great Britain*

Source: *Poor Law Commissioners on an Inquiry into the Sanitary Conditions of the Labouring Population of Great Britain* (London, 1842), pp. 369–372.

13. The views in the passage reflect which of the following trends in nineteenth-century England?
    (A) Liberalism shifted from laissez-faire to interventionist economic and social policies in response to the challenges of industrialization.
    (B) The mortality rate among Europe's population increased in the nineteenth century compared to the previous century.
    (C) The dominance of conservatism throughout the nineteenth century impeded much-needed reforms in dealing with living and social conditions.
    (D) The standard of living for the average European continued to decline throughout the century as cities became more overcrowded.

14. The main ideas of the passage along with other similar views in society resulted in which of the following?
    (A) The persistence of social tensions and urban violence in countries that failed to industrialize
    (B) The development of modern infrastructure in many European cities
    (C) The dominance of utopian socialism in the late-nineteenth century
    (D) The virtual disappearance of poverty and crime in England by 1900

15. The conditions cited in the passage were most likely a result of which of the following?
    (A) Political upheavals such as the French Revolution and nationalist revolutions in 1830
    (B) Increasingly bloody conflicts such as the Napoleonic Wars
    (C) Demographic changes due to the Industrial Revolution
    (D) Slow and uneven improvements in literacy throughout western Europe

Questions 16–19 refer to the passage below.

"…And they, or the greater Part of them, shall take order from Time to Time, by, and with the Consent of two or more such Justices of Peace as is aforesaid, for setting to work the Children of all such whose Parents shall not by the said Churchwardens and Overseers, or the greater Part of them, be thought able to keep and maintain their Children: And also for setting to work all such Persons, married or unmarried, having no Means to maintain them, and use no ordinary and daily Trade of Life to get their Living by: And also to raise weekly or otherwise (by Taxation of every Inhabitant, Parson, Vicar and other, and of every Occupier of Lands, Houses, Tithes impropriate, Propriations of Tithes, Coal-Mines, or saleable Underwoods in the said Parish, in such competent Sum and Sums of Money as they shall think fit) a convenient Stock of Flax, Hemp, Wool, Thread, Iron, and other necessary Ware and Stuff, to set the Poor on Work: And also competent Sums of Money for and towards the necessary Relief of the Lame, Impotent, Old, Blind, and such other among them being Poor, and not able to work, and also for putting out of such Children to be apprentices…"

An Act for the Releife of the Poor, 1601
Source: http://www.workhouses.org.uk/poorlaws/1601act.shtml

16. The passage above, when applied to the late-sixteenth and early-seventeenth centuries, represents a continued reflection of the definition of social power belonging to
    (A) those who had hierarchy and status
    (B) the Catholic Church
    (C) the monarchy
    (D) the feudal nobility

17. Based on the passage above and your knowledge, which of the following groups would have been most likely to have been directly affected by laws such as these?
    (A) Small merchants
    (B) Tradesmen in guilds
    (C) Landless farmers
    (D) Clergymen

18. In which of the following areas would institutions such as this be the *least* likely to be found?
    (A) England
    (B) France
    (C) The Netherlands
    (D) Russia

19. Based on the document and your knowledge, which of the following events most likely led to the need for laws such as these?
    (A) Protestant Reformation
    (B) Price Revolution
    (C) Scientific Revolution
    (D) French Revolution

Questions 20–22 refer to the image below.

Illustration in Peter Apian, *Cosmographia*, Antwerp, 1524

The text around the outside reads 'Empyrean Heaven, Home to God and All Chosen People.'

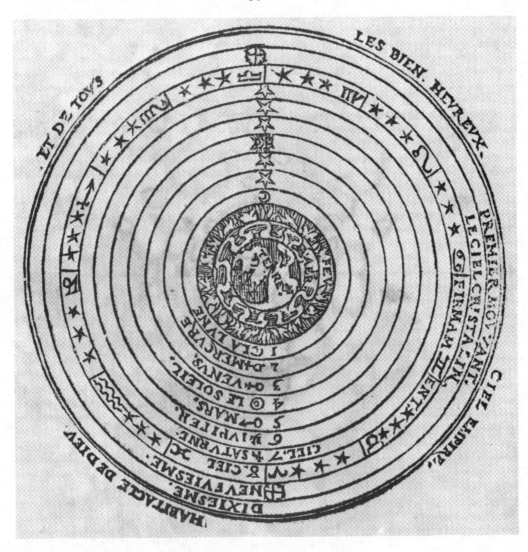

Source: Pictorial Press Ltd/Alamy Stock Photo

20. Which of the following conclusions best reflects the image?
   (A) The author supports the heliocentric theory.
   (B) The author represents traditional knowledge of the cosmos.
   (C) The author benefits from modern scientific instruments.
   (D) The author sees science and theology as completely separate branches of knowledge.

21. Which of the following would most likely have supported the views expressed in the illustration?
    (A) Ptolemy
    (B) Copernicus
    (C) Galileo
    (D) Newton

22. The underlying views of the image are most similar to which of the following?
    (A) Paracelsus
    (B) Vesalius
    (C) Harvey
    (D) Galen

Questions 23–26 refer to the image below.

Jacques-Louis David, **The Oath of the Horatii,** *1784–85*

Source: RMN-Grand Palais/Art Resource, NY

23. The image reflects which of the following artistic styles?
    (A) Baroque
    (B) Northern Renaissance
    (C) Rococo
    (D) Neoclassical

24. Which of the following most likely influenced the creation of the image?
    (A) Christian humanism
    (B) The Catholic Reformation
    (C) The Enlightenment
    (D) Mannerism

25. The ideals expressed in the image influenced which of the following?
    (A) The French Revolution
    (B) The English Civil War
    (C) The rise of absolutism
    (D) The Pugachev Rebellion

26. Which of the following represented a reaction against the philosophy underlying the image?
    (A) Capitalism
    (B) Classical liberalism
    (C) Romanticism
    (D) Impressionism

Questions 27–29 refer to the passage below.

"Immediately after the publication of the present decree, all suspect persons who are in the territory of the Republic and who are still at liberty shall be placed under arrest.

The following are considered suspect persons: first, those who by their conduct, their connections, their remarks, or their writings show themselves the partisans of tyranny or federalism and the enemies of liberty; second, those who cannot…justify their means of existence and the performance of their civic duties; third, those who have been refused certificates of good citizenship; fourth, public functionaries suspended or removed from their functions by the National Convention or its commissioners and not reinstated…; fifth, those of the former nobles, all of the husbands, wives, fathers, mothers, sons or daughters, brothers or sisters, and agents of the émigrés who have not constantly manifested their attachment to the Revolution; sixth, those who have emigrated from France…although they may have returned to France within the period fixed by that decree or earlier.

The committees of surveillance established according to the decree of March 21 last, or those which have been substituted for them, either by the orders of the representatives of the people sent with the armies and into the departments, or in virtue of special decrees of the National Convention, are charged to prepare, each in its district, the list of suspect persons, to issue warrants of arrest against them, and to have seals put upon their papers..."

The French National Convention, *The Law of Suspects*, September 17, 1793

Source: Jean-Baptiste Duvergier, *Collection complète des lois, décrets, ordonnances, règlements, avis du conseil d'état… de 1788 a 1830…*, 2d ed., 110 vols. (Paris, 1834–1906), 6:172–73.

27. Which of the following conclusions best reflects the content of the passage?
    (A) Revolutionary leaders supported a constitutional monarchy.
    (B) Revolutionary leaders had earlier abolished hereditary privileges.
    (C) Revolutionary leaders had earlier removed the influence of the sans culottes.
    (D) Revolutionary leaders sought to remove the influence of the bourgeoisie.

28. Which of the following individuals oversaw the policies in the passage?
    (A) Edmund Burke
    (B) Jean-Jacques Rousseau
    (C) Jacques Necker
    (D) Maximilien Robespierre

29. Those responsible for the ideas expressed in the passage later oversaw which of the following?
    (A) France's declaration of war against Austria and Prussia
    (B) The Tennis Court Oath
    (C) The introduction of the Code Napoleon
    (D) The institution of a de-Christianization campaign

"Jansenism made considerable progress among prominent families in Paris. They were opposed to the Jesuits and supported religious communities such as the convent in Port-Royal outside Paris. Jansenists, whose Augustinian theology resembled Calvinism, were known to live extremely pious and morally austere lives. In these respects, though firm Roman Catholics, they resembled English Puritans."

Donald Kagan, *The Western Heritage 12th edition* (Boston: Pearson Education, 2020) p. 352.

30. Which of the following is the most likely explanation for the appeal of Jansenism?
    (A) Louis XIV's revocation of the Edict of Nantes reassured Jansenists that they could worship without persecution.
    (B) Jansenists' faith aligned with traditional "Gallican Liberties" from papal authority now combined with a resistance to royal authority.
    (C) Jansenism supported the concept of "free will" and thus attracted followers from all religious denominations.
    (D) Louis XIV was known to be a secret Jansenist and although officially Catholic, he demonstrated considerable toleration for religious minorities.

31. In what way did movements like Jansenism offer challenges to the notion of "Divine Right of Kings"?
    (A) In war, such groups frequently offered aid and comfort to enemy forces.
    (B) Religious conformity was considered essential to political unity and stability.
    (C) Such movements often appealed to popular masses and thus threatened the existence of the state.
    (D) Kings were dependent on papal authority for their status, and thus monarchs like Louis XIV had little independence on religious matters.

32. What development later in French history offers validation for Louis XIV's views on absolutism?
    (A) It was religious minorities that provided the main stimulus for the French Revolution.
    (B) Persecution of minorities cost millions of francs and was a primary cause of later financial crises.
    (C) French wars pursued religious goals more commonly than geopolitical goals, thus contributing to the draining of state finances.
    (D) Nobles sought to entrench themselves in institutions like the *parlements* to shield them from royal power.

33. What other historical development had its origins in an issue similar to the one described in the passage?
    (A) The Decembrist Revolt in Russia
    (B) The various "partitions" of Poland
    (C) The Pragmatic Sanction of 1740
    (D) The English Civil War

Questions 34–37 refer to the image below.

1836 wood engraving created by George S. White

Source: White, G. S. (1967), Library of Congress Prints and Photographs Division [LC-USZ62-110375]

34. Which group of women typically composed the workforce depicted in the image above?
   (A) Middle-class married women
   (B) Rural peasants
   (C) Young, single women and widows
   (D) Middle-class unmarried women

35. What type of factory work did the women in the image above do?
   (A) Munitions production
   (B) Train engine construction
   (C) Manufactured steam engine parts
   (D) Textile production

36. The image best represents which of the following phases of technological development?
    (A) Proto-industrialization
    (B) The First Industrial Revolution
    (C) The Second Industrial Revolution
    (D) Introduction of the assembly line

37. Which of the following was an underlying cause for the economic activity seen in the image?
    (A) Capitalism
    (B) Socialism
    (C) Mercantilism
    (D) Corporate-syndicalism

Questions 38–41 refer to the passage below.

"…The Reform Act has effected a transfer of power from one domineering faction to another, and left the people as helpless as before…

Required as we are, universally, to support and obey the laws, nature and reason entitle us to demand, that in the making of the laws, the universal voice shall be implicitly listened to. We perform the duties of freemen; we must have the privileges of free men.

WE DEMAND UNIVERSAL SUFFRAGE

The suffrage to be exempt from the corruption of the wealthy, and the violence of the powerful, must be secret…

WE DEMAND THE BALLOT

The connection between the representatives and the people, to be beneficial must be intimate…To public safety as well as public confidence, frequent elections are essential…

WE DEMAND ANNUAL PARLIAMENTS

With power to choose, and freedom in choosing, the range of our choice must be unrestricted.

We are compelled by the existing laws, to take for our representatives, men who are incapable of appreciating our difficulties, or who have little sympathy with them; merchants who have retired from trade, and no longer feel its harassings; proprietors of land who are alike ignorant of its evils and their cure; lawyers, by whom the honours of the senate are sought after only as means of attaining notice in the courts…"

The People's Petition of 1838, issued by members of the Chartist movement,

Source: *The Life and Struggles of William Lovett* (New York: Knopf), 1920, pp. 478–481.

38. Within the context of the time period in which the passage was written, the point of view would have been considered
    (A) anarchist
    (B) liberal
    (C) radical
    (D) utopian

39. Which of the following groups does the passage most likely criticize?
    (A) The proletariat
    (B) The middle class
    (C) Monarchists
    (D) The peasantry

40. The views expressed in the passage are most similar to the views of which of the following in the mid-nineteenth century?
    (A) Socialists
    (B) Classical liberals
    (C) Nationalists
    (D) Mercantilists

41. Which of the following conclusions can be drawn based on the passage?
    (A) The ideals of the French Revolution inspired reformers to demand a republic in England.
    (B) The horrors of the Napoleonic Wars inspired conservatives to provide reforms for the lower classes.
    (C) The development of Marxism inspired several revolutions in England prior to 1850.
    (D) The influence of the bourgeoisie on society politically and economically was disproportionately high.

Questions 42–43 refer to the passage below.

"By the Grace of God WE, Alexander II, Emperor and Autocrat of All Russia, King of Poland, Grand Duke of Finland, etc., make known to all OUR faithful subjects:

…Examining the condition of classes and professions comprising the state, WE became convinced that the present state legislation favors the upper and middle classes, defines their obligations, rights, and privileges, but does not equally favor the serfs, so designated because in part from old laws and in part from custom they have been hereditarily subjected to the authority of landowners, who in turn were obligated to provide for their well being. Rights of nobles have been hitherto very broad and legally ill defined, because they stem from tradition, custom, and the good will of the noblemen. In most cases this has led to the establishment of good patriarchal relations based on the sincere, just concern and benevolence on the part of the nobles, and on affectionate submission on the part of the peasants. Because of the decline of the simplicity of morals, because of an increase in the diversity of relations, because of the weakening of the direct paternal relationship of nobles toward the peasants, and because noble rights fell sometimes into the hands of people exclusively concerned with their personal interests, good relations weakened. The way was opened for an arbitrariness burdensome for the peasants and detrimental to their welfare, causing them to be indifferent to the improvement of their own existence."

Tsar Alexander II, Emancipation Edict, 1861

Source: Nikolaevitch, Alexander II. "The Russian Emperor's Serf-Emancipation Manifesto." The Spectator, March 30, 1861, p. 6. http://archive.spectator.co.uk/article/30th-march-1861/6/the-russian-emperors-serf-emancipation-manifesto

42. Which of the following most likely occurred as a result of the passage?
    (A) Russia became more autocratic under the rule of Alexander II.
    (B) Reform and modernization emerged as important impulses in Russian society.
    (C) Former serfs received equality with other classes in Russian society by the eve of World War I.
    (D) Jews enjoyed more inclusion in Russian society as class distinctions slowly disappeared.

43. Which of the following was likely a cause of the author's motivations in the passage?
    (A) Russia's victory in the Crimean War inspired the tsar to reward serfs who had served as soldiers.
    (B) Russia's large middle class pressured the tsar to end feudal obligations of the peasantry.
    (C) Russia lagged behind Western European nations in its economic and industrial development.
    (D) Communist influences reached a critical level in Russia by the early 1860s.

Questions 44–47 refer to the passage below.

"Comrades, the workmen's and peasant's revolution, the need of which the Bolsheviks have emphasized many times, has come to pass. What is the significance of this revolution? Its significance is, in the first place, that we shall have a soviet government, without the participation of the bourgeoisie of any kind. The oppressed masses will of themselves form a government. The old state machinery will be smashed into bits and in its place will be created a new machinery of government by the soviet organizations. From now on, there is a new page in the history of Russia, and the present, third Russian revolution shall in its final result lead to the victory of Socialism… We shall secure the confidence of the peasants by one decree, which will wipe out the private property of the landowners. The peasants will understand that their only salvation is in union with the workers. We will establish a real labor control on production… We should now occupy ourselves in Russia in building up a proletarian socialist state. Long live the world-wide socialistic revolution!"

Vladimir Lenin, Speech after the Overthrow of the Provisional Government, 1917

Source: Aronsberg, Emanuel, trans. Frank A. Golder, ed., "Speech after the Overthrow of the Provisional Government," in *Documents of Russian History (1914–1917)* (New York: The Century Company, 1927), pp. 618–619.

44. Which of the following was most likely a cause for the contents of the passage?
    (A) The failure of the Revolution of 1905
    (B) The success of the Duma in achieving its objectives
    (C) The strains brought on by the First World War
    (D) The failure of Russia to industrialize sufficiently

45. The ideas in the passage are largely based on the ideas of which of the following?
    (A) Sigmund Freud
    (B) Friedrich Nietzsche
    (C) Georges Sorel
    (D) Karl Marx

46. Which of the following resulted from the development described in the passage?
    (A) Russia's eventual victory in the First World War
    (B) A civil war between communists and non-communist factions
    (C) The overthrow of Lenin by Joseph Stalin
    (D) The temporary expansion of the Ottoman Empire

47. In the 1920s, Lenin was forced to modify his views in the passage through the institution of which of the following?
    (A) The New Economic Policy
    (B) The Five-Year Plans
    (C) The collectivization of agriculture
    (D) Purges of "Old Bolsheviks"

Questions 48–51 refer to the passage below.

"If [they] were alone in this world, they would stifle in filth…they would try to get ahead of one another in hate-filled struggle and exterminate one another…So it is absolutely wrong to infer any ideal sense of sacrifice in [them] from the fact that they stand together in struggle, or, better expressed, in the plundering of their fellow men…Not through him does any progress of mankind occur, but in spite of him."

Adolf Hitler, *Mein Kampf*, 1923

Source: Adolf Hitler, *Mein Kampf*, English translation Houghton Mifflin Company (Boston, 1939).

48. The content of the passages convey which of the following?
    (A) Support for the Weimar Republic
    (B) Support for the Schlieffen Plan
    (C) Support for anti-Semitism
    (D) Support for *blitzkrieg* strategies

49. The purpose of the passages is most likely to justify the
    (A) institution of *lebensraum*
    (B) actions that occurred during "the Night of Long Knives"
    (C) Nazi-Soviet Non-Aggression Pact
    (D) creation of a new racial order

50. The ideas expressed in the passages resulted in which of the following?
    (A) The German invasion of Poland
    (B) The Holocaust
    (C) Nazi support for the Spanish Civil War
    (D) Creation of the Atlantic Charter

51. The views expressed in the passages are most similar to those of which of the following?
    (A) Ethnic cleansing in former Yugoslavia in the 1990s
    (B) Persecution of "guest workers" in post-war Western Europe
    (C) Terrorist activity in France in the early twenty-first century
    (D) European support for the Iraq War in 2003

Questions 52–53 refer to the passage below.

"Just a few words about the most insane system of all, the arms system, which every day reveals its absurdity anew. We have no desire to be utopian, or idealistic or removed from reality, unlike the politicians who keep talking about *dis*armament, and hail it as a victory for *dis*armament when *re*armament falls by a tiny one percent. We are talking about a stop or a freeze, and are enormously encouraged in this by the United States. Let us start with an arms freeze, and then let us see whether we can really disarm. There is a lot to be said about other systems too—the money and banking system, for example. Not even the so-called experts can make head or tail of this billion-dollar merry-go-round. Just one more absurdity after another? How much more absurdity can our minds cope with before we all go to pieces? How much technical expertise and sheer genius is being wasted on new weapons systems, which are then of no more use than a superior and very costly toy. If put to use they spell death and destruction…"

Petra Kelly, cofounder of the Green Party in West Germany, *Fighting for Hope*, 1983

Source: Petra Kelly, *Fighting for Hope*. Copyright © Lamuv Verlag GmbH, Martinstrasse 7, 5303 Bornheim-Merten, and Petra Kelly, 1983; Translation copyright ©1984 by Maryanne Howarth.

52 The views in the passage would most likely support
   (A) sustainable development
   (B) rising consumerism
   (C) laissez-faire policies
   (D) an increase in democratic principles

53. The views in the passage can best be understood within the context of the
   (A) rise of Vladimir Putin
   (B) Cold War
   (C) fall of the Soviet Union
   (D) *détente*

Questions 54–55 refer to the image below.

Photo of Berlin, 1989

Source: Régis BOSSU/Sygma/Getty Images

54. The image reflects which of the following trends?
    (A) The success of Solidarity in bringing about reform in Germany
    (B) Youth revolts that demanded an end to imperialism in Asia
    (C) Public reaction to the installation of nuclear missiles in NATO countries
    (D) The end of Soviet hegemony in Eastern Europe

55. Which of the following was most likely a cause of the event portrayed in the image?
    (A) The failure of Khrushchev's de-Stalinization campaign
    (B) The institution of the Brezhnev Doctrine
    (C) The failure of Gorbachev's *perestroika* policies
    (D) The creation of the European Union

489

SECTION I

PART B: SHORT-ANSWER QUESTIONS

Read the passage below and answer all parts of the question that follows.

"The term 'cold war' first came into currency in 1947. It was used to denote a sharp and unexpected deterioration in postwar relations between the Soviet Union and the United States. In 1945, the USA and the USSR—the two main victors of the Second World War—had proclaimed their commitment to postwar unity and co-operation. But by the end of 1947 this public harmony had been replaced by mutual recrimination about who was to blame for the postwar breakup of the allied coalition that had defeated Hitler. Each side blamed the other for generating the political, ideological, and military rivalry that divided Europe into competing blocs and spawned a dangerous global power struggle between communism and liberal democratic capitalism."

Geoffrey Roberts, British historian, 2009

Source: "Starting the Cold War," by Geoffrey Roberts. History Review, December 2000. Used by permission of the publisher, History Today. https://www.historytoday.com/geoffrey-roberts/starting-cold-war

Answer a, b, and c:
1. a) Describe one development during the 1940s that influenced the situation described in the passage.
    b) Explain one effect of the situation described in the passage on Western European nations prior to 1955.
    c) Explain one effect of the situation described in the passage on Central and Eastern European nations prior to 1955.

Read the passage below and answer all parts of the question that follows.

"A cruelty consecrated by the practice of most nations is torture of the accused during his trial, either to make him confess his crime or to clear up contradictory statements, or to discover accomplices, or to purge him of infamy in some metaphysical and incomprehensible way, or, finally, to discover other crimes, of which he might be guilty but is not accused.

No man can be called guilty before a judge has sentenced him, nor can society deprive him of public protection before it has been decided that he has in fact violated the conditions under which such protection was accorded him. What right is it, then, if not simply that of might, which empowers a judge to inflict punishment on a citizen while doubt still remains as to his guilt or innocence? Here is the dilemma, which is nothing new: the fact of the crime is either certain or uncertain; if certain, all that is due is the punishment established by laws, and tortures are useless because the criminal's confession is useless; if uncertain, then one must not torture the innocent, for such, according to the laws, is a man whose crimes are not yet proved."

Cesare Beccaria, On Crimes and Punishments, 1764

Source: Ingraham, E. D., trans. Cesare Beccaria. "The Greatest Happiness of the Greatest Number," *An Essay on Crimes and Punishments* (Philadelphia: H. Nicklin, 1819), pp. xii, 18–19, 47, 59–60, 93–94, 104–105, 148–149.

Answer a, b, and c:
2. a) Describe one factor that led to ideas such as those expressed in the passage.
   b) Describe one way in which ideas such as those expressed in the passage were disseminated during the eighteenth century.
   c) Explain one effect of ideas such as those expressed in the passage during the eighteenth century.

Directions: Answer **either** Question 3 **or** Question 4.

Answer a, b, and c:

3. a) Describe one significant <u>change</u> in the doctrine or practices of the Catholic Church from the beginning of the Reformation to the end of the Thirty Years' War.
    b) Describe one significant <u>continuity</u> in the doctrine or practices of the Catholic Church from the beginning of the Reformation to the end of the Thirty Years' War.
    c) Explain one significant effect of the Protestant Reformation on politics during the period 1517–1648.

Answer a, b, and c:

4. a) Describe one significant <u>change</u> in women's status in Europe during the twentieth century.
    b) Describe one significant <u>continuity</u> in women's status in Europe during the twentieth century.
    c) Explain how one political development affected women's status in Europe during the twentieth century.

SECTION II

PART A: DOCUMENT-BASED QUESTION

Question 1. Evaluate the extent to which nationalism led to the First World War.

Document 1

Source: Treaty Between Great Britain, Austria-Hungary, France, Germany, Italy, Russia and Turkey. (Berlin). July 13, 1878.

Article I. Bulgaria is constituted an autonomous and tributary Principality under the suzerainty of His Imperial Majesty the Sultan. It will have a Christian government and a national militia.

Article XXV. The provinces of Bosnia and Herzegovina shall be occupied and administered by Austria-Hungary. The government of Austria-Hungary, not desiring to undertake the administration of the Sanjak of Novi-Pazar [modern Kosovo Province], which extends between Serbia and Montenegro in a South-Easterly direction to the other side of Mitrovitza, the Ottoman administration will continue to exercise its functions there. Nevertheless, in order to assure the maintenance of the new political state of affairs, as well as freedom and security of communications, Austria-Hungary reserves the right of keeping garrisons and having military and commercial roads in the whole of this part of the ancient vilayet of Bosnia. To this end the governments of Austria-Hungary and Turkey reserve to themselves to come to an understanding on the details.

Article XXXIV. The High Contracting Parties recognize the independence of the Principality of Serbia, subject to the conditions set forth in the following Article.

Article XXXV. In Serbia the difference of religious creeds and confessions shall not be alleged against any person as a ground for exclusion or incapacity in matters relating to the enjoyment of civil or political rights, admission to public employments, functions, and honors, or the exercise of the various professions and industries, in any locality whatsoever. The freedom and outward exercise of all forms of worship shall be assured to all persons belonging to Serbia, as well as to foreigners, and no hindrance shall be offered either to the hierarchical organization of the different communions, or to their relations with their spiritual chiefs.

Source: R. B. Mowat, *Select Treaties and Documents to Illustrate the Development of the Modern European States-System*, (Oxford: Oxford University Press, 1915), pp. 79–83.

Document 2

Source: Heinrich von Treitschke, German politician and historian, *The Greatness of War,* from *Politics*, 1899–1900

Even as it is impossible to conceive of a tribunal above the State, which we have recognized as sovereign in its very essence, so it is likewise impossible to banish the idea of war from the world. It is a favourite fashion of our time to instance England as particularly ready for peace. But England is perpetually at war; there is hardly an instant in her recent history in which she has not been obliged to be fighting somewhere. The great strides which civilization makes against barbarism and unreason are only made actual by the sword. Between civilized nations also war is the form of litigation by which States make their claims valid. The arguments brought forward in these terrible law suits of the nations compel as no argument in civil suits can ever do. Often as we have tried by theory to convince the small States that Prussia alone can be the leader in Germany, we had to produce the final proof upon the battlefields of Bohemia and the Main.

Source: Heinrich von Treitschke, *Politics*, (Macmillan, New York, 1916), pp. 65–66. Trans. Blanche Dugdale

Document 3

Source: John Hobson, British social reformer, *Imperialism*, 1902.

…The decades of Imperialism have been prolific in wars; most of these wars have been directly motivated by aggression of white races upon "lower races," and have issued in the forcible seizure of territory. Every one of the steps of expansion in Africa, Asia, and the Pacific has been accompanied by bloodshed; each imperialist Power keeps an increasing army available for foreign service; rectification of frontiers, punitive expeditions, and other euphemisms for war are in incessant progress…Although the great imperialist Powers have kept their hands off one another…the self-restraint has been costly and precarious. Peace as a national policy is antagonized not merely by war, but by militarism, an even graver injury. Apart from the enmity of France and Germany, the main cause of the vast armaments which are draining the resources of most European countries is their conflicting interests in territorial and commercial expansion. Where thirty years ago there existed one sensitive spot in our relations with France, or Germany, or Russia, there are a dozen now; diplomatic strains are of almost monthly occurrence between powers with African or Chinese interests…

…It is not to the interest of the British people, either as producers of wealth or as tax-payers, to risk a war with Russia and France in order to join Japan in preventing Russia from seizing Korea; but it may serve the interests of a group of commercial politicians to promote this dangerous policy. The South African war [Boer War], openly fomented by gold speculators for their private purposes, will rank in history as a leading case of this usurpation of nationalism.…

From: John Atkinson Hobson, *Imperialism*, (James Nisbit and Co., London, 1902), pp. 79–83.

Document 4

Source: The Young Turks, Proclamation for the Ottoman Empire, 1908

3. It will be demanded that all Ottoman subjects having completed their twentieth year, regardless of whether they possess property or fortune, shall have the right to vote. Those who have lost their civil rights will naturally be deprived of this right.

4. It will be demanded that the right freely to constitute political groups be inserted in a precise fashion in the constitutional charter, in order that article 1 of the Constitution of 1293 A.H. [Anno Hegira=] be respected.

7. The Turkish tongue will remain the official state language. Official correspondence and discussion will take place in Turkish.

9. Every citizen will enjoy complete liberty and equality, regardless of nationality or religion, and be submitted to the same obligations. All Ottomans, being equal before the law as regards rights and duties relative to the State, are eligible for government posts, according to their individual capacity and their education. Non-Muslims will be equally liable to the military law.

11. The reorganization and distribution of the State forces, on land as well as on sea, will be undertaken in accordance with the political and geographical situation of the country, taking into account the integrity of the other European powers.

Source: "The Young Turks," trans. A. Sarrou, in *Civilization since Waterloo*, Rondo Cameron, ed. (Paris, 1912), pp. 40–42.

Document 5

Source: Punch, British satirical magazine, *The Boiling Point*, Oct. 1912

Document 6

Source: European Alliance System, 1914

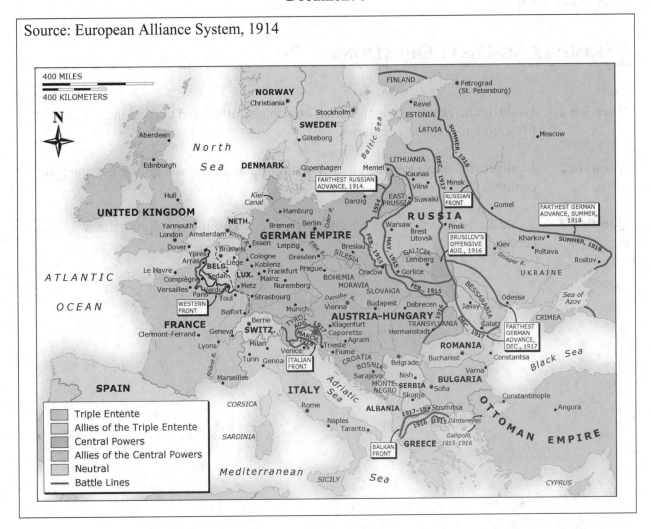

Document 7

Source: Kaiser Wilhelm II, Speech from the balcony of the Royal Palace, Berlin, Aug. 1, 1914*

I thank you from the bottom of my heart for the expression of your loyalty and your esteem. When it comes to war, all parties cease and we are all brothers. One or another party has attacked me in peacetime, but now I forgive them wholeheartedly. If our neighbors do not give us peace, then we hope and wish that our good German sword will come victorious out of this war!

* Germany declared war on Russia on Aug. 1, 1914

Source: http:// wwi.lib.byu.edu/index.php/Wilhelm_II%27s_War_Speeches l

SECTION II

PART B: LONG-ESSAY QUESTIONS

Question 1.   Evaluate the extent to which Italian humanism influenced the arts during the fifteenth and sixteenth centuries.

Question 2.   Evaluate the extent to which nationalism influenced the arts during the nineteenth century.

Question 3.   Evaluate the extent to which subjectivity influenced the arts during the twentieth century.

ANSWERS AND EXPLANATIONS: AP® PRACTICE TEST

SECTION I

PART A: MULTIPLE-CHOICE QUESTIONS

1   A   (KC: 1.2.I.A; LO: Unit 1 D) The passage represents the employment of Renaissance learning in the service of religious reform. This is one of the hallmarks of the Northern Renaissance.

2.   B   (KC: 1.2.I.A; LO: Unit 1 D) Erasmus was the most influential writer of the Northern Renaissance and the quintessential Christian Humanist.

3.   C   (KC: 1.2.I.B; LO: Unit 2 B) It has been said that "Erasmus laid the egg that Luther hatched." The powerful critiques of the Catholic Church by Erasmus and others inspired religious reformers such as Martin Luther to challenge Church practices that were seen as corrupt or outside the bounds of scripture. Christian Humanism thus led most directly to the Protestant Reformation.

4.   D   (KC: 1.2.III.B; LO: Unit 2 C) Habsburg rulers such as Charles V and Philip II supported Catholic uniformity in Europe and waged war against states that adopted Lutheranism and/or Calvinism. Therefore, the leaders of the Holy Roman Empire would most likely *disagree* with the views represented in the document.

5.   C   (KC: 2.1.I.B; LO: Unit 3 G) The French, English, and Dutch empires, among others, sought a favorable balance of trade—a key goal of mercantilism. To protect their respective economies, these governments heavily regulated trade. War was a common means of weakening an opponent's economic power.

6   D   (KC: 1.3.I.B; LO: Unit 1 H) Colbert was the principal architect of Louis XIV's mercantilist system. Under Colbert, France became the leading economic power in Europe.

7.   A   (KC: 2.1.III.C; LO: Unit 3 E) The competition among European empires in the Atlantic trade led to numerous wars throughout the seventeenth and eighteenth centuries. These include the Anglo-Dutch Wars of the mid-seventeenth century and four wars over North American territory between France and England between 1689 and 1763. The last of these wars—the Seven Years' War, led to France's removal from North America and established Britain as the most powerful empire in the world.

8.   B   (KC: 2.2.II.B; LO: Unit 3 C) The Atlantic slave trade, initially established by Portugal in the sixteenth century, became a central feature of the Atlantic trade in the seventeenth and eighteenth centuries. Britain, France, the Netherlands, Spain, and Portugal utilized millions of slaves in the New World for such activities as sugar production and mining.

9.   A   (KC: 1.2.I.B; LO: Unit 2 B) Martin Luther viewed the Reformation as a religious issue and criticized the abuses within the Catholic Church before eventually creating his own Protestant sect. However, Luther believed people were obligated to follow the authority of their secular rulers. He was offended that the peasants revolted violently against their noble lords while invoking his name.

10. B   (KC: 1.2.I.B; LO: Unit 2 B) While Luther believed that people should obey their secular rulers, John Calvin created a theocracy in Geneva where Calvinist leaders served as leaders of the state. Henry IV, Henry VIII, and Elizabeth I would all have agreed with Luther that people must obey their political rulers.

11. D   (KC: 1.2.II.A; LO: Unit 1 F) The English Reformation was not the result of noble revolts against Catholic authorities but rather Henry VIII's desire to secure an annulment from his first wife, Catherine of Aragon. All of the other answer choices speak to reactions to or resolutions of the issue of religious differences between nobles and Catholic authority.

12. C   (KC: 1.2.I.B; LO: Unit 2 B) The German peasants were deeply inspired by Luther's emphasis on all Christians being equals in the eyes of God. The peasants resented being exploited by German nobles and appealed for better treatment. When nobles refused to address peasant grievances, many peasants revolted, resulting in as many as 100,000 deaths in Germany.

13. A   (KC: 3.3.II.A; LO: Unit 6 J) Classical liberals of the eighteenth and nineteenth centuries advocated laissez-faire capitalism. By the early nineteenth century, however, liberals such as Jeremy Bentham and his protégé, Edwin Chadwick, sought government intervention to address negative social conditions brought about by industrialization. These interventions included laws restricting child labor, improvements in sanitation, and the eventual increase in suffrage for men.

14. B   (KC: 3.3.II.B; LO: Unit 6 J) Chadwick's "sanitary idea" influenced governments to install sewage systems to remove filth in cities, build aqueduct systems to pipe in clean water, and improve crowded living conditions to prevent epidemics such as cholera.

15. C   (KC: 3.3.II.B; LO: Unit 6 J) Overcrowding in towns and cities as a result of the Industrial Revolution exacerbated existing conditions that included poor housing and the existence of filth that was not removed regularly by municipalities.

16. A   (KC: 1.4.I.B; LO: Unit 1 N) Elites dominated local affairs throughout much of early-modern Europe. Nobles tended to dominate in the countryside while a growing commercial elite in towns and cities grew more influential in western Europe.

17. C   (KC: 1.4.I.B; LO: Unit 1 N) Landless farmers would have been most vulnerable to economic changes taking place, such as the early phase of enclosure, adverse impacts on farming such as weather, and a high mortality rate that wreaked havoc on poor families.

18. D   (KC: 1.4.II.C; LO: Unit 1 M) Western and northern European governments and church officials in early-modern Europe were more proactive in aiding the poor. Eastern European regions, such as Russia, experienced far fewer economic and political innovations while remaining dependent on serfdom.

19. B   (KC: 1.4.II.B; LO: Unit 1 M) The Price Revolution stimulated the commercialization of agriculture that led to some enclosing of fields in the sixteenth and seventeenth centuries. While landowners grew wealthier as a result, enclosure displaced some farmers in the English countryside.

20. B   (KC: 1.1.IV.A; LO: Unit 4 B) The image illustrates a geocentric view of the universe put forth by Ptolemy in the first century C.E. This view of the cosmos persisted in the sixteenth and seventeenth centuries within the Catholic Church despite advances made during the Scientific Revolution.

21. A (KC: 1.1.IV.A; LO: Unit 4 B) Although students are not expected to know Ptolemy, they should be able to identify Copernicus, Galileo, and Newton as instrumental in proving the heliocentric theory.

22. D (KC: 1.1.IV.B; LO: Unit 4 B) Galen was a Greek surgeon in the Roman Empire who built upon the humoral theory first developed by Hippocrates. Galen represents traditional knowledge in contrast to Vesalius, Paracelsus, and Harvey who advanced knowledge of the human body during the Scientific Revolution.

23. D (KC: 2.3.V.B; LO: Unit 4 F) The most notable Neoclassical artist of the late eighteenth century, Jacques-Louis David highlighted Roman republican values in *The Oath of the Horatii.*

24. C (KC: 2.3.V.B; LO: Unit 4 F) David was influenced by Enlightenment philosophy that emphasized constitutionalism and rejected absolutism. David later became one of the principal artists during the French Revolution.

25. A (KC: 2.1.IV.A; LO: Unit 5 D) Enlightenment philosophy deeply influenced the French Revolution. Enlightenment ideals are embodied in the Declaration of Rights of Man and Citizen.

26. C (KC: 2.3.VI.B; LO: Unit 5 I) While the Enlightenment emphasized science and reason, the Romantic era instead glorified human emotion and faith.

27. B (KC: 2.1.IV.B; LO: Unit 5 D) In August 1789, the National Assembly abolished feudalism in France thus stripping the nobility of its traditional hereditary privileges. In response to the increased violence against the noble class, thousands of aristocrats fled France to neighboring Austria and Prussia.

28 D (KC: 2.1.IV.C; LO: Unit 5 D) Robespierre emerged as the leading Jacobin in the National Convention by 1792. He sought the creation of a republic and the removal of King Louis XVI from power. He later oversaw the Reign of Terror from 1793–1794.

29. D (KC: 2.1.IV.C; LO: Unit 5 D) As a child of the Enlightenment, Robespierre believed in religious toleration and a dramatic reduction in influence of the Catholic Church. During the Reign of Terror, Robespierre and his fellow leaders of the Committee of Public Safety attempted to de-Christianize France completely. The replacement of the Christian calendar for the new Revolutionary Calendar is one such example.

30. C (KC: 1.2.I.B; LO: Unit 2 B) Jansenism supported the concept of "free will" and thus attracted followers from all religious denominations. Louis XIV saw Jansenism as a threat to his authority as he demanded all French people adhere to the official faith of the country—Catholicism.

31. B (KC: 2.1.I.B; LO: Unit 3 G) Religious conformity was considered essential to political unity and stability. For example, Louis XIV issued the Edict of Fountainbleau, which outlawed the practice of Calvinism.

32. D (KC: 2.2.II.A; LO: Unit 3 C) Hoping to preserve their traditional rights, such as exemptions from paying taxes, nobles sought to entrench themselves in institutions like the *parlements* to shield them from royal power. This can be seen on the eve of the French Revolution when nobles refused to accept tax increases sought by Louis XVI.

33. D (KC: 2.2.II.A; LO: Unit 3 C) Puritans and Presbyterians in Parliament resisted repeated tax increase requests by James I and Charles I of England. While both rulers believed in absolutism and "divine right of kings," members of Parliament disagreed and ultimately fought Anglican forces in the English Civil War.

34. C (KC: 3.2.I.A; LO: Unit 6 E) Young, single women and widows typically composed the workforce depicted in the image. They commanded lower wages than did male workers.

35. D (KC: 3.1.I; LO: Unit 6 B) The image shows women using machines to make cloth in a factory setting.

36. B (KC: 3.1.I; LO: Unit 6 B) The textile industry marked the beginning of the First Industrial Revolution. The Second Industrial Revolution occurred after 1850 and was marked by the use of far heavier machinery, typically worked by men.

37. A (KC: 3.1.I.B; LO: Unit 6 B) Entrepreneurs developed textile factories, in part, because the quality and quantity of cloth produced in the cottage industry was not sufficient. The use of steam engines to power textile machines required heavy private capital investment in England.

38. C (KC: 3.3.I.B; LO: Unit 6 H) Classical liberals of the nineteenth century and even more modern-leaning liberals during the first half of the nineteenth century would have scoffed at the notion of universal male suffrage—an idea quite radical for its time. Even with the passage of the monumental Reform Bill of 1832, the franchise was merely extended from approximately 6% of the male population to about 12%. Male suffrage in England would gradually increase through parliamentary legislation in 1867 and 1884 and, finally 1918 where all men in England had voting rights as well as women over the age of 30.

39. B (KC: 3.3.I.B; LO: Unit 6 H) The Reform Bill of 1832, to which the passage refers implicitly, gave the middle class in the House of Commons even more dominance over the House of Lords. Industrialism dramatically increased the wealth and influence of the middle class in England. Working-class people, such as the Chartists, resented this political domination and saw voting rights as a way to level the playing field politically.

40. A (KC: 3.3.I.D; LO: Unit 6 H) Socialists supported the working class and advocated voting rights for everyone, including women. They would certainly have sympathized with the goals of the Chartists.

41. D (KC: 3.2.I.A; LO: Unit 6 E) While the middle-class gentry in the House of Commons had long held the upper hand in English politics since the seventeenth century, the wealth brought about by the Industrial Revolution created an urban middle class that was increasingly influential in British politics and society.

42. B (KC: 3.4.II.D; LO: Unit 6 G) Russia's defeat in the Crimean War shocked Alexander II and other Russian leaders as they realized that Russia had fallen far behind Europe's other Great Powers militarily and economically. The tsar's efforts at modernization included the Emancipation Edict and industrial development. Although Alexander II's successor, Alexander III, proved far more conservative regarding social and political issues, industrial development, nonetheless, accelerated during his reign.

43. C (KC: 3.1.II.C; LO: Unit 6 B) See explanation to question 42.

44. C (KC: 4.2.I.A; LO: Unit 8 E) The horrors of World War I combined with poor leadership of Tsar Nicholas II led to the "February" Revolution of 1917 where the Provisional Government took over control of Russia and removed the tsar from power. As casualties and shortages mounted throughout 1917, the Provisional Government lost much of its support among the Russian people, leading to its overthrow by the Bolsheviks in November.

45. D (KC: 4.2.I.A; LO: Unit 8 E) Led by Vladimir Lenin, the Bolsheviks were rooted in Marxist ideology and hoped to create a new society where everyone was equal and

502

poverty was eliminated. Lenin differed from Marx in terms of strategy: while Marx believed the inevitable communist revolution would come from the workers themselves, Lenin believed that a small, professional group of revolutionaries would need to force the revolution forward—in effect, a revolution from above.

46. B (KC: 4.2.I.C; LO: Unit 8 E) The Bolsheviks nullified elections in early 1918 that were favorable to supporters of the Provisional Government. A catastrophic civil war broke out between the much-smaller Bolshevik forces and numerous factions of those who opposed Bolshevik rule. Millions died in the war and the economy was largely ruined under Lenin's War Communism policies.

47. A (KC: 4.2.I.D.i; LO: Unit 8 E) After the Bolsheviks prevailed in the Russian civil war, Lenin realized an economic compromise was necessary to bring the Russian economy back from ruin. The New Economic Policy (NEP) provided some market incentives for farmers and small merchants that allowed the economy to recover to some degree. These quasi-capitalist measures were removed by Stalin in 1928 when he instituted the first of his Five-Year Plans.

48. C (KC: 4.1.III.D; LO: Unit 8 L) Anti-Semitism is synonymous with anti-Jewish sentiment. It was at the root of Hitler's racial policies.

49. D (KC: 4.1.III.D; LO: Unit 8 L) Hitler sought to create a new racial order in Europe with the Aryans at the top of society and the Slavs and Jews forced into slave labor and eventual extermination. Other groups, such as the French, were tolerated. Aryan peoples in countries that Germany conquered during World War II, such as Denmark and Norway, were treated much better than the Slavic and Jewish populations in Poland and Russia who were murdered by the millions.

50. B (KC: 4.1.III.D; LO: Unit 8 L) Hitler's racial policies ultimately resulted in the Holocaust during World War II where six million Jews and nearly six million others were systematically murdered by the Nazis.

51. A (KC: 4.1.V; LO: Unit 9 E) Hundreds of thousands of Bosnian Muslims were murdered by Bosnian-Serbs supported by the Serbian regime led by Slobodan Milosevich. The Serbs sought to "ethnically cleanse" Bosnia of all Muslims. A similar effort began in Kosovo in the late-1990s but NATO forces prevented Milosevic from enacting the wholesale slaughter of Kosovars.

52. A (KC: 4.4.III.A; LO: Unit 9 N) Green Parties in post-war Europe increasingly emphasized ecological awareness in an age of growing pollution, stress on environmental resources, and globalization. They eschewed the nuclear arms race.

53. B (KC: 4.3.II.C; LO: Unit 8K) The Cold War resulted in a massive nuclear arms race between the United States and the Soviet Union.

54. D (KC: 4.2.V.C; LO: Unit 9 G) The image shows the beginning of the fall of the Berlin Wall in 1989. Economic strains in the Soviet Union forced Mikhail Gorbachev to give up control of the Soviet empire in Eastern Europe. Poland and Hungary had already broken away from one-party communist rule prior to the events in Berlin.

55. C (KC: 4.2.V.C; LO: Unit 9 G) Gorbachev introduced *perestroika* in the mid-1980s in an attempt to improve the Soviet economy through market reforms. The program failed miserably thus leading to Gorbachev's willingness to allow Eastern European countries to go their own way and the eventual collapse of the Soviet Union in 1991.

SECTION I

PART B: SHORT-ANSWER QUESTIONS

Sample Answers

Question 1
(KC: 4.1.IV, 4.2.IV; LO: Unit 9 B, C, D)

Possible responses to part a) include:
- Stalin's refusal to allow free elections in Eastern Europe after the war and Soviet domination of the region
- The temporary monopoly by the U.S. on atomic weapons
- Allied refusal to open a second front in Western Europe until 1944 causing Russia to suspect that the British and the Americans were delaying the much needed second front while fighting the Germans alone for an additional year
- U.S.-Britain collaboration on the atomic bomb project without consulting the Soviet Union
- Soviet support for communist insurgencies in Turkey, Greece, and later, support for communists in the civil war in China

Possible responses to part b) include:
- U.S. development of the Truman Doctrine and the Marshall Plan
- Stalin's blockade of West Berlin and Truman's Berlin airlift
- The creation of NATO
- The creation of two Germanies
- The emergence of a nuclear arms race
- U.S.-led military intervention on the Korean Peninsula

Possible responses to part c) include:
- East Germany, Czechoslovakia, Poland, Romania, Hungary, and Albania were dominated by one-party communist rule orchestrated by the Soviet Union.
- Eastern Bloc countries saw slow economic growth compared to Western Europe.
- Eastern Bloc countries were forbidden by the Soviets to receive Marshall Plan aid from the U.S.
- Eastern Bloc governments joined the Warsaw Pact as a defense against NATO.

Question 2
(KC: 2.3.I, 2.3.II; LO: Unit 4 C, D, F)

Possible responses to part a) include:
- Torture was common in the centuries prior to the Enlightenment (e.g., Star Chamber in England).
- Enlightenment philosophy emphasized natural rights of man and legal justice.

Possible responses to part b) include:
- The French *philosophes* spreading Enlightenment ideas
- The continued development of the popular press
- The salon movement

Possible responses to part c) include:
- Enlightened despots, such as Frederick the Great, Catherine the Great, and Joseph II, restricted or abolished torture and capital punishment in their realms.

505

Question 3
(KC: 1.2.I, 1.2.II, 1.2.III; LO: Unit 2 B, C, D)

Possible responses to part a) include:
- The Council of Trent that sought to reform the Church
- Reduction of abuses in the Church including simony, pluralism, nepotism, clerical ignorance
- Reduction in the use of indulgences
- Development of the Jesuit order to spread the Gospel and establish schools
- Development of the Ursuline order of nuns

Possible responses to part b) include:
- Reaffirmation of the seven sacraments
- Reaffirmation of clerical celibacy
- Continued use of indulgences (although to a lesser extent)
- Sponsoring military actions against the spread of Protestantism
- Use of the Spanish and Roman Inquisitions

Possible responses to part c) include:
- Spread of Lutheranism in northern Germany and Scandinavia
- Spread of Calvinism to Geneva, Scotland, the Netherlands, Scotland, and France
- Charles V's crusade against Protestantism in the Holy Roman Empire
- Habsburg-Valois Wars—Catholic France siding with Protestant German states to weaken the HRE
- English Reformation
- French Wars of Religion
- Dutch Revolt
- Spanish Armada
- Thirty Years' War
- English Civil War

Question 4

(KC: 4.4.II, 4.4.III; LO: Unit 8 M, Unit 9 H, O)

Possible responses to part a) include:
- Women gradually received the right to vote starting with Norway and Finland in the first decade of the century; Britain, Germany, and Russia after World War I; and France after WWII.
- Women increasingly played a larger role in the economy (e.g., WWI and WWII; postwar society)
- Second Wave Feminism led to an increase in economic opportunities starting in the 1960s
- Female leaders reached top positions of power in the late-twentieth century (e.g., Thatcher in Britain)

Possible responses to part b) include:
- Women in various countries were encouraged to maintain traditional roles (e.g. Fascist Italy, Nazi Germany).
- In the decade following WWII, women were encouraged to marry young and have children—a baby boom ensued.

Possible responses to part c) include:
- The Russian Revolution led to women's equality in the Soviet Union (theoretically).
- World War I and World War II increased women's role in the economy.
- The rise of fascism in Italy and Germany reversed gains women had made in those two countries.
- Second Wave Feminism led to the passage of laws that gave women equal access to educational and economic opportunities.

Section II

Part A: Document-Based Question

(KC: 3.3.I.F, 3.4.III, 3.5.III, 4.1.I; LO: Unit 7 B, D, I, Unit 8 B)

Question 1. Evaluate the extent to which nationalism led to the First World War.

Part A Thesis (0–1 point): The thesis should briefly explain whether nationalism did or did not lead to World War I. The thesis cannot merely restate the prompt.

Acceptable Thesis: Nationalism played a large role in leading to the First World War as Europe's major powers engaged in decades-long competition for colonies, prestige, and arms supremacy that led to increasing tensions among the two alliances.

Part B Contextualization (0–1 point): Students should give a broad overview of events prior to, during, and/or after the First World War. Acceptable responses should explain (not just mention) developments such as:
- The unification of Germany and the new balance of power that emerged in response
- The appeal of nationalism to the masses in various countries in the late-nineteenth and early-twentieth centuries
- Total war as an expression of nationalism (including the demonization of one's enemies)
- Anger in Germany after the Versailles Treaty and nationalism's role in the rise of the Nazis
- Extreme nationalism (i.e., fascism) and its role in events leading to World War II.

The above list is not exhaustive.

Part C Evidence (0–3 points): Evidence from the documents (up to 2 points) and Evidence beyond the documents (1 point):

Evidence from the documents
1 point—Student correctly uses the content of at least THREE documents

Acceptable:
- The Congress of Berlin created new countries in the Balkans that once belonged to the Ottoman Empire. (Doc. 1)
- Heinrich von Treitschke believes that war is a necessary means of solving disputes between nations. (Doc. 2)
- Hobson claims that imperialism and commercial interests have led to numerous wars. (Doc. 3)
- The proclamation by the Young Turks highlights Turkish nationalism by insisting that Turkish remains the national language of the Ottoman Empire. (Doc. 4)
- The political cartoon shows that tensions in the Balkans are growing so strong that European leaders can't contain them. (Doc. 5)
- The alliances systems that fought against one another for four years in World War I are clearly evident in the map. (Doc. 6)
- Kaiser Wilhelm's speech shows that he wants Germans to be united as one nation while fighting the war against the allies. (Doc. 7)

OR

2 points—Student correctly uses the content of at least SIX documents to support an argument/thesis

Acceptable:
- The creation of new countries as a result of the Congress of Berlin resulted in increased nationalist tensions in the Balkans that would lead to the First World War. (Doc. 1)
- Treitschke's view exemplifies the nationalistic view that nations must use force to achieve their political goals. This view resulted in a willingness to engage in warfare that contributed to Germany's aggressiveness at the beginning of World War I. (Doc. 2)
- Hobson views imperialism as an outgrowth of nationalism and sees imperialism as a source of increased nationalist tensions among the Great Powers in Europe. Imperialism became one of the major causes of the First World War. (Doc. 3)
- The Young Turks demands for a reorganization of the military and the imposition of Turkish as the national language highlight increased nationalistic tension in the region. Furthermore, the alliance with Germany was seen as a way for the Ottoman Empire to survive. (Doc. 4)
- The nationalistic tensions in the Balkans that existed prior to WWI are demonstrated in the cartoon where Europe's major powers are struggling to prevent the crisis in the Balkans from escalating into a wider conflict. (Doc. 5)

- Preserving the safety of one's nation became paramount in the late-nineteenth and early-twentieth centuries when alliance systems were created that included France, Russia, and Britain on the side of the Triple Entente and Germany, Austria-Hungary, and the Ottoman Empire on the side of the Triple Alliance. (Doc. 6)
- Kaiser Wilhelm's speech demonstrates the nationalism that existed in many countries at this time. He demands that all Germans set aside their differences and join forces to win the war. Victory in war has become a national mission. (Doc. 7)

Evidence beyond the documents

1 point--Student uses evidence not included in the documents. Common examples could include the following but must be explained.

Acceptable:
- German concerns about fighting Russia and France simultaneously led to Germany's creation of an alliance with Austria (a former enemy) in the late-nineteenth century.
- The assassination of Austrian Archduke Franz Ferdinand by Serbian nationalists became the immediate cause of the war.
- Russian mobilization against Austria prompted Germany to launch its Schlieffen Plan against Belgium and France.
- A naval arms race between Britain and Germany caused Britain to view Germany as a mortal threat.
- Conflicts between Germany and France over the issue of Morocco in 1906 and 1911 inspired the Entente Cordiale between Britain and France.

Part D Analysis and Reasoning (0–2 points):

1 point—Sourcing: Student explains the relevance of the document's audience, purpose, point of view, or historical situation in relation to the argument.

Acceptable example of audience:
The intended audience of Kaiser Wilhelm II's speech is most likely those who earlier opposed his policies. He is reaching out to those on the opposing political side to join him in working toward a German victory in the war. (Doc. 7)

Acceptable example of purpose:
The purpose of Hobson's book is to convince people that imperialism is ultimately destructive in achieving peace and security. (Doc. 4)

Acceptable example of point of view:
Document 5 comes from a satirical magazine, so it is likely an attempt to make the Great Powers look foolish as they try to contain escalating tensions in the Balkans that are spiraling out of control. (Doc. 5)

<u>Acceptable example of historical situation:</u>
The treaty in document 1 was an attempt to settle the "Eastern Question": how should European territories lost by the Ottoman Empire be treated? Should they be allowed to become independent or should empires such as Russia or Austria take control of them? (Doc. 1)

1 point—Complexity: Student demonstrates a complex understanding of both the prompt and the documents. Examples demonstrating complexity might include:

- Explaining a nuance by exploring various causes of World War I such as rising nationalism, militarism, imperialism, and rival alliances
- Explaining connections to other time periods such as causes of World War II
- Explaining nationalistic motivations of various powers such as Germany, Austria, and Russia
- Qualifying or modifying an argument by considering diverse or alternative views or evidence, such as other factors that caused the First World War such as military strategy (e.g., Schlieffen Plan) or balance of power politics

SECTION II

PART B: LONG-ESSAY QUESTIONS

Question 1: Evaluate the extent to which Italian humanism influenced the arts during the fifteenth and sixteenth centuries.
(KC: 1.1.I, 1.1.III; LO: Unit 1 B, C)

Possible responses to a larger extent:
- Painting: use of naturalism, geometric perspective, chiaroscuro, and individualism
- Sculpture: marble and bronze statues in the round, glorification of the human body
- Architecture: Greek temple architecture, Roman-style arches and domes
- Use of pagan themes from ancient Greece and Rome (e.g., Birth of Venus)
- Spread of humanism to Northern Europe (e.g., Durer)

Possible responses to a lesser extent:
- Christian themes remained paramount in the arts.
- Art remained important in conveying the power of the Church and temporal authority.

Question 2: Evaluate the extent to which nationalism influenced the arts during the nineteenth century.
(KC: 3.3.I.F, 3.6.1, 3.6.III; LO: Unit 7 B, J)

Possible responses to a larger extent:
- *Liberty Leading the People*
- Grimm's Fairy Tales

Possible responses to a lesser extent:
- Realism
- Impressionism
- Post-impressionism

Question 3: Evaluate the extent to which subjectivity influenced the arts during the twentieth century.
(KC: 4.3.IV; LO: Unit 9 O)

Possible responses to a larger extent:
- The Lost Generation
- Dadaism
- Modernism
- Expressionism
- Freudianism
- Surrealism
- Postmodernism

Possible responses to a lesser extent:
- Photography
- Movies
- Recording
- Functionalism (architecture)
- Soviet realism
- Ideological literature and totalitarian propaganda that glorified war and nationalism